COLONIALISM, NEO-COLONIALISM, AND ANTI-TERRORISM LAW IN THE ARAB WORLD

The threat of personal harm and destruction from terrorist attacks is nowhere near as great as in Arab nations. However, are counter-terrorism laws in the Arab world formulated and enforced to protect or oppress? *Colonialism, Neo-Colonialism, and Anti-Terrorism Law in the Arab World* examines the relationship between Western influence and counter-terrorism law, focusing on the Arab world, which is, on the one hand, a hostile producer of terrorist organizations, and on the other, a leader in countering 'terrorism.' With case studies of Egypt and Tunisia, Alzubairi traces the colonial roots of the use of coercion and extra-legal measures to protect the ruling order, which are now justified in both the West and the Arab world in the name of counter-terrorism. *Colonialism, Neo-Colonialism, and Anti-Terrorism Law in the Arab World* provides important lessons for counter-terrorism, not just in these countries but also elsewhere in the world.

Fatemah Alzubairi is an assistant professor in the international law department at Kuwait University. She holds a PhD from Osgoode Hall Law School (2017), an LLM from the University of Toronto (2011), and an LLB from Kuwait University (2003). Her area of specialization is counter-terrorism from international and comparative perspectives, counter-insurgency, colonialism, and neo-colonialism. Between 2005 and 2008, Alzubairi worked as a lawyer in the Legislative and the Human Rights committees at the National Assembly of Kuwait.

Colonialism, Neo-Colonialism, and Anti-Terrorism Law in the Arab World

FATEMAH ALZUBAIRI

Kuwait University

CAMBRIDGE
UNIVERSITY PRESS

CAMBRIDGE
UNIVERSITY PRESS

University Printing House, Cambridge CB2 8BS, United Kingdom

One Liberty Plaza, 20th Floor, New York, NY 10006, USA

477 Williamstown Road, Port Melbourne, VIC 3207, Australia

314–321, 3rd Floor, Plot 3, Splendor Forum, Jasola District Centre, New Delhi – 110025, India

79 Anson Road, #06–04/06, Singapore 079906

Cambridge University Press is part of the University of Cambridge.

It furthers the University's mission by disseminating knowledge in the pursuit of
education, learning, and research at the highest international levels of excellence.

www.cambridge.org
Information on this title: www.cambridge.org/9781108476928
DOI: 10.1017/9781108569262

© Fatemah Alzubairi 2019

First published 2019

Printed and bound in Great Britain by Clays, St Ives plc, Elcograf S.p.A.

A catalogue record for this publication is available from the British Library.

Library of Congress Cataloging-in-Publication Data
NAMES: Alzubairi, Fatemah, 1982- author.
TITLE: Colonialism, neo-colonialism, and anti-terrorism law in the Arab world /
Fatemah Alzubairi, Kuwait University.
DESCRIPTION: Cambridge, United Kingdom ; New York, NY, USA : Cambridge University Press, 2019. |
Based on author's thesis (doctoral – York University, Osgood Hall Law School, 2017)
issued under title: The Role of Colonialism and Neo-Colonialism in
Shaping Anti-Terrorism Law in Comparative and International Perspectives. |
Includes bibliographical references and index.
IDENTIFIERS: LCCN 2018034516 | ISBN 9781108476928 (hardback) |
ISBN 9781108701761 (pbk.)
SUBJECTS: LCSH: Terrorism–Prevention–Law and legislation–Arab countries. |
Terrorism–Prevention–Law and legislation–Egypt. | Terrorism–Prevention–Law and legislation–Tunisia.
| Law–Egypt–British influences. | Law–Tunisia–French influences.
CLASSIFICATION: LCC KMC982.T47 A5 2019 | DDC 344/.14927053257–dc23
LC record available at https://lccn.loc.gov/2018034516

ISBN 978-1-108-47692-8 Hardback

To Toronto

Contents

Acknowledgments

I would like to start off by thanking Kent Roach, whom I consider my mentor in law and human rights. It is owing to his support as well as expert guidance that this book came into existence. His knowledge, wisdom, and love of humanity as a whole both inspired and enriched this book and my view of life. Special gratitude goes to Anna Ezekiel, who read and generously commented on the entire book, and whose useful feedback saved me from many errors. I would also like to thank Veit Hillside for all her insightful views and reassuring support, and Liora Salter, who through challenging me, enabled me to clearly build my ideas. I greatly benefitted from the Middle East expertise of Sabal Alnasseri and from Jenny Hocking's criticism of counter-terrorism as counter-insurgency, which inspired this book. A number of colleagues and friends have influenced and made valuable comments on countless issues in this book. I thank Ghanim Al-Najjar, Rashid Al-Anezi, Domingo Lovera Parmo, and Stefanie Crispino. John Berger at Cambridge University Press has enthusiastically supported me in completing this book and has shown great competence in seeing it through the press. Discussions with my students have mirrored a mixture of disappointments on regional and global security and a desire for a brighter future. Their sense of hope highlights the importance of studying the roots and developments of counter-terrorism laws in order to make a difference. Last, but surely not least, I am grateful to my parents, Fakhriya Alharbi and Hussian Alzubairi, for their ongoing encouragement and love.

Introduction

This book investigates the link between colonialism, neo-colonialism, and counter-terrorism, particularly in the Arab world. The book focuses on the colonial rationale for crime control in the arena of national security, and the development of this logic within Egypt and Tunisia during and after colonialism. The unique contribution of this book is its attention to the connections between colonialism, neo-colonialism, and counter-terrorism. These connections have implications for global security in general, because they reveal the colonial roots of the use of coercion and extra-legal measures to protect the ruling order, which are currently justified in both the West and the Arab world in the name of counter-terrorism. Using case studies of Egypt and Tunisia, the book argues that colonialism has had a crucial impact on shaping postcolonial legal and penal systems, which include counter-terrorism laws and policy. In addition, colonialism affected the neo-colonial distribution of power, in which the West as well as Russia dominates the global war on terror, in particular through the United Nations Security Council. States have responded to the United Nation's (UN) promotion of anti-terror laws by broadening their laws regardless of their usefulness in crime control. As a result, global anti-terrorism approaches focus primarily on security at the expense of the progress of democracy or human rights, especially within the postcolonial world.

The subject of counter-terrorism and its relationship to unequal systems of power, such as colonialism and neo-colonialism, is timely. The counter-terrorism measures enforced following the 9/11 attacks on the United States are still in place; in fact, they have been developed further by the UN Security Council and by countries individually and collectively in order to combat the threat of Islamic State. This has led to concerns about the actual utility of contemporary counter-terrorism laws, and whether they serve crime control or deepen unequal systems of power. Although national and international efforts are required in this field, in practice, such efforts have often revealed misuse of power in the name of counter-terrorism. For instance, Egypt has long had a poor human rights record that the West has occasionally criticized. However, post-9/11, the UN Counter-Terrorism Committee (CTC) has turned a blind eye to Egypt's arbitrary anti-terrorism measures. Even worse, since 1998, the United States has transferred terrorist suspects into Egypt to be interrogated, taking advantage of the fact that Egypt is infamous for its willingness to use torture and other extra-legal measures.[1] The recent executive orders by the President of the United States, Donald Trump, which ban people of particular nationalities from entering the United States, reveal that the use of arbitrary measures is not exclusive to authoritarian countries like those in the Arab world. The global tendency to normalize this kind of exceptionalism in anti-terrorism practices suggests a meeting point between the West and the Arab world in terms of using counter-terrorism legislation to cement power. This book studies the roots of these practices in colonialism, and the way colonialism continues to play out in counter-terrorism legislation in the Arab world, with lessons for the West as well.

This book argues that current anti-terrorism approaches, in addition to being arbitrary, are inherited from colonial practices of crime and social control. Such practices are rooted in disregard for the rights and freedoms of the people they are imposed upon. It is the hope of this book that understanding the colonial roots of current patterns of political and social control will contribute to a move toward more balanced approaches to counter-terrorism in the Arab world and also the West.

The global nature of terrorism and its roots in oppression mean that understanding this phenomenon, and designing effective counter-terrorism measures, requires investigation of the power relations that have shaped it. This book examines the relationship between Western influence, whether under colonialism or neo-colonialism, and counter-terrorism law. The focus of this investigation is the Arab world, which is, on the one hand, a hostile producer of terrorist organizations, and on the other, a leader in countering "terrorism." The book tracks the roots and development of counter-terrorism by analyzing anti-terrorism and national security legislation and measures in two cases, Egypt and Tunisia, from colonial times to the present. The dynamic changes in the Arab world, particularly the so-called Arab Spring and the emergence of new and more radical terrorist organizations, suggest the failure of Arab policies of enduring strict anti-terror measures and national security, which have roots in colonial practices. This has important lessons for counter-terrorism not just in these countries but elsewhere in the world, including the West.

This book tracks historical evidence of colonial and neo-colonial influence on the development of counter-terrorism in the Arab world, which has received little scrutiny.[2] Some studies have covered the complexity of the connections between

[1] Kent Roach, *The 9/11 Effect: Comparative Counter-Terrorism* (New York: Cambridge University Press, 2011) at 80.
[2] See, however, Roach, *The 9/11 Effect*; Lynn Welchman, "Rocks, Hard Places and Human Rights: Anti-Terrorism Law and Policy in Arab States" in Victor Ramraj, Michael Hor & Kent

Arab legislation and colonial history.[3] However, there exists little work on the influence of colonial history specifically on Arab anti-terror legislation or on the continued influence of neo-colonialism. The book thus fills a gap between the study of Western and Arab approaches to counter-terrorism. While in colonial times, legislation was imposed on colonized countries involuntarily by colonizers, since the end of colonialism, migration of laws between countries is voluntary, at least on the surface. It does occur, including as a result of the increasing global obligations of states.[4] Counter-terrorism in the West thus has an impact on the Arab world and vice versa. The study of similarities and connections between Arab and Western counter-terrorism measures, in the context of the relationship between the West and the Arab world in colonialism and neo-colonialism, reveals the roots of current oppressive global counter-terrorism measures, exacerbated since 9/11, in colonial oppression. Therefore, such study is important because of the oppression that goes on in the name of counter-terrorism, exacerbated by the worrying developments in counter-terrorism post-9/11.

The problem with applying the colonial approach to counter-terrorism is that it is not limited to countering violent acts, but is also used to suppress other forms of nonviolent political activities and opposition. Today, methods similar to military ones that are supposed to be used against the enemy during wartime are used against opponents in domestic cases and during peacetime. The problem, then, is not colonialism or neo-colonialism per se, but the reappearance or continuance of aspects of colonialism in modern postcolonial states.

A NOTE ON TERMINOLOGY

Colonialism, Neo-Colonialism, and Imperialism

This book studies the effects of colonialism and neo-colonialism on anti-terror legislation. The term "imperialism" is used to denote a system of domination that functions through political and economic control; such a system is found in both colonialism and neo-colonialism. The book focuses on "new imperialism," which refers to the peak of Anglo-European imperialism during the eighteenth century onward, as opposed to sixteenth- and seventeenth-century imperialism that primarily sought raw materials and economic growth. New imperialism is often associated

---

Roach, eds, *Global Anti-Terrorism Law and Policy* (New York: Cambridge University Press, 2012).

[3] Nathan Brown, *The Rule of Law in the Arab World* (New York: Cambridge University Press, 1997); Sadiq Reza, "Endless Emergency: The Case of Egypt" (2007) 10:4 *New Criminal Law Review* 532.

[4] Kent Roach, "Comparative Counter-Terrorism Law Comes of Age" in Kent Roach, ed, *Comparative Counter-Terrorism Law* (New York: Cambridge University Press, 2015) at 18.

with the Western "civilizing mission" that was carried abroad through colonialism.[5] Nonetheless, as will be examined in Chapter 1, the influence of imperialism existed well before direct colonialism. According to Julian Go and Michael Mann, such influence, known as "informal empire," also dominates through forms of political and economic control.[6] After the fall of colonialism, informal empire has (re-)emerged in the form of neo-colonialism.

The book uses the term "colonialism" to refer to the European political occupation and expansion in the rest of the world that spread widely during the nineteenth and early twentieth centuries. Even though similar occupations have been carried out for thousands of years, I limit the scope of this investigation to British and French colonialism. Other empires, including the Russian (1721–1917), Austrian-Hungarian (1867–1918), and Ottoman (1844–1922) Empires, all vanished during the first two decades of the twentieth century. Also, the significance of Western imperialism is in its present impact over the globe. The colonial experience of Britain and France is complex and vast: together they once controlled over 31 percent of world land. One of the most important features of Western colonialism is that it successfully spread capitalism as the dominant economic system worldwide. Western influence is significant in its universality,[7] insofar as it established the basis of contemporary international investment and political relations.

The fading of colonialism paved the way for neo-colonialism to emerge as another form of Western hegemony. In the aftermath of colonialism, neo-colonialism arose as the use of economic and cultural domination to influence or control other countries. Neo-colonialism does not rely on permanent military occupation and expanding of territory; instead, its methods of control include globalization, capitalism, and cultural influence.[8] This means that neo-colonialism appears to be less coercive than colonialism; however, neo-colonialism continues to exert control and promotes the interest of the major powers.

This book identifies Western powers, above all the United Kingdom, the United States, and France, as the major neo-colonial players in the Arab world. These powers operate through direct relationships with inferior allies or client states. Their domination of these allies and clients takes several forms, including political pressure, migration of law, arms trade, the establishment of military bases, and economic

---

5 Julian Go, *Postcolonial Thought and Social Theory* (New York: Oxford University Press, 2016) at 3; Michael Mann, *The Sources of Social Power, Volume 3: Global Empire and Revolution, 1890–1945* (New York: Cambridge University Press, 2012) at 34–5.

6 Julian Go, *Patterns of Empire: The British and American Empires, 1688 to the Present* (New York: Cambridge University Press, 2011) at 3; Mann, *The Sources of Social Power, Volume 3*, at 18–20.

7 V. G. Kiernan, *Imperialism and Its Contradictions* (New York: Routledge, 1995) at 56–70; Mary Evelyn Townsend, *European Colonial Expansion since 1871* (Chicago: J. B. Lippincott, 1941) at 4.

8 Edward W. Said, *Culture and Imperialism* (New York: Knopf, 1993) at 7.

expansion. These relationships of influence also operate at a supra-national level. This is accomplished through, among other bodies, the UN Security Council, the North Atlantic Treaty Organization (NATO), and the Financial Action Task Force (FATF). These supra-national bodies are not by themselves neo-colonial powers, but they embody neo-colonial policies as imposed by their major member states.

Neo-colonialism is not limited to Western powers; Soviet Russia and contemporary Russia represent another neo-colonial power that dominates other parts of the world. Russia also controls through economic expansion, arms race, and developing nuclear programs for its allies and clients. Nonetheless, historically, Russia has shown little interest in the Arab world. Its bold domination has only emerged in recent years during the Syrian Civil War (2011–present). Its direct military interference in this conflict as well as its destructive role within the UN Security Council represent a shift in the neo-colonial distribution of power. This topic is examined in Chapter 3.

Many scholars do not use the term "neo-colonialism"; instead they refer to this form of control as "informal empire." This book prefers the term "neo-colonialism" for several reasons. "Neo-colonialism" reflects an era that followed colonialism, which represents a continuity with, or a reemergence of, the colonial rationale combined with "new" forms of control that suit contemporary times. These include cyber crimes and counter-terrorism financing – acts that can be practiced within a global electronic world. Another reason for using the term "neo-colonialism" is that the case studies of the book are former colonies, and their legal and political systems are highly influenced by their colonists, as will be shown in Chapters 4 and 6. This book uses the term "informal empire" for forms of control that are similar but occurred before or during colonialism, such as the Anglo-French Dual Control over Egypt's budget between 1879 and 1882.

Terrorism

We cannot talk about counter-terrorism without talking about the notion of terrorism. Attempts to define terrorism tend to be highly politicized. It is difficult to distinguish a terrorist from a revolutionary, or to distinguish violent acts from peaceful opposition, which could all be considered "terrorism." In other words, terrorism cannot be defined in neutral objective language. The problem of the definition of terrorism is also shared with other politicized terms such as "subversion" and "insurgency," which were used during colonialism.

This book does not suggest a direct colonial influence on the current definition of terrorism. Rather, it argues that the use of vague terms and broad definitions in current definitions of terrorism is derived from a colonial rationale in customizing criminal terms to opposing political movements and potential threats. The colonial rationale in criminology dealt with suspects based on a "catch-all" logic. This logic required identifying the enemy well before wrongdoing was carried out. Similarly, the war on terror justifies this logic under a "preemptive" approach.[9] The colonial rationale involved a highly politicized and militarized doctrine of counter-insurgency; this doctrine has reemerged in counter-terrorism thinking where it is undermining the role of the criminal law, and consequently, in the long run, security and justice.

Colonialism is not the only influence in counter-terrorism; neo-colonialism also plays a role in this respect. Jude McCulloch and Sharon Pickering argue that, like colonialism, neo-colonialism has established a set of terrorism-related crimes that aim to preempt terrorism.[10] Kent Roach observes that this kind of criminalization is problematic not only because of the unfair consequences that can result from preemptive practices like indefinite detention, but also because it is built on an assumed crime labeled "terrorism" rather than a clearly defined crime.[11] The counter-terrorism laws and measures established within this rationale have less to do with ensuring national and international security than with preserving the status quo of economic power that serves Western interests.

Part of the fundamental problem of counter-terrorism today is that it is carried out according to a set of stereotypical standards.[12] For instance, the fight against radical Islamist terrorism has led to targeting the large and diverse community of Muslims in general.[13] As is happening today, similar biased standards were used by the colonial powers in a form of racial segregation policy.[14] For example, the British colonial power dealt with protesters as insurgents using measures that included mass arrests and deportations.[15] Daily arrest, interrogation, and searching were part of counter-insurgency strategies that targeted specific groups that had not participated in violent activities.[16]

Today, in both the West and in Arab countries, in order to identify a terrorist, focus is given to the person's ethnicity and religion. While Arabs and Muslims are the target of counter-terrorism in the West, Islamists and/or ethnic minorities are

---

[9] Jude McCulloch & Sharon Pickering, "Counter-Terrorism: The Law and Policing of Pre-emption" in Andrew Lynch, Nicola McGarrity & George Williams, eds, *Counter-Terrorism and Beyond: The Culture of Law and Justice after 9/11* (New York: Routledge, 2010).

[10] Jude McCulloch & Sharon Pickering, "Suppressing the Financing of Terrorism" (2005) 45 *British Journal of Criminology* 470 at 473–6.

[11] Kent Roach, "The Criminal Law and Terrorism" in Victor Ramraj, Michael Hor & Kent Roach, eds, *Global Anti-Terrorism Law and Policy* (Cambridge: Cambridge University Press, 2005) at 138.

[12] Russell Hardin, "Civil Liberties in the Era of Mass Terrorism" (2004) 8:1 *The Journal of Ethics* 77 at 79–81.

[13] "Preempting Justice: Counterterrorism Laws and Procedures in France" (July 1, 2008) *Human Rights Watch*, online: www.hrw.org.

[14] Ambe Njoh, "Colonial Philosophies, Urban Space, and Racial Segregation in British and French Colonial Africa" (2008) 38:4 *Journal of Black Studies* 579 at 579.

[15] Barbara Watson Andaya, *A History of Malaysia* (Honolulu: University of Hawai'i Press, 2001) at 271.

[16] *Ibid.*

the targets in the Arab world. Selectivity in applying the law has less to do with crime control than with ensuring discipline that strengthens the state's sense of dominance.[17]

In today's world, the cross-boundary nature of the crimes of terrorism requires state cooperation at the international level in order to counter these crimes. However, these efforts are unlikely to succeed in the absence of a unified international definition of terrorism. This problem, and how it affects the war on terror, is examined in detail in Chapter 2 of this book.

COLONIALISM, NEO-COLONIALISM, AND COUNTER-TERRORISM

This book focuses on the colonial heritage found in modern anti-terrorism laws in the Arab world. These laws have been used as strategies of oppression and entrenchment of power rather than of protection and serving the public good. A key question in this respect is whether the government rationale for the use of power in crime control is in fact new. Does it represent a development of the modern state or a return to colonial state strategies and conceptions? I argue that law and crime control in Arab countries and in the West are closely related, both because the colonists left the roots of these strategies in the countries they had colonized, which have developed them further, and because colonists also continue to use them in a similar way in their homelands.

Many studies address the impact of colonialism on law in general, particularly in colonized India[18] and Africa,[19] but only a few address this relationship in the Arab world.[20] And while counter-terrorism has become a growing area for Western scholars, fewer writings are dedicated to this subject in the Arab world. Studies of terrorism in the Arab world focus on terrorist organizations and terrorism rather than addressing anti-terrorism laws.[21] Scholars have linked colonial counter-insurgency to

---

[17] Welchman, "Rocks, Hard Places and Human Rights," at 621–2.

[18] See e.g., Anil Kalhan, "Constitution and 'Extraconstitution': Colonial Emergency Regimes in Postcolonial India and Pakistan" in Victor V. Ramraj & Arun K. Thiruvengadam, eds, *Emergency Powers in Asia: Exploring the Limits of Legality* (Cambridge: Cambridge University Press, 2010); Kevin Tan, "From Myanmar to Manila" in Victor V. Ramraj & Arun K. Thiruvengadam, eds, *Emergency Powers in Asia: Exploring the Limits of Legality* (Cambridge: Cambridge University Press, 2010).

[19] See e.g., Jan Záhořík & Linda Piknerová, eds, *Colonialism on the Margins of Africa* (London: Routledge, 2018); Don Nardo, *The European Colonization of Africa* (Greensboro, NC: Morgan Reynolds Pub., 2010).

[20] Nathan Brown, "Retrospective: Law and Imperialism: Egypt in Comparative Perspective" (1995) 29:1 *Law & Society Review* 103; Brown, *The Rule of Law in the Arab World*; Roger Owen, *State, Power and Politics in the Making of the Modern Middle East* (London: Routledge, 2004).

[21] This tendency can be found in Nachman Tal, *Radical Islam in Egypt and Jordan* (Brighton: Sussex Academic Press/Jaffee Center for Strategic Studies, 2005); George Joffé, ed, *Islamist Radicalisation in Europe and the Middle East: Reassessing the Causes of Terrorism* (London: I. B. Tauris, 2013). For sources in Arabic, see Aḥmad M. Ṣubḥī & Zāmilīa Wālī, *Judhīr al-irhāb*

the theory and practice of counter-terrorism.[22] This book traces this connection specifically in Arab countries.

Colonial powers sought to secure their political and economic interests through the imposition of discipline against nationalists and political opponents who were viewed as insurgents, aiming to create a submissive society. According to David French, an "insurgency was more than simply an armed rebellion. Insurgents commonly employed not only different kinds of force, ranging from guerrilla warfare to urban terrorism, but also different kinds of political tools to subvert the colonial state."[23] In parallel, counter-insurgency was not limited to the use of force, but also included political, social, and economic measures. Nonetheless, coercion was a defining figure of the overall policy of colonial powers toward opposition groups.[24] Colonialism justified the use of coercion to prevent opponents' disobedience, which could lead to potential revolutions against the colonial rule.

Colonialism justified its oppressive practices to protect the imperial order, viewing it as the only legitimate order. Anti-colonialism was therefore seen as an evil that the colonial power countered through a wide range of politicized and militarized methods of control. Measures included the use of martial law, emergency legislation and special courts, which were inherited from colonial rule.[25] Scholars have found a connection between these military and exceptional strategies, which were carried over from the colonial power to current national security laws in postcolonial states.[26]

Many practices that were used to suppress insurgents in colonies were also used at some level in the colonists' homeland. From the eighteenth to the first half of the twentieth century, the European powers, particularly the British and French empires, produced national security laws and measures to respond to revolutions, anarchist, and communist movements, and the two World Wars. These events were considered a threat to the established Western values, and this identification of threat justified the use of militant principles and exceptional powers. The concept of "enemy aliens" was widely used during World War II to justify arbitrary detention

---

fī al-'aqīdah al-Wahhābīyah [The Roots of Terrorism in Wahhabism] (Beirut: Dār al-Mīzān, 2008); Aḥmad Abī al-Rīs, *al-Irhāb wa-al-taṭarruf wa-al-'unf fī al-duwal al-'Arabīyah [Terrorism and Extremism in Arab States]* (Alexandria: al-Maktab al-Jāmi'ī al-Ḥadīth, 2001).

[22] Jenny Hocking, *Beyond Terrorism: The Development of the Australian Security State* (St Leonards, NSW: Allen & Unwin, 1993); Jude McCulloch & Sharon Pickering, "Pre-Crime and Counter-Terrorism: Imagining Future Crime in the 'War on Terror'" (2009) 49:5 *British Journal of Criminology* 628.

[23] David French, *The British Way in Counter-Insurgency: 1945–1967* (Oxford: Oxford University Press, 2011) at 9.

[24] *Ibid.*

[25] Brown, *The Rule of Law in the Arab World*; Owen, *State, Power and Politics*; Reza, "Endless Emergency: The Case of Egypt."

[26] Tan, "From Myanmar to Manila"; Nasser Hussain, *The Jurisprudence of Emergency: Colonialism and the Rule of Law* (Ann Arbor, MI: University of Michigan Press, 2003).

of civilians.[27] That legacy can also be linked to the contemporary concept of "enemy combatant" that justifies the Guantanamo Bay detention camp operated by the United States. These measures, which were developed in the homelands of Western countries, still exist at some level in the West. The book argues that the United Kingdom and France have also transferred such measures to the Security Council anti-terrorism resolutions. Thus, there is an implicit unity between the Western and global anti-terrorism agendas.

Accordingly, this book argues that the Western culture of control has not ended with the fading of colonialism, but still dominates the global war on terror through neo-colonial forms of control. However, while the major players of colonialism were the United Kingdom and France, the neo-colonial powers include these two countries as well as the United States and, to a lesser degree, Russia. These countries continue to control global security measures, including counter-terrorism obligations, through their influence on the UN Security Council and other supra-national bodies like the FATF. Through these bodies, the neo-colonial powers impose global obligations on states regarding terrorism-related crimes. These include, among other acts, terrorism financing and speech associated with terrorism.

Highlighting the importance of the link between counter-terrorism and Western colonial and neo-colonial culture is not to deny the responsibility of Arab states for their continual use of harsh counter-terrorism measures. Rather, it is to show that counter-insurgency and counter-terrorism depend largely on colonial exceptional and wartime strategies to deal with mostly domestic peacetime crimes. These strategies are borrowed from the colonial past of each country and encouraged by international pressure from former colonial powers in the current era of neo-colonialism. This shows that the neo-colonial anti-terrorism policy does not necessarily serve to control crime and promote international security, but rather to maintain the status quo of an unequal position of powers. It also serves the authoritarian ambition of Arab rulers and dominant groups within the Arab world. The current wide and exceptional anti-terrorism powers that are being imposed in the Arab world and the West are applied to many forms of civil and political activities that are criminalized as terrorism alongside extreme violent acts.[28]

CASE STUDIES: EGYPT AND TUNISIA

Egypt and Tunisia have been selected for this study for several reasons. Both are republics, witnessed recent uprisings that led to regime changes, and are former colonies. Furthermore, in both countries, while several legal amendments are taking

---

[27] A. W. Brian Simpson, "Detention without Trial in the Second World War: Comparing the British and American Experience" (1988) 16:2 *Florida State University Law Review* 225.
[28] Jenny Hocking, "Orthodox Theories of 'Terrorism': The Power of Politicised Terminology" (1984) 19:2 *Australian Journal of Political Science* 103; Hocking, *Beyond Terrorism*.

place, the colonial heritage seems deeply rooted. However, Egypt was primarily under British administration (1882–1952) and earlier under the French (1798–1801), while Tunisia was only a French colony (1881–1956). Both countries are politically unstable owing to crimes like assassinations and "terrorism," and both combine legal and extra-legal measures to counter this instability. These similarities make the comparative approach useful for studying these countries, especially in light of the colonial heritage, which represents a common foundation for their national security laws.

In 2014, both Egypt and Tunisia adopted new constitutions. These amendments could reshape the policy of criminal law, in particular in relation to counter-terrorism.[29] The problem is that in Arab countries constitutions can be mere façade documents or hollow promises that reflect people's aspirations but ultimately leave them unfulfilled.[30] In both the old and the new constitutions of Egypt and Tunisia, rights are guaranteed, yet can be limited by law for public safety or during emergencies. This is an example of how constitutions are designed in "flexible" language that allows the authorities to limit constitutionalism and the rule of law by adopting arbitrary and subjective laws.[31] Authoritarian constitutions are designed to maximize state power and minimize state accountability, while minimizing the freedoms of the populace. For instance, all the common civil and political rights and freedoms, such as freedom of expression and association, are granted in the 2014 Tunisian constitution; however, Article 49 undermines the value of these rights by stating that:

> The law shall determine the limitations related to the rights and freedoms that are guaranteed by this Constitution and their exercise, on the condition that it does not compromise their essence. These limitations can only be put in place where necessary in a civil democratic state, with the aim of protecting the rights of others or based on the requirements of public order, national defense, public health or public morals.[32]

The constitution has become a tool of governing that expresses the state's authority without limiting it. It ensures the security of the state without protecting people from

---

[29] For instance, in March 2011 Egypt abolished Article 179 of the constitution, which is related to combating terrorism. The article states that: "The State shall seek to safeguard public security to counter dangers of terror. The law shall, under the supervision of the judiciary, regulate special provisions related to evidence and investigation procedures required to counter those dangers. The procedure stipulated in paragraph 1 of Articles 41 and 44 and paragraph 2 of Article 45 of the constitution shall in no way preclude such counter-terror action."

[30] Nathan Brown, *Constitutions in a Nonconstitutional World: Arab Basic Laws and the Prospects for Accountable Government* (New York: State University of New York Press, 2002) at 7–11.

[31] Jothie Rajah explains that the "'rule of law' signifies 'law' which, in content and in institutional arrangements, prevents 'arbitrary power and excludes wide discretionary authority[.]'" Jothie Rajah, *Authoritarian Rule of Law: Legislation, Discourse and Legitimacy in Singapore* (New York: Cambridge University Press, 2012) at 4.

[32] Article 49 of the 2014 Tunisian Constitution. The 2014 Egyptian Constitution included similar restrictions in Articles 56, 85, 62, 64, and 73.

the state's abuse of power. Nathan Brown observes that in the Arab world constitutions are not systematically violated; in fact, they are well respected and largely followed, yet their vague clauses allow flexible interpretation that serves those in power.[33]

Vague clauses, like the one mentioned above, have been added to many of the post-2011 revolution reforms in Egypt and Tunisia. The fact that authorities remain centralized and legal principles and human rights are mostly neglected mean that these reforms are not promising. Yet it is too soon to evaluate the outcomes of the post-revolution constitutional experience, since it requires some time to test the effectiveness of new constitutions. This is especially true of Tunisia. Unlike Egypt, which is still clinging to the military style of rule, Tunisia is still developing its method of governance. If Tunisia is able to keep its commitment to decentralize power, there is hope for a balanced legal system, and thus a balanced counter-terrorism law.

In addition to examining the laws themselves, this book investigates the major political events and terrorist attacks that had a direct impact on shaping anti-terrorism and national security laws in Egypt and Tunisia. The timeframe is from the 1800s until 2018. The reason for this wide range is to track any colonial legacy on Egyptian and Tunisian laws. The laws adopted post-9/11 are examined in order to explore whether neo-colonial influence has been a factor in shaping contemporary anti-terrorism laws in the Arab world.

HISTORICAL AND COMPARATIVE LEGAL ANALYSIS

This book takes a comparative and historical approach to the anti-terrorism law in Egypt and Tunisia. The objective of this approach is to provide a contextual description of the major historical events and cultural aspects – especially colonialism and neo-colonialism – that have shaped the ways in which Arab states understand terrorism. The comparative approach to law cannot be isolated from history, in which the development of national legislation is linked to historical and socio-political changes. Patterns from the past are not separated from the present unless they are associated with a choice to act differently. Law and policymaking are therefore not isolated from the dynamic historical conditions from which they emerged. The aim of the historical critical analysis is to highlight the unwanted patterns of extensive political control that drag Arab and other states into a circle of violence, in order to consciously replace them with wise patterns that can assure national and international security.

The cross-boundary nature of terrorism and counter-terrorism makes the comparative approach essential. Despite the increasing number of international

---

[33] Brown, *Constitutions in a Nonconstitutional World*, at 7.

obligations in counter-terrorism, most domestic laws reflect national interests. Uniting national efforts in crime control in international treaties may neglect the special geopolitical conditions of each nation and each region. However, common as well as contrasting features can be drawn from the various national laws, which can help enhance global anti-terrorism efforts. This book tracks and analyzes the origins of the problematic aspects of Egyptian and Tunisian anti-terror measures. The book does not just compare Egypt and Tunisia, or these two countries now and under colonial rule, but also puts legislation in Egypt and Tunisia in the context of the wider Arab world and relates the legislation in these two countries to Western legislative responses to terrorism and to international anti-terror legislation.

In both Egypt and Tunisia, the laws relevant to contemporary counter-terrorism measures are divided into two groups: those related to state security that were adopted before regulating the crime of terrorism, and those directly regulating the crime of terrorism under anti-terrorism laws. In the case of Egypt (examined in Chapters 4 and 5), the first group of laws includes the Penal Code of 1883, particularly the crimes of sabotage and sedition, and Law No. 162 of 1958 Concerning the State of Emergency. The book argues that these laws reflect the colonial rationale, which relies on vague politicized terms and exceptional measures. These also represent the bedrock of current anti-terrorism laws. The second group includes the Penal Code of 1992, which is the first to define the crime of terrorism in Egypt. As will be shown, the Egyptian definition of terrorism is over-broad with vague terminology that can be found in the harsh French Penal Code of 1810. In 2015, the same definition – with some insignificant changes – was added to the Law Regarding Regulating Terrorist Entities and Terrorists and the Anti-terrorism Law. The book examines the definition of "terrorism," speech related to terrorism, terrorism financing, and the procedural regulations. The aim of this investigation is to answer whether the current anti-terrorism regulations are influenced by neo-colonial factors, or whether they reflect an indigenous authoritarianism combined with a colonial heritage.

In Tunisia (examined in Chapters 6 and 7), the first group of laws includes the Penal Code of 1913, the Penal and Procedures Military Code No. 92 of 1957, and the Presidential Decree of January 26, 1978. The first of these focuses on the crimes of plotting and incitement, sabotage and rebellion. This Law, which is still active, was transplanted by the French colonist and reflects the colonial rationale. The book argues that these crimes represent the foundation for the current anti-terrorism regulations. The Penal and Procedures Military Code No. 92 was modified in 1979, expanding the jurisdiction of military courts to include crimes of rebellion committed during peacetime. Among the acts considered as rebellion is membership in a "terrorist organization." The colonial rationale appears in this law in the inclusion of vague terms like "rebellion" and "terrorist organization" without clearly defining them. It also appears in the trial of civilians before military courts. Lastly, my analysis of the State of Emergency regulated by the Presidential Decree of

January 26, 1978 aims to identify whether this represents another exceptional and colonial-based practice that is continually used in the current war on terror. The second group of laws includes those directly regulating the crime of terrorism under anti-terrorism laws. Tunisia first added a definition of "terrorism" to the Penal Code in 1993. Similar to the broad Egyptian definition, Tunisia included vague terms and acts that are lawful under other jurisdictions. From 1991 until 2005 Tunisia witnessed one terrorist attack, suggesting a secure environment. In response to this terrorist attack, carried out on Djerba Island in 2002, in 2003 Tunisia adopted the Law Concerning Support for International Efforts to Combat Terrorism and Prevent Money-laundering. It became the first Arab country to regulate terrorism in a separate law after the attacks of 9/11. As will be shown in Chapter 2, after the events of 9/11, the UN Security Council issued Resolution 1373 (2001) calling on states to combat terrorism crimes and terrorism financing through legal measures. The question that will be answered is whether Tunisia was under pressure from the Security Council to adopt a separate anti-terrorism law, or whether Tunisia took advantage of the global anti-terrorism movement to toughen up its law and target its opponents. After the "Arab Spring," Tunisia suffered a serious wave of terrorism. In response, in 2015 Tunisia adopted a new Law regarding Anti-terrorism and Money-laundering. The book examines the definition of "terrorism," speech related to terrorism, terrorism financing, and the procedural regulations. The investigation tracks the colonial or neo-colonial influence, if any, and the authoritarian ambition behind this Law.

In order to track the colonial influence in current anti-terrorism laws in Egypt and Tunisia, the book examines the related British and French laws. The main British law examined is the Defence of the Realm Consolidation Act (DORA) 1914, which was adopted during World War I. The importance of this law is that it influenced the global war on terror. For instance, DORA allowed issuing "regulations for securing the public safety and the defence of the realm."[34] Among these regulations is Regulation 14B, which deals with "hostile associations." DORA's regulations and spirit were also extended to other Acts, including Regulation 18B of the Defence (General) Regulations 1939[35] and the Restoration of Order in Ireland Act of 1920. Both of these Acts targeted those with "hostile origins or associations" and detained them without a trial. I argue that DORA is an early Act that normalized the exception. This normalization was done through repetition by constantly adopting similar regulations to deal with unpredictable situations, such as "rebellion," or unpredictable crimes, such as "terrorism."

---

[34] Defence of the Realm Consolidation Act as amended on 27 November 1914. See The National Archive of the United Kingdom, online: The National Archive.

[35] Regulation 18B was intended to suppress the Fascist movement and its leaders in Britain. See A. W. Brian Simpson, *In the Highest Degree Odious: Detention without Trial in Wartime Britain* (Oxford: Clarendon Press, 1992) at 69.

The British have a long history of using emergency and emergency-like powers in colonies.[36] Martial law, state of emergency, and military courts are all forms of emergency powers. For instance, during the British colonization of Egypt, and particularly during the World Wars, the British insisted on including a state of emergency in the Egyptian system.[37] Sadiq Reza argues that although the British introduced these forms of emergency powers, Egypt found such forms, which grant unlimited authority with no accountability, useful. Therefore, the Egyptian government willingly included them in the Egyptian constitution.[38] As will be shown in Chapters 1 and 4, the excessive British use of emergency powers had an impact on the current Egyptian system and on normalizing the exception.

The British influence is not limited to the period of colonialism but extends to the current war on terror. This is particularly significant at the level of the UN Security Council. The United Kingdom as a permanent member has been introducing resolutions that reflect its neo-colonial logic. For instance, in the aftermath of the 2005 London bombing, the United Kingdom promoted UN Resolution 1624 (2005).[39] This Resolution emphasizes condemning speech crimes related to terrorism. Such crimes include the "justification or glorification (*apologie*) of terrorist acts [.]"[40] The Resolution does not define "incitement" or "terrorism."

The French laws examined in the book include the Penal Code of 1810, the Press Law of 1881, and Act No. 86–1020 of September 9, 1986 on action against terrorism. In evaluating the French influence over former colonies, it should be observed that all Arab countries follow the French civil law system. This general tendency requires investigation. Nathan Brown argues that Middle Eastern countries, including those that were under British colonialism, French colonialism, or never colonized, adopted the French model. According to Brown, the French system centralizes authority within executive bodies. This centralization seemed appealing to Arab leaders and elites who sought political power.[41] The attractiveness of the French legal system is addressed in Chapters 1, 4, and 6.

The history behind Arab states adopting specific French laws differs from one country to another. For instance, Egypt borrowed its Penal Code from France and adopted other regulations selectively in accordance with its political interests (see Chapter 4). In the case of Tunisia, France played a direct role in transplanting its

---

[36] For more examples, see Kalhan, "Constitution and 'Extraconstitution'"; Tan, "From Myanmar to Manila"; Hussain, *The Jurisprudence of Emergency*.

[37] Brown, "Retrospective: Law and Imperialism," at 111.

[38] Reza, "Endless Emergency," at 535–7.

[39] Roach, *The 9/11 Effect*, at 55.

[40] UN Security Council, Security Council Resolution 1373, 2001 SC Res. 1373, UN SCOR, S/RES/1373 [Resolution 1373], para 1.

[41] Nathan Brown, "The Precarious Life and Slow Death of the Mixed Courts of Egypt" (1993) 25:1 *International Journal of Middle East Studies* 33 at 37.

laws and establishing new laws that worked for colonies (see Chapter 6). Regardless of how the French laws found their way into Arab legal systems, while France amended its laws by abandoning some harsh features that are not in line with human rights, such as the death penalty, the question is whether Arab states also amended their laws in accordance with human rights requirements.

An examination of current Arab and French security related laws shows little in common. However, when examining the early French laws, such as the French Penal Code of 1810 – also referred to in this book as the Napoleonic Penal Code – the similarity becomes noticeable. The Napoleonic Penal Code was infamous for containing draconian features and broad crimes that aimed to secure the French Empire under Napoleon Bonaparte. Chapter 4 examines these crimes while comparing them to the Egyptian Penal Code and its amendments. Similarly, the Egyptian and Tunisian penal codes include crimes against "public order" – a broad term that can be interpreted selectively. This concept of public order can be found in the French Law Regarding the State of Siege of 1849 (discussed in Chapter 1).[42] Most Arab countries still include the concept of public order in their laws regarding crimes against the state and in their current anti-terrorism laws.

At the regional level, the Arab Convention for the Suppression of Terrorism is examined in Chapter 3. The importance of this convention is that it represents the collective overview of national security policy in the Arab world. As will be shown, the definition of terrorism in the Arab Convention has a very similar wording to the Egyptian definition, which highlights the regional role of Egypt in imposing its view on other Arab states.

A historical and comparative study is ideal for understanding the current global shift in anti-terrorism law and other related fields like human rights and international humanitarian law. This book does not cover in depth these two latter fields, but some discussion of these topics cannot be avoided with the increased reliance on extra-legal measures by both Arab and Western states. The United States' war on Afghanistan and its Guantanamo Bay prison are examples of acting outside the scope of international humanitarian law and human rights law. Furthermore, the United States' war on terror has implicit global influence, in which countries with poor human rights records like Egypt find it acceptable to continue carrying out practices such as detention without trial and torture.

SOURCES

This book examines Arab national security and anti-terrorism laws and measures from their primary sources. Texts of the laws and decrees cited in this book are

[42] Article 8 of French Law Regarding the State of Siege of 1849. This law was adopted to secure the Second French Republic established in 1848, reflecting the "necessity" of that time.

available via each state's Ministry of Justice website and the Official Gazette.[43] Egypt's and Tunisia's reports to the Counter-Terrorism Committee (CTC) are also examined. Each country provided the CTC with four to six reports between 2001 and 2006; the CTC stopped publishing reports after 2006 for no obvious reason.[44] The importance of these reports is that they provide the official view of the national policy of counter-terrorism in each Arab country, as well as the CTC view of international security and the values that have priority of protection. These are good sources demonstrating the effects of neo-colonial policies on countries that justify repressive laws to satisfy an outside power.

In addition to the above sources, the argument is supported with judicial decisions on terrorist cases. It should be noted that judicial decisions from their primary sources are difficult to obtain in the Arab world, partly because in some periods in Egypt and Tunisia (as well as elsewhere) terrorist cases are seen by closed military courts. In addition, final judicial decisions are not necessarily posted by the government. Egypt, for instance, publishes some but not all judicial decisions on the Ministry of Justice website. Another source is the Arab Legal Portal sponsored by the United Nations Development Programme (UNDP),[45] which provides limited cases depending on what information each country supplies. To cover this gap, there are a few private Arab legal websites that provide legislation and judicial decisions. Still, not all court decisions are available, especially those related to terrorism and national security, since, as a manager of one of the websites claims, publishing them is prohibited by orders from the government. Owing to this limitation, the book does not seek a balanced account in viewing the terrorist cases in the two case studies, but rather gives an idea of how the judicial system functions in an authoritarian system.

This book includes appendices of an English translation of the Egyptian and Tunisian anti-terrorism laws. The translation covers only the most relevant articles of the anti-terrorism laws issued in 2015. Some of the articles in the Egyptian law are quoted from the translation provided by the Atlantic Council organization website.[46] The rest of the articles are my own translations. I have taken into account the linguistic differences between Arabic and English, and the ambiguity of some

---

[43] Egypt Official Gazette, online: www.alamiria.com/a/index.html; Tunisian Official Gazette, online: www.iort.gov.tn.

[44] The website of the CTC publishes reports dated from 2001 through 2006, but states, without providing reasoning, that "a decision was made not to make public subsequent reports on resolution 1373 (2001)." *Counter-Terrorism Committee*, online: www.un.org/en/sc/ctc/resources/countryreports.html.

[45] *Salah Al-Jasem Systems*, online: www.saljas.com; The Arab Legal Portal, sponsored by the *United Nations Development Programme* [UNDP], online: www.arablegalportal.org/criminal-laws/.

[46] "Egypt's Anti-Terror Law: A Translation," September 3, 2015, *Atlantic Council*, online: www.atlanticcouncil.org/blogs/menasource/egypt-s-anti-terror-law-a-translation. The quoted articles include articles 7, 8, 12, 14, 15, 16, 17, 21, 24, 25, 28, 30, 33, 34, 35, 37, 38, 50, 52, and 53.

clauses, and have attempted to offer a translation that would meet English legal standards without losing the structure of the original texts. In the translation provided of Arab laws, I use "he" and "his" because this is the exact wording of the texts, which reflects the Arab dominant patriarchal system and its biases.

THEORETICAL FRAMEWORK: THE FOUR PERSPECTIVES

The first chapter of this book develops the key theoretical framework for the analysis of colonialism and neo-colonialism. Theories of imperialism and postcolonialism are used to identify the main characteristics of the colonial rationale, its scope, and the justifications that were given for its theory and practice. Chapter 1 suggests four common features of colonialism and neo-colonialism: economic expansion, centralization, militarism, and exceptionalism. These features are considered throughout the book as the driving forces behind adopting legal and extra-legal reforms in the war on terror.

The first feature, economic expansion, refers to the efforts by Western colonial powers to expand their lands and find new markets to nourish their economy. This required introducing capitalism to the nations they colonized. In the neo-colonial context, former colonies and other developing nations remain largely dependent on Western financial aid, which allows Western powers to have some control over these countries. This has an impact on the war on terror through the use of counter-terrorism financing, controlled by supra-national bodies like the FATF.

The second feature, centralization, has its roots in the French monarchy,[47] and was extended to the Napoleonic system. This system has proved attractive to many countries, including Egypt and Tunisia, which have adopted it into their criminal systems. Global centralization has also emerged in the era of neo-colonialism, as supra-national powers like the UN Security Council and the FATF enjoy centralized powers regarding counter-terrorism.

The third feature, militarism, was a colonial tool that secured the imperial order and its economic interests through the use of arms. This aspect of counter-insurgency is reemerging in counter-terrorism today. At a national level, this aspect appears in the militarization of the police and security forces everywhere, including in the Arab world. At a global level, it appears in anti-terror military campaigns.

Finally, exceptionalism, which includes emergency and emergency-like powers, can be carried out with the aid of armies or in other forms, including arbitrary regulations within criminal justice systems that allow practices like referring civilians to special courts or indefinite detention. This book argues that martial law and the state of emergency, as practiced during colonialism, remain as a colonial legacy in the postcolonial world's anti-terrorism legislation.

---

[47] Centralization is also found in the British legal and political system but to a lesser extent, as this book explores in Chapter 1.

Although these features provide a theoretical foundation for colonial and neo-colonial practices, they do not provide a full explanation of why Arab states still cling to their colonial heritage. Therefore, after examining the case study of Egypt in Chapter 4, a fifth perspective is suggested: authoritarian ambition.

"Authoritarianism" refers to leadership, whether by a person, party, executive, or elites, who outline the law in accordance with their interests and create a state that allows them to be above the law whenever needed. An important feature of authoritarian regimes, such as those in the Arab world, is the lack of power-sharing, which creates either personal dictatorship or highly centralized authoritarianism, both of which limit political freedoms. "Authoritarian ambition" reflects the desire to control and even destroy legal and constitutional principles in order to enable the ruling individual or group to remain in power. It involves the expansion of authorities and normalization of exceptional powers under the pretext of national security or other alleged virtues. Arab states still cling to the colonial rationale as a "legal" way of securing their authoritarian regimes.

The perspective of authoritarian ambition provides a larger explanation for current anti-terrorism practices worldwide. Although when we talk about authoritarian regimes we mean governments with high centralization and limited political freedoms and mobilization, many colonial and neo-colonial practices are authoritarian in nature. For example, the obsession with monitoring, whether through censorship and speech restrictions, travel bans, or freezing funds, is part of a worldwide collective authoritarian ambition. Arab and Western governments are currently adopting similar anti-terrorism measures that are authoritarian in nature. I argue that the authoritarian ambition as a theoretical perspective, while capable of explaining practices in the Arab world, can also explain counter-terrorism practices in Western democracies.

This book will connect the theoretical framework to the case studies in order to show the convergence between Arab and Western approaches to counter-terrorism. The experience in Western democracies and in authoritarian regimes, like those in the Arab world, suggests that similar phenomena exist within both types of legal system. It is wrong to see authoritarian regimes such as those in the Arab world as totally alien to the Western experience and understanding of law and crime control, or to deny Western encouragement of Arab regimes.

1

On Imperialism, Colonialism, and Neo-Colonialism

Colonialism and neo-colonialism have a long and contested history, as does the related term imperialism; all three are central to the argument in this book. The first part of the chapter clarifies the way these terms are used in this book. The focus is on the law-shaping influence of imperialism and colonialism during the nineteenth and twentieth centuries, integrating them with the neo-colonial influence that evolved in the second half of the twentieth century. The aim of understanding the meaning of these notions is to identify any shared features, which are necessary for understanding the analysis of the case studies. The second part of the chapter analyzes the methods of control used in colonialism and neo-colonialism and identifies four common features that they share: economic expansion, centralization, militarism, and exceptionalism. These features are examined as the theoretical framework for the remainder of the book.

The purpose of the study is not to argue that colonialism is politically or morally right or wrong, but to identify its means and methods and see whether these continue to inform anti-terror legislation today. While in dealing with other crimes criminal law focuses primarily on wrongdoing, anti-terrorism law focuses on threat. Anti-terrorism law is a system that, unlike ordinary criminal law, includes overly broad definitions and lacks due process protection. This duality in the criminal legal system, in which one system exists for ordinary criminals and the other for suspected terrorists, is not new. The anti-terrorism measures being put in place in many countries today have results similar to the colonial dual legal system – one for the colonized peoples and one for the colonizers. This chapter provides the theoretical foundation for the rest of the book to answer whether this exceptional approach to counter-terrorism is borrowed from the colonial policy of crime control.

IMPERIALISM, COLONIALISM, AND NEO-COLONIALISM

This book investigates the influence of colonialism and neo-colonialism on current anti-terrorism measures in Arab states. But what do we mean when we speak of colonialism and neo-colonialism, and how do they relate to the similar term, imperialism? The meaning of any notion is often associated with a particular era and circumstances. To understand the meaning of imperialism, colonialism, and neo-colonialism, an understanding of the related historical and political conditions is essential. The first part of this chapter defines the meaning of colonialism, neo-colonialism, and imperialism as they are used in this book through an overview of the historical and political conditions related to these terms.

Although "imperialism" and "colonialism" are often used interchangeably, this book considers imperialism to be a governing tendency that manifests in the mainland of an empire as well as in colonialism and neo-colonialism. The description below begins with "empire" and the terms related to it, most importantly "imperialism," "new imperialism," and "informal empire," tracing the development of these models of rule in modern times. The discussion then addresses "colonialism" as a specific form of direct empire that was followed by "neo-colonialism" – a contemporary form of indirect control that can be seen as the modern version of informal empire.

The origin of the term "imperialism" is the Latin word *imperium*, which means command and supreme power. Its meaning was connected to Roman experience in expanding territory.[1] Within that timeframe, it also meant the sovereignty of the state over its subjects. An empire is a power that can practice its control by compulsion directly or indirectly over other territories. As Michael Mann defines it, an empire is

a centralized, hierarchical system of rule acquired and maintained by coercion through which a core territory dominates peripheral territories, serves as the intermediary for their main interactions, and channels resources from and between the peripheries.[2]

Mann's definition does not require that empires maintain control over their territories using military force, but leaves the possibility open for political and economic forms of coercion. Nonetheless, Mann explains that empires first expand and solidify their control through their militaries, but later tend to replace military power with economic coercion.[3] This suggests that an empire enjoys military power or the protection of a military power but does not necessary use it, as in employing threats of force.[4] This book identifies centralization, militarism, exceptionalism, and economic force as means by which empires maintain control.

[1] Ronald H. Chilcote, "Globalization and Globalism in Latin America and the Caribbean" (2002) 29:6 *Latin American Perspectives* 81.
[2] Mann, *The Sources of Social Power*, at 17.
[3] *Ibid.*
[4] Go, *Patterns of Empire*, at 10.

The term "imperialism" is derived from this broad concept of empire, and refers to the policies and practices of extending and maintaining the empire's supremacy and power. A distinctive feature of imperialism is that its policies can be applied in the mainland or the "core"[5] of an empire. Such imperial policies include the official use of coercive or exceptional measures *by* law – that is, measures that are written into law – without necessarily respecting the rule *of* law. In other words, rule by law does not limit the authority of the state and does not recognize individual rights as prior to such authority.[6] This rule by law is thus the expression of the will of the supreme ruler or sovereign, outside the framework of constitutionalism, according to which the sovereign is granted undefined authorities with no emphasis on accountability. The practice of the rule by law is particularly common during emergencies or what the sovereign considers as exceptional times.[7] For instance, the Defence of the Realm Act (DORA) of 1914, which granted exceptional powers to the British government during World War I and was applied in the United Kingdom of Great Britain and Ireland, is an example of imperial policy. Although such policies can be justified during emergencies, the problem is when such practices exceed the doctrine of proportionality and normalize the exception. Ruling through the exception is a theme of current anti-terrorism frameworks, which will be discussed throughout the book.

Imperial policy abroad takes several forms, including military, political, and economic pressure. As mentioned above, according to Mann, empires grow through using military power, but after an empire is established, political and economic means can be used as methods of control.[8] Mann suggests that through "economic imperialism" empires can replace the military with economic coercion, which can be done through a system of international banking and denial of foreign investment.[9] In some cases economic imperialism can occur without military intervention. For example, as is discussed in Chapter 6, in the 1860s Europe lent Tunisia loans with disadvantageous terms, which led Tunisia to declare bankruptcy. As a result, a European commission took control of Tunisia's budget until it had paid off its debts.

The latter form of control is considered by some as "informal empire."[10] Informal empire refers to the control of a superior power through indirect political control,

---

[5] See Mann's definition of "direct empire" in *The Sources of Social Power*, at 18.

[6] Martin Loughlin, *Sword and Scales: An Examination of the Relationship between Law and Politics* (Oxford: Hart, 2000) at 198.

[7] Carl Schmitt, *Dictatorship* (Cambridge: Polity Press, 2014) at 127.

[8] Mann, *The Sources of Social Power*, at 17. For Go, an empire can only be represented by state actors and official governmental control. Accordingly, the economic control of private corporations cannot be part of an empire. See Go, *Patterns of Empire*, at 7.

[9] Mann, *The Sources of Social Power*, at 19.

[10] Ibid, at 18; Go, *Patterns of Empire*, at 10–11; Juan Cole, *Colonialism and Revolution in the Middle East: Social and Cultural Origins of Egypt's 'Urabi Movement* (Princeton, NJ: Princeton University Press, 1993) at 55.

which can be economic, strategic, or even cultural in nature, with minimal or no military involvement and without claiming sovereignty. It suggests the exercise of the essence of an imperial policy without the direct engagement of the empire's formal representatives. The elites in the colonized territories often play a significant role in these imbalanced power relations, as they link the imperial power with its indigenous policymakers.[11] This form of control can exist prior to, after, or between periods of colonialism. For example, Juan Cole argues that during the eighteenth and nineteenth centuries, particularly in the Middle East, "colonies often existed before colonialism."[12] This means that imperialism dominated many parts of the world politically and economically whether or not direct colonization took place.[13] Informal empire still exists in our current time where it is described as "neo-colonialism" (discussed below).

This book is concerned with imperialism only within a specific timeline: the "new imperialism"[14] that prevailed from the eighteenth century onward, and its major Western players, above all Britain and France, and later the United States. Imperialism paved the way for direct colonialism. Britain and France engaged in direct colonial control all over the world including in the Arab region. The United States, although it did not have colonies in the Arab world, colonized the Philippines, Puerto Rico, Hawaii, Guam, Samoa, and the Virgin Islands.[15] Nonetheless, the United States remains a later colonial player than Britain and France, which were the most influential colonial leaders of their time.

Colonialism refers to the direct military and political occupation and expansion overseas by the European powers, which spread widely during the nineteenth and twentieth centuries and which sought to protect the colonists' political and economic interests. The British and the French colonial empires were the largest in the twentieth century. By 1922, the British colonial empire – the largest in history – held 22.6 percent of the earth's total land, whether as colonies, protectorates, or commonwealth.[16] Together, Britain and France held roughly 30 percent of the world's land area. This massive spread of European colonialism created a general worldwide pattern of Western domination.[17]

The dominant nature of earlier colonial empires such as that of the Spanish and Portuguese differed from British and French imperialism. While both kinds of empire sought territory and economic expansion, scholars of postcolonial theory

---

[11] Gregory A. Barton, *Informal Empire and the Rise of One World Culture* (London: Palgrave Macmillan, 2014) at 15.
[12] *Ibid.*
[13] Cole, *Colonialism and Revolution in the Middle East*, at 3.
[14] Go, *Postcolonial Thought and Social Theory*, at 3.
[15] For more, see Go, *Patterns of Empire*, at 25, 54–65.
[16] See Said, *Culture and Imperialism*, at 8; Barton, *Informal Empire and the Rise of One World Culture*, at 28.
[17] Said, *ibid*, at xi–xii.

explain that the latter claimed an idealistic purpose: the "civilizing mission."[18] From the imperial standpoint, it was an ethical duty and thus a "divine right" to save those societies they considered backward. This was done by teaching them the arts of governing and pulling them out of their isolation into a global market.[19] This imperial belief, whether French or British, in the colonizer's civilizing mission had the goal of legitimizing the imperial order. As for advancing what the empires saw as backward nations, many argue that the arts of self-government remained within the empires and were not truly granted in most colonies, except some commonwealth territories such as Canada and Australia.[20] J. A. Hobson describes the imperial tendency in the nineteenth and early twentieth century as lacking the intention to spread the skills of self-governing:

> [W]ithout discussing here the excellencies or the defects of the British theory and practice of representative self-government, to assert that our "fixed rule of action" has been to educate our dependencies in this theory and practice is quite the largest misstatement of the facts of our colonial and imperial policy that is possible. Upon the vast majority of the populations throughout our Empire we have bestowed no real powers of self-government, nor have we any serious intention of doing so [...]. Of the three hundred and sixty-seven millions of British subjects outside these isles, not more than eleven millions, or one in thirty-four, have any real self-government for purposes of legislation and administration.[21]

This selectivity in spreading and transplanting the arts of government guaranteed Western powers the upper hand over other nations. Edward Said calls this imbalanced relationship a "flexible positional superiority."[22] By keeping what imperialism viewed as backward nations where they are, there will always be a need for the knowledge and expertise of the West,[23] even after independence – as will be shown below with regard to neo-colonialism.

The classical form of colonialism is thus a manifestation of imperialism.[24] In the twentieth century, direct colonialism came to an end, primarily through armed and cultural resistance. With the rise of anti-colonialism and nationalism, imperial powers withdraw from formal imperialism or direct colonialism.[25] On the other hand, imperialism – the procreator of colonialism – still exists worldwide in the form of informal empire. Although colonialism has ended, neo-colonialism has emerged

[18] V. G. Kiernan, *The Lords of Human Kind: European Attitudes towards the Outside World in the Imperial Age* (Harmondsworth, UK: Penguin Books, 1972) at 24.
[19] V. G. Kiernan, "Tennyson, King Arthur, and Imperialism" in Harvey J. Kaye, ed, *Poets, Politics, and the People* (London: Verso, 1989) at 129–51.
[20] J. A. Hobson, *Imperialism: A Study* (New York: Gordon Press, 1975 [1902]) at 114–18.
[21] *Ibid*, at 114.
[22] Edward W. Said, *Orientalism*, 1st Vintage Books edn (New York: Vintage Books, 1979) at 7.
[23] Said, *Culture and Imperialism*, at 9.
[24] *Ibid*.
[25] *Ibid*.

as a less coercive and more indirect way of imperial control, reflected in the global domination of the Western – particularly American – cultural, political, economic, and social patterns.

In the aftermath of World War II, colonial powers such as the United Kingdom and France were politically and economically exhausted. They also had to respond to global anti-colonial movements. They did so by withdrawing their military forces from their colonies. Although these powers maintained strong ties with local elites and access to market manipulation, they left a political vacuum in many parts of the world, which were left without a solid constitutional and governance foundation. These factors paved the way for the United States to lead global economic and political reforms through modernization and globalization. In relation to the Arab world in particular, Lisa Hajjar and Steve Niva argue that during the 1970s, the "US commitment in the region grew dramatically, spurred by the 'vacuum' left by the British withdrawal from the Gulf, the rise of Saudi Arabia to global prominence following the 1973 war, and Anwar Sadat's embrace of the US during the same period."[26] The same pattern is visible across the world.

With the fading of colonialism and the growth of American imperial power, the term "neo-colonialism" has emerged to describe the new forms of control of the dominant global powers. Ella Shohat explains that the term "neo-colonialism" suggests that colonialism in its classical sense is in the past, but that its cultural, economic, and political effects are in the present, in a repetition of the old colonial rationale yet with new distinctive forms of practice.[27] Such practices are engaged in not only by states, but also by international corporations and supra-national bodies. Although these bodies may not be neo-colonial powers by themselves, they apply neo-colonial policies that benefit the powerful states behind them and strengthen the neo-colonial order. This order requires the maintenance of the dependency of developing and less developed countries on highly developed countries and their corporations.[28] Dominant powers control in a way that maintains their superiority over other countries. This kind of hegemony can thus be seen as a distinctive form of informal empire.

With the fading of colonialism after World War II, the United States became a great dominating power. While Britain, throughout its imperial history, controlled other territories through both formal and informal methods of imperialism, the United States has controlled primarily through informal imperialism.[29] The United

---

[26] Lisa Hajjar & Steve Niva, "(Re)Made in the USA: Middle East Studies in the Global Era" (1997) 205 *Middle East Report* 2 at 5.

[27] For an analysis of postcolonialism, see Ella Shohat, "Notes on the 'Post-Colonial'" (1992) 31/32 *Third World and Post-Colonial Issues* 99 at 105–6.

[28] Douglas Andrew Yates, *The Rentier State in Africa: Oil Rent Dependency and Neocolonialism in the Republic of Gabon* (Trenton, NJ: Africa World Press, 1996) at 4–5.

[29] Go, *Patterns of Empire*, at 26.

States spreads its control and influence worldwide primarily by making subordinate allies and client states. Through these forms of indirect control, the United States has emerged as a "not classical imperial power[,]"[30] as Said describes it. The United States did not use the colonial pretext of the "civilizing mission," but justifies its moves with the ideal of spreading the virtues of democracy and liberty. Said argues that the United States views itself as a "righter of wrongs," countering tyranny and defending freedom worldwide.[31] The Vietnam War, the Gulf War of 1991, and the 2003 invasion of Iraq are examples among many of the United States' role as a heroic state.[32]

The attacks of 9/11 gave the United States another reason for military intervention worldwide. However, it is possible that the underlying reason behind the American use of militarism has less to do with spreading democracy and liberty than with its own security and economic growth.[33] Go argues that the Cold War "had given justification for America's military power and economic hegemony, and served as the basis for a 'social compact' between the United States and the European capitalist states. The United States delivered peace and security in exchange for European deference."[34] Through this lens, in the above examples of military intervention the United States aimed to diminish communism in the Vietnam War, and to secure the flow of Gulf oil to the United States in the Gulf War. In the 2003 Iraq War the United States combined security with economic goals, aiming to get rid of Saddam Hussein, a former and not fully submissive ally. Being on the border of Iran, the location of Iraq is very significant to the American interests in the region. Iran has long represented a foe to the United States and an ally to Russia; by controlling Iraq, the United States strengthens its virtual defensive border against Russia.

This book argues that the contemporary war on terror can be seen as an extension of colonial policy under the new cloak of neo-colonialism. This can be seen in the use of militarism and exceptionalism. For instance, although colonialism used militarism and exceptionalism to spread "civilization" in colonies, the tendency is continued by neo-colonial powers but under a different pretext. Neo-colonialism uses militarism and exceptionalism to allegedly fight crimes and restore rights worldwide. In both colonialism and neo-colonialism, "virtue" adds legitimacy to militarized and exceptional practices, alongside other practices that include economic expansion and centralization, as examined below.

---

[30] Said, *Culture and Imperialism*, at 5.
[31] *Ibid.*
[32] *Ibid.*
[33] Noam Chomsky & Andre Vltchek, *On Western Terrorism: From Hiroshima to Drone Warfare* (Toronto: BTL, 2013) at 113–20.
[34] Go, *Patterns of Empire*, at 193.

THE COMMON FEATURES OF COLONIALISM
AND NEO-COLONIALISM

This book suggests that the colonial states ruled through the use of militarism and a combination of an exceptional and a political doctrine, which also extends to neo-colonial patterns of control. Both colonial and neo-colonial patterns of control share four common features: economic expansion and reforms, centralization, militarism, and exceptional regulations and measures. Exceptionalism, which is the set of measures regulated by law or necessity that allow temporary rule outside the umbrella of law, is treated in this book as the most important and most complex factor in securing colonial rule. This is due to the direct link between exceptional measures and counter-terrorism. Anti-terrorism law is a combination of several disciplines including criminal law, immigration law, and financial law, although the criminal nature of anti-terrorism remains central. However, many exceptions have been added to this field, in a way that makes anti-terrorism measures closer to exceptional powers. Forms of the exception include detention without trial and even declaring states of emergency for long periods, as is the case in Egypt.

This section does not treat these factors equally but gives each factor enough explanation while keeping in mind its relationship to the colonial and neo-colonial experience and their impact on contemporary counter-terrorism. The four above factors are at the core of imperial domination, emerging as colonialism in the eighteenth and nineteenth centuries and reemerging in the twentieth century as neo-colonialism. This section shows how each of these factors emerged as a strategy of domination of domination, remaining in place in former colonies after independence, and finally appearing again in neo-colonialism, specifically in the war on terror.

Economic Expansion and Reforms

Colonialism and neo-colonialism were driven by economic forces to secure their political power at home and abroad. In colonies, the focus was on integrating the capitalist economy and introducing these colonies to the global market.[35] By engaging colonies in the capitalist market, capitalism spread globally as the standard trade system. Sven Beckert provides an example of the global impact of the Western trade in cotton, which

> tie together Asia, the Americas, Africa, and Europe in a complex commercial web. [...] Never before had the products of Indian weavers paid for slaves in Africa to work on the plantations in the Americas to produce agricultural commodities for European consumers.[36]

[35] Patrick Chabal, *Power in Africa: An Essay in Political Interpretation* (New York: Springer, 2016) at 80.
[36] Sven Beckert, *Empire of Cotton: A Global History* (New York: Vintage Books, 2014) at 36.

This web functioned based on a hierarchal system created by European powers, who set the trading rules abroad in accordance with a master–subject relationship.[37] Beckert describes these relationships, which operated during different stages of colonialism:

> We associate industrial capitalism with contracts and markets, but early capitalism was based as often as not on violence and bodily coercion. Modern capitalism privileges property rights, but this earlier moment was characterized just as much by massive expropriations as by secure ownership. Latter-day capitalism rests upon the rule of law and powerful institutions backed by the state, but capitalism's early phase, although ultimately requiring state power to create world-spanning empires, was frequently based on the unrestrained actions of private individuals—the domination of masters over slaves and of frontier capitalists over indigenous inhabitants. The cumulative result of this highly aggressive, outwardly oriented capitalism was that Europeans came to dominate the centuries-old worlds of cotton, merge them into a single empire centered in Manchester, and invent the global economy we take for granted today.[38]

Although coercion is no longer systematically used in economic relations, the West still dominates the rest of the world through unequal positions of power. Western markets remained and expanded in the postcolonial world. Forms of economic control that emerged in the neo-colonial era include, among others, the arms trade, Western financial aid to former colonies and developing countries, and supranational financial supervision over states, organizations, and banks. Today, Western domination of the global economy is at the core of neo-colonialism. This section argues that the economic aspect is a driver of neo-colonial powers in the war on terror. The FATF is an example of a body that functions to place economic pressure on countries to adopt counter-terrorism financing regulations. This role represents a shift in global counter-terrorism policies, as is shown below.

In the neo-colonial era, supra-national bodies, above all the FATF, have been established as part of protecting and supervising national and global economic growth. The FATF is an inter-governmental body established in Paris in 1989 by the Group of Seven (G7). Its mandate originally included combating money laundering,[39] but was later expanded to regulate measures regarding combating terrorist financing.[40] This expansion was adopted in 2001 as a response to the 9/11 attacks. In its Special Recommendations on Terrorist Financing, the FATF called on states to implement UN Security Council Resolution 1373 and to criminalize terrorist financing.[41] Governments and bankers all around the world have responded

---

[37] *Ibid.*
[38] *Ibid.*
[39] FATF Members and Observers, *FATF homepage*, online: FATF www.fatf-gafi.org.
[40] This mandate was expanded once more in 2011 to include proliferation financing.
[41] See the Special Recommendations on Terrorist Financing, FATF IX Special Recommendations, October 31, 2001.

to the FATF by adopting more regulations regarding money laundering and terrorist financing.

The increasing influence of the FATF is not limited to its imposition of global regulations, but includes its growth in size from seven members to 37, mainly from the Organisation for Economic Co-operation and Development (OECD), and other observers and associate members. Among the associate members is the Middle East and North Africa Financial Action Task Force (MENAFATF), established in 2004. MENAFATF, as a sub-institution, is required to ensure the application of FATF recommendations and the relevant UN obligations within the MENA region.[42]

There is evidence that the FATF has significant financial and economic weight. It has been argued that governments have been responding to the FATF because they "have found themselves under heavy moral, political, and economic pressure"[43] that, if resisted, would risk putting them on the "non-cooperative countries and territories" list and the "name and shame" list.[44] Supra-national institutions like the FATF and the OECD have been accused, especially by those at risk of being listed, of adopting institutional imperialism and a neo-colonial policy.[45] J. C. Sharmen describes the FATF's moral and economic pressure as follows:

[B]odies such as the FSF, FATF, and even the OECD operate in an environment of "institutional Darwinism," i.e., of many close competitors operating to sustain any given regime, and member states who put increasing emphasis on getting "value for money," creating pressure to adapt and survive. International institutions that fail to live up to members' expectations or attract too much bad publicity may find themselves marginalized and strive of [sic] funds.[46]

Postcolonial nations remain largely dependent on Western and supra-national financial aid. This has created a de facto subordination to the West, which, through economic pressure, is able to direct political and global matters, including counter-terrorism. Terrorism financing in particular has become a part of most, if not all, national security laws, as will be shown in Chapter 2.

---

[42] Middle East and North Africa Financial Action Task Force, online: MENAFATF www .menafatf.org.

[43] Tim Parkman, *Mastering Anti-Money Laundering and Counter-Terrorist Financing* (Harlow: Pearson, 2012) at 154.

[44] Benn Steil & Robert E. Litan, *Financial Statecraft: The Role of Financial Markets in American Foreign Policy* (New Haven, CT: Yale University Press, 2008) at 36.

[45] George Gilligan, "Multilateral Regulatory Initiatives – A Legitimation-Based Approach" in Justin O'Brien, ed, *Governing the Corporation: Regulation and Corporate Governance in an Age of Scandal and Global Markets* (Hoboken, NJ: John Wiley & Sons, 2005) at 130; Ronen Palan, Richard Murphy & Christian Chavagneux, *Tax Havens: How Globalization Really Works* (New York: Cornell University Press, 2013) at 205, 216.

[46] J. C. Sharmen, "The Agency of the Peripheral Actors: Small State Tax Havens and International Regimes as Weapons of the Weak" in John M. Hobson & Leonard Seabrooke, eds, *Everyday Politics of the World Economy* (Cambridge: Cambridge University Press, 2007) at 52.

Economic expansion and reforms promoted the influence of Western powers over others in colonial times through domination and even force. Western powers were able to establish and transplant capitalism in former colonies as the global economic system; today they continue dominating through neo-colonial manifestations of this same tendency. Western countries have been politically influential over other countries through financial aid, which is an indirect way of maintaining a superior–inferior relationship. Collectively, Western neo-colonial powers have been setting new economic reforms and enforcing them worldwide through supranational bodies like the FATF, which allows countries that the FATF considers not cooperative in countering terrorism financing to be blacklisted. Granting the FATF the power to name and shame countries is a system that belongs to global centralization.

Centralization

Centralization offered empires of the nineteenth and twentieth century a legitimate way to monopolize political and military powers. France provides the most obvious model for centralization.[47] Modern French centralization can be linked to the Revolution and the Napoleonic government – both of which have had a large influence over Europe and worldwide. The historical conditions of the French Revolution required the newborn government to make order its priority.[48] Napoleon formed an excessively centralized government,[49] successfully involving himself in financial, legal, and military plans. He consolidated authoritarian powers, titling himself the First Consul. Whenever he did not get the approval of legislative or political bodies, he bypassed them through plebiscite, a practice that has become common in our contemporary time. It was through plebiscite that Napoleon obtained the position of First Consul for life, which granted him power over many authorities within the Prefects.[50]

Another important era for French centralization is the Second Empire (1852–70) under the rule of Louis Napoleon. Centralization was broadened further, allowing the emperor to dissolve the parliament and to declare a state of siege.[51] These authorities have been amended and contained in France, but they still exist in the

---

[47] This has been the case since the French monarchy, when powers were centralized within the hands of the ruler, forming a system close to authoritarianism. William W. Smithers, "The Code Napoléon" (1901) 49:3 American Law Register 127 at 130.

[48] Charles B. Wheeler, "The Code Napoleon and Its Framers" (1924) 10:3 American Bar Association Journal, 202 at 204.

[49] James T. Young, "Administrative Centralization and Decentralization in France" (1898) 11 Annals of the American Academy of Political and Social Science 24 at 28.

[50] David Nicholls, Napoleon: A Biographical Companion (Santa Barbara, CA: ABC-CLIO, 1999) at 65, 203.

[51] Kelly L. Grotke & Markus J. Prutsch, Constitutionalism, Legitimacy, and Power: Nineteenth-century Experiences (New York: Oxford University Press, 2014) at 98.

constitutions of most Arab countries, which adopted these measures from the French model, as will be shown in Chapter 3 and subsequent chapters.

By contrast, the British legal and political system is considered mostly localized, allowing "a high degree of local independence and activity" in its homeland and in the colonies.[52] Nonetheless, since the nineteenth century there has been a tendency toward British central control regarding certain matters.[53] These include the police and other national security bodies. Since the British forms of centralization are mostly exceptional or emergency-related, they will be addressed in the next section, which is dedicated to emergency and emergency-like powers.

Centralization as a system that legitimates the consolidation of authorities with those in power is also found within contemporary supra-national bodies, particularly the UN Security Council and the FATF. As will be shown in Chapter 2, these bodies have exclusive authorities that are similar to domestic executive powers. This book refers to this kind of centralization as "global centralization."

Global centralization arises in the modern context, including that of neo-colonialism. At the international level, privileges are granted to some nations over others. For example, the United Nations functions on the basis of equal sovereignties; this is particularly true within the General Assembly. On the other hand, this formal equality is limited by centralizing major powers within the Security Council. The domination of the Security Council in anti-terrorism policymaking reflects the actual power of its permanent members, particularly the United Kingdom, the United States, and France. Although this inequality existed in the aftermath of World War II, when colonialism still dominated, the Security Council did not evoke its executive-like powers until the late 1990s. Therefore, the book links global centralization to the period of neo-colonialism.

The UN Security Council, under Chapter VII of the UN Charter, has issued international obligations regarding criminalizing terrorism and terrorism financing, listing, travel restrictions and many other obligations. It has granted itself the absolute authority to list and de-list terrorists without sharing its reports, evidence, or reasons. The broad authority practiced by the Security Council derives from the fact the UN Charter did not set detailed limitations on the role of the Security Council. Thus, this book's critique of this role is based on general legal principles and human rights, rather than on any conflict of its actions with its mandate as specified in its founding document. Chapter 2 provides further analysis of the Security Council's role and its imperfect approach to counter-terrorism.

The FATF is another supra-national body that centralizes powers regarding counter-terrorism financing. Its role and impact were discussed in the previous section regarding the economic aspect of colonialism and neo-colonialism. To avoid

---

[52] James T. Young, "Administrative Centralization and Decentralization in England" (1897) 10 *Annals of the American Academy of Political and Social Science* 39 at 40.
[53] *Ibid*, at 41, 57.

repetition, I limit the discussion here to noting the current pattern of financially powerful forces such as the FATF tending to centralize their control, affecting the political and economic monopoly of power. Although the FATF is an executive-like body, its mandate allows it to issue global regulations and enforce them through a system of blacklisting incorporate countries. The use of such legislative and judicial-like powers by a financial institution affects nations' internal governance, leaving them with no choice but to submit to globally powerful bodies.

Militarism

The colonial powers used their militaries to secure the imperial order.[54] The basis of the colonial experience of militarism is therefore in the theory and practices of counter-insurgency. In this section, I argue that current methods of counter-terrorism are borrowed from colonial counter-insurgency. Jenny Hocking emphasizes that the importance of linking the theory of counter-insurgency to counter-terrorism is that it shows how a military approach that was used during colonial wartime is being applied during peacetime to a domestic crime (terrorism) that includes violent and non-violent acts.[55] Furthermore, the colonial rationale that justified the use of the military to suppress nationalists in the name of protecting the legitimate colonial government is the same that is used today in counter-terrorism. Lawful acts are being criminalized in both Western democracies and authoritarian regimes in the name of protecting society and its stability.

Colonial counter-insurgency was a militarized method of crime and social control. The British colonists, owing to their commitment to the principle of "minimum use of force," were less coercive than, for example, the French.[56] However, as French argues, the principle "minimum use of force" allowed the use of force, only not systematically.[57] Counter-insurgency thinkers saw the military approach as essential; however, they admitted that military action alone could not guarantee the objective of counter-insurgency, which is stability.[58] Therefore, suggests the British military officer Sir Robert Thompson, in order to counter insurgency, a strong administrative structure should be established that can "keep pace with the aspirations of the people while at the same time creating an atmosphere of order and stability[.]"[59] Thompson's suggestion of establishing an administrative structure as

---

[54] Kiernan, "Tennyson, King Arthur, and Imperialism," at 133.
[55] Hocking, *Beyond Terrorism*, at 14–16.
[56] *Ibid*, at 75–9.
[57] *Ibid*.
[58] See Robert Thompson, *Defeating Communist Insurgency: Experiences from Malaya and Vietnam* (New York: F. A. Praeger, 1966); David Galula, *Counterinsurgency Warfare: Theory and Practice* (New York: Praeger, 1964).
[59] Thompson, *Defeating Communist Insurgency*, at 70.

part of counter-insurgency policy grants the military and related security bodies greater centralization and executive powers.

Martial law is another militarized method of domination, which combines militarization and exceptionalism. For this reason, martial law is discussed in more detail in the following section on exceptionalism and emergency powers. Here, it is enough to note that martial law is a system of suspending law and providing the military with immunity from accountability. Under colonialism, the necessity of security justified the temporary suspension of ordinary law in favor of martial law.

Whether because of a rebellion, a civil war, or a threat of an invasion, the utility of martial law is claimed to be that of maintaining order and security. When the ordinary authority is unable to secure the right to life and to protect property during emergencies, the military is authorized to take control and bring peace and order.[60] According to Nasser Hussain, by suspending ordinary law, martial law aims to reflect the "legal maxim *Salus populi suprema est lex* (safety of the people is the supreme law)."[61] This represents the highest law and the state of no law at once.[62] Thus, lawful violence remains the tool of enforcing the supreme law.

In the aftermath of World War II and the fading of colonialism, there has been a decrease in the use of armed force. However, Western intervention, led primarily by the United States and its allies, as well as NATO, has affirmed the reemergence of militarism as a political tool of control. For example, under the pretext of security necessity, between 1960 and 2005 France launched 46 military operations in its former African colonies.[63] This form of military intervention is part of the neo-colonial policy and practices. Other examples that are directly related to counter-terrorism are the post-9/11 reactive American military attack on the Taliban in Afghanistan and the more recent military campaigns on the Islamic State of Iraq and Syria (ISIS) in Syria and other air strikes against the Syrian regime. These events suggest a reemergence of a militarized colonial rationale.

In addition, militarizing the police has become a growing practice in the neo-colonial period.[64] Specialized police forces have been created to deal with specific

[60] *Ibid*, at 407.
[61] Hussain, *The Jurisprudence of Emergency*, at 102.
[62] *Ibid*.
[63] Christopher Griffin, "French Military Interventions in Africa: Realism vs. Ideology in French Defense Policy and Grand Strategy" (2007) Paper prepared for the International Studies Association Annual Convention, February 28–March 3, 2007, Chicago.
[64] The root of specialized security units can be found in the British experience in Northern Ireland. Britain established military counter-insurgency units such as the Auxiliary Division, as well as police counter-terrorism units, including the Royal Irish Constabulary Special Reserve, known as the Black and Tans. The utility of such units was often controversial owing to their excessive use of violence. See Anna Oehmichen, *Terrorism and Anti-Terrorism Legislation: The Terrorised Legislator? A Comparison of Counter-terrorism Legislation and Its Implications for Human Rights in the Legal Systems of the United Kingdom, Spain, Germany, and France* (Antwerp: Intersentia, 2009) at 62; Lawrence James, *The Rise and Fall of the British Empire* (New York: Abacus, 1995) at 381–4.

responsibilities and crimes, such as the Civil Nuclear Constabulary in the United Kingdom and the Northern Ireland Security Guard Service. The specialization of police forces on its own is not a problem. In fact, it can enhance the productivity of crime control. However, despite the "police" label on their chests, the heavy guns that are carried by these forces – and the authority granted to them to "shoot to kill" suspects even when there is no direct and immediate threat to the lives of civilians[65] – shifts their civil role of protecting society and enforcing law into a militarized role of combating the enemy.

The current war on terror thus adopts some of the features of militarism. This adoption of militaristic measures reflects an explicit effort to apply counter-insurgency measures to the war on terror. Paul Wilkinson, a member of the London-based Institute for Study of Conflict, suggests that counter-insurgency measures must be considered when countering terrorism. He argues that "it is possible to draw from the recent experience of low-intensity and counter-insurgency operations certain basic ground rules which should be followed by liberal democracies taking a tough line against terrorism."[66] Such justification paved the way for gradual penetration of using militarized approaches in domestic peacetime situations.

In both its colonial and neo-colonial application, there is a close relationship between militarism and the elite. Sabah Alnasseri observes that security has always represented a concern to the elite, who seek to protect their status. The elite, therefore, tend to use their influence to militarize the state through military protection and establishing bases of both internal and external origin.[67] Alnasseri links the need to secure the elite to the phenomenon of terror, and more importantly to the war on terror, or, as he describes it, a "war of terror."[68] The militarized approach of ruling is an extension of imperial norms that aims to serve the elite and their relations with imperial powers.

Exceptionalism and Emergency Powers

Exceptionalism is a set of extraordinary measures regulated by law or outside the framework of law.[69] Among the four characteristics of colonialism and

---

[65] Oehmichen, *Terrorism and Anti-Terrorism Legislation*, at 152.
[66] Paul Wilkinson, *Terrorism versus Liberal Democracy* (London: Institute for the Study of Conflict, 1976) at 10.
[67] Sabah Alnasseri, "Understanding Iraq" in Leo Panitch & Colin Leys, eds, *Global Flashpoints: Reactions to Imperialism and Neoliberalism* (Wiltshire: Merlin Press, 2007) at 80–1.
[68] Pepe Escobar, interview with Sabah Alnasseri, "Basra: Class Struggle, Not Civil War" (April 1, 2008) online: *The Real News* therealnews.com.
[69] The legitimacy and necessity of emergency powers are discussed by Schmitt's theory of the exception. Schmitt's definition of the exception is derived from his understanding of the meaning of the sovereignty, which is "he who decides on the exception." Schmitt was able to establish a sophisticated legal theoretical framework that justifies the extraordinary powers of the

neo-colonialism that this chapter explores, exceptionalism represents the main link between the past and the present – between an imperial–colonial rationale and the neo-colonial influence on the current war on terrorism. The reliance on emergency powers in counter-terrorism, especially post-9/11, has brought the theory and practice of the exception to the surface. Practices like establishing special courts and detention without trial have a long history in the precolonial state, but colonialism was a direct way of spreading and legalizing these practices.

This section starts with an examination of the colonial use of exceptionalism. It addresses the British experience followed by that of the French, with greater focus on the British experience, for two reasons. First, unlike France, which used exceptionalism at home and in its colonies, Britain created a duality in its application of exceptionalism. For example, martial law was declared in British colonies but never in Britain, whereas the French applied their state of exception in both mainland France and its colonies. Unlike France, Britain has a dual exceptional system, which is discussed below in two parts: the policy of the exception as it was applied in British colonies, and as it was applied in Britain. Forms of the exception reflected in the British colonial experience include martial law and state of emergency. On the other hand, the experience within the United Kingdom includes exceptional measures of detention without trial and other restrictions on meetings and associations as implemented in the Defence of the Realm Act 1914 (DORA). The investigation of the forms of the exception applied in colonies and in Britain shows that the British exceptional measures have had a great influence on postcolonial counter-terrorism in countries such as Egypt.

The French experience with exceptional powers, discussed next, included two similar exceptional systems to the British: the state of siege and the state of emergency. However, the French adopted a revolutionary doctrine in their colonies that justified the use of coercion. A similar logic still exists in the postcolonial world, as is shown in Chapter 7 in relation to the Tunisian postcolonial experience.

---

state practiced within the context of dictatorship, or the so-called constructional dictatorship. For Schmitt and other writers such as Clinton Rossiter who support the state of exception, the historical perspective seems to play a great role in shaping their thought. Such writings are delivered in the aftermath of an emergency. In the aftermath of World War I, Schmitt attempted to support the Nazi regime by placing "democracy" over "liberalism," whereas Rossiter in *Constitutional Dictatorship* seeks to justify emergency powers in the name of protecting liberal democracies. Carl Schmitt, *Political Theology: Four Chapters on the Concept of Sovereignty* (Chicago: University of Chicago Press, 2005 [1922]) at 5–6; Clinton Rossiter, *Constitutional Dictatorship: Crisis Government in the Modern Democracies* (New York: Harcourt Brace & World, 1963) at 3–8.

   Schmitt and Rossiter's reactive intellectual approach lacks a holistic view of the nature of the actual and legal dimensions of the use of the state of exception within a dynamic social order. Agamben criticizes both Schmitt's and Rossiter's writings as works of "self-serving." Giorgio Agamben, *State of Exception* (Chicago: University of Chicago Press, 2005) at 47.

After looking at the British and French experiences, the chapter examines the neo-colonial manifestations of exceptionalism and emergency powers. Exceptionalism has roots in colonialism but continues to be a powerful force used today in the counter-terrorism frameworks of former colonies and globally within the UN Security Council.

The British Experience of Exceptionalism

THE BRITISH EXPERIENCE WITHIN ITS COLONIES The British ruled their colonies according to the rule of law, which was generally designed on the basis of what the British viewed as political necessity. Necessity, however, allowed the British to establish exceptional systems like martial law and state of emergency that paralyzed the rule of law. These systems are discussed next. The use of martial law in particular to bypass law for the sake of preserving legal order presents a critical issue regarding the legitimacy of martial law – at least outside the framework of conventional wars and invasions. This issue resonates in post-9/11 debates,[70] as will be discussed at the end of this chapter.

Martial Law

Martial law, as it has been known and applied in the nineteenth century and onward, is basically a system that suspends ordinary law and replaces it with the will of the military commander during wartime or an emergency.[71] Since the rule of Charles I (1625–49), Britain has restricted the exercise of this undefined power within the parliament.[72] It should be noted that the British Parliament has never declared martial law in Britain.

Ireland, despite its official status as part of the United Kingdom between 1801 and 1922, was subject at times to excessive coercive measures. For this reason, this book treats the coercive measures in Ireland, particularly against Irish rebels, as part of the British colonial rationale. Martial law was among the militarized measures that exceptionally used in Ireland. For instance, in British colonies and in Ireland, the authority for declaring martial law was not parliament; martial law was regulated by the common law, and the royal governors and military commanders had the authority to declare it.[73] The fact that parliament did not have exclusive authority to declare martial law in colonies, whereas it did in mainland Britain, suggests a duality and inequality in applying legal systems.

---

[70] David Dyzenhaus, "The Puzzle of Martial Law" (2009) 59 *University of Toronto Law Journal* 1, at 3.
[71] French, *The British Way in Counter-Insurgency*, at 75.
[72] William E. Birkhimer, *Military Government and Martial Law* (Kansas City, MO: F. Hudson, 1914) at 374.
[73] Joseph B. Kelly & George A. Pelletier, Jr., "Theories of Emergency Government" (1966) 11 *South Dakota Law Review* 42 at 47.

In "Round up the Usual Suspects: The Legacy of British Colonialism and the European Convention on Human Rights,"[74] The legal historian A. W. Brian Simpson describes the arbitrariness behind martial law under British rule:

Martial law belongs to a world in which, in effect, government makes war on those who do not accept its authority and makes no bones about what it is doing. This was, for example, what happened in the case of the Indian Mutiny, and in 1865, when Governor Eyre suppressed a supposed Jamaican insurrection. These government wars are not wars of an international character. Rather, they are wars waged against persons regarded as rebels or insurgents who, if not killed in military operations or summarily punished under martial law, may be tried as traitors or criminals. In the period when the imposition of martial law was a normal response to insurrection, it was not thought that the rebels acquired the rights of combatants in a war between states. In a sense, the rebels were treated worse than combatants in regular wars or than criminals under normal conditions.[75]

During martial law, the colonial authority had the power to suspend the constitution and to try civilians before martial law courts established during World War I, all of which had exceptional forms, measures, and procedures.[76] "Subversives" were tried before military courts and sentenced to death in places like Palestine and Malaya,[77] and trials *in camera* were allowed in Kenya.[78] These practices have become part of former colonies' national security laws, as will be shown in the case of Egypt in Chapter 4.

After independence, former colonies adopted imperfect democratic systems. They borrowed strategies of exceptionalism, such as emergency and emergency-like powers, special courts, and detention without trial, and incorporated them in national security laws and measures. They also accepted continued control from their former colonizers through different political and economic channels, as evidenced in the machinations of industrialism, the global market, and the arms trade.

State of Emergency

The gap between the British and the colonized people increased because of the reliance on the military and martial law. This led the British to limit their use of martial law; instead, they established another exceptional form of rule: the state of emergency.[79] According to French, emergency powers allowed the British "to maintain the outward appearance of legality and simultaneously employ as much

---

[74] A. W. Brian Simpson, "Round up the Usual Suspects: The Legacy of British Colonialism and the European Convention on Human Rights" (1953) 41:4 *Loyola Law Review* 629 at 634.

[75] *Ibid.*

[76] Brown, *The Rule of Law in the Arab World*, at 77.

[77] *Ibid*, at 90–91.

[78] *Ibid.*

[79] French, *The British Way in Counter-Insurgency*, at 57, 103.

or as little coercion and violence as they chose[.]"[80] Without declaring martial law, civil power was not given to the military. It has been argued that the shift from martial law to emergency powers aimed to replace the military with an executive political power.[81] Despite the political nature of emergency powers, militarism continued aiding the British authority in its colonies.

The case of Malaya shows a combination of exceptional and militarized measures. For instance, in 1948 the British adopted the Enemy Regulations Ordinance to suppress the insurgency of the Malayan Communist Party during a state of emergency. According to the Ordinance, the High Commissioner of the Federation of Malaya has the power to issue regulations that are "necessary or expedient for securing the public safety or for the maintenance of public order."[82] I should point out that in British colonies insurgency was not limited to violent crimes, but also included strikes and public meetings. Major-General Frank Kitson, who served in the British army in Kenya, Malaya, and Northern Ireland from 1946 to 1985, is one of the best-known counter-insurgency thinkers. He argues in his book *Low Intensity Operations*[83] that pickets, street corner meetings, and mass meetings, although nonviolent acts by themselves, can persuade others to revolt. According to Kitson,

> if they can once be got onto the streets, even in relatively small numbers, it may be possible for the extremists to goad the authorities into taking some violent action against the moderates which will at least attract the sympathy of the uncommitted part of the population, some of whom may even align themselves with them[.][84]

As this example indicates, repressing associations was part of the theory and practice of counter-insurgency.

After independence, former colonies included exceptional powers in their constitutions. Kevin Tan observes that many former British territories embodied the "state-of-exception" powers in their constitutions. Tan links the tendency of adopting the colonial rationale to the short history and limited experience of constitutional traditions in Southeast Asia, where most states achieved independence after World War II. This short history of constitutionalism contributed noticeably to the way reserve and emergency powers were transplanted into the legal sphere of most Southeast Asian states.[85] Nathan Brown suggests that postcolonial Arab states adopted constitutions that granted rulers the same exceptional powers that colonists enjoyed. According to Brown, the British transplanted emergency powers into its Arab

---

[80] *Ibid*, at 74, 103.
[81] *Ibid*; Mark Neocleous, "From Martial Law to the War on Terror" (2007) 10:4 *New Criminal Law Review* 489 at 496.
[82] Section 20 (1) of Enemy Regulations Ordinance 1948, quoted in Kevin Tan, *Marshall of Singapore: A Biography* (Pasir Panjang: Institute of Southeast Asian Studies, 2008) at 259.
[83] Frank Kitson, *Low Intensity Operations* (London: Faber and Faber, 1971).
[84] *Ibid*, at 82–3.
[85] *Ibid*, at 151.

colonies, but did not transplant constitutionalism.[86] This transplantation suggests that the colonial emergency powers have been normalized in postcolonial laws related to security. The transplanting of British emergency powers into its colonies led colonies to adopt an imperfect democratic system that focuses on strengthening national security laws and measures that normalize the exception and neglects the rule of law.

Another violation by law was the practice of trying insurgents by committee rather than courts, which relied on secret intelligence without providing judicial safeguards. According to French, the model of counter-insurgency by committee was developed as an alternative way of imposing martial law. Since the civil authorities and police were not under the control of the army, as was the case under martial law, the British established centralized administrative committees that had control over political, civilian, and military powers. This led, among many things, to underestimating the role of courts. As mentioned earlier, trials *in camera* were used in some colonies.[87]

In addition to the above examples, detention without trial was a common practice in colonies and Britain during the World Wars. Holding suspects without prosecuting in the courts is an abuse of power and a violation of a person's liberty. One of the main reasons the British believed that detention without trial was necessary was that they did not want to disclose evidence and information from their secret sources. French argues that the British context indicates that "many people were detained on the basis of flimsy evidence or mere suspicion[.]"[88] The British legal justification for detaining people without trial in the colonies was simply based on previous practices carried out in Britain during World War II under Defence Regulation 18B. However, the scale of detention in the colonies significantly exceeded the numbers of detainees in Britain between 1939 and 1945.[89]

THE BRITISH EXPERIENCE WITHIN THE UNITED KINGDOM Britain was not immune to internal and external crises. The eighteenth and nineteenth centuries were a starting point for the adoption of emergency statutory provisions to face potential threats of war, revolution, and economic depression. Among the series of statutes adopted by Britain are the Riot Act of 1714, the Telegraph Act of 1863, and the Wireless Telegraphy Act of 1904. The latter two allowed the government "to take over the nation's means of communications[.]"[90] The British–Irish conflict in particular produced exceptional laws and measures.

The British have long experience in developing special laws. One of the most controversial British laws is the Civil Authorities (Special Powers) Act (Northern

[86] Brown, *Constitutions in a Nonconstitutional World*, at 72–82.
[87] *Ibid.*
[88] *Ibid*, at 112.
[89] *Ibid.*
[90] Rossiter, *Constitutional Dictatorship*, at 137.

Ireland) of 1922. One scholar describes it as "the most wide-sweeping Act passed in the United Kingdom."[91] The Act criminalized, among other activities, "offences against the regulations" of this Act. Article 2 paragraph 4 states that "If any person does any act of such a nature as to be calculated to be prejudicial to the preservation of the peace or maintenance of order in Northern Ireland and not specifically provided for in the regulations, he shall be deemed to be guilty of an offence against the regulations."[92] This Act was later repealed by the Northern Ireland (Emergency Provisions) Act 1973.[93] The essence of these statutes was to allow the executive to take action during emergencies – justifying by law the combination of exceptionalism and centralization.

This combination of power developed more clearly with the events of World War I and the economic depression of the early 1930s.[94] I will not go through the detailed history of emergency powers in Britain but will focus on the major emergency Acts and measures that impacted civil life, and will later relate them to the laws that have arisen during the current war on terror. The British laws I will look at are the Defence of the Realm Act 1914 (DORA) and the Emergency Powers (Defence) Act 1939. I will also address the consequences doled out to accused transgressors in Britain, which included detention without trial and the trial of civilians in military or special courts.

The Defence of the Realm Act, known as DORA, was passed a few days after the United Kingdom entered World War I. Clinton Rossiter suggests that DORA is the foundation of the virtual state of siege in the United Kingdom during the two World Wars.[95] DORA is a written declaration on the legality of transferring governmental powers to the executive. It granted the executive and the army vast powers and placed limitations over citizens' rights.[96] The Act states in one of its articles:

(1) His Majesty in Council has power during the continuance of the present war to issue regulations for securing the public safety and the defence of the realm, and as to the powers and duties for that purpose of the Admiralty and Army Council and of the members of His Majesty's forces and other persons acting in his behalf; and may by such regulations authorise the trial by courts-martial, or in the case of minor offences by courts of summary jurisdiction, and punishment of persons committing offences against the regulations and in particular against any of the provisions of such regulations designed:

---

[91] Oehmichen, *Terrorism and Anti-Terrorism Legislation*, at 137.
[92] Article 2 paragraph 4 of the Civil Authorities (Special Powers) Act (Northern Ireland), 1922. See *Conflict and Politics in Northern Ireland*, online: CAIN cain.ulst.ac.uk/hmso/spa1922.htm. See also Oehmichen, *Terrorism and Anti-Terrorism Legislation*, at 137.
[93] Northern Ireland (Emergency Provisions) Act 1973.
[94] A chronological account of the crisis and emergency powers adopted in England can be found in Rossiter, *Constitutional Dictatorship*, at 133–203.
[95] *Ibid*, at 153.
[96] Agamben, *State of Exception*, at 19.

(a) to prevent persons communicating with the enemy or obtaining information for that purpose or any purpose calculated to jeopardise the success of the operations of any of His Majesty's forces or the forces of his allies or to assist the enemy; or

(b) to secure the safety of His Majesty's forces and ships and the safety of any means of communication and of railways, ports, and harbours; or

(c) to prevent the spread of false reports or reports likely to cause disaffection to His Majesty or to interfere with the success of His Majesty's forces by land or sea or to prejudice His Majesty's relations with foreign powers; or

(d) to secure the navigation of vessels in accordance with directions given by or under the authority of the Admiralty; or

(e) otherwise to prevent assistance being given to the enemy or the successful prosecution of the war being endangered.[97]

Simpson, in his masterpiece *In the Highest Degree Odious: Detention without Trial in Wartime Britain*,[98] examines the executive detention of citizens and aliens in Britain during World War II. Likewise, F. H. Hinsley had written earlier a comprehensive history of this dark period of British history, *British Intelligence in the Second World War*.[99] Both describe the detention of more than 25,000 enemy aliens, but focus primarily on the 2,000 British citizens detained without trial under Regulation 18B of the Defence (General) Regulations 1939 (18B)[100] and the Emergency Powers (Defence) Act 1939. Again, the parallels between the acts of detention that took place in this period and counter-terrorist measures in the modern West are striking.

Under 18B, the detention of citizens was based on the allegation that they were of "hostile origins or associations" or were "concerned in acts prejudicial to the public safety or the defence of the realm."[101] The term "hostile origins or associations" indeed included former enemy citizens or individuals who were of enemy citizenship, but it also included citizens who had enemy friends or relatives.[102] Sir Eric Holt-Wilson, the head of MI5, defined citizenship as "not the nationality by place of birth, or by law, but nationality by blood, by racial interests, and by sympathy and friendship that is taken as the deciding factor in all classifications of possible enemy agents and dangerous persons."[103] As with the term "terrorist" today, there was no

---

[97] Defence of the Realm Consolidation Act as amended on November 27, 1914.

[98] Simpson, *In the Highest Degree Odious*.

[99] F. H. Hinsley & C. A. G. Simkins, *British Intelligence in the Second World War: Volume 4. Security and Counter-Intelligence* (Cambridge: Cambridge University Press, 1990).

[100] Regulation 18B was intended to suppress the Fascist movement and its leaders in Britain. See Simpson, *In the Highest Degree Odious*, at 69.

[101] *Ibid.*

[102] *Ibid*, at 15.

[103] Mark E. Neely, "In the Highest Degree Odious: Detention without Trial in Wartime Britain by AW Brian Simpson" (1995) 13:1 *Law and History Review* 177 at 177.

official definition of the term "of hostile origin"; this was left to be determined by the facts of each particular case.[104] Simpson shows that the exceptional practices used during World War II were not invented in 1939 but were used earlier in colonies during emergencies. Such practices vary in their degree of coercion, starting with detention and ending with a shoot-to-kill policy.[105] This suggests that colonial policies mirrored the willingness of empires to rule through the exception and "necessity." Simpson observes that during the World Wars foreign nationals were a source of fear to the British government. While Irish nationalists were deemed to present a threat, the central perceived threat was from Germans, who could engage in sabotage and espionage in Britain. This led the British government to establish the Special Branch within its Security Service. The task of Special Branch was to prevent aliens from committing political terrorist crimes.[106] In his argument against Regulation 18B, Simpson states that:

[I]t was the assumption in Whitehall that war could only be carried on in conditions in which civil liberty had, as a matter of law, been abolished, and the executive armed with even more draconian powers than had existed in the earlier war. I do not know of any paper setting out in a coherent form argument in favour of this belief; it was simply taken for granted.[107]

The significance of the British experience during World War II is its impact in shaping modern national security policy, including current counter-terrorism laws and measures. In other words, contemporary national and international security changes have been shaped by the wars of the twentieth century and the experiences of the colonial powers in these wars.[108]

The French Experience of Exceptionalism

The French, like the British, regulated some forms of the exception within law, including the state of siege and state of emergency. However, unlike the British, in their colonies the French adopted an overall revolutionary doctrine derived from the French Revolution: *la guerre révolutionnaire*. David French argues that this doctrine allowed the army to take control of all military and civil operations, as well as engaging in practices of "dirty wars," including the use of systematic torture.[109] The meaning of *la guerre révolutionnaire* has never been entirely clear, but according to George A. Kelly, it indicates the "values of French nationalism[.]"[110] Kelly notes

---

[104] Simpson, *In the Highest Degree Odious*, at 20.
[105] *Ibid*, at 2.
[106] *Ibid*, at 8.
[107] *Ibid*, 46.
[108] *Ibid*, at 177.
[109] French, *The British Way in Counter-Insurgency*, at 138–9.
[110] George A. Kelly, *Struggles in the State: Sources and Patterns of World Revolution* (New York: Wiley, 1970) at 419.

that, because insurgency was seen as a revolutionary threat, it required a similar antidote to that facing the revolution of communism, that is, a parallel revolutionary countering doctrine, a *guerre contre-révolutionnaire*.[111] The assumption of the legitimacy of the imperialist order meant that the French colonist was right and anti-colonialism was wrong. This mindset reinforced the notion of "otherness," which not only created two different groups, but made the French colonist superior to the colonized other. This justified the use of forms of the exception to maintain order.

Within the French system, the state of siege is an emergency system that deals with the most severe crisis,[112] whereas the state of emergency deals with less dramatic events. The revolutionary nature of the French state of siege can be seen in the fact that the circumstances that can be considered as an emergency are broad and vague, and include "imminent danger to internal or external security."[113] The intolerance to what French authority views as threat to its security and the desire to fundamentally end it is revolutionary in its essence.[114] The revolutionary aspect can also be seen in the state of emergency, which granted the militarized police forces exceptional measures including raids, surveillance, and house arrests that target people based on their identity and associations, as will be shown in the two following sections.

In contemporary history, there has been more reliance on the state of emergency, which can be declared by the president. For instance, in the aftermath of the November 2015 Paris attacks, a state of emergency was declared by President François Hollande and extended by the parliament until November 1, 2017. The long period of the state of emergency raised concerns among civil society organizations about its necessity and efficiency.[115] It should be noted that when France lifted the state of emergency, it adopted a new anti-terrorism law, which includes many exceptional and emergency-like powers. This suggest a shift in anti-terrorism law from a penal nature to exceptionalism.

STATE OF SIEGE The defining French state of exception occurred in the aftermath of the French Revolution, when in 1791 the French Constituent Assembly adopted a law that divided military operations into three categories, with different laws applying to each: state of peace, state of war, and state of siege.[116] An important modification was made in 1797, which allows a state of siege to be declared in case of foreign invasion or rebellion. The problem was that "rebellion" was defined to include any

---

[111] *Ibid*, at 423–5.
[112] Rossiter, *Constitutional Dictatorship*, at 79, 84.
[113] Article 1 of the law of 1849, quoted in Rossiter, *Constitutional Dictatorship*, at 85.
[114] See Agamben, *State of Exception*, at 53.
[115] Chloe Farand, "Thousands March in the Paris Rain to Protest against the State of Emergency" *Independent* (January 31, 2016) online: *Independent News* www.independent.co.uk.
[116] Albert H. Y. Chen, "Emergency Powers: Constitutionalism and Legal Transplants: The East Asian Experience" in Victor V. Ramraj & Arun K. Thiruvengadam, eds, *Emergency Powers in Asia: Exploring the Limits of Legality* (New York: Cambridge University Press, 2010) at 59.

type of domestic disturbance.[117] Both Napoleon I and Napoleon III targeted political opposition through this statute.[118]

As part of the civil law tradition, the state of siege is framed by the constitution and defined by statute. Rossiter and William Feldman call this the "extreme legality"[119] of a system that denies law.[120] Along similar lines, Giorgio Agamben suggests that "it is important not to forget that the modern state of exception is a creation of the democratic-revolutionary tradition and not the absolutist one[.]"[121]

In the French colonies, the declaration of the state of siege was left to the governor of the colony.[122] The state of siege has been declared in several colonies, including Algeria, Tunisia, and Vietnam. For instance, in response to World War I, the state of siege was declared in Algeria "for the duration of the war[.]"[123] The state of siege should be specified for a particular duration, but in the above case it referred to the state of war regardless of when it would end. (More details on the state of siege in colonies are given when examining the case of Tunisia in Chapter 6.)

On the other hand, French law places some restrictions on declaring the state of siege in France. In France, according to the Law Regarding the State of Siege of 1849 and 1878, declaring a state of siege is part of the legislature's authority.[124] No authority can suspend the rule of law except the one that makes it in the first place.[125] Parliament's supremacy was granted in a law made in 1878, to contain the earlier executive abuse of the state of siege.[126] In a state of siege, the cabinet was able to issue administrative ordinances.[127] The duration of a state of siege, which is considered an *acte de gouvernement* or *acte politique*, must be restricted for a limited

---

[117] William Feldman, "Theories of Emergency Powers: A Comparative Analysis of American Martial Law and the French State of Siege" (2005) 38:3 *Cornell International Law Journal* 1021 at 1024.

[118] *Ibid.*

[119] *Ibid*, at 1022; Rossiter, *Constitutional Dictatorship*, at 79.

[120] French, *The British Way in Counter-Insurgency*, at 75; Max Radin, "Martial Law and the State of Siege" (1942) 30:6 *California Law Review* 634 at 635.

[121] Agamben, *State of Exception*, at 5.

[122] Article 4 of Law Regarding the State of Siege (August 9, 1849); Article 10 of French Decree (April 29, 1857); Article 4 of Law Regarding State of Siege of 1878. See Birkhimer, *Military Government and Martial Law*, at 624–5; Feldman, "Theories of Emergency Powers," at 1026.

[123] Quoted in Rossiter, *Constitutional Dictatorship*, at 92.

[124] Article 2 of Law Regarding the State of Siege (August 9, 1849) states: "The National Assembly has the sole power to declare the state of siege." Quoted in Birkhimer, *Military Government and Martial Law* 174, at 624. A new constitution, however, was established in 1852, which transferred the authority of declaring a state of siege from the Parliament to the head of state. This shift was part of the establishment of the Second Republic under Louis Napoleon, who transferred the Republic into an Empire. Nonetheless, the authority was granted again to the Parliament by law in 1878. Feldman, "Theories of Emergency Powers," at 1025; Radin, "Martial Law and the State of Siege," at 638.

[125] Rossiter, *Constitutional Dictatorship*, at 84.

[126] *Ibid.*

[127] *Ibid*, at 87.

time of weeks or months, and can be renewed by issuing a new law.[128] The regulation of the state of siege came in direct response to a period, beginning in 1870, when parts of France were under a state of siege for over five years with no obvious reason.[129]

In a state of siege, the powers of the police are transferred to the army. This, significantly, relates to the enforcement of criminal justice, and includes the judicial process. Any civilian who commits a crime of a public nature during the state of siege will be sent to a military court, unless the military authority agrees that the case may be seen by ordinary courts.[130] The military found several advantages in military courts during the World War I enforcement of the state of siege, including quick procedures and rigorous penalties. Permanent army courts were established in each military district. The military tribunals looked upon cases involving civilians regarding public safety, which were formerly regulated by the Penal Code; these included espionage, treason, and communicating and trading with the enemy. These tribunals also dealt with crimes that had no direct impact on public safety, as catalogued by Rossiter: "frauds in connection with the quality of provisions furnished the armed forces or in their sale, attempted robbery in a railroad station, insults to public officials engaged in their duties, the misdemeanor of *vagabondage*, the embezzlement of letters by a post-office agent[.]"[131] As the war came to a close, the severity and broad jurisdiction of these courts were largely deemed unacceptable by the public. The legislature had to reduce the harshness of military jurisdiction by introducing the right to appeal and allowing for pardons.

In 1958, with the establishment of the Fifth Republic, a new constitution was issued that broadened centralization by strengthening the powers of the executive. Among several wide powers, it granted the president the power to take any "measures required" should the "institutions of the Republic, the independence of the nation, the integrity of its international commitments [be] gravely and immediately threatened and the regular functioning of the constitutional public authorities [be] interrupted."[132] This article was invoked in 1961 when it was feared that the Algerian revolt would spread to France.[133] Under this article, President Charles de Gaulle established special military tribunals, monitored censorship, and granted the police more powers to search and arrest suspects.[134] This amendment indicates the relationship between exceptionalism and executive powers, both of which can be used to bypass ordinary measures.

---

[128] Article 1 of Law Regarding the State of Siege of 1878.
[129] Rossiter, *Constitutional Dictatorship*, at 88.
[130] *Ibid*, at 86–7.
[131] *Ibid*, at 95.
[132] Article 16 of the 1958 Constitution. Quoted in Kelly & Pelletier, "Theories of Emergency Government," at 47.
[133] *Ibid*.
[134] *Ibid*.

One of the important yet dangerous consequences of the use of state of siege is in the broad authorities granted to the military. The French Law Regarding the State of Siege of 1849 grants jurisdiction to military tribunals to try all persons for all crimes "against the safety of the Republic, against the Constitution, against public peace and order, whatever be the status of the principal perpetrators and their accomplices."[135] As we will see in Chapters 5 and 7, the army and other militarized security forces are still involved in the civil life of Egypt and Tunisia. In addition, the protection of the constitution and public peace and order is found in current Arab national security and counter-terrorism laws.

STATE OF EMERGENCY (*ÉTAT D'URGENCE*) Like the British, the French found the state of emergency a useful political tool that offered control without the direct control of the military. This shift allowed the French, at least on the surface, to protect the civilized appearance of the state. However, the French state of emergency remains a system of exceptional powers that could violate civil liberties.

State of emergency is regulated in France by a law adopted in 1955[136] and the constitution of 1958. It allows the president to declare a state of emergency for up to 12 days,[137] and can be extended by the parliament. State of emergency allows the use and expansion of exceptional powers, including censorship, administrative searches, and seizures without judiciary review.

Article 16 of the French Constitution of 1958 shows that in France, the state of emergency can be declared in the following cases: when "the independence of the Nation, the integrity of its territory or the fulfilment of its international commitments are under serious and immediate threat, and where the proper functioning of the constitutional public authorities is interrupted[.]" The wording does not include the vague term "public order," but it does include another broad concept, which is threats to the "constitutional public authorities." Article 16 of the constitution also gives the President the right to "take measures required by these circumstances[.]" While the measures are defined in the law regarding the state of emergency, the above article of the constitution reflects the "flexible" French approach to national security.

Unlike the state of siege, the state of emergency was not used in colonies. However, it has been declared many times in France, including in relation to the Paris attacks in November 2015. The attacks left 130 persons dead and hundreds injured. President Hollande declared a state of emergency, which was extended by law for almost two years.[138] According to the law regarding the state of emergency,

---

[135] Article 8 of the French Law Regarding the State of Siege of 1849.
[136] Law No. 55–385 of April 3, 1955.
[137] This authority granted to the president is stated in Article 12 of the French Constitution of 1958, which reads: "Le Président de la République peut, après consultation du Premier ministre et des présidents des assemblées, prononcer la dissolution de l'Assemblée nationale."
[138] "French MPs Vote to Extend State of Emergency after Paris Attacks" (November 19, 2015) *The Guardian*, online: www.theguardian.com.

any person may be placed under house arrest if "there are serious reasons to believe that a person's behaviour constitutes a threat to security and public order[.]"[139] The application of the above article shows no limits for such residence orders.[140] Other exceptional measures that can be taken during a state of emergency include banning meetings,[141] dissolving associations, and carrying out searches without a warrant.[142]

In practice, these measures have often been used arbitrarily and selectively. According to a report about the French state of emergency by Amnesty International in 2016, several mosques were shut down and other Islamic associations were dissolved without clear charges.[143] Scholars argue that most of the emergency legislation and powers have been adopted as preventive systems.[144] Joseph B. Kelly and George A. Pelletier, Jr. describe emergency policies in general and the French ones in particular as "worried only about past or already present exigencies rather than any carefully thought out long-term approach to the problem."[145] Experience shows that because governments provide no long-term plans, the prediction criterion is left open to include almost all acts that the state or the military government do not feel comfortable with. As a result, emergency powers can become a weapon against the "enemy" and a tool to suppress rights and liberties.

Neo-Colonial Exceptionalism and the War on Terror

In the example of the Paris attacks of November 2015, other external measures were taken by the army. For example, the French Air Force launched a military operation against the Islamic State.[146] The United States and its allies have launched several attacks against ISIS in Iraq and Syria. Russia has done the same against ISIS in Syria. Other air strikes led by the United States targeted chemical weapons sites in Syria. Since 9/11, militarism and exceptionalism have become interrelated as neo-colonial aspects of counter-terrorism.

Contemporary counter-terrorism measures, both national and international, are controversial primarily owing to their normalization of many practices that are exceptional in nature, such as martial law. Mark Neocleous[147] argues that there has been a "liberalization" of the principles of martial law. These principles have been

[139] Article 6 of Law No. 55–385 of 3 April 1955 regarding the state of emergency [law regarding the state of emergency].
[140] *France: Upturned Lives: The Disproportionate Impact of France's State of Emergency* (February 4, 2016) *Amnesty International*, online: www.amnesty.org/en/documents/eur21/3364/2016/en/.
[141] Article 8 of law regarding the state of emergency.
[142] Article 14–1, *ibid.*
[143] Amnesty International, *Upturned Lives.*
[144] Feldman, "Theories of Emergency Powers," at 1039; Kelly & Pelletier, "Theories of Emergency Government," at 46.
[145] Kelly & Pelletier, "Theories of Emergency Government," at 68.
[146] Ben Brumfield, Tim Lister & Nick Paton Walsh, "French Jets Bomb ISIS Stronghold of Raqqa, Syria; Few May Have Been Killed" (November 16, 2015) online: CNN edition.cnn.com.
[147] Mark Neocleous, "From Martial Law to the War on Terror" (2007) 10:4 *New Criminal Law Review* 489 at 490.

normalized within the legal and political systems of liberal democracies,[148] as well as in Arab countries. This normalization is not exclusive to martial law; it also includes the use of the military internally during states of emergency and the militarization of police powers outside martial law and outside emergencies. According to Neocleous, this shift of liberalization "occurred as new forms of the exceptional practices under martial law, with legal covers that make them accepted in liberal terms."[149]

Neocleous claims that a revival of "new liberal authoritarianism"[150] combines past exceptional powers with a contemporary modern system. Others justify the exception within militant democracy, in which protecting democratic values justifies violating law and liberties.[151] Agamben argues that the theory of the exception in Western democracies is "clear in principle, but hazier in fact[.]"[152] He refers to the terrorist attacks of 9/11 as an event that allowed President George W. Bush to use his "presidential claim to sovereign powers[,]"[153] which is a form of the exception. The same approach has been taken by many other countries against ISIS.

The problem is that, unlike any conventional war or any state of emergency, the war on terrorism is endless, and this shifts the exceptional nature of such presidential powers and many other extra-legal measures into the norm.[154] Scholars have questioned post-9/11 counter-terrorism measures and whether they should be classified as part of law or of the suspension of law.[155] Similarly to martial law, these measures are regulated by law, and also similarly to martial law, they justify extra-legal measures, such as detention without trial and prisons controlled by the military.[156] However, the necessity and (il)legitimacy of the use of emergency and exceptional powers is not our main concern. Our concern is the continuous clinging to colonial practices that have a cultural and political foundation of coercion.

Neo-colonialism operates in a context of centralization in global policymaking and decisionmaking. By establishing politically and financially powerful supranational bodies like the UN Security Council and FATF (discussed in Chapter 2), the influence of neo-colonialism is practiced and achieved through political pressure. These supra-national bodies have been increasingly involved in establishing international obligations regarding counter-terrorism. They are imposing the Western agenda of crime and culture control, leaving no choice to other nations except to continue complying with the system. These obligations have justified the use of militarism without clear limitations on their role. The use of militarism, while

[148] *Ibid.*
[149] *Ibid.*
[150] *Ibid.*
[151] Carl J. Friedrich, *Constitutional Reason of State: The Survival of the Constitutional Order* (Providence, RI: Brown University Press, 1957) at 13.
[152] Agamben, *State of Exception*, at 9.
[153] *Ibid*, at 22.
[154] *Ibid.*
[155] Dyzenhaus, "The Puzzle of Martial Law," at 3.
[156] Neocleous, "From Martial Law to the War on Terror," at 490.

accepted during the state of war, must not be confused with the war on terror – which has no clear beginning and is unlikely to have an end.

CONCLUSION: UNEQUAL POSITIONS OF POWER

A colonial culture of control comprised the basic logic and rationale for a conservative distribution of authority and centralization driven by economic expansion, as well as ruling through militarism and exceptions. This rationale gradually percolated into the colonies in the late nineteenth and early twentieth centuries. This rationale continued in post-independence former colonies and reemerged in new forms in neo-colonialism. According to David Garland, the Euro-American culture of control is a "reconfigured complex of interlocking structures and strategies that are themselves composed of old and new elements, the old revised and reoriented by a new operation context, the newer elements modified by the continuing influence of working practices and modes of thought dating to the earlier period[.]"[57] The culture of control of colonialism and neo-colonialism has led to changes in the field of crime control, and particularly counter-terrorism. This culture of control signifies that this legal field reflects the relationship between the past and the present, between the colonial rationale of control and the neo-colonial contention of liberties versus security.

It is crucial to pinpoint the origins and ongoing causes of patterns of control in order to understand the impact that these changes have had on the criminal system and on society as a whole. This book's later chapters on anti-terrorism measures in Egypt and Tunisia will support the claim that both imperialism and colonialism set the foundations of modern legal systems in former colonies, and neo-colonialism has continued normalizing the colonial rationale. The neo-colonial experience may not be identical to colonial practices, but the foundation of state security policy is the same. In both cases, this policy is based on a national and global hierarchical system that unequally distributes powers between nations.

Imperialism did not necessarily transplant European ideology or project European laws directly on to colonies or informal colonies, but by being the dominant power, empires did universalize their logic of rule. The current legal system in many former colonies may, therefore, continue to bear the influence of the imperial cultures that colonized them. The Westernization of the global framework of politics and economy is a consequence of the vast British and French empires, which dominated the trade market and the elites in their former colonies.[158] This role was later largely replaced by the United States, which empowered and contained democratic capitalism and neo-liberalism. Whether because of voluntary cooperation, coercive pressure, or adjusting to the Western model as the one

---

[57] David Garland, *The Culture of Control* (New York: Oxford University Press, 2001) at 23.
[158] Barton, *Informal Empire*, at 28.

absolute option,[159] informal empire has become the most legitimate and least aggressive – and to a lesser extent cheapest – means of Western domination. The Western imperial and colonial powers of the nineteenth and twentieth century have become the great powers that function at a neo-colonial level. These powers include, above all, the United Kingdom, France, and the United States, all of which operate individually through political pressure and financial aid, and collectively through supra-national bodies like the UN Security Council and FATF (discussed in Chapter 2).

Russia is another neo-colonial power that plays a significant role in the current war on terror, particularly in Syria. Nonetheless, the Russian Empire had no colonial history in the Arab region, which means that no direct role can be traced. Soviet Russia built political and economic ties with some Arab states, through alliances and client states. Yet unlike the United States, which has a superior–inferior relation with its Arab allies, Russia had seemingly equal relations: a client pays, and Russia provides weapons or develops nuclear programs. Russia's role as a neo-colonial superior power only emerged after the "Arab Spring," a topic discussed in Chapter 3.

Despite the difference in details between British and American and between Western and Russian imperialism, colonialism and neo-colonialism, all these models share a desire for economic expansion, and for rule through centralization, militarism, and exceptionalism. These aspects shaped the legal and political systems in former colonies as part of the colonial legacy. Yet colonized people challenge the colonial existence and its legacies, aiming for complete self-governance. The inter-action between colonial powers and colonial peoples produced conflicting policies after independence: prioritizing self-governance and desiring more power to defend the newborn governments from external and internal threats. These are three goals that could not be achieved, fully or partially, without clinging to the colonial rationale and without allying with neo-colonial powers. These conflicting relationships are explored throughout the following chapters.

[159] *Ibid.*

Terrorism and Counter-Terrorism at the International Level: A Challenge in the Postcolonial World

Regulating counter-terrorism has not been an easy task. The major difficulty is in agreeing on a unified definition of terrorism at the international level. Several international conventions have dealt with specific acts of terrorism,[1] but no convention has yet defined the general term "terrorism." The lack of an international definition of terrorism raises questions about the legal foundation of international counter-terrorism measures. This chapter explains the international framework for counter-terrorism policy, focusing on the United Nation's role in directing the war on terror.

In the years following World War II, the role of the UN was significant in shaping the road to international peace and security. This was done primarily through the UN Charter, which prohibits state violence. The focus of the UN at that time was on prohibiting of state aggression, with virtually no expectation of any serious threat from non-state actors.[2] The Charter therefore does not incorporate the collection of acts and actors that are currently interpreted as terrorism and terrorists.[3]

This miscalculation synchronized with the global withdrawal of the colonial state. Liberation movements worldwide steadily increased, and anti-colonialist movements adopted tactics associated with terrorism to expel the colonizer and attract the attention of the international community to peoples exercising their right of self-determination. For instance, during the 1930s and 1940s the Jewish liberation group, Irgun, carried out violent operations against the British in Palestine. Bruce Hoffman

---

[1] Tokyo Convention, 1963, Aviation Safety: Convention on Offences and Certain Other Acts Committed on Board Aircraft; Hague Convention, 1970, Aircraft Hijacking: Convention for the Suppression of Unlawful Seizure of Aircraft; Montreal Convention, 1971, Aviation Sabotage: Convention for the Suppression of Unlawful Acts against the Safety of Civil Aviation; Supplement to 1971 Montreal Convention on Air Safety: Protocol for the Suppression of Unlawful Acts of Violence at Airports Serving International Civil Aviation.

[2] Victor D. Comras, *Flawed Diplomacy: The United Nations and the War on Terrorism* (Dulles, VA: Potomac Books, 2010) at 8.

[3] See Chapter I: Purposes and Principles of the UN Charter.

describes Irgun's attacks as a strategy to spread fear in Palestine in order to under-mine the British ability to maintain order.[4] The violent attacks continued until the Israeli case gained international support for the establishment of a Jewish state in Palestine.[5] Other examples that adopted a similar strategy include Algeria against the French and South Africa against the British: both used violence until they achieved their independence.[6] The independence of these countries added legitimacy to the actions of freedom fighters. The challenge has thus become defining the line between the right to struggle and terrorism crimes.

Today, terrorism is taken to represent a serious threat to national and international peace and security. The wave of terrorism that was associated with the right of self-determination has faded, and another wave of what is known as "Islamic terrorism" has emerged. Each wave has been met with a wave of countermeasures. The aim of this chapter is to evaluate the rationale and utility of the related national and international countermeasures, and the impact of global counter-terrorism policy on domestic policies and vice versa.

Debates about counter-terrorism are often limited to a discussion of the deterrent function of counter-terrorism measures. However, equally central to a full discussion of the issue is the importance of balancing the powers granted to governments to ensure the prevention of terrorist acts with a counterbalancing check on these powers to prevent their misuse.[7] For instance, the UN Security Council has the centralized power to blacklist terrorist individuals and entities. The listing procedure is not compliant with human rights because of the executive nature of the Security Council's work, and because of the politicized understanding of "terrorism." Although the Security Council's decisions may be appealed, those who are listed have minimal space to view and challenge the evidence against them. No basic human rights guarantees or effective crime control can be achieved without a clear definition of "terrorism." The increasing international significance of terrorism and counter-terrorism did not bring with it a universal agreement on what terrorism is. As we will see, the lack of an international definition was a result of the imperfect policy of the UN Security Council, represented by the major neo-colonial powers, which empowered states to enact broad terrorism laws without insisting on a definition of terrorism.

This chapter examines international attempts to define terrorism in three phrases. The first is in the aftermath of World War II. That period was also the fading years of

---

4   Comras, *Flawed Diplomacy*, at 52.
5   By United Nations General Assembly Resolution No. 181 (1947) the Jewish state "Israel" came into official existence.
6   Bruce Hoffman, *Inside Terrorism* (New York: Columbia University Press, 2006) at 56–65; Walter Laqueur, *The New Terrorism* (New York: Oxford University Press, 1999) at 22–4; Oehmichen, *Terrorism and Anti-Terrorism Legislation*, at 65–70.
7   Victor Ramraj, Michael Hor & Kent Roach, eds, *Global Anti-Terrorism Law and Policy* (New York: Cambridge University Press, 2012) at 1.

colonialism. The UN General Assembly put in serious efforts to define terrorism, yet without a result. The historical conditions of that time meant any attempt to define "terrorism" was bound by anti-colonial thought, which in practice valued the right of groups to struggle, even with the use of violence, over the need for security. This view was represented by the Arab position, which refused to consider violent attacks by Palestinians as terrorism.

The second phase of international attempts to define terrorism was in the 1990s. This phase represents the emergence of neo-colonialism. During this phase, the UN Security Council started to take a direct part in setting the rules of counter-terrorism. As will be shown, the Arab bloc vanished in response to events like the Gulf War, which led to a *de facto* American presence in many Arab states through its military bases. Such states no longer dare to oppose America, which dominates globally through many forms of informal empire, but more importantly through its position in the Security Council. Thus the Security Council view on important issues like counter-terrorism is one-sided.

The third phase is post-9/11: the peak of neo-colonialism. In this phase, the UN Security Council dominates global decisionmaking regarding terrorism, commanding almost complete global obedience to the obligations it imposes. The chapter places greater focus on this phase because the Security Council has issued a number of obligations that require a detailed investigation.

Terrorism financing, speech related to terrorism, and violent extremism are the major themes of criminalization that are examined in this chapter. The Security Council's executive-like powers, including blacklisting, freezing funds, and travel bans, are also examined. The chapter questions whether such powers reflect a positive development in international security or a form of neo-colonial control in the name of counter-terrorism.

ATTEMPTS BY THE UNITED NATIONS TO DEFINE TERRORISM
DURING THE FADING OF COLONIALISM

In the mid-twentieth century, the understanding of the term "terrorism" was only linked to state terrorism. This can be found in the 1954 Draft Code of Offences against the Peace and Security of Mankind[8] framed by the UN International Law Commission. Article 2(5) defines an offense "against the peace and security of mankind" as "undertaking or encouragement by the authorities of a State of terrorist activities in another State, or the toleration by the authorities of a State of organized activities calculated to carry out terrorist acts in another State."[9] The wording of the

---

[8] International Law Commission, "Draft Code of Offences against the Peace and Security of Mankind" (Part I), in ILC 6th Session Report (June 3–July 28, 1954), UN Doc A/2693, as requested by UNGA Res 177(II) (1947).

[9] Article 2(6), *ibid.*

article clearly indicates that the thinking around terrorism in the 1950s was related to one state's intervention in the affairs of another state, through means of violence and associated terror.

The same approach is evident in a later UN General Assembly resolution adopted in 1970. The 1970 Declaration on Friendly Relations states that "Every State has the duty to refrain from organizing, instigating, assisting or participating in acts of civil strife or terrorist acts in another State[.]"[10] It should be noted that the resolution acknowledges self-determination as a protected principle.[11] Although "terrorist acts" were not defined, they were clearly linked to state terrorism with no reference to non-state actors. According to Victor Comras, there was no expectation that the principle of "self-determination of peoples" would be used by non-state actors as a justification for a form of terrorism that is closer to our modern idea of what terrorism is.[12]

The attempts by the UN to define terrorism escalated in the aftermath of the Munich Olympics massacre in September 1972.[13] As a response, the General Assembly adopted Resolution 3034 (XXVII) of 1972, which includes measures to prevent international terrorism, as well as preparing a study of "the underlying causes of those forms of terrorism and acts of violence which lie in misery, frustration, grievance and despair and which cause some people to sacrifice human lives, including their own, in an attempt to effect radical changes."[14]

The resolution does not represent an attempt to define terrorism, but rather an attempt to arrive at an understanding of terrorist acts by focusing on their causes. The clear suggestion is that these causes are largely encompassed by "colonial and racist regimes and other forms of alien domination" that undermine the right to self-determination and independence of the perpetrators of terrorist acts.[15] The resolution explicitly excludes from its definition of terrorism acts of violence undertaken in the name of the right to self-determination, which is at least partially self-contradictory, partly owing to the lack of a clear differentiation between terrorism and the type of "freedom-fighting" that would later be protected by UN Resolution

---

[10] General Assembly on October 24, 1970 (Resolution 26/25 (XXV).
[11] *Ibid*, Article 1.1.7 and 5.1.
[12] Comras, *Flawed Diplomacy*, at 8.
[13] In September 1972, the Palestinian group Black September killed two and kidnapped nine other Israeli athletes, followed by blackmailing the German government to get an airplane, and demanding the release of 234 Palestinians and others held in Israel, along with two German radicals held in Germany. The incident ended with the killing of all the Israeli hostages, one German policeman, and five of the kidnappers. See Hoffman, *Inside Terrorism*, at 31–2; Comras, *Flawed Diplomacy*, at 17–18.
[14] UN General Assembly Resolution 3034 (XXVII) adopted on December 18, 1972 "Measures to prevent international terrorism which endangers or takes innocent human lives or jeopardizes fundamental freedoms, and study of the underlying causes of those forms of terrorism and acts of violence which lie in misery, frustration, grievance and despair and which cause some people to sacrifice human lives, including their own, in an attempt to effect radical changes."
[15] *Ibid*.

40/61.[16] The members of the Ad Hoc Committee established by the above resolution agreed on the importance of addressing the causes of terrorism, but they were unable to successfully identify these causes or evaluate their impact on international security.[17] In general, Western states could not successfully negotiate a method to practically explore the causes and significance of these acts.[18]

As for the Arab position on defining terrorism within the UN General Assembly, Arab countries insisted on distinguishing the right to struggle and self-determination from any definition of terrorism. The dominant Arab thinking defined one clear cause for acts that were being interpreted as terrorism in much of the Western world: a legitimate struggle for self-determination. This view was represented most audibly by Jamil Baroody, Saudi Arabia's UN representative, who considered the Palestinians as anti-colonial and national liberation actors, regardless of the forms of violence they carried out against other states or civilians.[19]

THE INTERNATIONAL DEFINITION OF TERRORISM IN A NEO-COLONIAL ERA

The emphasis within the UN and Western discourse around the elimination of terrorism and the problematically overlapping right for people to struggle to achieve self-determination occurred in the early 1990s. Besides the fall of the Soviet Union and the division of the Republic of Yugoslavia, the Gulf War beginning in 1991 created new allies for the West. The spreading impact of the Gulf War among Arab states, in particular the Arabian Peninsula states, was to greatly shape the future conversation around terrorism.

At this time, these nations entered into a significantly different phase of their relationship with the United States. Saudi Arabia, which continued to have great influence over Arab countries in the UN General Assembly, allowed the Bush administration to establish US bases on its soil. This measure was taken in order to protect its borders during the Iraqi invasion of Kuwait. The Iraqi invasion had divided Arab states into two categories: those who were for and those who were against waging war against Iraq. The states that favored the American action against Iraq included Egypt, Syria, and the Gulf oil countries, but the motivations of these states were not identical. Egypt was in receipt of extensive financial aid from the United States, while the Syrian president, Hafez al-Assad, was a personal enemy of Saddam Hussein. The Gulf oil countries feared that a successful expansion of Hussein's invasion could undermine their economic interests. On the other hand, Hussein had the support of Libya, the Palestine Liberation Organization, and

---

[16] Ben Saul, *Defining Terrorism in International Law* (New York: Oxford University Press, 2008) at 71.
[17] For more, *see ibid*, at 71–8.
[18] *Ibid*, at 72.
[19] Comras, *Flawed Diplomacy*, at 19, 21.

Jordan – poorer Arab countries that supported Hussein for his promises to equalize the distribution of oil wealth among Arab people.[20] The language of terrorism was greatly affected by the fallout of these alliances and the course of the war and its aftermath. The division of support among Arab countries for either the United States or Iraq had a direct impact on the treatment of the Palestinian–Israeli conflict, which had long influenced the debate on terrorism. Arab states that allied with the United States no longer supported Palestine at the same level or validated its status as a nation: this was due to its decision to ally with Hussein. As a result, the language used in UN General Assembly resolutions has shifted: the long-supported right to struggle is now a decidedly lower priority than resolutions on the elimination of terrorism.

The realignment of alliances following the Gulf War paved the way for the neo-colonial influence regarding global counter-terrorism to expand. The 1990s witnessed a shift in global counter-terrorism policy in which the UN Security Council was engaged in decisionmaking. In October 1999, after a series of bombing attacks carried out by Al-Qaeda, the Security Council adopted Resolution 1267 as the first measure to call for sanctions against the Taliban government that hosted Al-Qaeda. The resolution established what is known as the "Al-Qaeda and Taliban sanctions regime."[21] It was easy for the Security Council, rather than the General Assembly, to adopt such a resolution, since Al-Qaeda represents a common enemy to both the United States and Russia. The Security Council includes 15 members, five permanent and ten non-permanent. The five permanent members, China, France, Russia, the United Kingdom, and the United States, all have different experiences with terrorism. The United Kingdom and France have domestic and colonial experience; the United States and Russia have experience with earlier anarchists and current Islamic extremists; China has experience with radical Islamists and more importantly with ethnic separatism movements. This suggests that these powerful states individually and collectively share a common interest in suppressing terrorism. Thus, resolutions adopted by the Security Council represent the will of these powers that dominate within a neo-colonial framework.

The above sanctions regime contains a series of resolutions[22] that have been described as "the most elaborate system of sanctions" set up by the Security Council.[23] The sanctions regime requires all states to freeze the assets and implements of Al-Qaeda and the Taliban, and creates a mechanism for the listing and

---

[20] William L. Cleveland & Martin P. Bunton, *A History of the Modern Middle East* (Boulder, CO: Westview Press, 2013) at 7, 114, 145–8.

[21] UN Security Council, Security Council Resolution 1267, 1999 SC Res. 1267, UN SCOR, S/RES/1267.

[22] These include UN Security Council Resolutions 1267 (1999); 1333 (2000); 1363 (2001); 1390 (2002); 1452 (2003); 1455 (2003); 1526 (2004).

[23] Paz Andrés-Sáenz-De-Santa-María, "Collective International Measures to Counter International Terrorism" in Pablo Antonio Fernández-Sánchez, ed, *International Legal Dimension of Terrorism* (Leiden: Martinus Nijhoff, 2009) at 95.

de-listing of individuals and entities known or believed to be associating with Al-Qaeda or the Taliban. An account of the problematic consequences and the lack of minimum legal standards of evidence and transparency of this sanctions regime is not within the scope of this book; however, the policy of listing in accordance with UN Security Council Resolution 1267 is based on a politically subjective standard. In other words, this process creates terrorists without defining the *actus reus* of terrorism or of being a terrorist.

By the end of the 1990s, terrorist financing had become an important theme that led the General Assembly to adopt the 1999 International Convention for the Suppression of the Financing of Terrorism.[24] This convention is the first that provides international guidance on the definition of terrorism. Article 2(1)(b) defines terrorism as:

> [A]ct[s] intended to cause death or serious bodily injury to a civilian, or to any other person not taking an active part in the hostilities in a situation of armed conflict, when the purpose of such act, by its nature or context, is to intimidate a population, or to compel a government or an international organization to do or to abstain from doing any act.

Despite the guidance provided by the above article, states did not rely on it in their domestic anti-terrorism legislation, in part because later Security Council resolutions, particularly 1373 (2001), implicitly allowed broad definitions to be established. By ignoring the importance of defining terrorism, the Security Council encouraged states to adopt or continue to adopt broad definitions. The fact that the Security Council adopted resolutions with a wide range of demands on states to counter terrorism, including counter-terrorism financing, restrictions on speech, and travel bans, has forced states to adopt broad definitions of terrorism in order to implement these demands. The Security Council plays an active role in demanding states to counter terrorism, and a passive role by not emphasizing the importance of defining terrorism.

THE DEFINITION OF TERRORISM POST-9/11: THE PEAK
OF NEO-COLONIALISM

In the wake of the 9/11 attacks, the United States' victimization and subsequent rhetorical and militaristic responses spurred much of the global community to reach a consensus: terrorism is a serious threat that must be suppressed at all costs. While terrorists use violence to achieve their goals, the state is supposed to use the law to counter terrorism. Nonetheless, an international definition of "terrorism" as part of anti-terrorism measures remains neglected, especially by the UN Security Council. The aim of this section is to explain the executive nature of the Security Council's

---

[24] International Convention for the Suppression of the Financing of Terrorism, Adopted by the General Assembly of the United Nations in Resolution 54/109 of December 9, 1999.

resolutions regarding counter-terrorism, which embodies a collective neo-colonial policy of domination.

Practicing neo-colonial dominance, the United States has been pushing the Security Council into embodying an active role regarding counter-terrorism.[25] A few weeks after 9/11, the United States took the lead by calling secretly for informal consultation with the Security Council's other permanent members, followed by proposing a draft convention on September 28, 2001. As Roach points out, the resolution was drafted in secrecy based on the United States' informal consultations with the other permanent members and approved in a five-minute meeting; no explanation was provided on the members' voting. The whole process took a little more than a 48-hour period. This makes it similar in essence to decisions made by national executive powers.[26] Such executive-like powers are instances of what I call "global centralization" (discussed earlier in Chapter 1).

The UN Security Council, as a supra-national power, practices its global centralization of issuing binding resolutions under Chapter VII of the UN Charter. According to Article 39 of the Charter, "The Security Council shall determine the existence of any threat to the peace, breach of the peace, or act of aggression and shall make recommendations, or decide what measures shall be taken [...] to maintain or restore international peace and security."[27] The Security Council considered the terrorist attacks of 9/11 "a threat to international peace and security." Accordingly, it approved the American draft mentioned above by issuing Resolution 1373 (2001). This resolution is discussed in detail in the following section.

The concept of "threat to the peace" mentioned in Article 39 of the UN Charter is not clearly defined, leaving a flexible space for the Security Council to determine its meaning. This, however, does not mean that the Charter did not place limits on the Security Councils' legislative authority. Article 41 of the UN Charter states that:

> The Security Council may decide what measures not involving the use of armed force are to be employed to give effect to its decisions, and it may call upon the Members of the United Nations to apply such measures. These may include complete or partial interruption of economic relations and of rail, sea, air, postal, telegraphic, radio, and other means of communication, and the severance of diplomatic relations.[28]

Scholars have explained that the role of the Security Council is limited to a particular issue within an actual situation.[29] Stefan Talmon argues that the Charter

---

[25] Hilde Haaland Kramer & Steve A. Yetiv, "The UN Security Council's Response to Terrorism: Before and after September 11, 2001" (2007) 122:3 *Political Science Quarterly* 409 at 426.

[26] See Roach, *The 9/11 Effect*, at 31–2.

[27] Article 39 of the UN Charter. Chapter VII: Action with Respect to Threat to the Peace, Breach of the Peace, or Act of Aggression.

[28] Article 41, *ibid.*

[29] Stefan Talmon, "The Security Council as World Legislature" (2005) 99:1 *American Journal of International Law* 175 at 182; Luis Miguel Hinojosa Martínez, "The Legislative Role of the

does not treat the Security Council as a world legislator, but as "a single-issue legislator."[30] For instance, when one state invades another, the Security Council may place sanctions on the invader. However, it cannot issue general regulations that apply to all invaders.

Post-9/11, the Security Council has replaced this conventional process of single-issue legislation.[31] This has been done through frequently adopting general resolutions regarding counter-terrorism and placing general obligations on states to domestically criminalize terrorism and terrorism-related crimes. The general nature of these obligations and their global domain suggest that the Security Council is acting as a global executive-legislator. This shift has not been challenged by states despite its impact on sovereignty.[32] On the contrary, states have explicitly or implicitly approved the general role of the Security Council in counter-terrorism. For instance, the representative of Spain to the UN praised the role of the Security Council by stating that

> resolution 1373 (2001) is of historic significance. It establishes for the first time a series of binding measures to be applied by all States in combating terrorism, setting a deadline for each of them to provide information about provisions adopted in compliance with that resolution.[33]

Even though this speech was given in January 2002, before more resolutions regarding counter-terrorism were adopted, the representative is right in his assumption that Resolution 1373 was the first among a series of resolutions that are still being continuously issued even more than ten years later. The series of resolutions regarding counter-terrorism have broadened global obligations in counter-terrorism; terrorism is no longer restricted to violent crimes like bombing and hijacking, but includes speech that apologizes for terrorism and funding terrorism. These forms of crime control have their roots in colonial history (as discussed in Chapter 1 and later in Chapter 2). The neo-colonial mindset, represented by the Security Council, continues to cling to such methods with limited or no willingness to learn from the colonial history that failed in providing long-term national and international peace and security.

Security Council in Its Fight against Terrorism: Legal, Political and Practical Limits" (2008) 57:2 *The International & Comparative Law Quarterly* 175 at 334–5.

[30] Talmon, "The Security Council as World Legislature," at 182.

[31] For more, see Martínez, "The Legislative Role of the Security Council," at 334–5; Stefan Talmon & Nico Krisch, "The Rise and Fall of Collective Security: Terrorism, US Hegemony, and the Plight of the Security Council" in Christian Walter et al, eds, *Terrorism as a Challenge for National and International Law: Security versus Liberty?* (Berlin: Springer Science & Business Media, 2004) at 879, 883.

[32] See UN Doc. S/PV.4453 (2002).

[33] *Ibid* (Spain).

The following sections explore the series of Security Council resolutions adopted post-9/11, the wide list of obligations they include, and the continuing neglect of the need to define terrorism.

UN Security Council Resolution 1373 (2001)

Resolution 1373 is considered one of the most influential sources of post-9/11 counter-terrorism.[34] It establishes a global counter-terrorism system that requires states to prevent the financing of terrorism, become parties to the 1999 International Convention for the Suppression of the Financing of Terrorism, deny terrorists a safe haven, update criminal laws, bring terrorists to justice, improve border controls, control arms trafficking, and cooperate with and exchange information with other states. It also establishes a Counter-Terrorism Committee (CTC). Despite its length, I find it important to quote the related parts of the resolution. These state that:

> *The Security Council* [...] *Acting* under Chapter VII of the Charter of the United Nations,
> 1. *Decides* that all States shall:
>   (a) Prevent and suppress the financing of terrorist acts;
>   (b) Criminalize the wilful provision or collection, by any means, directly or indirectly, of funds by their nationals or in their territories with the intention that the funds should be used, or in the knowledge that they are to be used, in order to carry out terrorist acts;
>   (c) Freeze without delay funds and other financial assets or economic resources of persons who commit, or attempt to commit, terrorist acts or participate in or facilitate the commission of terrorist acts; of entities owned or controlled directly or indirectly by such persons; and of persons and entities acting on behalf of, or at the direction of such persons and entities, including funds derived or generated from property owned or controlled directly or indirectly by such persons and associated persons and entities;
>   (d) Prohibit their nationals or any persons and entities within their territories from making any funds, financial assets or economic resources or financial or other related services available, directly or indirectly, for the benefit of persons who commit or attempt to commit or facilitate or participate in the commission of terrorist acts, of entities owned or controlled, directly or indirectly, by such persons and of persons and entities acting on behalf of or at the direction of such persons;
> 2. *Decides also* that all States shall:
>   (a) Refrain from providing any form of support, active or passive, to entities or persons involved in terrorist acts, including by suppressing recruitment

---

[34] According to the representative of France at the UN, Resolution 1373 is "one of the most important resolutions in its history." UN Doc. S/PV.4453, at 7 (2002) (France).

of members of terrorist groups and eliminating the supply of weapons to terrorists;

(b) Take the necessary steps to prevent the commission of terrorist acts, including by provision of early warning to other States by exchange of information;

(c) Deny safe haven to those who finance, plan, support, or commit terrorist acts, or provide safe havens;

(d) Prevent those who finance, plan, facilitate or commit terrorist acts from using their respective territories for those purposes against other States or their citizens;

(e) Ensure that any person who participates in the financing, planning, preparation or perpetration of terrorist acts or in supporting terrorist acts is brought to justice and ensure that, in addition to any other measures against them, such terrorist acts are established as serious criminal offences in domestic laws and regulations and that the punishment duly reflects the seriousness of such terrorist acts;

(f) Afford one another the greatest measure of assistance in connection with criminal investigations or criminal proceedings relating to the financing or support of terrorist acts, including assistance in obtaining evidence in their possession necessary for the proceedings;

(g) Prevent the movement of terrorists or terrorist groups by effective border controls and controls on issuance of identity papers and travel documents, and through measures for preventing counterfeiting, forgery or fraudulent use of identity papers and travel documents;

3. *Calls* upon all States to [...]

(d) Become parties as soon as possible to the relevant international conventions and protocols relating to terrorism, including the International Convention for the Suppression of the Financing of Terrorism of 9 December 1999;

(e) Increase cooperation and fully implement the relevant international conventions and protocols relating to terrorism and Security Council resolutions 1269 (1999) and 1368 (2001); [...]

6. *Decides* to establish, in accordance with rule 28 of its provisional rules of procedure, a Committee of the Security Council, consisting of all the members of the Council, to monitor implementation of this resolution, with the assistance of appropriate expertise, and *calls upon* all States to report to the Committee, no later than 90 days from the date of adoption of this resolution and thereafter according to a timetable to be proposed by the Committee, on the steps they have taken to implement this resolution[.]

Despite the variety of obligations, the resolution focuses primarily on terrorism financing. The logic of the Security Council is that, if the financial position of terrorist groups is weakened, they will be unable to function, and terrorism will vanish. Without identifying what terrorism is it is not possible to accurately and fairly identify terrorists and their funders.

On the Definition

Resolution 1373 does not provide a definition of or guidance on the meaning of "terrorist acts." Roach suggests that this imperfect side of the resolution is a result of the quick reactive approach in criminalization. Such legislative responses often lack a comprehensive view of the multidimensional aspects of the situation.[35] Eric Rosand, United States Mission to the UN, states that the sponsors of the resolution wanted to pass it without going through the problems of the definition that could not be solved by the General Assembly for more than three decades, and which would complicate negotiations.[36] This resolution, which is globally binding in the obligation to criminalize terrorist acts under each state's domestic system, has thereby increased the complexity of the definition instead of solving it.

This imperfect international approach to issuing obligations without appending an adequate definition of terrorism had two major consequences: terrorism was defined much too broadly at the domestic level in most UN member countries, and countries with poor human rights records proudly report their anti-terrorism measures without fear of further criticism.[37] Roach describes Security Council Resolution 1373 as a "panic global legislation," in which the resolution came about in a climate of near-hysteria, and the Security Council enacted the resolution with limited information about 9/11.[38] This unsound resolution and subsequent legislation and actions built around it have led to various definitions of terrorism based on each state's national interests. These definitions may be arrived at arbitrarily, and are frequently far too broad, encompassing lawful actions and behaviors that are subsequently criminalized.

Furthermore, a retrospective consideration of the events of 9/11 casts doubts on the idea that there was a need for a global shift in crime control. This shift manifested as a widespread drive to establish laws aimed at preventing crimes and threats. Threat-based criminalization risks human security and national justice systems. McCulloch and Pickering examine the shift in the criminal approach that deals with terrorism. For McCulloch and Pickering, preventing violent mass attacks is indeed necessary, but preempting threats that have not yet become a reality is a major concern. To prevent terrorist attacks, the focus is on the prohibited criminal conduct; however, to preempt, the focus is on individuals who are considered a threat based on their identity or associations.[39] McCulloch and Pickering reject the preemptive approach because, whereas legislators and policymakers assume that this approach can reduce the terrorist threat and enhance security, there is no evidence that supports this

---

[35] Roach, *The 9/11 Effect*, at 31.
[36] Eric Rosand, "The UN Security Council's Counter-Terrorism Efforts" in Roy Lee, ed, *Swords into Plowshares: Building Peace through the United Nations* (Leiden: Martinus Nijhoff, 2006) at 74–5.
[37] Roach, *The 9/11 Effect*, at 31.
[38] *Ibid.*
[39] McCulloch & Pickering, "Counter-Terrorism: The Law and Policing of Pre-Emption," at 14.

assumption. Even in societies where there are a number of convictions for terrorist offenses, convictions are a guide to the effectiveness of law enforcement and do not necessarily show success in preventing future crimes.[40]

This argument makes me question the effectiveness of law enforcement in the Arab world, where convictions may only reflect the overbroad definitions, making the indictment process arbitrary, as will be shown in Chapters 4 and 6. The importance of a definition of terrorism is to send a clear message to society and law enforcement agencies about the wrongful acts, allowing terrorism to be distinguished from other crimes and from lawful acts. Current practice suggests an overlap between these three categories, in which a mass school shooting in the United States or a military attack on civilians in neglected parts of the world can be politically less threatening than a Facebook "like" on a terrorist video.

Counter-Terrorism Financing

The task of counter-terrorism, especially post-9/11, has been to anticipate the movement and growth of terrorist organizations in order to preempt their terrorist acts. To this end, the UN Security Council has established a counter-terrorism regime that aims to target terrorist organizations, primarily by weakening their financial position. Resolution 1373 emphasizes the prevention of terrorism financing. As mentioned earlier, there were previous international attempts to prohibit terrorism financing, including the International Convention for the Suppression of the Financing of Terrorism. Even though this convention was adopted in 1999, it was signed and ratified by only a few states. Resolution 1373 promotes this convention by calling on states to become parties to it,[41] which has been achieved through their gradual ratification of the convention. The convention now has 132 signatories and 188 parties.[42] However, the efficiency of counter-terrorism financing is worth examining, especially since the 1991 Al-Qaeda and Taliban sanctions regime mentioned earlier did not prevent the attacks of 9/11.

While great global emphasis has been placed on counter-terrorism financing, this focus has shown limited efficacy. For instance, the massive attacks of 9/11 were estimated to have cost the plotters between $400,000 and $500,000,[43] an amount that can be readily collected with or without financial sanctions. The focus on suppressing the financing of terrorists comes from an assumption that terrorist organizations, especially Al-Qaeda, which was led by the wealthy Osama bin Laden,

---

[40] *Ibid*, at 15–16.
[41] UN Security Council Resolution 1373, para 3(d).
[42] International Convention for the Suppression of the Financing of Terrorism, online: UN Treaty Collection treaties.un.org.
[43] National Commission on Terrorist Attacks upon the United States (9–11 Commission) [The 9/11 Commission Report] (2004) online: National Commission on Terrorist Attacks upon the United States www.9-11commission.gov/report/, at 172.

have great assets and access to financial liquidity, which must be frozen. However, a report by the National Commission on Terrorist Attacks upon the United States (9/11 Commission) shows that Al-Qaeda's major source of funds was not bin Laden's personal inheritance or network of businesses as the United States and the world thought, but donations.[44] Such donations were made by charities located in the wealthy Gulf countries, particularly Saudi Arabia.[45] It should be mentioned that not all donors were Al-Qaeda sympathizers; some did not know the final destination of their donations.[46] This suggests that, unlike funds coming through money laundering from organized crime, which involve large amounts of money, terrorism financing may involve small transfers that can come from legitimate sources.[47]

The post-9/11 counter-terrorism experience has shown the limited effectiveness of terrorism financing laws. However, states were required to update the CTC with their counter-terrorism financing laws and measures.[48] This suggests that, regardless of the efficacy of terrorism-financing laws, the obligation listed in Security Council Resolution 1373 must be adhered to, and states must adopt new laws to satisfy the neo-colonial powers that dominate the Security Council. The obligations of Resolution 1373 enable the control of potential terrorist groups more than terrorist activities, and this in turn accords with a colonial counter-insurgency approach, which attempts to control social conduct through politics.

Counter-Terrorism Committee (CTC): No Emphasis on the Definition of Terrorism

Resolution 1373 established the Counter-Terrorism Committee (CTC). The CTC is comprised of all 15 Security Council members, with the assistance of appropriate expertise. Its mandate is to monitor the implementation of Resolution 1373. States should provide the CTC with annual reports on the steps they have taken to implement this resolution.

Resolution 1373 requires countries to report their anti-terrorism measures to the CTC within 90 days of its issuance in September 2001. This short period was understood by a number of countries as a deadline to adopt anti-terrorism laws. To respond to Resolution 1373, many countries, including those that already had anti-terrorism laws, rushed to expand their existing laws. In an attempt to comply with the obligations established in this resolution, many states took the definition in the United Kingdom Terrorism Act (2000) as their guidance. Roach observes that the United Kingdom has great global influence, especially over its former colonies. Britain has a long history of dealing with combating terrorism in Northern Ireland

---

[44] *Ibid*, 169–70.
[45] *Ibid*, at 170.
[46] *Ibid*.
[47] Roach, *The 9/11 Effect*, at 35.
[48] 2006 is the year of the last published report on the CTC website.

and other colonies.[49] The British Terrorism Act defines terrorism – with a focus on the motive element – as occurring when:

> [...] (b) the use or threat is designed to influence the government [or an international governmental organization] or to intimidate the public or a section of the public, and
> (c) the use or threat is made for the purpose of advancing a political, religious[, racial] or ideological cause.
>
> (2) Action falls within this subsection if it—
> (a) involves serious violence against a person,
> (b) involves serious damage to property,
> (c) endangers a person's life, other than that of the person committing the action,
> (d) creates a serious risk to the health or safety of the public or a section of the public, or
> (e) is designed seriously to interfere with or seriously to disrupt an electronic system.[50]

Throughout the years following the establishment of the CTC, countries reported their broad anti-terrorism measures to the CTC without fear of being criticized. In practice, the role of the CTC was mainly to follow up on how stern domestic anti-terrorism laws and measures were, despite the fact that some laws and measures were unnecessarily broad and repressive. Roach has criticized the CTC by arguing that countries that were disapproved of before 9/11 for their poor human rights records in dealing with suspected terrorists were proudly reporting their anti-terrorism measures to the CTC without fear of further criticism.[51] For instance, in its first report to the CTC, Egypt confidently reported its tough counter-terrorism penalties, including the death penalty. Egypt's report states that "the legal texts regarding terrorist acts provide severe penalties [...,] the maximum penalty being death and the minimum being lifelong hard labour[.]"[52] Egypt also reported to the CTC the sufficiency of its Penal Code to meet the standards of Resolution 1373 by covering "all criminal acts, as well as attempted offences and complicity, including incitement, conspiracy and assistance."[53] It goes further in mentioning the use of its infamous State of Emergency Law, stating that "paragraph 1 of article 3 of law no. 162 of 1958 permits the

---

[49] Roach, The 9/11 Effect, at 228.
[50] Section 1(1) of the Terrorism Act 2000.
[51] Roach, The 9/11 Effect, at 3, 48–9.
[52] "Letter dated 20 December 2001 from the Permanent Representative of Egypt to the United Nations addressed to the Chairman of the Security Council Committee established pursuant to Resolution 1373 (2001) concerning counter-terrorism," S/2001/1237 [Egypt's Report to the CTC, 2001], at 11.
[53] "Letter dated 20 January 2003 from the Permanent Representative of Egypt to the United Nations addressed to the Chairman of the Security Council Committee established pursuant to Resolution 1373 (2001) concerning counter-terrorism," S/2003/277 [Egypt Report to the CTC, 2003], at 8.

competent authorities to arrest any suspect person or persons presenting a threat to security and public order and to search them and search their homes."[54] CTC reports in following years do not show criticism of Egypt's wide authorities under its Penal Code or State of Emergency Law.

Arab States' Responses to Resolution 1373

The general response of Arab states to Resolution 1373 showed no rush in adopting new anti-terrorism laws. Unlike the rest of the world, Arab states did not immediately adopt new anti-terrorism laws. Countries like Egypt and Syria that had already criminalized terrorism within their criminal codes did not see a need to expand their existing overly broad laws. Other countries, like Bahrain and Jordan, which found their criminal code and national security laws more than adequate to fight terrorism, later adopted special anti-terrorism laws between 2005 and 2006 in a response to opponents and internal threats.

On the other hand, Tunisia responded to Resolution 1371 differently than the rest of the Arab states by adopting a new anti-terrorism law. In 2002 Tunisia reported to the CTC that a draft law on counter-terrorism was being prepared.[55] The law was passed in December 2003 by Act No. 75 of 2003 concerning Support for International Efforts to Combat Terrorism and Prevent Money-Laundering.[56] The Act criminalizes terrorism, terrorism financing, and money laundering in one law, an approach that is criticized by Tunisian lawyers.[57] Tunisian lawyers have pointed out that Tunisia took advantage of the event of 9/11 to broaden its national security laws, restricting rights and liberties in the name of counter-terrorism.[58]

With the exception of Tunisia, which enacted a new anti-terrorism in 2003 as a response to a terrorist attack on Djerba Island (addressed in Chapter 7), most Arab states were relatively slow in adopting new anti-terrorism laws. However, they have shown no hesitation in adopting regulations regarding financing. The laws are primarily dedicated to money laundering, with less or even no focus on terrorism financing. Some countries, such as Egypt and Lebanon, prohibit terrorism financing as part of prohibiting money laundering.[59] Both of these countries refer to the

---

[54] *Ibid.*
[55] "Note verbale dated 30 August 2002 from the Permanent Mission of Tunisia to the United Nations addressed to the Chairman of the Security Council Committee established pursuant to Resolution 1373 (2001) concerning counter-terrorism," S/2002/1024 [Tunisia's Report to the CTC, 2002], at 3–4.
[56] Tunisian Act No. 75 of 2003 concerning Support for International Efforts to Combat Terrorism and Prevent Money-Laundering.
[57] Khawla Zatyaqi, "Terrorism Law: Between the Urge to Counter the Phenomenon and Protecting Human Rights" (August 14, 2014) *Attounissia*, online: www.attounissia.com.tn/details_article.php?t=41&a=132012.
[58] Sameh Samear, "New 'Terrorism' Law Enhances Fascist Laws" (February 8, 2014) *Mohamoon*, online: www.mohamoon.com/montada/Default.aspx?Action=Display&ID=14904&Type=3.
[59] Article 2 of Egyptian Law No. 80 of 2002 on Anti-Money Laundering. Article 1 of the Lebanese Law No. 318 of 2001 on Combating Money Laundering.

definition of terrorism stipulated in their Penal Code. Other countries, like the United Arab Emirates (UAE), also prohibit terrorism financing as part of prohibiting money laundering, but the UAE did not provide a definition of terrorism until it adopted its first anti-terrorism law in 2004.[60]

An overall observation regarding Arab states' response to Resolution 1373 is that they all rushed into adopting money-laundering laws; some immediately included terrorism financing while others did so in following years. The motive behind the collective adoption of such laws can be seen in the case of Egypt in relation to the FATF. In 2001, Egypt was listed by the FATF as a noncooperative country,[61] a measure that can be taken by the FATF against countries that have weak measures regarding money laundering – and terrorism financing, as added to the FATF's mandate post-9/11. Lebanon was also blacklisted in a previous year.[62] In order for such countries to be de-listed, the FATF requires a modification of legislation that ensures the prevention and punishment of crimes regarding money laundering and terrorism financing in accordance with international standards.[63] Egypt thus modified its legislation and was de-listed in 2004. In a report to the CTC, Egypt, while demonstrating its counter-terrorism measures, also reveals its efforts to meet FATF standards. It states that:

> Since June 2001, Egypt has been subject to assessment by the Financial Action Task Force (FATF) aimed at monitoring the extent of Egypt's commitment to implementing the FATF recommendations on terrorist financing and money-laundering. Egypt had been included on the list of non-cooperative countries and territories (NCCTS), but was removed from the list in February 2004 in view of the institutional and practical changes it had introduced in that area.[64]

Egypt's experience shows that compliance with FATF requirements, which are part of Security Council Resolution 1373 obligations, is done, whether partially or entirely, in order to be removed from the FATF blacklist. In this respect, Alain Damais, Executive Secretary of the FATF, argues that the FATF's measures have

> had long-lasting effects on a much broader range of countries than the [blacklisted countries], as it has created a global incentive for countries to either create or improve [their anti-money laundering and counterterrorist financing] regime, and better cooperate at the international level. In addition, this initiative encouraged

---

[60] United Arab Emirates Law No. 1 of 2004 regarding Combating Terrorist Crimes.
[61] For more on Egypt, see Financial Action Task Force, "Review to Identify Non-Cooperative Countries or Territories: Increasing the Worldwide Effectiveness of Anti-Money Laundering Measures," June 22, 2001, at 3, 14, 18.
[62] "Financial Action Task Force on Money Laundering 2000–2001 Report Released," PAC/ COM/NEWS (2001) 58 Paris, June 22, 2001, at 1–3.
[63] *Ibid.*
[64] "Note verbale dated 29 April 2005 from the Permanent Mission of Egypt to the United Nations addressed to the Chairman of the Counter-Terrorism Committee," S/2005/288 [Egypt's Report to the CTC, 2005], at 10.

many other countries and territories to adopt and implement measures for the prevention, detection and punishment of money laundering and terrorist financing, to prevent any listing by FATF.[65]

Damais' statement supports our argument that Arab states adopted counter-money laundering and terrorist financing laws in order to avoid being blacklisted by the FATF. Whether or not terrorism is effectively countered, the tool of blacklisting, among other tools of financial control, has served the FATF and UN Security Council in maintaining their position of influence. This position allows them to continue centralizing the global power to regulate in the name of counter-terrorism.

UN Security Council Resolution 1566 (2004): Late Guidance on the Definition of Terrorism

Resolution 1566 was adopted in October 2004 after the killing of more than 300 children and adults by Chechen rebels in the Beslan school siege in Russia.[66] It was adopted under Chapter VII of the UN Charter, reminding states of their responsibilities to combat terrorism. The resolution also attempts to fill one of the gaps of Resolution 1373 by providing a general definition for "terrorism." Resolution 1566 defines terrorism as follows:

> [C]riminal acts, including against civilians, committed with the intent to cause death or serious bodily injury, or taking of hostages, with the purpose to provoke a state of terror in the general public or in a group of persons or particular persons, intimidate a population or compel a government or an international organization to do or to abstain from doing any act, which constitute offences within the scope of and as defined in the international conventions and protocols relating to terrorism[.][67]

This definition provides international guidance on the meaning of terrorism. It focuses on violent acts that physically harm the population and spread fear among the populace. It avoids the political or religious motive element required in the British and other Western definitions. Roach observes that this guidance provides a "minimal definition that focused on intentional" acts of serious harm, and that is in line with criminal law principles.[68] The focus on the most serious and violent crimes will help reduce the ambiguity related to many national definitions of terrorism. However, it is unlikely to be implemented since many countries complied with Resolution 1373 and had already adopted anti-terrorism laws that applied to a broader range or a different set of offenses than those covered by the new definition.

---

[65] Alain Damais, "The Financial Action Task Force" in Wouter H. Muller, Christian H. Kalin & John G. Goldsworth, eds, *Anti-Money Laundering: International Law and Practice* (London: John Wiley & Sons, 2007) at 78.
[66] "Beslan School Siege Fast Facts" (August 15, 2016) *CNN Library*, online: www.cnn.com.
[67] UN Security Council Resolution 1566 (2004), para 3.
[68] Roach, *The 9/11 Effect*, at 52.

Since 2004, countries have frequently amended their anti-terrorism laws, but with no consideration to the above definition. This suggests a duality in states' responses to international obligations. On the one hand, they rush into broadening their anti-terrorism legislation in accordance with Resolution 1373, and on the other, they neglect the guidance provided by Resolution 1566. This duality will continue as long as the issue of the definition of terrorism is not a priority for the Security Council.

UN Security Council Resolution 1624 (2005): Speech Crimes

The UN Security Council adopted nonbinding Resolution 1624 in September 2005 as a response to the 2005 London bombing. The resolution emphasizes speech crimes related to terrorism. Despite the fact that this resolution is nonbinding, it calls upon states to adopt measures that prohibit and prevent incitement to commit a terrorist act. The resolution reads:

> Condemning also in the strongest terms the incitement of terrorist acts and *repudiating* attempts at the justification or glorification (*apologie*) of terrorist acts that may incite further terrorist acts,
>
> Deeply concerned that incitement of terrorist acts motivated by extremism and intolerance poses a serious and growing danger to the enjoyment of human rights, threatens the social and economic development of all States, undermines global stability and prosperity[.][69]

Resolution 1624 does not define the terms "incitement" and "glorification" of terrorism. It leaves interpreting such acts to national jurisdictions. However, such terms are often defined vaguely or broadly in order to allow national authorities to penalize those who encourage or glorify terrorism and radical ideologies without necessarily being part of inciting or planning any specific attacks. The impreciseness of the wording of the resolution broadens the capacity of speech crimes to include certain uses of the internet and social media.[70] Extending speech crimes in this way risks violating the right to free speech, which is protected under international conventions, including the Convention for the Protection for Human Rights and Fundamental Freedoms and the International Covenant on Civil and Political Rights (ICCPR).

Even though freedom of speech is granted by international human rights law, it has been suggested that freedom of speech may legitimately be restricted when it is misused.[71] This view represents the overall European tradition as observed from the

---

[69] UN Security Council, Security Council Resolution 1566, 2004 SC Res. 1566, UN SCOR, S/RES/1566 [Resolution 1566], para 1.

[70] "Letter dated 2 September 2015 from the Chair of the Security Council Committee established pursuant to Resolution 1373 (2001) concerning counter-terrorism addressed to the President of the Security Council," S/2015/683, at 4–5.

[71] Daphne Barak-Erez & David Scharia, "Freedom of Speech, Support for Terrorism, and the Challenge of Global Constitutional Law" (2011) 2 Harvard National Security Journal 1 at 5.

collective European national laws and regional conventions.[72] For example, France reported to the CTC that it prohibits incitement in its Penal Code and in its Law on the Freedom of the Press of July 29, 1881 (Press Law). Incitement is defined in Article 23 of the Press Law as:

> [S]peeches, shouts or threats proffered in public places or meetings, or by written words, printed matter, drawings, engravings, paintings, emblems, pictures or any other written, spoken or pictorial aid, sold or distributed, offered for sale or displayed in public places or meetings, either by posters or notices displayed for public view, or by any means of electronic communication.[73]

The French Press Law of 1881 can thus be viewed as the legal foundation for the restriction of freedom of expression in France and its colonies, as we will see in Chapters 6 and 7. France continues explaining in its report to the CTC that incitement is punishable even if no further offense is committed.[74] As we will see in Chapters 5 and 6, the above article has migrated to former French colonies, including Egypt and Tunisia.

The United Kingdom, which promoted Resolution 1624, also has a long history of legislating on speech crimes. Several laws were adopted by the United Kingdom to counter the threat of Irish "rebels." These include the 1833 Act for the More Effective Suppression of Local Disturbances and Dangerous Associations in Ireland, the Prevention of Crime (Ireland) Act of 1883, and the Restoration of Order in Ireland Act of 1920, which targeted Irish rebels, as discussed in the introduction to this book. Speech crimes were further regulated in Northern Ireland. During the 1970s, the British security forces took suppressive measures against Catholics in Northern Ireland, which exacerbated the sense of hatred toward the British forces.[75] To preempt Catholics from taking further angry actions, "incitement" to hatred was criminalized in the 1970 Prevention of Incitement to Hatred Act (Northern Ireland). Article 1 of the Act states that:

> 1. A person shall be guilty of an offence under this Act if, with intent to stir up hatred against, or arouse fear of, any section of the public in Northern Ireland—
> (a) he publishes or distributes written or other matter which is threatening, abusive or insulting; or
> (b) he uses in any public place or at any public meeting words which are threatening, abusive or insulting;

---

[72] For more, see *ibid.*
[73] "Letter dated 14 July 2006 from the Permanent Representative of France to the United Nations addressed to the Chairman of the Counter-Terrorism Committee," S/2006/547 [France's report to the CTC, 2006], at 3.
[74] *Ibid.*
[75] Robert Post, "Hate Speech and Democracy" in Ivan Hare & James Weinstein, eds, *Extreme Speech and Democracy* (New York: Oxford University Press, 2009) at 481.

being matter or words likely to stir up hatred against, or arouse fear of, any section of the public in Northern Ireland on grounds of religious belief, colour, race or ethnic or national origins.[76]

This law is another foundation of incitement and speech crimes in the United Kingdom and its former colonies. The above regulations were adopted later in the United Kingdom in the Public Order Act 1986.[77] These Acts did not explicitly list incitement to terrorism, but their wording includes the arousing of fear, which can be linked to the current crimes of terror.

The British experience in Malaya shows that emergency powers in this colony included restrictions on freedom of expression, including Emergency (Publications – Control of Sale and Circulation) 1950 and Emergency (Newspaper) Regulations 1951, mentioned in Chapter 1. Such restrictions are extended to the contemporary laws of Singapore, particularly the Internal Security Act 1960. According to this Act, the "Minister charged with the responsibility for printing presses publications" may prohibit any print item that:

(a) contains any incitement to violence;
(b) counsels disobedience to the law or to any lawful order;
(c) is calculated or likely to lead to a breach of the peace, or to promote feelings of hostility between different races or classes of the population; or
(d) is prejudicial to the national interest, public order or security of Singapore,
        he may by order published in the Gazette prohibit either absolutely or subject to such conditions as may be prescribed therein the printing, publication, sale, issue, circulation or possession of such document or publication.[78]

Prohibiting speech that encourages or apologizes for terrorism is a direct threat to freedom of expression and the future of democracy. The UN Special Rapporteurs on counter-terrorism and freedom of expression suggest avoiding criminalizing "glorification" or "justifying" terrorism so that freedom of expression is not arbitrarily narrowed in a way that effects normal conduct by ordinary people, journalists, and researchers.[79] According to their report, such offenses "must be prescribed by law in precise language, including by avoiding reference to vague terms such as 'glorifying' or 'promoting' terrorism[.]"[80] The ambiguity of speech crimes allows opponents to

---

[76] Prevention of Incitement to Hatred Act (Northern Ireland) 1970.
[77] Part III of the Public Order Act 1986.
[78] Article 20 of the Singapore Internal Security Act 18 of 1960 as amended by Act 15 of 2010.
[79] UN Human Rights Office of the High Commission, Special Rapporteur on the Promotion and Protection of Human Rights and Fundamental Freedoms while Countering Terrorism, A/HRC/16/51, December 22, 2010, para 39.
[80] Ibid, para 31.

be charged with terrorism even when no violent acts are planned, which risks civil and political liberties.

As the above examples show, a strong colonial legacy has been extended to national and global legislation. Vague measures against glorification in colonial legislation continue to influence current global anti-terrorism measures. Such a legacy prioritizes security over rights, yet without evidence of the effectiveness of such measures. In fact, colonial history shows that coercive measures have often resulted in more violent social and political responses. This point is discussed in more detail in Chapter 6 when examining the Tunisian experience under French colonialism.

UN Security Council Resolution 2178 (2014): Foreign Terrorist Fighters

The UN Security Council adopted Resolution 2178 in September 2014 to deal with the increasing wave of foreign terrorist fighters. Under international law, foreign fighters are individuals who leave their home countries to take part in armed conflicts abroad by joining nonstate armed groups.[81] According to the resolution, foreign terrorist fighters are "individuals who travel to a State other than their States of residence or nationality for the purpose of the perpetration, planning, or preparation of, or participation in, terrorist acts or the providing or receiving of terrorist training, including in connection with armed conflict."[82] While the resolution points out foreign terrorist fighters as a phenomenon, it particularly refers to Islamic State in Iraq and Syria (ISIS) and other cells derivative of Al-Qaeda. The question of treating ISIS as a distinctive global threat has been concerning academics and the international community.[83] Both ISIS and Al-Qaeda carried out worldwide massive attacks. In this section, the threat of ISIS is addressed, followed by the obligations imposed under Resolution 2178, their effectiveness and rationale.

The Global Threat of Islamic State (ISIS)

ISIS, declared in April 2013, is a jihadist group that seeks the establishment and expansion of the Islamic Caliphate through military conquest.[84] Following the Salafi–Wahhabi tradition, ISIS's ideology is similar to that of Al-Qaeda. While ISIS is more focused on territorial control in the region of Iraq and the Levant, it also calls for violence in countries that have joined the international military campaign against it.[85]

---

[81] "Foreign Fighters under International Law" (October 2, 2014) 7 *Geneva Academy of International Humanitarian Law and Human Rights*, online: www.geneva-academy.ch, at 5.

[82] UN Security Council Resolution 2178 (2014).

[83] Jessica Stern & J. M. Berger, *ISIS: The State of Terror* (New York: Ecco Press, 2015); Michael Weiss & Hassan Hassan, *Isis: Inside the Army of Terror* (New York: Regan Arts, 2015).

[84] Charles C. Caris & Samuel Reynolds, "ISIS Governance in Syria" (July 2014) *Institute for the Study of War*, online: www.understandingwar.org/report/isis-governance-syria, at 9–10.

[85] Stewart Bell, "ISIS Takes Credit for Inspiring Terrorist Attacks that Killed Two Canadian Soldiers" (November 21, 2014) *National Post*, online: news.nationalpost.com.

The threat of the radical ideology of ISIS increases with its reliance on foreign fighters from all around the world, who consequently spread the culture of violence. It should be noted that the phenomenon of foreign fighters is not new. Mercenaries and terrorists have been engaging in international armed conflicts and civil wars throughout history. For instance, Arab–Afghan warriors played a major role in the Soviet War in Afghanistan (1979–89). Other examples include the Spanish Civil War (1936–9) and the Palestine–Israeli conflict (1948–present).[86]

The threat of foreign terrorist fighters to some extent differs from the threat of major terrorist groups like Al-Qaeda. While both ISIS and Al-Qaeda adopt a radical ideology and carry out violent and massive attacks, ISIS differs insofar as it has a geographical existence in Iraq and Syria and an ambition to expand its territory.[87] A report by the UN Analytical Support and Sanctions Monitoring Team shows that, after the ousting of the Taliban regime in 2001, the survivors established new bases in countries that had no history of jihadism, above all Iraq and Syria.[88] ISIS has attracted many supporters, traveling from different parts of the world to join the fight. There has been a radical increase in the number of foreign fighters from some thousands in the last decades to currently more than 25,000.[89] In addition, in the past decade terrorist fighters came from a few countries, but now they come from over 100 countries.[90] The spread of terrorist fighters all around the world has motivated the Security Council to adopt obligations that focus on terrorist movement and funding.

ISIS has been involved in many forms of illegal funding, including taxation and oil production from occupied territories, human trafficking, and looting of cultural properties. Each of these terrorism-related crimes is a serious crime by itself that both international and national laws have criminalized. Therefore, to combat such complex crimes, states should apply existing criminal laws combined with regional and international cooperation in crime control. Introducing new anti-terrorism laws and measures could fill a political need by sending a symbolic message of the seriousness of the war on terror; however, this move would have minimal impact on global security.[91]

---

[86] *Ibid.*
[87] Roach, "Comparative Counter-Terrorism Law Comes of Age," at 5; Thomas Hegghammer, "The Rise of Muslim Foreign Fighters: Islam and the Globalization of Jihad" (2010/11) 35:3 *International Security* 53 at 57.
[88] "Letter dated 19 May 2015 from the Chair of the Security Council Committee pursuant to Resolutions 1267 (1999) and 1989 (2011) concerning Al-Qaida and associated individuals and entities addressed to the President of the Security Council," at 6.
[89] *Ibid*, at 7–8.
[90] *Ibid.*
[91] See Kent Roach, *September 11: Consequences for Canada* (Montreal: McGill-Queen's University Press: 2003) at 23–5.

The Obligations of Resolution 2178: Counter Violent Extremism
Resolution 2178 is adopted under Chapter VII, emphasizing obligations from Resolution 1373 (2001), including blacklisting and financial restrictions. Roach points out that while Resolution 1373 provides a global response to Al-Qaeda, Resolution 2178 plays a similar role in setting the foundation for responding to the threat of ISIS.[92] Resolution 2178 also emphasizes preventing the movement of terrorists through effective border controls and controls on issuing travel documents. It engages both states and airlines in providing information on listed passengers to competent authorities.[93] As we will see in Chapter 7, countries such as Tunisia, which has many people thought to be traveling to join ISIS, have responded to the travel ban obligation by imposing unfair restrictions on traveling that do not respect the right to movement or the rule of law.

Resolution 2178 refers to the concept of "violent extremism,"[94] and encourages states to counter this threat. However, this is another concept that is left without a clear definition and without clear guidance on how to counter it. According to Resolution 2178, violent extremism "can be conducive to terrorism"[95]; therefore, violent extremism must be countered in order to prevent terrorism.[96] The resolution acknowledges that military operations, law enforcement, and the use of intelligence alone are not enough to counter violent extremism and terrorism, and that a "nonviolent alternative"[97] must be developed in order to resolve and prevent conflicts. The resolution encourages states to enhance their efforts in countering violent extremism by preventing radicalization,[98] countering incitement to terrorism or extremism, encouraging religious tolerance, and adopting economic and social solutions.[99]

The wide range of measures can be linked to the model of "winning hearts and minds" established within counter-insurgency thinking, which combines military and political measures.[100] The neo-colonial regulations differ from colonial practices by being relatively less coercive; however, they are similar in adopting unfair measures. In the aftermath of the Paris attack in November 2015, the Security Council adopted Resolution 2253,[101] which neglects the holistic approach suggested in Resolution

[92] *Ibid*, at 14–15.
[93] Para 9 of Resolution 2178 (2014).
[94] Para 15–18 of UN Security Council, Security Council Resolution 1566, 2004 SC Res. 1566, UN SCOR, S/RES/1566 [Resolution 1566].
[95] Preamble and para 15 of UN Security Council, Security Council Resolution 2178, 2014 SC Res. 2178, UN SCOR, S/RES/2178 [Resolution 2178].
[96] *Ibid.*
[97] *Ibid.*
[98] Para 15, *ibid.*
[99] Preamble, *ibid.*
[100] The practice and theory of this model is discussed in Chapter 1.
[101] UN Security Council, Security Council Resolution 2253, 2015 SC Res. 2253, UN SCOR, S/RES/2253.

2178 by emphasizing blacklisting, travel bans, freezing funds, and restrictions on speech. Thus, neo-colonial measures allow the restricting of democratic freedoms in a way similar to how counter-insurgency undermined self-government and liberties. In addition to the above obligations, Resolution 2178 also requires states to comply with international human rights law. However, this obligation has been largely ignored. Democracies are responding to the threat of ISIS through exceptionalism and militarism. The United States-led war against ISIS (2014–present) has used a combination of laws of wars and exceptionalism. The basis of this war is the order of the United States President Barack Obama in August 2014. His order authorized two military operations in Iraq,[102] followed by over twenty operations in about three years.[103] While evaluating the il/legitimacy of this war is beyond the scope of this book,[104] it is worth pointing out that neo-colonial powers still adopt colonial counter-insurgency measures, which rely on militarism, centralization of power, and exceptionalism in the contemporary war on terror and violent extremism.

CONCLUSION: NEO-COLONIAL DOMINATION THROUGH
THE UN SECURITY COUNCIL AND FATF

This chapter has shown that the formal and informal influence of neo-colonial powers, particularly Western states through the UN Security Council and FATF, are the major factors in directing the current global war on terror. In its resolutions, the Security Council has emphasized techniques derived from the colonial and neo-colonial experiences of its permanent members, particularly the United Kingdom. These techniques include financial regulations, blacklisting, travel bans, and restrictions on speech, all of which may be unfairly used against suspects, and all of which have limited effectiveness in countering terrorism.

The Security Council and FATF's focus on counter-terrorism financing has led to a global shift in counter-terrorism legislation. States have adopted financial regulations regarding terrorism financing and money laundering, regardless of the actual effectiveness of such regulations. For instance, Egypt has adopted a wide

---

[102] The White House, Office of the Press Secretary (August 7, 2014) online: www.whitehouse.gov/the-press-office/2014/08/07/statement-president.

[103] Justin Carissimo, "US Airstrikes 'Kill at Least 250 Isis Militants' in Iraq" (June 29, 2016) *Independent*, online: www.independent.co.uk.

[104] According to international law, the kind of attacks carried out against ISIS constitute an armed conflict similar to the one that took place in Afghanistan in October 2001 between the Taliban forces backed by Al-Qaeda and the Northern Alliance forces backed by US forces. Although the term "armed conflict" is not defined in the four Geneva Conventions, it is generally understood as the involvement of the use of force between two or more states. This would be international armed conflict, while violence over a certain threshold between a state and armed groups, or between armed groups within a state, would be a noninternational armed conflict. While any military countermeasures taken against ISIS must be governed under international humanitarian law, the practice suggests that there has been a tendency toward normalizing the exception in the war on terror.

range of laws and regulations in this regard even though experience shows that accessing of the local banking system is low.[105] According to a report by MENA-FATF, only 20 percent of the Egyptian population has bank accounts, and the most common way of conducting financial transactions is with the use of cash.[106] This observation, while it does not apply to all states, is also a reflection of the limited effectiveness of financial regulations in preventing the funding of terrorists and in preventing violent operations.

The Security Council, on the other hand, dominates through political central-ization of what has become the norm of "global legislation." The frequent use of Chapter VII in adopting mandatory general obligations regarding counter-terrorism creates unequal positions of power. The inequality is in granting the Security Council, as a supra-national body, powers that allow it to skip the regular channels of legislation. In my view, the expansion of the Security Council's authorities should be seen as a normalization of the exception. Some could argue that this expansion of the Security Council's powers is necessary to respond to the increasing threat of bloody terrorist attacks; however, post-9/11 measures by the Security Council have not reduced terrorist groups or terrorist attacks.

The problem with the Security Council's approach to counter-terrorism is that it encourages states to adopt broad laws without insisting on a definition of terrorism that enhances national and international security. Resolution 1373 (2001) failed to address the definition; rather, it focused on broad measures that resulted in the expansion of the meaning of "terrorism" by including inciting and encouraging terrorist acts and financing terrorists. Although Resolution 1566 (2004) came up with guidance on the meaning of "terrorism," it was too late. Resolution 1566 and later resolutions did not insist that states must adopt a clear definition that is in line with the guidance provided in the resolution. The definition of terrorism is the founda-tion of the criminalization of other terrorism-related crimes, including terrorism financing and speech crimes. Without a clear and precise definition of terrorism at both the national and international level, attempts to combat terrorism and terrorism-related crimes will fail to meet basic standards of justice and fairness.

The FATF and the Security Council are not the only powers to embrace neo-colonial policy that direct the global war on terror. The United States and its allies are launching military interventions against terrorist cells. These interventions include the post-9/11 war in Afghanistan and the current intervention against ISIS in Syria and Iraq, which are examples of the destructive outcome of the unwise use of militarism and exceptionalism in counter-terrorism. Besides the fact that thou-sands of civilians have been killed in these interventions, the attack against Al-Qaeda in Afghanistan has resulted in the spread of the remaining Al-Qaeda supporters into

---

[105] "Mutual Evaluation Report: Anti-Money Laundering and Combating the Financing of Terrorism, Egypt" (May 19, 2009) *MENAFATF*, at 18.
[106] *Ibid.*

areas that previously had no history of jihadism. Until this attack, Al-Qaeda was contained in Afghanistan; killing its members did not end its ideology; rather, the ideology reemerged in the form of ISIS, this time more influential with more supporters and fighters carrying out more attacks worldwide.

The Security Council responded to the enormity of the threat of ISIS by encouraging the countering of "violent extremism" in order to prevent terrorism. However, the Security Council is not clear on the methods required to counter violent extremism. Does countering violent extremism mean the use of colonial counterinsurgency tactics? Does it mean working on a civil program that focuses on educational, economic, and political progress? Or is it a combination of military and political tactics – winning hearts and minds? The practice shows overall approval of the United States-led war on terror, as well as the methods of travel bans, blacklisting, and counter-terrorism financing, with little or no emphasis on a gradual program to solve the issues of radicalism and violence.

Radicalism and violence are two issues from which the Arab world has long suffered. Even though Arab states collectively and individually have long faced the threat of extremism and violence with tough national security policies, these threats remain uncontrolled.

3

Terrorism and Counter-Terrorism in the Arab World

Arab countries individually and collectively had broad national security laws well before the attacks of 9/11. This makes them ahead in the war on terror compared with the UN Security Council. This chapter shows the development, and influences on the development, of counter-terrorism measures in the Arab world. The chapter analyses the development of terrorism and the legal steps taken at a regional level to define and counter terrorism. The chapter tracks the rise and fall of movements perceived as threats to government and society in the Arab world, and the legal responses to these common threats. This historical development is broken into four phases: the war on communism; the war on Islamic terrorism; collective efforts to counter terrorism under the Arab Convention for the Suppression of Terrorism (Arab Convention) of 1997; and regional developments in the first twenty years of the twenty-first century.

Beginning in the 1920s and up until the 1960s, communism spread rapidly in the Arab region. Communism, which aimed to challenge the tyranny of Arab monarchies, was soon suppressed. This section focuses on a case study of Iraq, and an initial analysis of the situation in other Arab countries. The aim of this examination is to determine to what extent the measures adopted against communism were influenced by colonial practices and agendas, and to what extent these measures are extended to the current war on terrorism.

The second section examines Islamic terrorism as the common enemy in the neocolonial era. This section examines the emergence and development of Islamic movements in the Arab world. Islamic scholars argue that Islamic extremism and Islamic terrorism were results of conflicting postcolonial political and cultural values.[1] Most Arab countries sought "modernity" and to "Westernize" the political

---

[1] Rashid al-Ghanoushi, *al-Ḥurrīyāt al-'āmmah fī al-dawlah al-Islāmīyah* [*Public Liberties in the Islamic State*] (Beirut: Markaz Dirāsāt al-Waḥdah al-'Arabīyah, 1993) at 60; Mohammad Hussain Fadlallah, *Hiwarat filfikr wa esyasa wa elejtima'* [*Dialogues in Thought, Politics and Sociology*] (Beirut: Dar al-Malak: 1997) at 50.

77

system, which neglected Islamic values.[2] In addition, economic reforms largely served the few in power, affirming a system of local and global elitism. This section aims to show that the war on Islamic terrorism is, at least partially, a war of protecting the political and economic interests of neo-colonial powers and postcolonial authoritarian regimes. This makes the war on terror similar to the war on communism: both protect the status quo. In addition, national and global efforts to combat common enemies, whether communists or Islamists, focus on the identity of the enemy rather than the causes of its emergence or the nature of its wrongdoing. This has led to short-term peace and security at best.

However, this short-term peace and security did not prevent radical violence and the emergence of new terrorist groups. The Arab world responded to the increasing threat of terrorism by adopting the Arab Convention in 1997. This convention is an Egyptian product and reflects the Egyptian definition of terrorism adopted in its Penal Code in 1992. It also reflects the collective Arab view regarding issues of self-determination, overprotecting heads of state, and political crimes. The importance of the Arab Convention is that it shows that the Arab world was ahead of the West in the war on terrorism. This suggests that the Arab world had an interest in criminalizing terrorism well before the post-9/11 global shift in counter-terrorism.

Finally, the chapter examines twenty-first-century regional developments on security and counter-terrorism. The twenty-first century witnessed major events, including the attacks of 9/11 and the "Arab Spring." The former shaped the current global anti-terrorism framework, while the latter reshaped the distribution of power globally and regionally. This section examines the chaotic events that impacted Arab authoritarianism, which includes the influence of Egypt and Saudi Arabia over the Arab region. It also examines global neo-colonialism, which includes Western support of authoritarian regimes. Another neo-colonial power that has involved itself in the Arab region is Russia. In the aftermath of the "Arab Spring," Russia entered the Arab world as a neo-colonial power that empowered the Syrian dictator Bashar al-Assad through the UN Security Council by vetoing resolutions that condemn the Syrian regime. Russia's interference in Syria sends a symbolic message regarding Russia as a dominant neo-colonial power.

"TERRORISM" AND THE COMMON ENEMY

The term "terrorism," understood as referring to acts of violence, including bombing and hijacking, that target civilians, was not codified in the Arab world until the 1940s. Lebanon and Syria were among the first Arab countries to criminalize terrorism. The Lebanese Penal Code of 1943 defines terrorism as "all acts [that] aim to create a state of panic and are committed by means such as explosives and inflammable materials, toxic or burning products, epidemiological or microbial

---

[2] Al-Ghanoushi, *ibid*, at 60–2; Fadlallah, *ibid*, at 50–7.

factors that could cause a public danger."[3] This general definition, which focuses on the element of fear, inspired Syria to adopt the same definition in its Penal Code of 1949.[4] However, before these definitions were adopted, "terror" was associated with the threat of communism and its attempts to overthrow tyrannical regimes. This interpretation can be seen in the Egyptian experience. In 1946, Article 98(b) was added to the Egyptian Penal Code, condemning "whoever promotes in the Egyptian Republic in any way to change the fundamental principles of the constitution [...] or to overthrow the state's fundamental social or economic system [...] when the use of force or terror or any other illegal means is noticeable."[5] This article was adopted during the war on communism in Egypt. The article does not criminalize "communism" per se, but its judicial application shows that it targeted communists. A detailed examination of the application of this article in Egypt is addressed in Chapter 5.

While between the 1920s and 1960s communism was the common enemy that threatened monarchies and colonialists, Islamic terrorism has become the common enemy that currently threatens Western democracies and Arab authoritarian regimes. This section examines these two movements in the Arab world.

Communism: The Common Enemy during Colonialism

After the Russian Revolution of 1917, communism spread all over the world including to different parts of the Arab region, promoting social revolutions against the dominant capitalist regimes. Arab communist movements sought social, economic, and political reforms to protect people and particularly workers from the unfair distribution of power. This desire to close the gap between classes threatened the interests of colonists and local ruling classes and elites. These capitalism-driven powers responded by adopting legal and exceptional measures to suppress the emerging threat of communism. The war on communism was a war on ideology and not on particular violent acts. It targeted all acts associated with communist thought regardless of whether they included action, planning, or mere speech, and regardless of whether such speech was expressed publicly or privately.

The background and influences on communism in the Arab world differ from one place to another. For example, Iraqi and Syrian communist movements were connected to the international and particularly the Soviet movement of communism but were developed locally.[6] Communism in Syria was suppressed by the dominant Syrian Socialist Ba'ath Party, particularly during the union with Egypt

---

[3] Article 314 of the Lebanese Penal Code No. 340 of 1943.
[4] Welchman, "Rocks, Hard Places and Human Rights," at 639.
[5] Article 98(b) of the Egyptian Penal Code added by Law No. 117 of 1946.
[6] Maxime Rodinson, *Marxism and the Muslim World* (London: Zed Press, 1979) at 61.

(1958–71). Syrian members of communist parties were accused of being loyal to the Soviet Union and were exiled to remove their social threat.[7]

The Egyptian communist movement did not have direct connections with the Soviet Union, but was at first influenced by Greek, Italian, and Russian residents in Egypt. However, the movement was established and developed locally.[8] Egypt's experience in developing national security laws and measures goes back to the time of the monarchy (1922–53), which was seen by nationalists as an ally to the colonial power. At that time, Islamic groups had no significant role in political life, whereas liberals and communists did. These latter two groups sought to change the political and socioeconomic system, which represented a threat to the monarchy and to the colonial interests in the region.[9] Egyptian authorities suppressed communist members through accusations of criminal "overthrowing the regime," as will be shown in Chapter 4. In Tunisia, the Tunisian Communist Party was less popular. Unlike the Iraqi Communist Party, which included thousands of members, the Tunisian Communist Party had only a few hundred. Nonetheless, the communist agenda threatened the French colonist and the local government, who fought communism by banning communist papers,[10] arresting communist figures,[11] and convicting them of conspiracy.[12] A detailed review of the suppressive measures in Tunisia is provided in Chapters 6 and 7.

Among Arab states, communism played a significant role, particularly in Iraq. Before examining the role of communism in Iraq, I start with a brief background of the colonial experience and the British influence in Iraq. The Kingdom of Iraq under British Administration was established in 1920. The British had great influence and control in the area. They chose the ruler of Iraq, King Faisal ibn Husayn, and established a system of elitism that favored the minority of Sunni Arabs over the rest of the Iraqis.[13] The British granted the elite the effective political and economic positions in the country. On the other hand, the Iraqi monarchy and the elite became puppets of the British administration. This system secured the mutual interests of each: the ruling family enjoyed nominal power, the local elite held the key political and economic positions in the country, and the British secured

---

[7] Götz Nordbruch, *Nazism in Syria and Lebanon: The Ambivalence of the German Option, 1933–1945* (London: Routledge, 2009) at 120; Michel Aflaq, "Our Political Position on Communism," online: *Fi Sabeel Al-Ba'ath* [For the Sake of Ba'ath] albaath.online.fr/Volume%20IV-Chapters/Fi%20Sabil%20al%20Baath-Vol%204-Ch79.htm.

[8] *Ibid*, at 61–2.

[9] *Ibid*, at 156, 178.

[10] Khamis Arfawi, *Al-Qaḍā' wa-al-siyāsah fī Tūnis zaman al-isti'mār al-Faransī, 1881–1956* [*The Judiciary and Politics in Tunisia during French Colonialism: 1881–1956*] (Ṣafāqis: Ṣāmid lil-Nashr wa-al-Tawzī', 2005) at 43.

[11] Donald F. Busky, *Communism in History and Theory: Asia, Africa, and the Americas* (Westport, CT: Greenwood Publishing Group, 2002) at 96.

[12] Arfawi, *The Judiciary and Politics in Tunisia*, at 208–9.

[13] Elizabeth F. Thompson, *Justice Interrupted: The Struggle for Constitutional Government in the Middle East* (Cambridge, MA: Harvard University Press, 2013) at 178.

their route to India and benefitted from the Iraqi oil supply and investment.[14] This scenario was repeated in many colonies, but the case of Iraq represented "the most tyrannical state in the Middle East[,]"[15] as historian Elizabeth F. Thompson puts it. The situation of the elite ruling in their own interests while neglecting the mass of people was fertile ground for communism, which worked for the people against the elite.

The Iraqi Communist Party (ICP) was the most popular and the most targeted by repressive measures. It attracted workers and students who protested and rebelled against the unfair social order, shortage of food, and poverty.[16] The influence of the ICP threatened the monarchy and the existence of the British in Iraq. For instance, during the 1920s, a communist group named Mutadarisi al-Afkār al-Ḥurrah published a journal called *al-Ṣaḥifah*, which was soon closed down under the allegation that it attacked religion.[17] Censorship was one of the least coercive measures used to suppress opposition. The infamous Prime Minister Nuri al-Said ordered other exceptional measures, which included detention, torture, and execution of communist figures.[18]

Examining the war on communism in the Arab world shows that communists represented the common enemy of imperialism and Arab monarchism. There was a concern that allowing the spread of the ideology of communism would lead to a large insurgency war. Galula describes this concern:

> The East–West conflict that today covers the entire world cannot fail to be affected by any insurgency occurring anywhere. Thus, a Communist insurgency is almost certain to receive automatic support from the Communist bloc. Chances for Communist support are good even for non-Communist insurgents, provided, of course, that their opponent is an "imperialist" or an ally of "imperialism[.]"[19]

In their war against communism, Arab countries were influenced directly or indirectly by the Western imperial agenda. Arab governments dealt with communism based on the assumption that it was an extension of a foreign ideology that differed from the local political and economic system. The irony is that Arab governments did not question the economic and legal norms inherited from colonialism.

While communism has faded in the Arab world, the idea of the common enemy has not. The enemy can be opposition groups or minorities that governments view

[14] Ian Rutledge, *Enemy on the Euphrates: The Battle of Iraq and The Great Arab Revolt 1914–1921* (London: Saqi, 2015), 18–19.
[15] Thompson, *Justice Interrupted*, at 178.
[16] *Ibid*, at 193.
[17] "A History of The Iraqi Communist Party: Interview with University of East Anglia's Johan Franzén" (July 15, 2015) *Musings in Iraq* (blog), online: musingsoniraq.blogspot.ca/2014/07/a-history-of-iraqi-communist-party.html.
[18] Thompson, *Justice Interrupted*, at 178.
[19] David Galula, *Counterinsurgency Warfare: Theory and Practice* (New York: Praeger, 1964) at 30.

as sources of national insecurity and instability. Laws and measures have been designed to identify the "enemy" based on their group affiliation rather than on their engagement in criminal conduct. Exceptional measures such as censorship and detention without trial give a sense of security to citizens who believe that they will be safer if the "enemy" is being put under the microscope. This mentality has been carried over into efforts against Islamic groups, which have become the new global enemy.

Islamic Terrorism: The Common Enemy during Late Colonialism and Post-Independence

The emergence of Islamic movements during the 1920s did not occur in a vacuum. These groups were a response to the changes in the political structures that colonialism and anti-colonialism produced. A major change was the rise of the nation-state.[20] Egyptian and Tunisian rulers did not mind allying with Western powers in order to be "liberated" from the Ottoman rule; in fact, these rulers did not insist on fully self-governing nations. It was the people who steered the wheel of independence. Arab states consider their people as subjects who should follow the will of their ruling governments. Conflicting interests have resulted from this hierarchal relationship: people seek more rights whereas Arab governments seek more power.

Arab rulers sought to express their authority through political autonomy even if such autonomy was partial or nominal. Hence the existence of a colonial power or informal empire did not interfere with their interests. In fact, Arab rulers secure their positions through maintaining strong ties with colonists and informal empires. To keep these ties, the economic and political systems in Arab countries have to meet Western standards. However, the transformation in Arab countries is only partly Westernized; the other part is theologized. In Egypt and Tunisia, rulers have shown a tendency toward a dual system of semi-secular politics and theological norms. For instance, these countries allied with the West against the ambition of other powers, making foreign affairs subject to globalized rather than religious policy. Such globalized policy also covered diplomatic relations and economic trade. However, internal affairs are subject to different standards. Although the form of Arab governance may have been drawn from Western models, it was given a theological foundation. For example, a common Sharia rule prohibits disobeying the ruler "by carrying weapons against him";[21] in other words, rulers have "divine" protection from being overthrown.

Theological norms also control the underlying sociopolitical life of many people, above all Islamic thinkers. In the 1960s and 1970s, Said Qutab, a student of the

---

[20] Cemil Aydin, *The Idea of the Muslim World: A Global Intellectual History* (Cambridge, MA: Harvard University Press, 2017) at 204.
[21] الخروج على الحاكم [*khuruj ealaa alhakim*].

Muslim Brotherhood's founder Hassan Al-Bana, responded to the tyranny of the Egyptian government through an intellectual interpretation of deep-rooted theological norms. He interpreted jihad as the way to fight tyrannical regimes and their Western supporters.[22] Qutab inspired radical movements such as Al-Gama'a al-Islamiyya and the Takfir wal-Hijra (Excommunication and Exile), which emerged in Egyptian prisons.[23] This wave of extremism has carried out mass bombings and shootings worldwide, seeking a return to the original political-religious state or Caliphate.

Multiple factors lay behind this violent phenomenon. Islamic scholars explain the emergence of Islamic terrorism as the result of the disappointing post-independence governments that, among their many socioeconomic failures, disregarded the original Islamic heritage and mimicked Western culture.[24] Islamic thinkers agree that with the rise of imperialism and Western influence, the Arab ruling elites became more secular, and Islam became secondary in political life.[25] Yet parts of marginalized society remained religious, and found in religion a sanctuary from the corrupt secular rulers. The distrust between rulers and people led to the emergence of politicized Islamic groups that sought to counter the state's tyranny through violence. Given the use of violence by these groups, they are considered terrorists who represent a serious threat to the safety of civilians and the security of the state. The problem is in including other peaceful Muslim opponents of the government as terrorists based on their identity and beliefs.

Tunisia too, with its bold secular approach, fought the presence of Islamists, which also led to the emergence of extremists, but to a different degree than their emergence in Egypt. In both Egypt and Tunisia, nationalism, which took control of post-independence life, did not fulfill people's aspirations. Authoritarian governments were formed and a set of draconian national security laws and measures were adopted. These governments fought Islamists in order to secure the position of those in power. The suppression of Islamists led to more resistance and the emergence of countless Islamic extremists.

THE ARAB CONVENTION FOR THE SUPPRESSION OF TERRORISM:
"LEGAL" AUTHORITARIANISM

Arab states have long countered "terrorism" through tough national security laws and measures. Yet, unlike their position in the UN, in which they refuse to define terrorism and primarily focus on the causes of terrorism, these causes are intentionally neglected at Arab regional and domestic levels. Under the leadership of Egypt,

---

[22] Said Qutab, *Fi Zilal Al-Qur'an* [*In the Shade of the Qur'an*] (Beirut: Al Shurooq, 2003) at 8–26.
[23] Gilles Kepel, *Muslim Extremism in Egypt* (Berkeley, CA: University of California Press, 1986) at 97.
[24] Al-Ghanoushi, *Public Liberties in the Islamic State*, at 60.
[25] *Ibid.*

Arab states have reached an agreement regarding defining terrorism. However, contrary to their early view in the UN, which emphasized excluding the right to struggle and self-determination from the definition of terrorism, the legitimacy of this right is not granted at the regional level, as we will see in discussing the Arab Convention.

The importance of the Arab Convention in this book lies in two factors: its timing, and the leading role of Egypt in its creation. As for the first point, it was adopted after the independence of Arab countries and pre-9/11. In other words, there cannot be a direct colonial influence on this convention. What we need to know, though, is whether neo-colonialism played any role in influencing Arab states to establish this convention. And if not, what are the other factors that shaped it? Answering this question requires looking into the second point, which is the leadership role of Egypt in shaping this document. As we will see, the definition of terrorism in this convention is almost the same as that added to the Egyptian Penal Code in 1992. While Egypt's leading role in framing the Arab Convention is undeniable, we still need to examine the collective motives of the Arab states in adopting this convention.

In 1998, Arab governments, under the League of Arab States, adopted the Arab Convention for the Suppression of Terrorism, which came into force in 1999. The definition of terrorism in the Convention is almost word-for-word the definition in the 1992 Egyptian Penal Code, which will be discussed in Chapter 5.[26] Arab governments consider the convention to be a remarkable achievement in suppressing terrorism regionally. However, civil society groups, especially human rights organizations, consider it to be flawed because it restricts individual freedoms and increases governments' power.[27] My goal is to reveal the failures related to the definition of terrorism in some of the convention's articles in an attempt to determine the utility of its definition of terrorism. The broad definition of terrorism and the political reasons behind this document will be a key to answering the question: What interests and values do Arab states tend to protect through anti-terrorism legislation?

The Arab Convention is a controversial regional document that is highly politicized because of its broad definitions and word usage. "Terrorism" is defined in Article 1(2) as:

> Any act or threat of violence, whatever its motives or purposes, that occurs in the advancement of an individual or collective criminal agenda and seeking to sow panic among people, causing fear by harming them, or placing their lives, liberty or security in danger, or seeking to cause damage to the environment or to public

[26] Article 86 of Law No. 97 of 1992, *Official Gazette 29bis*, July 18, 1992.
[27] Abdu-al Hussan Sha'ban, *Islam and International Terrorism* (London: Dar Al-Hikma, 2002), at 81; Mahmoud Samy, "The League of Arab States" in Giuseppe Nesi, ed, *International Cooperation in Counter-Terrorism* (Aldershot: Ashgate, 2006) at 156–7.

or private installations or property or to occupying or seizing them, or seeking to jeopardize a national resource to danger.[28]

This definition requires the element of violence or threat of violence, which is broad enough to include any criminal act the state wishes to consider as terrorism. This could include acts of vandalism against private property for the motive of revenge, which do not necessarily involve violence against persons. Such acts are still condemned under criminal law.

Amnesty International considers this convention a serious threat to human rights.[29] The meaning and boundaries of the terms "violence" and "threat of violence" are not clarified, and as a result there is a higher risk of charging innocent people.[30] The term "violence" included in the definition is left undefined, and it is not clear whether it exclusively refers to unlawful acts of violence or includes all violent acts. Another point is that the statement "seeking to cause damage to the environment or to public or private installations or property" does not require any actual damage to be done.[31] Article 1 suggests considering a wide range of actions as terrorism – acts that in other legislation would be no more than arson and property damage crimes.

The purpose of condemning and criminalizing terrorism is not clear in the Arab Convention. It is unclear whether the protected value is security or the suppression of any political opposition. In fact, common practice suggests the second option. Anti-government groups in the Arab world, such as political opponents, nonviolent critics including suspected Islamists and communists, human rights defenders and journalists, have become the targets of anti-terrorism measures,[32] especially in those states that have permanent or semi-permanent states of emergency.

It should be noted that the Arab Convention has been ratified by most Arab states, which means that the above definition is part of their domestic laws. Syria is one state that has ratified and utilized the convention. In its first report to the CTC, Syria claimed that, because UN Resolution 1373 did not define terrorism, it relies on the definition in the Arab Convention, which "distinguishes between terrorism and legitimate struggle against foreigner occupation."[33] While Syria considers financing terrorists against Israeli citizens to be legitimate struggle,[34] it considers financing all

---

[28] Article 1(2) of the Arab Convention for the Suppression of Terrorism [Arab Convention].

[29] Amnesty International, "The Arab Convention for the Suppression of Terrorism: A Serious Threat to Human Rights" (January 9, 2002) online: amnestyinternational.org.

[30] Welchman, "Rocks, Hard Places and Human Rights," at 630; Saul, *Defining Terrorism in International Law*, at 154.

[31] Saul, *ibid*, at 145.

[32] Welchman, "Rocks, Hard Places and Human Rights," at 628.

[33] "Letter dated 13 December 2001 from the Permanent Representative of the Syrian Arab Republic to the Chairman of the Security Council Committee established pursuant to Resolution 1373 (2001) concerning counter-terrorism" (December 13, 2001), S/2001/1204 [Syria's Report to the CTC, 2001].

[34] Roach, *The 9/11 Effect*, at 93.

other opposition groups as terrorism. This is indeed a result of the lack of international guidance, which allows states to understand and define terrorism broadly and to justify coercion against civilians under the pretext of the right to struggle.[35]

Article 1(3), which defines "terrorist offence," was amended in November 2006. This version offered a new paragraph, which reads that a "terrorist offence" would also include "incitement to commit or praise terrorist crimes, or publish, print, or prepare writings, prints, or records in any form, for distribution or to show it to others with the aim of encouraging committing such crimes."[36] This paragraph was added after the establishment of UN Security Council Resolution 1624 (2005) regarding incitement and glorification of terrorism, which was discussed earlier in Chapter 2. The neo-colonial influence of the Security Council regarding incitement is clear in this example.

Despite this neo-colonial influence, colonial speech regulations preexisted in the Arab world. For instance, the French colonists had long suppressed people through speech regulations. These include the application of the French Press Law of 1881 in protectorate Tunisia. This law prohibits speech and publications that incite hatred or violence.[37] Article 24 of this Law states that "Shall be punished [...] those who, by one of the means set forth at Article 23, incite hatred or violence against a person or group of persons on account of their origin or membership or non-membership of a given ethnic group, nation, race or religion."[38] The vague wording of "incite hatred or violence" can be selectively used against opponents.

The ordinary crimes of incitement and sedition have long been part of many domestic criminal codes. The problem is the difficulty in drawing a line between legitimate and illegitimate speech or other forms of expression. This line is more blurred in the Arab world, where there are limited actual safeguards on individuals' rights. For instance, in 2005 the State Security Court of the UAE charged an offender for "promoting in speech Al-Qaeda as a terrorist organization by wearing shirts that have his leader's picture to make him more acceptable among people [...] and call[ing] in public places for not hating [bin Laden]."[39] The offender, who was a Sudanese citizen, was charged and exiled based on the 2004 Counter-Terrorism Act.

In addition to including some acts that should not be considered terrorism, the convention excludes some actions that either should be included (or at least that Western countries include) or that could be used to exclude some acts that would

[35] *Ibid*, at 93.
[36] The new paragraph as it is stated in the Arabic version of the Convention:
وكذلك التحريض على الجرائم الإرهابية أو الإشادة بها ونشر أو طبع أو إعداد محررات أو مطبوعات أو تسجيلات أيا
كان نوعها للتوزيع أو لاطلاع الغير عليها بهدف تشجيع ارتكاب تلك الجرائم.
[37] Article 23 of the French Press Law 1881.
[38] Article 24, *ibid*.
[39] State Security Case No. 237:33 (May 30, 2005), UAE University Press, Ministry of Justice, vol 61:27 (2005) at 616.

otherwise seem to be included in the definition. For example, after proposing the definition of "terrorism" and "terrorist acts," the convention excludes the case of armed struggle against foreign occupation from the definition of "terrorism." Article 2(a) states:

> All cases of struggle by whatever means, including armed struggle, against foreign occupation and aggression for liberation and self-determination, in accordance with the principles of international law, shall not be regarded as an offence. Such cases shall not include any act prejudicing the territorial integrity of any Arab state.[40]

This clause suggests that armed struggle for self-determination is excluded from terrorist offenses. Apparently, the continuous conflict between Israel and Palestine, as well as the battles involving Israel and other Arab states like Lebanon and Syria, is the reason behind the creation of this article. Some Arab scholars argue that this clause was created to distinguish between terrorism and lawful resistance.[41]

Mahmoud Samy, Legal Advisor for the Permanent Mission of Egypt to the UN (2002–6), claimed that Arab states, unlike the rest of the countries in the UN, share a clear view of what is and what is not terrorism: "They clearly differentiate between criminal acts of terrorism and other acts that fall within legitimate rights of people to struggle against foreign occupation and aggression."[42] By reading the clause carefully, however, we see that Arab states offer a double standard for the meaning of the right to self-determination. The convention creates an exception in which the right to self-determination "shall not apply to any act prejudicing the territorial integrity of any Arab State[,]"[43] meaning that Arab states have created an arbitrary dual meaning to deal with rebellions and opponents.

The motive behind this clause is directly related to Morocco's interests. While drafting the convention, Morocco insisted on adding this part of the article so that the struggle by the national liberation movement Polisario Front in Western Sahara would be considered terrorism.[44] In 1975, in the Western Sahara Case, the International Court of Justice (ICJ) pointed out that the 1960 UN Declaration on the Granting of Independence to Colonial Countries and Peoples[45] "allows a people to

---

[40] Article 2(a) of the Arab Convention.
[41] Rajaa Anaser, "al etifaqia alarabia le mukafahat al erhab: hal tasluh asasan leda'wa ela moatmar dawli li mukafahat alerhab?" ["The Arab Convention for the Suppression of Terrorism: Is it Suitable to Call for an International Conference?"] *Damascus Center for Theoretical and Civil Rights Studies*, online: www.mokarabat.com/mo3-3.htm.
[42] Mahmoud Samy, "The League of Arab States" in Giuseppe Nesi, ed, *International Cooperation in Counter-Terrorism* (Aldershot: Ashgate, 2006) at 157.
[43] Article 2 (a) of the Arab Convention.
[44] Anaser, "The Arab Convention for the Suppression of Terrorism," at 415.
[45] Declaration on the Granting of Independence to Colonial Countries and Peoples Adopted and Proclaimed by United Nations General Assembly Resolution 1514 (XV) of 14 December 1960.

choose from three options: to emerge as an independent state, to associate with an independent state, and to integrate with an independent state."[46] Although the right to self-determination for people in Western Sahara is internationally respected, it is not respected by Morocco. In October 2009, the Moroccan authorities arrested three "Sahrawi activists" for their visit to refugee camps in Algeria, which are run by the Polisario Front. They have been accused of "undermining [Morocco's] internal security."[47] Other Sahrawi activists were also arrested and charged with "undermining [Morocco's] external security"[48] and its "territorial integrity."[49] This is another example of the actual use of the term "terrorism," which tends to serve political interests rather than combating terrorism and ensuring security. The authoritarian ambition thus appears clearly in the collective agenda of Arab states.

The convention also excludes political crimes from the common extradition norms. Article 2(b) excludes the offenses that are defined and listed in the convention from being considered political offenses, even if they were committed for political reasons, and, as a result, such offenders lose any protection applied to political criminals. Article 2(b) lists examples of terrorist offenses that cannot be considered political offenses. For instance:

(iv) Premeditated murder or theft accompanied by the use of force directed against individuals, the authorities or means of transport and communications;

(v) *Acts of sabotage and destruction* of public property and property assigned to a public service, even if owned by another Contracting State. [emphasis added]

Sabotage is one of the crimes that were first included in Arab penal codes, and is borrowed from the French Napoleonic model. This point is further examined in Chapters 5 and 7. Amnesty International points out that this article "defines what is not a 'political crime,' but does not define what is a political crime."[50] Even though distinguishing between terrorist crimes and political crimes is not easy, it is very important in the matter of extradition. The problem is that, in the absence of guidance that clarifies the meaning of terrorism, and by leaving the distinction to the executive rather than the courts, there is a risk of charging and extraditing innocent people and political activists.

[46] Kent Roach, "Defining Terrorism: The Need for a Restrained Definition" in Craig Forcese & Nicole LaViolette, eds, *The Ottawa Principles on Human Rights and Counter-Terrorism* (Toronto: Irwin Law, 2008) at 144.

[47] "Sahrawi Activists on Trial for Visiting Refugee Camps" (October 13, 2010) *Amnesty International*, online: www.amnesty.org.

[48] *Ibid.*

[49] *Ibid.*

[50] Amnesty International, *Upturned Lives: The Disproportionate Impact of France's State of Emergency* (2016).

Another point to discuss in relation to the Arab Convention is the security of state leaders. Such protection is not a new concept.[51] An early codification can be found in the French Penal Code of 1810. According to Article 86 of this code, "An attempt or plot against the life, or against the person of the emperor, is a crime of high treason (*lèse majesté*); this crime is punishable as parricide; and, moreover, infers the confiscation of property."[52] This law, created under Napoleon, aimed to protect the emperor from those opposed to the French Revolution. Article 87 of this Napoleonic Code also provides wide protection to the imperial family:

> Every attempt or plot against the life or the person of any member of the imperial family;
> Every attempt or plot, the object of which shall be,
> Either to destroy or change the government, or the order of succession to the throne;
> Or to incite the citizens or inhabitants to arm themselves against imperial authority,
> Shall be punished with death and confiscation of property.[53]

The same tendency can be seen in the Arab Convention. It, however, considers such crimes as terrorism. Article 2 of the Arab Convention states:

> (b) None of the terrorist offences indicated in the preceding article shall be regarded as a political offence. In the application of this Convention, none of the following offences shall be regarded as a political offence, even if committed for political motives:
>   (i) Attacks on the kings, Heads of State or rulers of the contracting States or on their spouses and families.

In regard to protection of heads of state, the Arab Convention goes too far by protecting their families, especially when we look at the Arabic version, which includes "the ancestors and descendants" of the head of state. Members of royal families can absolutely abuse such protection. A hypothetical example can be pondered in which a grandson of an Arab head of state, while visiting another Arab State or within his own state, fights with a waitress for refusing to pay the bill. In such a case, the waitress would be considered a terrorist. The Diplomatic Agents Convention, on the other hand, has listed internationally protected persons in the same way as the Arab Convention; however, they are followed by two conditions,

---

[51] It is considered in the 1973 Convention on the Prevention and Punishment of Crimes against Internationally Protected Persons (Diplomatic Agents Convention), which was signed in New York.
[52] Article 86 of the French Penal Code of 1810.
[53] Article 87 of *ibid*.

which as stated in Article 1(1)(a) are: "whenever any such person is in a foreign State, as well as members of his family who accompany him." The protection is for those who are outside their country, and for the family members who are accompanying state leaders. Based on the Arab Convention, the family members of a head of state are protected wherever they are, in their country or abroad, whether or not they are accompanied by the head of state. This wide protection shows how Arab leaders are more concerned with their positions and personal safety under the cover of anti-terrorism than with public safety, which reflects an authoritarian ambition. The convention includes many other failures related to the lack of safeguards against the risk of torture and the death penalty, of guarantees to a fair trial, and of rights in general, especially the rights to privacy and freedom of expression.[54]

The Arab Convention also shows that Egypt is the most influential leader within the Arab region. Egypt has significant political and legal influence over the rest of the Arab world. Roach observes that Arab countries, including Jordan, Iraq, Qatar, and Bahrain, have adopted a definition of terrorism based on the Egyptian model. Similarly to Egypt, they included vague concepts like "threats to national unity" and "disturbing public order" in their definition of terrorism.[55]

Kuwait is one of the few Arab countries, if not the only Arab country, that has not ratified the Arab Convention and has not adopted a separate anti-terrorism law or even criminalized "terrorism" within its penal code.[56] Nonetheless, Kuwait includes the concept of threatening public order in its Press and Publication Law No. 3 of 2006. Article 21 criminalizes "incitement to violate public order or to violate the laws or to commit crimes even if they are not committed.]"[57] This migration of elements of the Egyptian definition of terrorism was done voluntarily without direct pressure from Egypt.

In this respect, the influence of Egypt is similar to the influence of the United Kingdom, although the former is regional and the latter is global. However, Egypt's reliance on Western aid keeps it in a submissive position. This relative duality of being a leader at the regional level and a follower at the global level has created a complex political condition, which is examined in Chapter 4.

---

[54] Welchman, "Rocks, Hard Places and Human Rights," at 632.
[55] For more, see Roach, "Comparative Counter-Terrorism Law Comes of Age," at 36–8.
[56] Despite this fact, Kuwait defined "terrorist acts" within its Law No. 106 of 2013 regarding Combating Money Laundering and Terrorism Financing. Article 1 states: "any act or attempt inside or outside Kuwait committed in the following cases: if the act intended to cause death or serious injury to civilians, or against any person who did not take part of aggression acts during armed conflict, when the purpose of such act, by its nature or context intended to intimidate the population or to compel a government or an international organization to take a specific action or to refrain from taking it."
[57] Article 21 of Kuwaiti Press and Publication Law No. 3 of 2006.

TWENTY-FIRST CENTURY REGIONAL DEVELOPMENTS IN SECURITY AND COUNTER-TERRORISM

Accustomed Authoritarianism

In the first ten years of the twenty-first century, the Arab world was adjusting to the global changes in counter-terrorism. It focused on adopting new financial regulations regardless of whether it seriously intended to activate them. Arab states have been accused of financing terrorists. According to the US State Department 2007 International Narcotics Control Strategy Report, "Saudi donors and unregulated charities have been a major source of financing to extremist and terrorist groups over the past 25 years."[58] Aside from Saudi Arabia, the report lists Egypt and other Gulf states as "source and transit countries" for terrorist groups.[59]

As mentioned in Chapter 2, since 9/11 Arab countries have taken financial legal reforms, but these reforms did not prevent terrorism financing. According to a 2009 report revealed by Wikileaks, US Secretary of State Hillary Clinton expressed her concern about donors in Saudi Arabia who represent a major source for funding Sunni terrorists worldwide. She complained that it was an "ongoing challenge to persuade Saudi officials to treat terrorist funds emanating from Saudi Arabia as a strategic priority."[60] In 2003 in a lawsuit involving Saudi Arabia in funding Palestinian terrorists, the Saudi authorities replied by saying that "[we] didn't know that some of the people we were sending money to were relatives of suicide bombers."[61] Whether a result of the difficulty of complying with anti-terrorism financing laws or the lack of willingness to combat terrorism, Arab states have been, at least to some extent, countering terrorism financing selectively and politically.[62]

Another practice during the early twenty-first century is the post-9/11 American extraordinary rendition of terrorists to foreign countries, including Egypt, Syria, and Jordan.[63] Extraordinary rendition means forced disappearance of individuals who are not charged with crimes and are subject to indefinite detention.[64] The United States has been engaged in this practice since the 1990s, but post-9/11 it adopted a harsher and more intolerant policy toward suspects in terrorist cases.[65] Torture was

---

[58] Christopher M. Blanchard & Alfred B. Prados, "Saudi Arabia: Terrorist Financing Issues" (September 14, 2007) *Congressional Research Service*, online: www.osenlaw.com/sites/default/files/uploaded/Useful_Links/SaudiArabiaTerroristFinancingIssues.pdf
[59] *Ibid.*
[60] Declan Walsh, "WikiLeaks Cables Portray Saudi Arabia as a Cash Machine for Terrorists" (December 5, 2010) *The Guardian*, online: www.theguardian.com
[61] Quoted in Blanchard & Prados, "Saudi Arabia: Terrorist Financing Issues."
[62] For more on accusations against Arab states for funding terrorists, see *ibid.*
[63] Mark J. Murray, "Extraordinary Rendition and U.S. Counterterrorism Policy" (2011) 4:3 *Journal of Strategic Security* 15 at 16.
[64] *Ibid*, at 17.
[65] *Ibid*, at 18.

commonly practiced against detainees.[66] The United States' global anti-terrorism policy encourages countries with poor human rights records, like Egypt and Syria, to become accustomed to extra-legality as a common practice.

During the 2010s, the retreat from human rights led to crucial changes in the Arab world. The 2010–11 "Arab Spring" rocked the region, resulting in the overthrow of the presidents of both Egypt and Tunisia. Other parts of the Arab world, including Syria, Bahrain, and Yemen, witnessed bloody uprisings. The circumstances in each of these countries is different, but a common outcome is a regression in regional and national security and a failure in democratic development. Terrorism has been continuously carried out in Egypt and Tunisia, and ISIS has penetrated in many Arab countries, particularly Iraq and Syria. To combat terrorism and stabilize their regimes, Arab governments have shown no hesitation in breaking legal principles and safeguards. In Egypt, Abdel Fattah el-Sisi allowed himself to win a fake presidential election, presenting himself as a strong authoritarian figure who can rule through the military and the exception. In Syria, despite the long lasting civil war, Assad remains in power because of his authoritarian approach and Russia's support of him. In Tunisia, a state of emergency has been in place since November 2015 until the time of writing, allowing the security forces and judicial bodies to take extra-legal measures against suspects in terrorism-related cases.[67] Arab states have become accustomed to such exceptional practices in their war on terror.

External powers, above all the United States and Russia, have played a significant role in strengthening authoritarianism in the Arab world. The United States has been backing Saudi Arabia through its continuous blessing for Saudi Arabia's regional and internal coercive approach against terrorism. On the other hand, Russia has been supporting Syria's dictator Assad. Russia's interference in Syria makes it a new neo-colonial player in the Arab region.

The American–Saudi Impact on the Region

In 2017, Donald Trump became the president of the United States. His impact on global policy has been controversial. In May of that year, he started his foreign tour by visiting Saudi Arabia, selling it arms for allegedly $110 billion. It should be noted that the UN and NGOs have been criticizing Saudi Arabia for its destructive role in the war in Yemen,[68] which has led to the killing of thousands of people,

---

[66] *Ibid.*

[67] "Tunisia: 'We Want an End to the Fear': Abuses under Tunisia's State of Emergency" (February 13, 2017) *Amnesty International*, online: www.amnesty.org/en/documents/mde30/4911/2017/en/; "Tunisia: Open Letter Urges Government to End Impunity for Security Forces" (March 13, 2018) *Amnesty International*, online: www.amnesty.org/en/latest/news/2018/03/tunisia-open-letter-urges-government-to-end-impunity-for-security-forces/.

[68] "Yemen: Events of 2017," *Human Rights Watch*, online: www.hrw.org/world-report/2018/country-chapters/yemen.

displacement of more than 3 million, and putting the population on the edge of famine.[69] By arming Saudi Arabia, Trump is implicitly approving the Saudi intervention in Yemen and disregarding the humanitarian crisis. The same tendency can be seen in Bahrain. During the Obama administration, Bahrain was prevented from buying F-16 fighter jets and other arms worth $2.8 billion because of its human rights violations against the majority Shiite opposition. However, since Trump has come to power, these human rights conditions have been lifted.[70] This retreat from committing to human rights encourages authoritarian practices. As will be shown in Chapter 4, Trump has also been supporting el-Sisi in Egypt through military aid.

Since Trump's visit to the Arab region in May 2017, Saudi Arabia and Egypt have become bolder in their exercise of their authoritarian influence in the region. They led a boycott campaign against Qatar for funding terrorist groups. Among several reasons for the boycott, Qatar's support of the Muslim Brotherhood in the region irritates many countries including Egypt, UAE, and Saudi Arabia. This brings us to the crimes related to terrorism; the logic suggests that because Qatar is a financier of terrorism, Qatar's sympathizers can be accused of supporting terrorism. The authorities in Saudi Arabia, Bahrain, and UAE have banned people from expressing sympathy toward Qatar. Violators of these executive orders – not laws – are punishable by up to fifteen years of imprisonment and a fine.[71] In addition, Saudi Arabia, UAE, Jordan, and Egypt have blocked several Qatari websites and media outlets.[72] Suppressing sympathizers and controlling media are reminiscent of exceptional periods such as the two World Wars, when the enemy's media could disturb order and stability. Such policy was also embodied during the war on communism.

The continuation of American support despite these Saudi laws being so oppressive encourages greater authoritarianism in the region. In November 2017, Saudi Arabia adopted a new Anti-Terrorism Act. The fact that Saudi Arabia is authoritarian and backed by the United States could influence other countries in the region toward greater authoritarianism, even though Saudi is not generally influential in terms of legislation. The chapter does not discuss this Act in depth, but briefly highlights the most draconian articles, aiming to show the contradiction between Saudi's alleged modernization and its neglect of the rule of law, which plays a role beyond Saudi itself.

---

[69] Angela Dewan, "Saudi Blockade Pushing Yemen toward 'Worst Famine in Decades'" (November 9, 2017) *CNN*, online: https://edition.cnn.com/2017/11/09/middleeast/yemen-famine-saudi-arabia/index.html.

[70] David E. Sanger & Eric Schmitt, "Rex Tillerson to Lift Human Rights Conditions on Arms Sale to Bahrain" (March 29, 2017) *The New York Times*, online: www.nytimes.com.

[71] "Bahrain Detains Citizen for Sympathising with Qatar" (June 14, 2017) *Reuters*, online: www.reuters.com/article/gulf-qatar-bahrain/bahrain-detains-citizen-for-sympathising-with-qatar-agency-reports-idUSL8N1JB5F6.

[72] "Media Blocked, Threatened in Dispute with Qatar: Actions by Other Middle Eastern Countries a Blow to Free Speech" (June 14, 2017) *Human Rights Watch*, online: www.hrw.org/news/2017/06/14/media-blocked-threatened-dispute-qatar.

In the Saudi Anti-Terrorism Act, a "terrorist act" is defined as

Any conduct committed by the offender to advance an individual or collective criminal plan, directly or indirectly, that aims to disturb public order, shake the security of the community and the stability of the state, expose its national unity to danger, or suspend all or parts of the basic system of governance, or damage the state's facilities or its natural or economic resources, or attempt to force the authority to carry out or prevent it from carrying out an action, or harm an individual or result in his death, when the purpose—by its nature or context—is to terrorize people or force a government or international organization to carry out or prevent it from carrying out an action, or the threat or the incitement to commit acts that would lead to the mentioned purposes and aims.[73]

This overbroad definition includes violent and nonviolent acts. It contains the Egyptian vague clauses of "disturbing public order" and endangering "national unity." The Saudi Act considers incitement of terrorism as a crime punishable by up to 20 years' imprisonment.[74] It is also a terrorist crime to criticize the king or the crown prince in a way that directly or indirectly undermines the king or crown prince's religion or justice.[75] This is an application of authoritarianism under the "divine protection" of royals in the Arab world. Authoritarian legality is a way to manipulate "justice" in accordance with ambiguous terms that can be interpreted selectively to serve those in power.

The Act also violates due process by granting executive bodies legal jurisdiction over terrorist cases. According to the Act, the Head of State Security has the authority to directly ban suspects from traveling.[76] Although his orders should be referred to the Public Prosecution, with the above broad definition anyone can be a suspect of terrorist acts. The Act excludes the Public Prosecution and grants the Ministry of Internal Affairs and the Head of State Security the authority to investigate terrorist crimes. The Act admits that this is an exceptional step but justifies it by stating that the Ministry of Internal Affairs and the Head of State Security are authorized to practice the jurisdiction over terrorist cases for two years or more "until the necessary resources are available."[77] Human Rights Watch has provided a detailed criticism of this Act, describing it as a law that "enables abuse" and "criminalizes a wide range of peaceful acts that bear no relation to terrorism."[78] In May 2017, prior to issuing the above Act, Ben Emmerson, UN Special Rapporteur

---

[73] Article 1 (3) of the Saudi Regulations of the Anti-Terrorism and Financing Act. Royal Decree No. 21 issued on November 6, 2017, *Saudi Official Gazette*, online: www.uqn.gov.sa/editions/4696/4.

[74] Articles 34 and 43 of Saudi Anti-Terrorism and Financing Act.

[75] Article 30, *ibid.*

[76] Article 10, *ibid.*

[77] The preamble, *ibid.*

[78] "Saudi Arabia: New Counterterrorism Law Enables Abuse: Criminalizes Criticisms of King and Crown Prince as Terrorism Offense" (November 23, 2017), *Human Rights Watch*, online: www.hrw.org/news/2017/11/23/saudi-arabia-new-counterterrorism-law-enables-abuse.

on human rights and counter-terrorism, criticized the Saudi anti-terrorism measures and "handed the Government a list of priority cases for urgent review."[79] It included the broad definition of terrorism and ill-treatment and torture during investigation.[80] Despite the above criticism, Saudi Arabia issued its new law without addressing these human rights concerns.[81]

Saudi Arabia enjoys regional political power, backed by the United States. Despite their cultural and religious differences, they share economic and political ties. Saudi Arabia is the third largest supplier of oil to the United States, and one of the largest importers of arms from the United States. In 2015, Saudi Arabia led the establishment of the Islamic Military Counter Terrorism Coalition. The actual role of this inter-governmental alliance in fighting terrorism has not become clear as yet, but it reflects a symbolic significance of the Saudi regional influence in suppressing the threat of terrorist groups like ISIS as well as other groups and states accused of financing or supporting what this alliance views as terrorism. Although the actual role of this alliance has not been shaped yet, it could justify the reliance of military approaches rather than peace talks. This could further delay taking serious political reforms to establish functioning democracies in the Arab region and the Islamic world.

Although Saudi Arabia is openly shifting toward "modernization," its legal system still lacks rule of law and basic human rights, making it one of the boldest authoritarian countries in the region. Through coercion, whether intimidation or military intervention, Saudi Arabia has shown an aggressive pattern in dealing with its neighbors. Its positions in Yemen, Qatar, and Syria show unwillingness to advance regional security. The fear is that at local and regional levels, Saudi Arabia's coercive approach could culturally shape young Muslim minds into more violence.

Russian Impact on the Region

Since the "Arab Spring," Russia has been involving itself in the Arab region through military and political actions. Through the Security Council, Russia has been frequently blocking international attempts to engage in the Syrian crisis. It has also sent its troops to Syria and established a naval base in the city of Tartus. This section investigates Russia's role as an emerging neo-colonial player in the Arab region.

Historical Background

During the nineteenth and early twentieth centuries, the Russian Empire had no geopolitical interest in the Arab world. However, the Russian Empire showed

[79] "Saudi Arabia Must Reform 'Unacceptably Broad' Counter-Terrorism Law – UN Rights Expert" (May 5, 2017) *UN News*, online: news.un.org/en/story/2017/05/556742-saudi-arabia-must-reform-unacceptably-broad-counter-terrorism-law-un-rights.
[80] *Ibid.*
[81] "Saudi Arabia: Allegations of Abuse, Death in Custody" (March 14, 2018) *Human Right Watch*, online: www.hrw.org/news/2018/03/14/saudi-arabia-allegations-abuse-death-custody.

interest in nearby regions, particularly the Mediterranean. The Mediterranean is geographically significant to Moscow, linking Russia to the rest of Europe, northern Africa, and most importantly the Suez Canal. The Mediterranean also has symbolic religious importance to Moscow. Rajan Menon argues that, in suppressing Christians in areas like Greece, the Ottoman Empire provoked Russia's moral duty to intervene.[82] During Greece's struggle for independence, the Russians, with the British and the French, sent troops and defeated the Ottoman Empire in 1827.[83] On another occasion, the Russian Empire sent its troops in 1877–8, ending the Ottoman Empire's mass killing of Bulgarians.[84] These occasional Russian interventions in Eastern Europe reflected an imperial policy of militarism and imposing hegemony.

Pre-Soviet Russia had no role in the Arab world. Russia's interest in the Arab world began in the aftermath of World War II. At that time, the Soviet Union sought alliances with countries that leant toward a socialist system, such as Algeria, Egypt, Iraq, and Libya. The relationship between the Soviet Union and these Arab states focused on developing their military power and nuclear programs. This is a common aspect of the Cold War, in which the Soviet bloc sought to empower countries that were not friends with the Western bloc and vice versa. This empowering was not part of the colonial "civilizing" mission, but a strategic mechanism aiming to set geopolitical boundaries between the two blocs. The Soviet Union did not invade Arab states and did not intimidate them. It took advantage of its military and nuclear progress and shared it with countries that were fed up with direct Western colonialism or its remote informal empire. Thus, Arab states were not submissive to the Soviet Union. They were clients interested in arms trade and willing to pay for it, with no promises of political support. For instance, although post-independence Egypt allied with the Soviet Union, in 1972 Egyptian president Sadat expelled Soviet military advisors, a step that showed Sadat's favoring of the American side.

After the fall of the Soviet Union, Russia's economic and political power diminished compared to the Western bloc. Despite this weakness, it kept its old policy toward its allies, supplying them with arms and developing their nuclear programs. One of the biggest buyers of Russian weapons was Iraqi president Saddam Hussein. However, the Russian–Iraqi alliance did not mean Russia's full support of Hussein. When he invaded Kuwait in 1990, Russia showed its disapproval at the Security Council by voting against the invasion in a series of resolutions, demanding Iraq withdraw its forces,[85] and authorized using "all necessary means" to evict Iraq from

---

[82] Rajan Menon, *The Conceit of Humanitarian Intervention* (New York: Oxford University Press, 2016) at 79.
[83] *Ibid*, at 78.
[84] *Ibid*.
[85] UN Security Council, Security Council Resolution 660, 1990 SC Res. 660, UN SCOR, S/RES/660 [Resolution 660].

Kuwait.[86] This example suggests that Russia during the 1990s had a policy of minimum support to its Arab allies. Nonetheless, two decades later, the "Arab Spring" reshaped the Russian role in the region. This coincided with Vladimir Putin's desire of making Russia a "great power."[87]

Russia's Neo-Colonial Policy in the Arab World

Putin was president of Russia from 1999 to 2008 and again since 2012. From 2008 to 2012, Putin held the position of prime minister. During these years, he has shown a desire to bring back the glory of the Russian Empire. Since the mid-2000s, Russia has expanded its military.[88] Through selling arms comes economic growth, but this has not been Russia's only way to empower its economy; Russia has shown interest in oil and gas deals in the Arab world. Despite these desires, Russia's role dramatically expanded in the aftermath of the "Arab Spring."

The "Arab Spring" opened the road for Russia's involvement in the Arab region. In 2011, Russia took a middle position to supporting Libya's former president Muammar Gaddafi, who was one of its allies. On March 17, 2011, Russia abstained from voting at the Security Council when it issued Resolution 1973 (2011) approving a no-fly zone over Libya. On March 19, NATO led a military intervention in Libya, which ensured the ending of Gaddafi's rule. In terms of security, Libya became a place of chaos and terror. Russia later expressed its regret for not vetoing Resolution 1973.[89] In 2017, Russian foreign minister, Sergei Lavrov, said "By distorting the mandate obtained from the UN Security Council to secure a no-fly zone, NATO simply interfered in the war under the flag of protecting the civilian population."[90] Whether a result of the chaotic consequences of intervening in Libya or an attempt to save its allies, Russia has since been blocking resolutions at the Security Council regarding military interventions in Syria.

The ultimate support for Syria's president Assad represents a shift in Russia's policy in the region. It is boldly a supporter of a dictator, despite the humanitarian crisis and the accusation of the use of chemical weapons.[91] Analysts and scholars have explained that Russia's involvement in Syria has a geopolitical motive.[92] The

---

[86] UN Security Council, Security Council Resolution 678, 1990 SC Res. 678, UN SCOR, S/RES/678 [Resolution 678].

[87] Imran Rahman-Jones, "Why Does Russia Support Syria and President Assad?" (April 11, 2017) *BBC News*, online: www.bbc.co.uk/newsbeat/article/39554171/why-does-russia-support-syria-and-president-assad.

[88] *Ibid.*

[89] "Russia Has a Serious Stake in Libya's Uncertain Future" (June 20, 2017) *The Conversation*, online: theconversation.com/russia-has-a-serious-stake-in-libyas-uncertain-future-79371.

[90] *Ibid.*

[91] "Amid New Reports of Chemical Weapons Use in Syria, United Nations Top Disarmament Official Says International Community Obliged to Enact Meaningful Response" (February 5, 2018) *UN Meeting Coverage*, online: www.un.org/press/en/2018/sc13196.doc.htm.

[92] Alexey Malashenko, "Russia and the Arab Spring" (October 2013) *Carnegie Moscow Center*, at 12.

Russian scholar Alexey Malashenko argues that Russia desires to "maintain an image of a global power[,]" which requires establishing a military base in the Mediterranean.[93] The Syrian port of Tartus represents an ideal choice for Russia's military and economic interests in the Mediterranean.[94] The Russian base also sends a symbolic message to the world of Russia's power.[95]

Regarding anti-terrorism laws and policies – the main theme of this book – Russia has no direct role in shaping them. However, by supporting Assad, Russia encourages the authoritarian approach in counter-terrorism. And through Russia's military intervention and the establishment of a military base in Syria, as well as its extensive vetoing at the Security Council, it solidifies the neo-colonial aspects of militarism, exceptionalism, and global centralization. These moves make Russia a late yet significant neo-colonial player in the Arab region.

CONCLUSION: ADJUSTED AUTHORITARIANISM, AND APPROVAL FROM THE WEST AND RUSSIA

After viewing Arab counter-terrorism policy, the conclusion is that crime control in the Arab world starts at a sociocultural level. This is done through restrictions on expression, thoughts, and beliefs. Arab intellectuals and people are suppressed through censorship, imprisonment, and other unfair measures. The same policy is applied against the common enemy, whether communists or Islamists. This policy has its roots in the colonial practice against communists worldwide. This policy, however, has remained in the postcolonial Arab world because it continues serving those in power. In addition, it serves the neo-colonial powers and their interests in the region.

The Arab world, led by Egypt, has codified the inherited colonial legacy and indigenous authoritarian practices in the Arab Convention. This convention defines terrorism broadly in a way that allows targeting of the "enemy" rather than establishing clear and precise wrongdoings, and provides maximum protection for the state and its ruling elites. The amendment made to the convention in 2006, in which incitement through speech or writing is also considered terrorism, reflects the colonial origin of these practices, which have long restricted freedom of expression. More importantly, it shows that the Arab world is bound by UN Security Council Resolution 1624 (2005), which reflects neo-colonial policy in global counter-terrorism.

Although the United States is aware of Saudi Arabia's poor human rights record, it abstains from seriously criticizing it. This used to create a duality between internal

---

[93] *Ibid.*
[94] Rajan Menon, "What's Russia Doing in Syria and Why" (August 2, 2013) *Huffington Post*, online: www.huffingtonpost.com/rajan-menon/whats-russia-doing-in-syr_b_3375715.html.
[95] *Ibid.*

and external American policy, when the United States worshipped its democratic values and human rights. However, since Trump's presidency, such values have devolved, along with the rise of American authoritarianism.

Russia's role in Syria signifies a neo-colonial policy of militarism, exceptionalism, and centralization that serves Russia's image as a global power. Russian intervention in Syria was alleged to counter ISIS, but experience has shown it also countered Assad's opposition. Regionally, Russia's support of Assad's tyranny encourages Arab states to continue ruling through the colonial legacy of militarism and exceptionalism combined with authoritarian practices of coercion and excluding dictators from accountability.

4

The Colonial and Neo-Colonial Experience in Egypt

Egypt is located in the heart of the Arab world, bridging Western Asia and North Africa. The Canal Zone has long made Egypt a strategic cosmopolitan center that attracts regional and global powers. Its significant geographical location and lack of natural barriers has affected its political status. In the past, this made it vulnerable to invasion by the Greeks, Romans, Arabs, Ottomans and later by the French and the British. At the same time, this allowed it to become more receptive to cultural, political, and legal progress. Egypt's contemporary counter-terrorism approach has thus been shaped by complex factors of Western influence and internal ambition for control.

This chapter is dedicated to modern Egypt and is divided into five main parts: Egypt under French colonialism (1798–1801); the subsequent period of informal imperialism (mainly between the 1850s and 1870s); under British colonialism (1882–1914); postcolonialism; and lastly the current era of neo-colonial economic dependency and political submission. The chapter will look at the development of legal and political frameworks through the lenses of the four perspectives defined in Chapter 1, namely, economic expansion, centralization, militarism, and exceptionalism. The question is to what extent these approaches were used by the colonial power in shaping national security in Egypt, and to what extent postcolonial Egypt uses them. In addition, this chapter asks if there has been neo-colonial pressure in this respect.

THE FRENCH OCCUPATION (1798–1801)

The French, under the leadership of Napoleon Bonaparte, invaded the Ottoman province of Egypt in 1798 and continued ruling it until 1801. The French army was too advanced to be resisted by locals, who soon surrendered. Napoleon's primary intention went beyond Egypt itself: by occupying Egypt, he aimed to challenge

British expansion in the Middle East and obstruct the British from getting to India easily.[1]
This motivation had an impact on Napoleon's policy in Egypt. He adopted – at least on the surface – a relatively tolerant policy toward local Egyptians, as their support was needed in the face of any external competitor. According to Paul Strathern, Napoleon proclaimed a compassionate approach toward Islam.[2] His tactic was to draw near to the *ulema*, or scholars of Muslim religious law, of Al-azhar Mosque. Napoleon also raised questions with Arab Egyptians that could provoke a sense of patriotism and ethnocentrism: "Why has the Arabic nation submitted to Turks? How come fertile Egypt and holy Arabia are under the domination of a people from the Caucasus?"[3] Breaking Egyptian society into smaller opposing groups was part of the colonial strategy of divide and rule. Napoleon was aware of the internal conflicts and social gap between Arab Egyptians and the dominant groups, which were the Ottoman *pashas* and the Mamluk household. Using these divisions to his advantage, Napoleon proclaimed that he would bring justice to Arab Egyptians. In his pronouncement when he invaded Egypt he declared:

> People of Egypt! [T]hey will tell you that I come to destroy your religion. Believe it not! Answer that I come to restore your rights, to punish the usurpers [Mamluks], and that I respect, more than the Mamelukes do, God, his Prophet, and the Koran.[4]

Under the cloak of the spirit of the French Revolution, Napoleon claimed to be a liberator. Egypt was viewed by the French as a producer of tyranny and injustice, where slavery and inequality dominated social and political culture. In Paris, the occupation was seen as part of the Western civilizing mission. French legislator Joseph Eschasseriaux argued:

> What finer enterprise for a nation which has already given liberty to Europe [and] freed America than to regenerate in every sense a country which was the first home to civilization [...] and to carry back to their ancient cradle industry, science, and the arts, to cast into the centuries the foundations of a new Thebes or of another Memphis.[5]

The French, despite their policy, which appeared to be tolerant in Egypt, were strict in bringing order, and, whenever they needed to be, were violent and terrifying. Any opposition acts by local Egyptians were faced with official terror. This can be seen, for example, in an incident in the Egyptian village of Alkam, when the locals killed Capitan Thomas Prosper Jullien and another 15 Frenchmen. As a

---

[1] Juan Cole, *Napoleon's Egypt: Invading the Middle East* (Basingstoke: Palgrave Macmillan, 2007) at 9.
[2] Paul Strathern, *Napoleon in Egypt* (New York: Bantam Books Trade Paperbacks, 2009) at 139.
[3] Quoted in *ibid.*
[4] Quoted in *The Quarterly Review* 75 (London: John Murray, Albemarle Street, 1845) at 541.
[5] Quoted in Cole, *Napoleon's Egypt*, at 16.

response, Napoleon ordered the village to be destroyed by fire, and it was completely burned.[6] This can also be seen in the Revolt of Cairo in October 1798, which the French suppressed with artillery bombardment. The French were serious about maintaining order and harsh with their opponents.[7]

Cole argues that the French wanted to bring their revolutionary sense into Egypt – to overthrow the old regime of Ottoman-Egypt and replace it with a government that guaranteed "liberty" and "rights."[8] Nonetheless, those who did not respect the government were considered "enemies"; as a result, they lost their liberty and rights.[9]

The French unwillingly left Egypt after less than four years. In 1801, Britain and Ottoman troops forced France to leave Egypt and restore it to the Ottoman Empire.[10] This short period of occupation explains the limited French colonial influence in Egypt. The French did not fundamentally change the political and social life of Egyptians. Nevertheless, the French introduced centralization and liberal ideas to Egypt. Arab states, including those that were colonized by Britain or those that remained independent, adopted a French legal system.[11] Brown argues that Arab states willingly adopted the French model because of its usefulness in centralizing the power of the dominant groups. Brown suggests that the French system offered a unified legal code and a nationwide hierarchy of courts to enforce it.[12] The French-style legal system constructed in Arab states over the past century and a half has been maintained precisely because of the benefits it provides to centralizing and reformist regimes. Centralization is discussed further in Chapter 5.

Despite the departure of France, its influence – as well as the influence of the British – can be seen in the years immediately after the short period of colonization. A few years after the French left Egypt, Khedive Muhammad Ali ruled Egypt from 1805 to 1848. Muhammad Ali, known as the "Father of Modern Egypt," was attracted to the French system. He desired to build a modern state based on European models. Security was a priority, so he established an organized army

---

[6]   *Ibid*, at 172.
[7]   Gebre Tsadik Degefu, *The Nile: Historical, Legal and Developmental Perspectives* (Victoria, BC: Trafford, 2003) at 29.
[8]   Cole, *Napoleon's Egypt*, at 172.
[9]   Carlos Gómez-Jara Díez, "Enemy Combatants versus Enemy Criminal Law: An Introduction to the European Debate Regarding Enemy Criminal Law and Its Relevance to the Anglo-American Discussion on the Legal Status of Unlawful Enemy Combatants" (2008) 11:4 *New Criminal Law Review: International and Interdisciplinary Journal* 529 at 530–62.
[10] Juan Cole, *Colonialism and Revolution in the Middle East: Social and Cultural Origins of Egypt's 'Urabi Movement* (Princeton, NJ: Princeton University Press, 1993), at 25.
[11] Nathan Brown, "Retrospective: Law and Imperialism: Egypt in Comparative Perspective" (1995) 29:1 *Law and Society Review* at 103–4; Nathan Brown, "The Precarious Life and Slow Death of the Mixed Courts of Egypt" (1993) 25:1 *International Journal of Middle East Studies* at 37.
[12] Brown, "Retrospective: Law and Imperialism," at 117.

and military schools supervised by the French officer Joseph Anthelme Sève.[13] He also sent many who belonged to the elite ruling class to European military academies. Even though he bought warships and weapons from Europe, he sought independence through establishing arms factories.[14] Despite the military reforms, Muhammad Ali was aware that he was unable to defeat major powers like the British who had interests in Egypt. Therefore, to avoid an occupation, he granted the British grain for their army, favorable trading rights, and secure lines of communication to India.[15] This was an early economic–political trade. Other aspects of Muhammad Ali's and subsequent eras were the tendency to abandon Islamic Sharia and adopt laws based on the French model, and sometimes the application of French law directly, while considering local customs.[16]

The most significant legacy that the French left in Egypt was centralization. Egyptian politicians and lawmakers found that the French system fostered their ambitions in increasing their own power by "centralizing state elites."[17] In Africa, India, and the Arab world, the European system was adopted mainly for those benefits. Brown suggests that principles such as "no punishment without a text" were used to benefit the new regime by guaranteeing that criminalization and interpretation were within their power and based on their views and interests.[18] Brown also observes that the timing of this legal shift in Egypt suggests a gradual legal evolution rather than an external imperial transplanting.[19]

INFORMAL IMPERIAL CONTROL (1790S–1920S)

In addition to the traces of influence left from the occupation, the French remained an influential power in Egypt even after ending their military occupation. Two of the ways in which this influence manifested itself were in scientific and archaeology campaigns, and economic control. The first method focused on studying the history and culture of a particular place as a step toward controlling it through "knowledge." The second method focused on the financial (in)stability of a country, providing it with loans and controlling its budget when it failed to pay its debts. Both of these methods attracted other Western powers, particularly the British, to expand their

---

[13] Jamal Badawi, *Muhamad Ali wa awladah* [*Muhamad Ali and His Sons*] (Cairo: Matabie' alhaya' almasriya alama' lilkitab, 1999) at 90–5.
[14] Abdu-rahman aRifa'ee, *Tareakh alharaka alqawmiya wa tatawur nitham alhukom* [*History of Nationalist Movement and the Development of the Ruling System*] (Cairo: Matabie' alhaya' almasriya alama' lilkitab, 2000) at 327–50.
[15] Andrew McGregor, *A Military History of Modern Egypt: From the Ottoman Conquest to the Ramadan War* (Westport, CT: Praeger Security International, 2006) at Ch. 5.
[16] *Al-kitab al-dahabi li-lmahakim al-ahliyya* [*The Gold Book of the National Courts*], vol 2 (Cairo: Al-matba'a al-amiriyya bi-bulaq, 1937) at 282.
[17] Nathan Brown, *The Rule of Law in the Arab World* (New York: Cambridge University Press, 1997) at 57.
[18] Brown, "Retrospective: Law and Imperialism," at 118.
[19] *Ibid.*

informal imperial control in the region away from direct colonization. The import-ance of such methods is that they are similar to the neo-colonial ways of control, in which a system of hierarchy is established that grants the West superior authority economically, politically, and culturally, without the need for a direct military occupation. Such methods of control later formed the core of neo-colonialism.

Scientific Expeditions and Control through "Knowledge" (1798–1920s)

Europeans established an effective security system not only through crime control, but also through what I will refer to as "knowledge-control." Said argues that knowledge means the attempts to study and understand others' culture based on their history, social life, and political system in order to manipulate their self-understanding, which allows Europeans to dominate these nations.[20] Michel Fou-cault uses the term "power-knowledge" in suggesting that observing people, their behavior, and studying their history provide the state with the knowledge that allows it to manipulate and control. According to Foucault, this knowledge becomes a source of the state's power. Foucault seems to view colonialism as just one manifest-ation of a form of state power that includes this type of knowledge.[21] Foucault's notion of "power-knowledge" signifies that power – importantly, power to enforce social discipline and conformity – is constituted through forms of knowledge and scientific understanding.[22] Said follows Foucault's view; yet, unlike Foucault, who focuses on the West, Said applies his argument to the unequal positions of power between the Orient and the Occident.

Said argues that the West implanted the idea that the Orient is backward, has always been ruled by dictatorships, is unable to rule, does not respect women, is lazy, and lacks democracy. In addition, he argues that the West's interference is not to rescue the Orient from its backwardness, but to continue ruling it with different methods yet within the same logic.[23] And because the West studies the Orient and its culture and history, it has the superiority to control it. This control can be direct, as was the case during colonialism, but it can also be indirect, for example in influencing the Orient to believe it has a "fixed" identity that requires a ruling hand to control it.[24]

Said suggests that imperialism conceives knowledge within a politicized utilitar-ian approach that makes the apprehension and outcome of such investigations one-sided and biased. He argues that the aim is not to serve the highest good of

---

[20] See Said, *Orientalism*, at xv.
[21] Michel Foucault, *Discipline and Punish: The Birth of the Prison* (New York: Pantheon Books, 1977) at 12.
[22] *Ibid.*
[23] Said, *Orientalism*, at xv.
[24] *Ibid*, at 336.

knowledge itself, but the interest of the colonial or imperial power.[25] Said differentiates between knowledge and "knowledge-control":

> [T]here is a difference between knowledge of other peoples and other times that is the result of understanding, compassion, careful study and analysis for their own sakes, and on the other hand knowledge—if that is what it is—that is part of an overall campaign of self-affirmation, belligerency, and outright war. There is, after all, a profound difference between the will to understand for purposes of coexistence and humanistic enlargement of horizons, and the will to dominate for the purposes of control and external dominion.[26]

This logic of knowledge-control was cleverly used by the imperial powers in their overseas colonies. For instance, the French occupation of Egypt was not merely military; besides the army and the naval forces, Napoleon brought along teams of scientists and researchers to examine and explore Egyptian culture and history.[27] The actual military occupation did not last for more than four years, but the imperial scientific and scholarly expedition continued for decades. This gave French imperialism the privilege of monitoring the Egyptians through "knowledge."

Said claims that because of the knowledge that the West has about the Orient, a belief was set into the Oriental mind about its identity and its position within a system of superiority and hierarchy.[28] Said suggests that the identity of the Orient is a Western invention that is based on manipulating interpretations of the Oriental culture. Such culture is viewed as different, inferior, backward and aggressive, which justifies categorizing the Orient as "other."[29] According to Said, this conflict of identity creates a "flexible *positional* superiority, which puts the Westerner in a whole series of possible relationships with the Orient without ever losing him the relative upper hand."[30]

In Egypt, knowledge-control was not only used by the French. The British also justified their superiority because of their "knowledge." In 1910, Arthur James Balfour worked on convincing the House of Commons about the privilege Britain had because of its knowledge about Egypt:

> I take up no attitude of superiority. But I ask [Robertson and anyone else...] who has even the most superficial knowledge of history, if they will look in the face the facts with which a British statesman has to deal when he is put in a position of supremacy over great races like the inhabitants of Egypt and countries in the East. We *know* the civilization of Egypt better than we know the civilization of any other

---

[25] *Ibid*, at xix.
[26] *Ibid*.
[27] "The Napoleonic Invasion of Egypt" *Linda Hall Library*, online: napoleon.lindahall.org/learn .shtm.
[28] Said, *Orientalism*, at 58.
[29] *Ibid*, at 5–11, 98.
[30] *Ibid*, at 7.

country. *We know it* further back; *we know it* more intimately; *we know more* about it. It goes far beyond the petty span of the history of our race, which is lost in the prehistoric period at a time when the Egyptian civilisation had already passed its prime. Look at all the Oriental countries. Do not talk about superiority or inferiority.[31] [emphasis added]

"Knowledge," as explained by Balfour, seems to justify the British occupation of Egypt. This justification is derived from the characteristics of the Oriental political identity, which is seen as despotic. Balfour suggested that Egypt has always been ruled by dictatorships, so why not allow the British colonizer to correct the course of history:[32]

> You may look through the whole history of the Orientals in what is called, broadly speaking, the East, and you never find traces of self-government. All their great centuries—and they have been very great—have been passed under despotisms, under absolute government [. . .]. It is not a question of superiority and inferiority [. . .].
>   Is it a good thing for these great nations—I admit their greatness—that this absolute government should be exercised by us? I think it is a good thing [. . .] which not only is a benefit to them, but is undoubtedly a benefit to the whole of the civilised West [. . .]. We are in Egypt not merely for the sake of the Egyptians, though we are there for their sake; we are there also for the sake of Europe at large.[33]

Through their "knowledge" of Egyptian history and culture, the British assumed they could be more reasonable and just than Egyptians in ruling Egypt, and that, hopefully, Egyptian rulers would learn from British colonialism the "right" way to self-govern. At the same time, the British could benefit from Egypt's strategic Suez Canal and natural resources. The "civilized West" would thus further advance their economic and political positions.

Political and Economic Control (1850s–1870s)

European pressure had an early impact on Egypt's political, economic, and legal systems. The impact of this informal imperial political and economic control provides a precedent for post-9/11 pressures (discussed further in the section titled Neo-colonialism in Egypt). Colonial economic policy was not isolated from law. In fact, law was, whenever needed, designed to serve colonial economic ambition. Byron Cannon argues that informal empire played a significant role in shaping law and politics in Egypt for economic ends. He gives the example of the Mixed Courts, which were active from 1875 until 1949. This judicial system, which streamlined legal issues between foreigners and between foreigners and Egyptians, was an

---

[31] Quoted in *ibid*, at 32.
[32] See *ibid*, at 32–3.
[33] Quoted in *ibid*, at 32–3.

Egyptian invention. This system was founded before the British occupation. However, despite the fact that at that time Egypt was not officially a colony, it was under great political and economic pressure from Europe, particularly France and Britain.[34]

According to Cannon, the tactics of informal empire started with France allowing itself to impose its will on the Egyptian legal system and defy the will of Egyptian powers regarding the functioning of the Mixed Courts.[35] The power of France was not derived from any formal position as colonizer, but from its economic position as an informal imperial power in Egypt.[36] In other words, the *de facto* power of imperialism made Arab countries, and their legal systems, subject to the control of an imperial power that controlled the economy.[37]

During the 1870s Egypt went through financial crisis and declared its inability to pay a debt borrowed from Europe. As a result, the Anglo-French Dual Control committee was established to supervise the Egyptian budget. This Anglo-French expert body was not only responsible for the budget, but also for practicing political pressure that resulted in replacing the ruler Isma'il Pasha with Khedive Tawfiq. This can be seen as the starting point of the puppet government in Egypt, which gradually deepened and became most evident in the 1950s during King Farouk's reign. The relationship between the British and the Egyptian rulers, whether the sultan or the king, was a superior–subordinate relationship. For instance, the first sultan of the Sultanate of Egypt, Hussein Kamel, came into power after the British forces deposed the khedive, at that time Abbas II Hilmi.[38] The stability of any ruler depended largely on the approval of the British.

The increased European control in Egypt led to a nationalist uprising, known as the 'Urabi Revolt (1879–82), led by nationalist officer Ahmed 'Urabi against Tewfiq Pasha's rule. 'Urabi was described on different occasions by Khedive Tawfiq as a "rebel" who committed "anarchist acts" and "treason."[39] These terms were misused well before a penal code was established in Egypt (explained in Chapter 5). The revolt was a threat not only to the khedive, but also to European interests in Egypt, which were seen as exploitation of Egypt's natural and financial resources. The revolt paved the way for the British occupation, which ended the revolt and secured the rule of the khedive.

---

[34] Byron Cannon, *Politics of Law and the Courts in Nineteenth-Century Egypt* (Salt Lake City: University of Utah Press, 1988) at 50–1.
[35] *Ibid.*
[36] Cole, *Colonialism and Revolution in the Middle East*, at 3.
[37] Cannon, *Politics of Law*, 50.
[38] Naguib Mahfouz, *Palace Walk* (New York: Anchor Books, 1991) at 12.
[39] Aḥmad Urābī, *Mudhakkirāt al-Za 'īm Aḥmad 'Urābī: kashf al-sitār 'an sirr al-asrār fī al-naḍah al-Miṣrīyah, al-Mashhurah bi-al-Thawrah al-'Urābīyah, fī 'āmay 1298 wa-1299 al-hijrīyatayn, wa-fī 1881 wa-1882 al-mīlādīyatayn [Ahmad Urabi's Memoir]* (Cairo: Dār al-Hilāl, 1989) at 10–12.

THE BRITISH OCCUPATION (1882–1952)

The direct reason for the British occupation was to crush the 'Urabi revolt, which aimed to end European political and economic control in Egypt. Thus, in 1822 Britain sent its troops to Egypt, fought 'Urabi in the Battle of Tel el-Kebir, and secured the khedive's government.[40] This event suggests that militarism as a colonial tool seeks to protect the imperial economy abroad.

'Urabi's trial is a case that shows the actual influence the British had in criminal matters. The trial was arranged between the British and the Egyptians. The Egyptians aimed to punish 'Urabi with death, but the British insisted on several things: a "fair" and public trial, that the charge must be for acts of rebellion, and that the death sentence must be replaced with life in exile to one of Britain's colonies, Ceylon.[41] This arrangement suggests a direct British influence on judicial process. The Egyptian Penal Code was introduced around the same time, but it is not clear from the available documents whether the British had a similar role in influencing or approving the Egyptian Penal Code.

After the occupation, the Egyptian government was no longer able to take a major decision without British approval.[42] In this regard, Nathan Brown describes the British position in Egypt as follows:

> The British never assumed direct control of the Egyptian government (even though British personnel were employed at all levels of Egyptian administration), but British power was exercised regularly and even heavy-handedly in the country. No Egyptian government could take an action that the British actively opposed [. . . T]he British unilaterally declared the country independent in 1922 but refused to concede control over important issues, including defense and protection of foreigners.[43]

This suggests that at the administrative level the British used methods of informal imperialism that allowed indirect involvement in decisionmaking. According to David French, the British colonials relied on local elites to rule and direct people on their behalf – a cheaper way to rule.[44] This required building a strong network with the ruling class and elites.

During colonialism, the British secured the khedive's government, yet it was a nominal government with limited authority. The actual governor was Evelyn Baring, also known as Lord Cromer, who ruled Egypt on behalf of Britain until

---

[40] *Ibid.*
[41] Earl of Cromer, *Modern Egypt*, vol 1 (New York: The Macmillan Company, 1908) at 336–7.
[42] *Ibid*, at 336.
[43] Brown, "Retrospective: Law and Imperialism," at 107.
[44] David French, *The British Way in Counter-Insurgency: 1945–1967* (Oxford: Oxford University Press, 2011) at 16.

1907.[45] Unlike in India, where a coercive policy was enforced in order to change the native mentality, and which was faced with violent resistance, there was relatively limited coercion in Egypt. The colonialists attempted to accommodate natives' needs without compromising their imperial agenda.[46] Cromer's policy in ruling Egypt was to identify the "oriental mind." He advised that "British officials in Eastern countries should be encouraged by all possible means to learn the views and the requirements of the native population."[47] Said argues that this attempt was undertaken not in order to cooperate with the natives, but to manipulate them according to imperial standards.[48] The British managed to combine methods of informal imperialism and colonialism in ruling Egypt. Both of these forms dissatisfied Egyptians who sought complete self-government.

Egyptian nationalists were aware that a revolt against the British would probably end up like the 'Urabi revolt. And, recognizing that "the Oriental" was not an equal competitor, they faced the colonizer with a method that would be acknowledged as equal – the French system. Egyptian laws and institutions were based on a French model, which is discussed in more detail in Chapter 5. This allowed Egyptian nationalists to negotiate with the British on a more equal footing and be confident in pushing for independence.

In 1922, Egypt gained a nominal independence, declaring itself a monarchy. The substance of this independence was to end the British protectorate that had been announced in 1914 at the start of World War I. British troops, however, remained in Egypt, especially in the Suez Canal. This nominal independence did not satisfy nationalists, who saw the new monarchy as an extension of the "puppet government." As an objection to the British existence in Egypt, in the 1940s Islamic violence, carried out particularly by the Muslim Brotherhood, emerged. Bombings and other forms of violent attacks were carried out against British troops, as well as constant assassinations of Egyptian officials. Over time, especially post–World War II, the Brotherhood's influence increased rapidly, establishing schools and hospitals, as well as a secret army, which was viewed by the monarchy as carrying a potential threat of establishing another state within Egypt.[49] A suppression policy was carried out against the Brotherhood as a group and against its members. This suppressive policy consisted in banning publications by the Brotherhood, dissolving the group, and arbitrary arrest and imprisonment of its members.[50] This policy continued after

---

[45] Sean Lyngaas, "Ahmad Urabi: Delegate of the People's Social Mobilization in Egypt on the Eve of Colonial Rule" (Spring 2011) *The Fletcher School Online Journal for Issues Related to Southwest Asia and Islamic Civilization*, online: fletcher.tufts.edu/Al-Nakhlah, at 6.

[46] *Ibid.*

[47] Evelyn Baring, *The Government of Subject Races* (Cambridge: Cambridge University Press, 2011) at 27.

[48] Said, *Orientalism*, at 207.

[49] Richard P. Mitchell, *The Society of the Muslim Brothers* (London: Oxford University Press, 1969) at 58–61.

[50] "Profile: Egypt's Muslim Brotherhood" (December 25, 2013) *BBC*, online: www.bbc.com/news.

the establishment of the republic and until this day. As we will see in the next section and in Chapter 5, the British methods of crime and social control, including state of emergency and special courts, were adopted by postcolonial Egypt in its war on terror.

The British Legacy of Martial Law

Britain was able to pull Egypt, at least to some extent, toward a Western political culture of modernization. During the British occupation of Egypt, Britain avoided being directly involved in decisionmaking or policymaking in Egypt. It prepared Egypt for a gradual political and cultural shift. Nonetheless, in terms of martial law and state of emergency, Britain had a direct role in transplanting these forms of the exception to Egypt.

The first time martial law was declared in Egypt was by the British in 1914. That was when Britain declared Egypt a protectorate as a result of declaring war with the Ottoman Empire, of which Egypt was nominally a province. A British governor headed the Egyptian military, and military actions were provided immunity from the jurisdiction of the courts. This martial law remained active until the declaration of Egypt's independence in 1922.[51]

In 1936, an Anglo-Egyptian treaty was signed, which allowed the British military two things: to remain in Egypt, and to request the declaration of martial law. Accordingly, and as a necessary response to World War II, Egypt declared martial law in 1939, which lasted until the end of the war in 1945.[52] The law imposed limitations on rights and liberties, but its significance during the two World Wars was that it provided immunity to the military from lawsuits by forbidding claims to revoke any military decision or action or claims for compensation.[53]

Martial law was a useful tool to protect the military during the two World Wars. For this reason, the British insisted on including martial law in the 1923 Egyptian constitution.[54] Although Nathan Brown plays down the role of colonialism in imposing law in general, when it comes to the field of national security, he explains the adoption of these laws as part of the colonial legacy.[55]

Reza argues that the advantages of martial law, in which the military can enjoy unlimited authority without accountability, encouraged the newly liberated Egyptian elite to regulate it further in the 1923 Egyptian constitution and its subsequent

[51] Sadiq Reza, "Endless Emergency: The Case of Egypt" (2007) 10:4 *New Criminal Law Review*, at 535.
[52] *Ibid*, at 536; Brown, *The Rule of Law in the Arab World*, at 82.
[53] Article 10*bis* of the Egyptian Law No. 15 of 1923 on the System of Martial Law.
[54] Brown, "Retrospective: Law and Imperialism," at 111; Reza, "Endless Emergency," at 535–7.
[55] Brown, *The Rule of Law in the Arab World*, at 72–82; Reza, "Endless Emergency," at 535–6; Roach *The 9/11 Effect*, at 82.

amendments.[56] A piece of legislation regarding martial law was also established in 1923.[57] Article 1 of this law states that "Martial law may be declared whenever security or public order in the Egyptian territory or part of it is at risk, whether due to an armed enemy raid or due to internal disturbance."[58]

This law granted the military governor several areas of authority outside the field of war, including searching persons and houses, monitoring newspapers before they are published, suspending or closing any press without prior notice, monitoring mail and teleconferences, as well as preventing associations or public meetings and resolving them by force.[59] These restrictions to rights and libraries were justified as part of securing the mission of the military in protecting the stability of the state by suppressing any propaganda by the enemy during wartime. Among these authorities was the right to open fire in cases of disobedience. In one occasion in 1951, the British army opened fire on a car that disregarded the army's order to stop. The result was the killing of a female passenger and wounding of the male driver.[60] This action broadens the right to open fire to include cases of disobedience without the use of force. This rationale is borrowed from the colonial counter-insurgency experience. According to French, in "Cyprus, and Nyasaland [the British] could create free-fire zones where the security forces could engage suspected insurgents with lethal force."[61] Treating civilians equally to "insurgents" suggests that discipline rather than crime control is the ultimate goal of the colonial order. The British transplanted their militarized approach into Egypt yet covered it with legal principles that neutralized the actions of military forces.

British colonialism, with its commitment to the principle of "minimum use of force," was less coercive than that of the French.[62] However, a minimum use of force is a principle without clear definitions, which allows the use of force, especially during martial law. For instance, in the early 1950s counter-insurgency campaigns were carried out in Egypt, particularly across the Canal Zone. In January 1952, the British troops launched Operation Eagle by firing on the Egyptian police, who were considered insurgents. The operation resulted in the killing of around 40 and injuring of over 60 Egyptians.[63] The excessive use of force was faced with an increased number of attacks on British figures and troops. This led the British to replace the unnecessary use of force with low-intensity counter-insurgency operations.[64]

---

[56] Reza, "Endless Emergency," at 535.
[57] Law No. 15 of 1923 on the System of Martial Law.
[58] Article 1, *ibid*.
[59] Article 3, *ibid*, replaced by Law No. 533 of 1954.
[60] French, *The British Way in Counter-Insurgency*, at 108.
[61] *Ibid*, at 80.
[62] *Ibid*, at 75–9.
[63] *Ibid*, at 114–15.
[64] *Ibid*.

The British Legacy of Special Courts

The British legacy in Egypt included special courts – another form of exceptionalism. In Egypt, when crimes were committed against the British troops by locals, extreme emergency measures were imposed. These included establishing special courts and invoking collective responsibility.[65]

In Egypt, the British granted military actions, including actions that are practiced during peacetime, immunity from prosecution. For example, one special tribunal sentenced several Egyptian villagers to death and others to flogging because of a conflict with pigeon-hunting British troops.[66] The British were not comfortable with the Egyptian national system, especially regarding the judiciary and the police. Therefore, "sensitive cases" were not brought to the National Courts. Lord Cromer complained of "the delay which constantly occurs, in the Native Courts, in dealing with offences against British soldiers."[67] As a result, the British justified establishing special tribunals, where harsh verdicts were acceptable.[68]

The British distrusted Egyptian National Courts; this led to calls for Anglicization.[69] In 1912, after an Egyptian court acquitted two men accused of carrying out an alleged attack on a French engineer, Lord Kitchener, British consul-general in Egypt, wrote:

> All authorities agree that the case was fully and satisfactorily proved against the two men accused, one of whom had been twice tried for attempted murder in the last four years; yet they were both acquitted by Egyptian judges. These judges were known to be Nationalists, and it is naturally considered that race and religious feeling alone can account for their finding.[70]

British officials, in particular Lord Cromer, complained about the Egyptian tendency to apply legal procedures too strictly, which often resulted in setting free the guilty.[71] National Courts did not recognize confessions under torture, which upset both the Egyptian government and the British. As a response, the British established a tradition of special procedures to deal with those convicted by officials and not judges.[72] Such a legacy still exists in Egypt, and is addressed in more detail in Chapter 5.

---

[65] Brown, "Retrospective: Law and Imperialism," at 121.
[66] Brown, *The Rule of Law in the Arab World*, at 45.
[67] Quoted in *ibid*.
[68] Earl of Cromer, *Modern Egypt*, vol 2 (New York: The Macmillan Company, 1908) at 32–3.
[69] Brown, *The Rule of Law in the Arab World*, at 45.
[70] Quoted in *ibid*, at 46.
[71] *Ibid*, at 52.
[72] *Ibid*.

POSTCOLONIALISM: COLONIAL HERITAGE BLENDING
INTO LOCAL AUTHORITARIANISM

The Free Officers Movement was organized to end the *de facto* colonialism of the British. The movement included, among others, Muhammad Naguib, Gamal Abdel Nassar, and Anwar Sadat, who became the first three presidents of Egypt. In July 1952, a coup was carried out that forced King Farouk to leave Egypt, and the Republic of Egypt was established in July 1953. Naguib was the first president of the Republic of Egypt from July 1953 to November 1954. Naguib had a democratic stance and a desire to limit the authority of the army.[73] However, he was forced to leave office by Nasser and other officers after only 16 months.

Nasser was the next president. He ruled Egypt with a military and authoritarian approach. Although other presidents have since taken over, the military and authoritarian approach still continues until the day of writing this book. Freedoms were limited through censorship and travel restrictions. Powers were centralized within the personal control of the president, with the aid of some members of the army and the Ministry of the Interior.[74] Other economic activities and international trade were limited within a socialist policy.[75]

Nasser, although a revolutionary ruler, could not commit to the aspirations and goals of the revolution, and designed a constitution that allowed him to back out of the promises made in it. For instance, while the constitution listed individual rights, it also granted the president the right to dissolve the parliament and declare a state of emergency. This failure to observe a national constitution has been a common shortcoming of statesmen in other modern states. Karl Loewenstein observes that "Mussolini, Goebbels, Peron, Ngo Dinh Diem, Nasser and *tutti quanit* are modern men and no fools. They cannot believe in what their constitutions proclaim, and their elections produce."[76] Brown describes these documents as "generally viewed as elegant but insincere expressions of aspirations that rulers issue in an effort to obscure the unrestrained nature of their authority."[77] This description of constitutions fits well with those that are adopted in post-independence Arab countries, including Egypt.

The reaction toward this extreme authoritarian approach led to an attempted assassination of President Nasser in 1954. As a response, hundreds of members of the

---

[73] Nissim Rejwan, *Arabs Face the Modern World: Religious, Cultural, and Political Responses to the West* (Gainesville, FL: University Press of Florida: 1998) at 87.

[74] Clement Henry Moore, "Authoritarian Politics in Unincorporated Society: The Case of Nasser's Egypt" (1974) 6:2 *Comparative Politics* 193 at 196.

[75] Thomas W. Lippman, *Egypt after Nasser: Sadat, Peace and the Mirage of Prosperity* (New York: Paragon House, 1989) at 5.

[76] Karl Loewenstein, *Political Power and the Governmental Process* (Chicago: University of Chicago Press, 1957) at 146.

[77] Nathan Brown, *Constitutions in a Nonconstitutional World: Arab Basic Laws and the Prospects for Accountable Government* (New York: State University of New York Press, 2002), at 2.

Brotherhood who were suspected of having taken part in the assassination attempt were arrested and some were sentenced to either death or life imprisonment.[78] Egyptian prisons became filled with Brotherhood members – a factor that had counterproductive results. Prisons became the birthplace of many influential radical figures and groups.[79]

Nasser was clear in his war against the Brotherhood and other Islamist groups. He relied on exceptional courts and measures. Several exceptional courts were established by decree, such as the Court of Ethics, the Court of Sequestration, and the Court of the Revolution. These extra-ordinary courts had vague tasks that allowed the authority to protect itself under the pretext of protecting the public order. These courts can be seen as part of the British legacy in Egypt. These measures have continued to be used since Nasser, showing an extension of a colonial legacy. Such practices have thwarted democratic progress and consolidated authoritarianism in post-independence Egypt.

NEO-COLONIALISM: ECONOMIC DEPENDENCE
AND POLITICAL SUBMISSION

Sadat came to power in 1970 after the death of Nasser. Sadat adopted a less strict policy at the national level and a friendly policy toward the West. Internally, he released political prisoners in an attempt to culturally contain Islamists and other opposition groups.[80] His foreign policy welcomed a "partnership" with the United States.[81] He hoped to secure economic prosperity for Egypt by obtaining financial and technological support from the United States.[82]

Sadat signed the Egypt–Israel Peace Treaty in the United States in 1979. On the one hand, this step made him hated among Egyptians and most Arab rulers, and led to his assassination in 1981 by solders belonging to the al-Jihad group.[83] On the other, it improved Sadat's relations with the West. Since the date of signing the peace treaty with Israel, Egypt has been the second-largest recipient of American foreign aid.

Hosni Mubarak, another military officer, came to power in 1981. He first ruled Egypt through a middle course. He satisfied the West while taking Egypt back to its

---

[78] Anthony Nutting, *Nasser* (New York: E. P. Dutton, 1972) at 73–4.
[79] Jeffery T. Kenney, *Muslim Rebels: Kharijites and the Politics of Extremism in Egypt* (Oxford: Oxford University Press, 2006) at 129–33.
[80] Gilles Kepel, *Jihad: The Trail of Political Islam*, trans Anthony F. Roberts (London: I. B. Tauris, 2006) at 83.
[81] Brad Plumer, "The U.S. Gives Egypt $1.5 Billion a Year in Aid. Here's What It Does" (July 9, 2013) *Washington Post*, online: www.washingtonpost.com.
[82] Thomas W. Lippman, *Egypt after Nasser: Sadat, Peace and the Mirage of Prosperity* (New York: Paragon House, 1989) at 13.
[83] William L. Cleveland & Martin P. Bunton, *A History of the Modern Middle East* (Boulder, CO: Westview Press, 2013) at 229.

leadership role in the Arab region.[84] He recognized the necessity of foreign economic and military support in order to keep the peace with Israel and maintain internal security. This was achieved primarily through American aid.[85] Egypt receives annual aid from the United States of $2.1 billion ($1.3 billion for the military; $815 million in economic aid).[86]

This relationship between Egypt and the United States suggests a new form of subordination to the Western neo-colonial powers, at least financially, which could give the superior the upper hand regarding other political matters. Despite these unequal positions of power, the relationship encouraged Mubarak's authoritarian tendencies. Post-9/11, Mubarak found the global war on terror a new justification for the endless state of emergency and other restrictive measures. Yet he also had to keep pace with global countermeasures, especially regarding terrorism financing, which will be discussed further in Chapter 5. The Egyptian subordination to the West is what kept a dictator like Mubarak secure for all these years. As one scholar puts it, the "firm backing of the United States and a formidable Egyptian security apparatus were for thirty years safeguards to Mubarak's throne."[87]

American aid continued during the presidency of Mohamed Morsi.[88] Morsi's presidency – which began in June 2012 and ended in July 2013 – was too short to evaluate the American influence over Egypt during that one year. The coup that ended the rule of Morsi was supposed to end American military aid. According to the United States Foreign Assistance Act, "None of the funds appropriated or otherwise made available pursuant to this Act shall be obligated or expended to finance directly any assistance to the government of any country whose duly elected head of government is deposed by military coup or decree."[89] However, after the election in June 2014 of President el-Sisi, the leader of the coup, the United States, while reducing the funding, had released $575 million in military aid to Egypt.[90]

President Trump has been carrying out the same approach of reducing military and economic aid to Egypt as his predecessors, yet with more controversial policies.

---

[84] Tony Karon, "What the U.S. Loses If Mubarak Goes" (January 31, 2011) *TIME*, online: content .time.com.
[85] Jeremy M. Sharp, "Egypt: Background and U.S. Relations" (January 10, 2014) *Congressional Research Service*, online: www.crs.gov, at 18–38.
[86] Robert Satloff & Patrick Clawson, "U.S. Economic Aid to Egypt: Designing a New, Pro-Growth Package" (July 7, 1998) *The Washington Institute*, online: www.washingtoninstitute .org/policy-analysis/view/u.s.-economic-aid-to-egypt-designing-a-new-pro-growth-package.
      Peter Baker, "In a Shift, Trump Will Move Egypt's Rights Record to the Sidelines" (March 31, 2017) *The New York Times*, online: www.nytimes.com/2017/03/31/world/middleeast/in-major-shift-trump-taking-egypts-human-rights-issues-private.html.
[87] Lyngaas, "Ahmad Urabi," at 10.
[88] "Obama: Egypt Is Not US Ally, Nor an Enemy" (September 13, 2012) *BBC*, online: www.bbc .com.
[89] United States Foreign Assistance Act 1961.
[90] "US Unlocks Military Aid to Egypt, Backing President Sisi" (June 22, 2014) *BBC*, online: www .bbc.com.

On the one hand, in its Country Reports on Human Rights Practices for 2016 the US Department of State criticizes Egypt's excessive use of force by security forces, deficiencies in due process, and many other suppressive practices against civil liberties.[91] On the other, President Trump has frequently praised el-Sisi's policies. On one occasion, Trump stated that el-Sisi has "done a fantastic job in a very difficult situation. We are very much behind Egypt and the people of Egypt."[92] However, Trump's alleged alliance with Egypt may be no more than rhetorical pronouncements. In action, the Trump administration has denied and delayed about $290 million in military aid to Egypt, allegedly primarily for Egypt's poor human rights record. However, analysts have referred to Egypt's bilateral relations with North Korea as the reason for the aid cut.[93] Since the 1970s, Egypt has developed military relations with North Korea, and Egypt invited North Korean pilots to prepare Egyptian pilots for the 1973 war with Israel.[94] The necessities of that era no longer exist, because of the peace treaty between Israel and Egypt, and while the UN Security Council has been condemning North Korea's ballistic missiles and other nuclear productions and tests,[95] but Egypt has continued its military cooperation with North Korea. In 2016, North Korea tried, using one of its ships, to smuggle to Egypt more than 30,000 rocket-propelled grenades – a number that is suitable for an army and not a terrorist group.[96]

In response to pressure from Washington, Egypt has cut its military and economic relations with North Korea, and only maintains limited diplomatic representation.[97] Still, Washington has concerns about Egypt allowing North Korea to illegally trade arms under diplomatic cover in the Middle East.[98] Future United States financial aid to Egypt may depend not only on Egypt's willingness to completely cut its ties to North Korea, but also on other efforts to regain the United States' trust. However, the American withdrawal of the $290 million remains insignificant compared to the $1.3 billion in military aid, most of which Egypt continues to receive. The aid cut is a symbolic step that suggests the superiority of the United States.

---

[91] "Country Reports on Human Rights Practices for 2016" (April 29, 2018), *US Department of State*, online: www.state.gov/j/drl/rls/hrrpt/2017/nea/277239.htm.

[92] Gardiner Harris & Declan Walsh, "U.S. Slaps Egypt on Human Rights Record and Ties to North Korea" (August 22, 2017), *The New York Times*, online: www.nytimes.com/2017/08/22/us/politics/us-aid-egypt-human-rights-north-korea.html.

[93] Declan Walsh, "Need a North Korean Missile? Call the Cairo Embassy" (March 3, 2018), *The New York Times*, online: www.nytimes.com/2018/03/03/world/middleeast/egypt-north-korea-sanctions-arms-dealing.html.

[94] Harris & Walsh, "U.S. Slaps Egypt on Human Rights Record and Ties to North Korea."

[95] UN Security Council, Security Council Resolution 2397, 2017 SC Res. 2397, UN SCOR, S/RES/2397 [Resolution 2397].

[96] Joby Warrick, "A North Korean Ship Was Seized Off Egypt with a Huge Cache of Weapons Destined for a Surprising Buyer" (October 1 2017), *The Washington Post*, online: www.washingtonpost.com.

[97] Walsh, "Need a North Korean Missile? Call the Cairo Embassy."

[98] *Ibid.*

In 2018, el-Sisi's regime corrupted the Egyptian presidential election through disqualifying potential candidates or forcing them to withdraw. Washington has turned a blind eye to this obvious violation, which el-Sisi may understand as an implicit approval of his policy. This means that although the United States disapproves of, for instance, Egyptian relations with North Korea, it is prepared to deal with a corrupt government and use aid cuts to force it to change policies that interfere with the American agenda. The American support of the authoritarian government in Egypt protects the neo-colonial structure and its security without advancing Egypt's human rights and democracy.

Internally, the lack of constitutional safeguards and external criticism has allowed Egypt to expand its authoritarian ambition through surveillance. Surveillance is a form of knowledge-power that gradually developed in areas of political life, most importantly in policing and secret intelligence. Egypt has several secret intelligence bodies, including an intelligence unit in the Ministry of Interior Affairs, an intelligence unit in the Ministry of Defense, the General Intelligence Directorate, and the Technical Research Department – an independent unit in the General Intelligence Directorate.[99] According to a report by the Privacy International organization, during Mubarak's regime, the Technical Research Department was established, allowing him to monitor his political opponents when the General Intelligence Directorate refused to carry out certain activities.[100] Although little has been documented about its function in Egypt, political opponents and journalists have shared their experience with the state's secret intelligence threat. In the aftermath of the "Arab Spring," journalists have expressed their concern about the increasing use of surveillance in recent years and the excessive monitoring of their social media communications as well as their private lives.[101] Female opponents have claimed that taped phone calls and personal photos have been shared online in an attempt to publicly shame them.[102] The systematic surveillance of private communications and tracing individuals and groups based on their associations has increased the sense of social and political insecurity among people.

Another way of bringing social life under full control is in mobilizing religious bodies. Egyptian authorities view mosques as a set of organizations that might produce state opponents. Therefore, Egypt brought religious establishments under

---

[99] "The President's men? Inside the Technical Research Department, the Secret Player in Egypt's Intelligence Infrastructure" (February 2016) *Privacy International*, online: privacyinternational. org/sites/default/files/2018–02/egypt_reportEnglish_0.pdf, at 5–6.

[100] *Ibid.*

[101] Marwa Morgan, "How Surveillance, Trolls, and Fear of Arrest Affect Egypt's Journalists" (June 12, 2017), *Committee to Protect Journalists*, online: cpj.org/blog/2017/06/how-surveillance-trolls-and-fear-of-arrest-is-affe.php.

[102] *Ibid*; Sarah Carr, "Sexual Assault and the State: A History of Violence" (July 7, 2014), *Mada Media Organization*, online: www.madamasr.com/en/2014/07/07/feature/politics/sexual-assault-and-the-state-a-history-of-violence/.

the umbrella of its control by officializing the positions of *mufti* (the clergy) and paying them salaries.[103] Egyptian presidents have often relied on *fatwa* (religious opinion) to justify their political actions.[104] Even in more secular states like Tunisia, the position of *mufti* still exists, as will be shown in Chapter 6.[105] By containing religious positions within the state and placing limits on freedom, the state is controlling society through the "winning hearts and minds" approach.

Other professions were also brought under the supervision of the state, such as judges, teachers, and journalists. Replacing existing judges was not always easy; therefore, the state found a way of reducing the role of jurisdiction through establishing exceptional courts in colonial times and subsequently. This is a combination of centralization and exceptionalism that solidifies the authoritarian rule in Egypt.

CONCLUSION: AUTHORITARIAN AMBITION AS AN ADDITIONAL PERSPECTIVE

The common features of imperialism, colonialism, and neo-colonialism discussed in this and the previous chapter do not explain all the postcolonial legal and extra-legal practices in the Arab world. This requires an inquiry into the unique features of Arab states as mostly authoritarian regimes. An important feature of such regimes is the lack of power-sharing, which creates either personal dictatorship or highly centralized authoritarianism. Both limit political freedoms.

In the aftermath of independence, in order to secure the newly independent states, Arab rulers transformed the former colonized regimes into authoritarian governments. The duality in modern Arab legal systems – a European legal system with a colonial model regarding national security – could be viewed as a consequence of ambivalent colonial policy: preparing states for independence while protecting imperial interests in these colonies. The policies in former Arab colonies mirror the paradoxical juxtaposition of these two goals.

Arab states sought to increase their domestic power. This was done through replacing colonial control with local control. A combination of centralization, special courts, and extra-legal authorities served the regimes' purposes well. The state aimed to bring under its supervision all opponents. In this respect, regulations were applied to educational bodies by imposing national programs and restricting students' political activities.[106]

---

[103] Roger Owen, *State, Power and Politics in the Making of the Modern Middle East* (London: Routledge, 2004), at 29.
[104] *Ibid.*
[105] Article 79 of the 2014 Constitution: "The President of the Republic is responsible for: Appointing and dismissing the General Mufti of the Tunisian Republic."
[106] Owen, *State, Power and Politics*, at 28–9.

Controlling through "knowledge," such as through scientific expeditions and political and economic control during informal imperialism, has been adopted in Egypt by the secret intelligence services. Egyptian authorities have been monitoring people's communications and associations in an attempt to preempt the threat of criminals and opponents alike. Egypt's obsession with identifying the "enemy" of the state has led to breaching people's privacy and threatening their sense of security. Such practices dovetail with their authoritarian ambition, which aims to maintain the president and his corrupted government in their position.

The American support of Egypt undermines any internal attempts for political reforms. The United States has been turning a blind eye to Egypt's extra-legal practices and excessive emergency powers in a way that encourages the Egyptian government to remain authoritarian. The United States and Egypt share the common enemy of Islamic terrorism, which justifies all means, including exceptionalism and militarism. While these means have not ended terrorism or even decreased it, they keep the Egyptian authoritarian government well secured.

The chapter concludes that authoritarian ambition is also spreading to the West. Authoritarian ambition makes Arab states seem right in influencing the West to adopt or cling to suppressive laws that reflect the counter-insurgency tradition. For instance, on September 26, 2001, US Secretary of State Colin Powell praised Egypt's anti-terrorism approach by stating that "Egypt, as all of us know, is really ahead of us on this issue. They have had to deal with acts of terrorism in recent years in the course of their history. And we have much to learn from them and there is much we can do together."[107] This statement suggests a devolution in global and Western counter-terrorism and a justification of the Arab authoritarian approach.

Even though, when talking about authoritarian regimes, the focus is on governments with high centralization and limited political freedoms and mobilization, such as the government in Egypt, many colonial and neo-colonial practices are authoritarian in nature. The obsession with monitoring, whether through censorship and speech restrictions, travel bans or freezing funds, is part of a worldwide collective authoritarian ambition. This means that authoritarian ambition as a theoretical perspective, while capable of explaining practices in the Arab world, can also explain counter-terrorism practices in Western democracies.

---

[107] Quoted in "September 11, 2001: Attack on America Secretary Colin L. Powell Remarks with Egyptian Minister of Foreign Affairs Ahmed Maher; September 26, 2001" *Yale Law School Avalon Project*, online: avalon.law.yale.edu/sept11/powell_brief21.asp,.

5

Counter-Terrorism in Egypt

A dramatic scene has been dominating Egyptian political life for decades. The opposition has been mixed up with terrorism, and national security necessity has overlapped with excessive control. This chapter examines the development of the Egyptian war on terror and the possible influence of colonialism and neo-colonialism and of indigenous authoritarian ambition in shaping anti-terrorism law and measures. The question raised in this chapter is: Are the anti-terror and national security laws in Egypt established to keep pace with the evolving require-ments of our time, or are they an extension of a deep-rooted colonial rationale? To answer this question, I examine the early laws that were adopted in the 1880s. The timing of the earlier laws is important because some of them were enacted during colonialism. These laws will reflect one or a mix of the following influences: colonial influence, an oppositional approach to colonialism, and local authoritarianism.

The chapter starts by discussing the Egyptian national security laws and measures. It examines the origin of the Penal Code, which goes back to 1883. Three crimes are selected for analysis from this law: sabotage, rebellion, and sedition. Examining these crimes shows that they form the basis of the later anti-terrorism law. The chapter then examines Law 162/1958 Concerning the State of Emergency, followed by the Egyptian application of special courts. The analysis of these suggests a direct colonial influence, which, in the case of Egypt, combines with authoritarian ambi-tion. I argue that these regulations are extended in the war on terror.

The chapter then provides an overview of the emergence of the term "terror" during the war on communism. "Terror" and other vague terms like "sabotage" were intensively used against communists during both the monarchy and the early stages of the republic. During that period, the Egyptian courts, including the Court of Cassation, sentenced hundreds of people for "revolutionary acts," including "membership in communist organizations." The importance of these verdicts is in showing how vague terms like "sabotage" were applied against opponents, and how the term "terrorism" first emerged and was applied in Egypt. More importantly, it shows the patterns of control adopted by the state to deal with enemies.

After the historical background of the internal war on communism, the chapter then discusses current counter-terrorism policy. It starts with an overview of the Egyptian approach to counter-terrorism, the constitutional amendments that centralized powers with the president, the use of the state of emergency as an anti-terrorism tool, and the exceptional nature of the internal war on terror. Egyptian laws were extremely broad well before 9/11. This section provides a criticism and evaluation of the legal framework for counter-terrorism. It covers the broad definitions and the problematic criminalization of terrorism-related crimes, including terrorism financing and speech related to terrorism. This includes problems of vagueness, excessive discretion for emergency powers, and violations of constitutional and procedural rights.

The chapter then examines other security-related laws and measures, which include the 2017 Law for Regulating the Work of Associations and Other Institutions Working in the Field of Civil Work (NGOs Law). This law significantly tightens the role of NGOs and civil society. It explicitly refers in some of its articles to the potential role of NGOs in financing terrorism. It thus grants the Egyptian government excessive authorities to monitor and limit NGOs' work. Finally, the chapter looks at a cyber crime draft law, which suggests great censorship of social media. In addition, the chapter stresses the practices of exceptionalism, special courts, and regulations of speech and associations that are most related to the colonial legacy. It also examines the theme of dualism – the fact that the Egyptian postcolonial anti-terrorism offenses are broader than those inherited from or accepted in the United Kingdom or France.

LAWS AND MEASURES REGARDING NATIONAL SECURITY: THE INFLUENCE OF COLONIALISM

Prior to regulating the crime of terrorism, there were far-reaching laws regarding crimes against the state in Egypt. Crimes against the state are undeniably dangerous: whatever affects the stability and the safety of the state will directly or indirectly affect society. In this part, my aim is not to argue for or against the different meanings of the notion of "state security," but to show how this concept is conceived in Egypt. It is important to look at the values that are protected and the rationale of state security laws as part of evaluating the current criminal system.

This section examines the colonial influence in shaping national security laws and measures. It starts by discussing the Penal Code of 1883 and the current Penal Code of 1937. It should be noted that the British granted Egypt nominal independence in 1922, but full independence was not obtained until 1952, or arguably even later in 1965 when all the British troops left the Canal Zone. According to Nathan Brown, it was only post-1922 and later that the Egyptian government had full autonomy in legislation related to its local citizens. In this period, Egypt codified a new set of political crimes, mostly protecting the king and the regime. These legal reforms were meant to strengthen the state.[1]

A subsequent section examines the exceptional measures inherited from colonial practice. These include Law 162/1958 Concerning the State of Emergency, and the Egyptian application of special courts. In examining these laws and measures and their legal and political roots, the book compares them with the current war on terror.

The Penal Code and Its Amendments

The current Egyptian Penal Code was established in 1937 after Egypt obtained nominal independence. The law has been amended several times since then. However, the very first modern penal code was established in 1883. The 1883 code was the first to criminalize sedition, sabotage, and any attempt to change the governmental system. These regulations still exist in the current Penal Code.

The Penal Code of 1883 was replaced in 1904 and again in 1937. Each of these laws was expanded by including broad and vague terms. For instance, in 1923 an amendment was made to the Penal Code of 1904, which condemns incitement of revolutionary ideas. Article 105 criminalizes "dissemination of revolutionary ideas"[2] and "advocating changing the basic social system through force or terror."[3] The underlying wrongdoing can be categorized as "sedition," "sabotage," and "rebellion." At the time of adopting the above article, Islamic movements were not yet visible in the political arena. In principle, this article was designed to protect the monarchy from any potential threat, particularly that of communism. The following sections discuss in detail the crime of sabotage and its relationship to rebellion, as well as the crime of sedition. I argue that these acts, which are drawn from the 1883 and 1904 Penal Codes, are the basis of all subsequent national security crimes, including terrorism.

Rebellion and Sabotage

In Egypt, there is not a distinctive crime under the term "rebellion." However, the history of Egypt is rich with those labeled as rebels, such as Ahmad 'Urabi and Saad Zaghloul, who were exiled during British colonialism. Instead, the Penal Code uses the terms "revolutionary crimes" and "sabotage." Even though there is not much written on the background of the first Penal Code of 1883, the facts suggest that the failure of the 'Urabi revolt (discussed in Chapter 4) led to the shaping of the Penal Code in a way that served the victorious government. The significance of the case of

[1] Brown, *The Rule of Law in the Arab World*, at 60.
[2] Article 151 (2) of Law No. 37 of 1923 on Adding Provisions to the Penal Code no. 3 of 1904.
[3] Article 151 (3), *ibid.*

'Urabi in shaping the Penal Code, which was adopted a year later, can be seen in two codifications: the labeling of anti-government acts with terms like "rebellion" and "sabotage," and the criminalizing of unlawful association.

The 1883 Penal Code embodied a tough approach to revolutionaries and anti-government groups. Article 77 of the code focuses on incitement, even unsuccessful instigation. It states that "Whoever instigated the population to take arms to fight the government, shall be punished with death whether there were full or partial outcomes, though if no outcomes occur from such instigation, the punishment shall be life in exile." Although this article does not use the term "rebellion," its wording implicitly suggests that open political resistance is not allowed.

The root of this law can be seen in colonial and imperial practice. As mentioned earlier, the defeat of 'Urabi by the British may have been influential in adopting an anti-revolutionary policy. However, a more direct influence can be seen in the French Penal Code of 1810. Egypt willingly built its Penal Code based on the French model (the attractiveness of the French model is addressed in Chapter 4). The *Gold Book of the National Courts* (1937), which documents the development of law and national courts in Egypt, confirms the French origin of the Egyptian Penal Code. It states that the Egyptian Penal Code of 1883

> cut the link with the past [...] in adopting the approach of the French law of 1810, with some variations that consider the cultural difference between the Egyptian civilization and its mentality and the Western civilization and its mentality, particularly the French.[4]

This requires a direct examination of the French Penal Code of 1810.

Section IV of the French Penal Code of 1810, "Resistance, Disobedience, and other Defaults, in regard to the Public Authority," addresses crimes of "rebellion" in at least ten articles. For instance, Article 217 states that:

> Whoever shall have incited a rebellion, either by discourses pronounced in any public places or assemblies, or by bills posted up, or by printed writings, shall be punished as guilty of such rebellion. In case the rebellion shall not have taken place, the inciter (provocateur) shall be punished with an imprisonment of not less than six days, nor more than one year.[5]

French history is full of revolutions, so it is not surprising that the First French Empire, which adopted this law, was aware that a revolution could threaten its stability. In addition to the French Penal Code, France targeted rebels based on its state of siege regulations adopted in 1797 (mentioned in Chapter 1). According to the 1797 regulations, a state of siege can be declared in case of "rebellion." However, the definition of rebellion remained unclear, which allowed domestic disturbance

---

[4] *The Gold Book of the National Courts*, at 5.
[5] Article 217 of the French Penal Code of 1810.

to be included.[6] The Egyptian monarchy probably found the French approach useful, especially after its experience with the 'Urabi revolt. Codifying the crime of rebellion adds legitimacy to the state and its countermeasures.

In addition to crimes associated with rebellion, the Egyptian Penal Code of 1883 focuses on the crime of sabotage. For instance, Article 83 states, "Whoever burned or sabotaged intentionally and malevolently buildings, stores or suchlike of government property shall be punished with death."[7] Another article punishes with death those involved in "temptation that is intended to incite the population to fight each other or to sabotage [state institutions.]"[8] The Egyptian authority places special protections on public property, regardless of the motive. The same tendency is extended to the current counter-terrorism approach, examined in a subsequent section regarding the definition of "terrorism."

The Egyptian legislation also borrowed the above crimes of sabotage from the French Penal Code of 1810. For instance, Article 95 of the French Penal Code states that "Whoever shall have set fire to, or destroyed by the explosion of a mine, any buildings, magazines, arsenals, ships, or other property, belonging to the state, shall be punished with death and confiscation of property."[9] The death penalty and life imprisonment are among the distinctive features of the Napoleonic Code that Egypt willingly clings to until this day.

In Egypt, the articles regarding rebellion and sabotage regulated in the Penal Code of 1883 were transferred to the subsequent Penal Code of 1904, and they still exist in the current Penal Code of 1937[10] but with different wording. For instance, Article 90 of the current Penal Code states that:

Shall be punished with imprisonment for no more than five years everyone who intentionally damages [sabotages] buildings or public property [. . .].
And shall the maximum limit of this punishment be multiplied if the crime was committed for a terrorist purpose.
And shall the punishment be life imprisonment if the crime was committed during a time of agitation or civil strife or with the intention to place terror or anarchy among people.
And shall a death penalty be imposed if the crime caused death of a person[.][11]

It is not clear in this article what "sabotage" means. Is it exclusive to damaging property partially or completely through bombs or weapons? Does it include acts of vandalism, such as breaking the glass or the lamps of a building, or creating graffiti?

[6] William Feldman, "Theories of Emergency Powers: A Comparative Analysis of American Martial Law and the French State of Siege" (2005) 38:3 *Cornell International Law Journal*, at 1024.
[7] Article 83 of the Egyptian Penal Code of 1883.
[8] Article 78, *ibid.*
[9] Article 95 of the French Penal Code of 1810.
[10] Articles 89*bis* and 90 of the Egyptian Penal Code of 1937.
[11] Amended by Law No. 120 of 1962, and later by Law No. 97 of 1992.

The wording of the above article does not propose any limits. Moreover, it suggests that if property damage is undertaken for the purpose of intimidating the government, it will probably be categorized as terrorism.

While the punishment of life in exile no longer exists, partly because of the end of colonialism, which enabled the colonial power to send its enemies to any of its outspread colonies, and partly because of the evolution of human rights, the punishment is multiplied when the same violent acts are committed for a "terrorist" motive. In practice and in theory, determining such a motive will not be possible as long as terrorism is ill-defined. C. A. J. Coady suggests that it is important to have a definition of terrorism that leaves open the possibility of non-terrorist revolutionary violence to occur and be morally legitimate against oppressive governments.[12] However, as long as there are governments that use the anti-terrorist campaign to suppress internal or secessionist opposition, such a suggestion may seem too idealistic, especially in authoritarian regimes like those in the Arab world.

Sedition
Sedition is commonly understood as any politically motivated action, especially in speech or writing, that promotes a rebellion against the government or the socio-economic system. There is no doubt that acts that target the stability of the state and its order are considered serious offenses. However, in Egypt, in order to prevent such serious acts, criminalization is extended to include expressions of ideas that are viewed by the state as dangerous. The problem is that the definition of "dangerous ideas" is not specified; it is left to the state to be determined and applied arbitrarily in each case.

In Egypt, crimes under the umbrella of sedition were regulated in the 1883 Penal Code. According to Article 88 of this code, "whoever speaks out shouting or singing to provoke civil strife [*fitan*] shall be punished with eight days to one-year imprisonment and a fine[.]"[13] This restriction on speech is drawn from Article 23 of the French Press Law of 1881 (mentioned in Chapter 3). Briefly, the French Press Law condemns "speeches, shouts or threats proffered in public places or meetings, or by written words[.]"[14] Both the Egyptian and the French texts leave the door open for the state to tighten freedom of expression and suppress opposing voices. The above Egyptian article, with the exact wording, still exists in the current Penal Code of 1934.[15]

In 1957, Article 102*bis* was added to the Penal Code of 1934,[16] which imposes more restrictions on freedom of expression. It condemns anyone who "deliberately

[12] C. A. J. Coady, "Defining Terrorism" in Igor Primoratz, ed, *Terrorism: The Philosophical Issues* (Basingstoke: Palgrave Macmillan, 2004) at 40.
[13] Article 88 of the Egyptian Penal Code of 1883.
[14] Article 23 of the French Press Law of 1881.
[15] Article 102 of the Egyptian Penal Code of 1934.
[16] Egyptian Law No. 112 of 1957.

diffuses news, data, or false or tendentious rumors, or propagates controversial propaganda, if they disturb public safety or spread terror among people or harm public interest."[17] The article also condemns anyone who "holds prints or publications [. . .] intended for distribution"[18] that aim to disturb public order. The wording of this article is similar to the restriction stated in the British Defence of the Realm Consolidation Act 1914 (DORA) (discussed in Chapter 1). To remind the reader, DORA condemns "the spread of false reports or reports likely to cause disaffection to His Majesty or to interfere with the success of His Majesty's forces by land or sea or to prejudice His Majesty's relations with foreign powers[.]"[19] The *Gold Book of the National Courts* explicitly states that the Egyptian Penal Code of 1881 and its amendments were influenced by the British approach. It states,

> the British influence and mentality appeared clearly in the current Penal Code [of 1904 and as amended in 1923] and its preparation works, including the borrowed quotes from the Indian, Sudanese, and British laws. The British influence, however, did not overturn the [Egyptian] Penal Code, but left it with its origins borrowed from the French law[.][20]

This suggests that the British did not force Egypt to adopt legal provisions from the British law. However, it also suggests that even after the nominal independence of Egypt in 1922, the British represented an influential and perhaps an attractive power to Egypt, which may have influenced their legislation.

As the *Gold Book of the National Courts* suggests, the Egyptian Penal Code continued to reflect its French origin. The restriction on expression in the above Article 102*bis* does not significantly differ from the restriction drawn from the French Press Law mentioned earlier. In addition, the Egyptian Penal Code borrowed the concept of "public order" from the French Law Regarding the State of Siege of 1849 (mentioned in Chapter 1). This law does not clarify the meaning of this concept, but it allows civilians who commit crimes against "public order" to be tried.[21] Protecting public order was restricted to exceptional times, such as the state of siege. However, adding this phrase to the Egyptian Penal Code suggests a normalization of the exception – a theme that is seen in other practices in Egypt, including the endless state of emergency and the application of special courts.

Exceptionalism and Militarism

When Colonel Jamal Abdu Nasser was elected as president, Egypt entered a period of military control, as opposed to rule according to social consensus. In 1954, a new

---

[17] Article 102*bis* of the Penal Code of 1934.
[18] *Ibid.*
[19] Defence of the Realm Consolidation Act as amended on November 27, 1914.
[20] *The Gold Book of the National Courts*, at 10.
[21] Article 8 of French Law Regarding the State of Siege of 1849.

martial law was established that strengthened the military's powers and broadened the military courts' jurisdiction. Several military courts were established by decree. They had vague tasks that allowed the authority to protect itself under the pretext of protecting the public order. Nasser imposed martial law in November 1956 with the outbreak of the Suez Crisis,[22] and reimposed it in 1958 upon the socialist union with Syria.[23] Egypt followed in British footsteps by limiting the use of martial law and replacing it with emergency legislation. The postcolonial Egyptian regime established a new emergency law in 1958[24] that strengthened military power by transferring some of the authority of individual ministers or the cabinet to the military.[25] The following two sections will discuss separately Egypt's use of state of emergency and special courts.

Law No. 162 of 1958 Concerning the State of Emergency

Egypt has a long history of ruling under the exception, whether by martial law or state of emergency. The state of emergency was a useful replacement for martial law, the latter of which was declared during the British occupation of Egypt, especially during World War II.[26] The discontent of Egyptians with martial law paved the way for the adoption of Law No. 162 of 1958 Concerning the State of Emergency (State of Emergency Law), which softened the measures of martial law.[27] Nonetheless, the state of emergency continued to be a problematic measure in suspending the constitution and violating political and civil rights.

A state of emergency was first declared in Egypt in 1958 until 1980.[28] It was declared again a year later, when President Sadat was assassinated by Islamist militants, and was continually renewed for another three decades.[29] The state of emergency was due to expire in 2006, and President Mubarak promised to end it and to replace it with a new anti-terrorism law that was intended to be influenced by the post-9/11 Western approach. Despite this promise, Mubarak declared a state of emergency in 2006, alleging that the anti-terrorism draft law had not been completed.[30] The state of emergency lasted until 2012, after Mubarak left the presidential office. Since then, it has been declared across the country for three months in

---

[22] The Suez Crisis or Suez War was between, on the one hand, Egypt and the Palestinians, and, on the other, Israel, the UK, and France.
[23] Reza, "Endless Emergency," at 536.
[24] Law No. 162 of 1958 Regarding State of Emergency.
[25] See Reza, "Endless Emergency," at 537.
[26] *Ibid*, at 536.
[27] *Ibid*; Brown, *The Rule of Law in the Arab World*, at 83.
[28] Reza, "Endless Emergency," at 536–7.
[29] *Ibid*, 537.
[30] "Egypt and The Impact of 27 Years of Emergency on Human Rights" (May 28, 2008) *Egyptian Organization for Human Rights*, online: web.archive.org.

August 2013,[31] for three months in April 2017 – extended for another three months twice[32] – and is still declared frequently in Sinai.[33]

By law, a declaration of state of emergency must specify the period, the area, and the reason,[34] and must be referred to the People's Assembly for approval.[35] However, practice shows centralization in decisionmaking that mostly leaves declaring a state of emergency solely to the president. According to Article 1 of the State of Emergency Law, a state of emergency may be declared "whenever public safety or order is threatened [. . .] whether because of war or a state threatening the eruption of war, internal disturbances, public [natural] disasters, or the spread of an epidemic."[36] The broad concept of "public order" is borrowed from the French Law Regarding the State of Siege, as mentioned in the previous section regarding the crime of sedition. In addition, the concept of "public safety" is listed in DORA (discussed in Chapter 1). The British adopted DORA during World War I, which justified the broad wording that suits the necessity of war. In reality, however, broad and vague terms are frequently used in Egypt in specifying domestic and peacetime crimes. The Egyptian use of state of emergency has created a *de facto* normalization of the exception in a way that exceeds colonial practice.

The State of Emergency Law grants vast exceptional powers to the president. According to Article 3, upon a declaration of emergency the president may, "by an oral or written order," do the following:

(1) Restrict people's freedom of assembly, movement, residence, or passage in specific times and places; arrest suspects or [persons who are] dangerous to public security and order [and] detain them; allow searches of persons and places without being restricted by the provisions of the Criminal Procedure Code; and assign anyone to perform any of these tasks.

(2) Order the surveillance of letters of any type; supervise censorship; seize journals, newsletters, publications, editorials, cartoons, and any form of expression and advertisement before they are published, and close their publishing places.

(3) Determine the times of opening and closing public shops, and order the closure of some or all of these shops.

---

[31] "Egypt Declares National Emergency" (August 14, 2013) *BBC*, online: www.bbc.com.
[32] Presidential Decree No. 157/2017 issued on April 10, 2017; Presidential Decree No. 510/2017 issued on October 10, 2017.
[33] "President Sisi Extends State of Emergency in North Sinai for 3 Months" (May 4, 2016) *Ahram Online*, online: english.ahram.org.eg.
[34] Article 2 of Egyptian Law No. 162 of 1958 Regarding State of Emergency.
[35] Article 3, *ibid*.
[36] Article 1, *ibid*.

(4) Confiscate any property or building, order the sequestration of companies and corporations, and postpone the due dates of loans for what has been confiscated or sequestrated.

(5) Withdraw licenses of arms, ammunitions, explosive devices, and explosives of all kinds, order their submission, and close arms stores.

(6) Evict some areas or isolate them; regulate means of transport; limit means of transport between different regions.[37]

During the nearly endless state of emergency, practice has shown abusive searching without warrants, systematic practices of indefinite and incommunicado detention, and torture.[38] Reza argues that excluding the application of this law from the provisions of the Criminal Procedure Code, as is stated in the first paragraph, means that there are no limits to authoritarian practices.[39] However, as part of the minor but positive outcomes of the more recent uprising in Egypt, in 2013 the Constructional Court held part of paragraph 1, which granted the president "the power to authorize arresting, detention, and searching people and places without being bound by the provisions of the law Criminal Procedure[,]" to be unconstitutional.[40]

The Application of Special Courts

The State of Emergency Law authorizes the establishment of special courts, which is another form of exceptionalism. According to a presidential decree adopted in 1981, the president has the authority to refer several ordinary crimes to these courts.[41] The decree is a combination of centralization and exceptionalism – an ultimate authoritarianism.

The experience of Egypt in establishing and depending on exceptional courts is unusual. During colonialism, both the British and the Egyptians relied heavily on exceptional courts. These included the 1882 exceptional court to try 'Urabi and those involved in that revolt,[42] the 1884 Commissions of Brigandage under the jurisdiction of the Ministry of the Interior,[43] the special courts to try offenses against

---

[37] Article 3, *ibid.* Translation quoted in Reza, "Endless Emergency," at 538.

[38] "Egypt: Systematic Abuses in the Name of Security" (April 2007) *Amnesty International*, online: amnesty.org/resources/Egypt/pdf/2007_04_amnesty_international_egypt_report.pdf.

[39] Reza, "Endless Emergency," at 538–9.

[40] Constitutional Court, case 17 of 2013, issued on June 2, 2013, *Eastlaws*, online: www.eastlaws.com.

[41] Reza, "Endless Emergency," at 539.

[42] Brown, *The Rule of Law in the Arab World*, at 77.

[43] During and in the aftermath of the 'Urabi revolt, Egypt witnessed an interior distribution and an increasing phenomenon of brigandage; it was the British who took action by arresting 54 brigands. Later, the idea of establishing the Commissions of Brigandage came from the pro-British Prime Minister of Egypt, Nubar Pasha. See Harold Tollefson, *Policing Islam: The British Occupation of Egypt and the Anglo-Egyptian Struggle over Control of the Police, 1882–1914* (London: Greenwood Publishing Group, 1999) at 27–9.

the British army, and the martial law courts established during World War I, all of which had exceptional measures and procedures.[44] After declaring the independence of Egypt in 1922, the Egyptian government responded to British pressure by codifying martial law, which allowed the trial of civilians in military courts.[45]

One might think that the need for exceptional courts would be over by the end of colonialism and the major wars surrounding that period, or that such courts would be exclusive to wartime. However, the experience in Egypt suggests that exceptional courts and exceptional rule like the state of emergency have become the norm rather than the exception in Egypt. While it is true that at one point Egypt faced external threats, mainly from Israel, that period has been over since the signing of mutual peace agreements in 1978. This clinging to exceptional rule requires a deeper look.

Following the 1952 Revolution by the Free Officers Movement and the coup that overthrew the monarchy, the new government did not hesitate in bringing back the old legacy of exceptional rule. Egypt, with its newborn authoritarian regime, avoided the regular courts and instead relied on special courts for sensitive political cases.[46] By avoiding the regular procedures, the regime hoped to achieve quick adjudication in its own favor, which could deter opponents through harsh punishments.

Between 1952 and 1954, four exceptional courts were established.[47] Among them was the People's Court, which was established to try the Muslim Brotherhood for their attempt to assassinate President Nasser.[48] The court's mandate was to try "actions considered as treason against the Motherland or against its safety internally and externally as well as acts considered as directly against the present regime or against the bases of the Revolution."[49] This text sets no limits for interpretation. Its scope could include the members of the Brotherhood as well as Brotherhood sympathizers.

The People's Court had a broad scope.[50] It disregarded the right to appeal and allowed trials *in absentia*.[51] The members of the courts were from the military with no judicial background. Furthermore, trials aimed to embarrass the enemies of the regime rather than to punish wrongdoers; in other words, they were show trials.[52] These show trials, with their overbroad mandate and collective punishment,

---

[44] Brown, *The Rule of Law in the Arab World*, at 77.
[45] Reza, "Endless Emergency," at 535–7.
[46] Brown, *The Rule of Law in the Arab World*, at 77.
[47] These include the Court of Treason; the special court against Egyptian communists; the Court of Revelation; and the People's Court.
[48] Brown, *The Rule of Law in the Arab World*, at 77.
[49] Quoted in *ibid*, at 80.
[50] *Ibid*, at 77.
[51] *Ibid*, at 78–81.
[52] *Ibid*.

managed to deter the "enemy" by targeting individuals and groups based on their associations.

The motive behind the People's Court, according to the account of the American Embassy in Cairo, is that "it had been demonstrated that the Civil Courts could not be trusted to deal adequately with the Muslim Brotherhood and hence the People's Court had to be set up [for another year to] secure the Revolution first."[53] President Nasser alleged that the special courts were a way to avoid involving the judiciary in the new regime's political activity.[54] No judiciary appeal can challenge the special courts' flawed orders. Bringing authorities that initially belong to the judiciary under special courts that function within an executive-like framework established a highly centralized authoritarian government that can arbitrarily suppress its political opponents.

Besides the People's Court, courts-martial were active almost constantly in Egypt from 1952 until 1958. While courts-martial combined judges and military officers, when needed they included military officers only.[55] Judgments were final and not subject to appeal.[56] Nonetheless, the law gave the military governor the right to commute sentences or abolish the verdict.[57] This form of pardon, which individualizes the punishment,[58] grants the military governor more exceptional powers that have little or no impact on correcting the course of justice that is fundamentally breached by special courts.

Similar to courts-martial are State Security Courts,[59] which were established under the 1958 Law of State of Emergency. According to Nathan Brown, the "Law of Emergency is a direct descendant of measures taken by the British during the occupation[.]"[60] This colonial legacy has become an aid and a justification to continue ruling through the exception. In its interpretation of a state of emergency, the Supreme Constitutional Court states that:

> The origin of a state of emergency is that it is not announced except to face serious threats to national interests, or imminent risks that could affect the stability of the state or its security or safety. [...] considering the conditions [of the emergency situation, justify adopting] proper exceptional measures necessary to face the situation. These measures are not necessarily limited to crimes threatening the internal or external state security, but include in many ways of their application other crimes beyond this range, and there is no argument about the danger [of these crimes] and

---

[53] Quoted in *ibid*, at 77.
[54] *Ibid*, at 78.
[55] Article 8 of Law No. 533 of 1954 of the System of Martial Law.
[56] Article 11, *ibid*.
[57] Article 13, *ibid*.
[58] René Lévy, "Pardons and Amnesties as Policy Instruments in Contemporary France" (2007) 36:1 *Crime and Justice* 551 at 552–3.
[59] Article 8 of Law No. 162 of 1958 Regarding State of Emergency.
[60] Brown, *The Rule of Law in the Arab World*, at 112.

the rationale for treating them under the exceptional measures that require quick judgment to deter the offenders and to maintain national safety.[61]

The decision suggests that state security is above the rule of law. This broad understanding is a serious threat to individual rights and long-run state stability. The Egyptian use of special courts suggests a strong attachment to centralization, exceptionalism, and militarism. These qualities, which are noticeable in colonialism, as discussed in Chapter 1, have been absorbed by the Egyptian authoritarian system.

Another special court is the special military court to try Egyptian communists established in 1953.[62] Little has been published about this court since its verdicts remain confidential.[63] However, ordinary courts have tried many other communist cases, some of which are examined in the following section. Ordinary courts are supposed to grant suspects a fair trial with criminal procedure guarantees; however, the fact that the applicable law is politicized with vague wording could undermine the role of courts in delivering justice.

THE EMERGENCE OF THE TERM "TERROR" DURING
THE WAR ON COMMUNISM

During the monarchy and the early stages of the newborn Republic, communism was considered a serious threat to the state, as described in Chapter 3. The threat of communists was in their organized civil acts aiming to overthrow the government and change the political system. The importance of these cases is in showing two major things: the early use of the term "terror" and its relation to group identity rather than wrongdoing, and the inefficiency of ordinary courts as long as the penal code is exceptionally broad.

Communism was a common threat to Western empires as well as Arab regimes. The large volume of material regarding Anglo-Egyptian history and law does not provide detailed indications of colonial pressure to adopt suppressive measures against communists. Nonetheless, there is evidence of colonial influence to be drawn from the similarities in the legislation. Furthermore, the period of British involvement in Egypt was one of virtually continual difficulty in keeping order, and British influence over Egyptian officials in terms of amending the Penal Code is difficult to detect in the available documents – the Foreign Office officials must have been far too clever to commit anything overt to paper. However, the following discussion avoids making assumptions about the existence of external influence in this regard and will examine this period in accordance with the available material.

[61] جلسة 30 يناير سنة 1993, الطلب رقم 1 لسنة 15 , أحكام المحكمة الدستورية العليا
    [January 30, 1993, request 1/15, Part 5 no. 2, High Constitutional Court Decisions] *Moha-moon*, online: www.mohamoon-ju.net.
[62] Brown, *The Rule of Law in the Arab World*, at 78.
[63] *Ibid.*

The related national security laws suggest a strong tendency toward an authoritarian and centralized form of ruling. While the Egyptian Penal Code does not mention the term "communism," the code was written in general and vague language that ensured the protection of the dominant groups in power. This can be observed in Article 98(b), which was added in 1946. It states that:

> Shall be punished for a period not exceeding five years and a fine not less than fifty Pounds and not exceeding five hundred Pounds whoever promoted in the Egyptian Republic in any way to change the fundamental principles of the constitution or the basic systems of the social body, or to dominate one social class, or to overthrow the state's fundamental social or economic system, or to destroy any system of the fundamental systems of the social body when the use of force or terror or any other illegal means is noticeable.[64]

This article was established during the monarchy, which adopted capitalism as it was introduced by imperial and colonial powers. Therefore, any call to change the economic system, especially by communists, was a threat to several dominant groups: the ruling class represented by the Egyptian monarchy, capitalists represented by both the Egyptian landowners and merchants and the European corporations, and lastly the colonial power and its political interests. Joel Beinin and Zachary Lockman argue that the Egyptian monarchy was so tyrannical that it did not consider Egyptian workers as a class that deserved rights. Instead, it suppressed any threat to the ruling class and the British colonist.[65] Even though these dominant groups had different priorities, they shared a common enemy: communism. In their eyes, this justified the war on communism that took place in special and military courts as well as in regular courts.

For example, in a case during the monarchy, the Court of Cassation upheld the conviction of the defendants for several acts: unlawful association, sedition, and the use of violence and terror. The verdict states that:

> [First,] the defendants joined an organization that aims to dominate one social class over the others, and to end a social class and overthrow the state's fundamental social and economic systems [. . .] and *the use of force and terror were noticeable* [. . . . The defendants] joined a secret organization that works on eliminating the capitalist class and [ensuring] the dominion of the working class [. . .] along the lines of the Russian revolutionary style adopted by Lenin and Stalin by instigating workers to assault and violate others' rights to work and instigating them against some owners and capitalists in a way that disturbs the public peace. And second, [they] promoted in the Egyptian monarchy to change the fundamental constitutional principles [. . .] with the use of

---

[64] Article 98(b) of the Egyptian Penal Code added by Law No. 117 of 1946.
[65] Joel Beinin & Zachary Lockman, *Workers on the Nile: Nationalism, Communism, Islam, and the Egyptian Working Class, 1882–1954* (Cairo: American University in Cairo Press, 1998) at 350.

force, terror, and illegal means [. . .] by issuing bulletins, forming cells, and promoting ideas [encouraging] the rule of the working class.[66] [emphasis added]

The court's interpretation of the meaning of "terror" was that it was not a distinctive crime, but a method used to commit criminal wrongdoing. This can be understood from the language used in Articles 98(a)[67] and 98(b),[68] which condemn attempts to overthrow the state's social or economic system with "the use of force or terror or any other illegal means noticeable." Thus, in order to consider the organization illegal, or, as it was labeled, "subversive," two conditions had to be met. The first is related to the objective of the crime, and the second to the means. The objective is to destroy the capitalist class and replace it with another. As for the means, which I will focus on, there must be a noticeable use of force, terror, or any other illegal means. The court defines the meaning of "use of force" as "all means of physical violence over people or the threat to use weapons." It defines "terror" as "all means of pressure, damage, sabotage, or obstructing facilities." While each of these terms needs to be defined, the court went further by leaving open the meaning of "other illegal means," stating that "it is not necessary for the other illegal means to reach a limit of a crime."[69]

The earlier verdicts show that the court condemned defendants based on the argument that communism as it is practiced in Russia calls for the use of force. As a result, the court did not look into whether or not there was an actual use of force in each case, especially considering broad clauses like "other illegal means," which do not require the use of violence. Consequently, freedom of expression and association were tightened based on the assumption that these groups were dangerous. When defendants argued that their actions were not associated with the use of force, the court dismissed this argument, claiming that the use of force or terror are not part of the crime, but aggravating circumstances. According to the court, "considering the explanatory notes, the use of force, terror, or illegal means are not part of the elements of this crime [. . . It] is not required to be mentioned explicitly in the text [of Article 98(a)*bis*] to use force, violence, or terror, which are considered by the legislature as aggravating circumstances."[70] "Terror" while not considered a crime by itself, was linked to acts that aim to overthrow the government or change the system. The early use of the term "terror" at the legal level was to protect the regime, not necessarily from violent acts, but from civil acts that included speech and meetings.

[66] جلسة 11 مارس سنة 1952 (208)، القضية رقم 419 سنة 21 القضائية, أحكام النقض
[March 11, 1952 (208), case no. 419/21, appealing decisions] *Mohamoon*, online: www .mohamoon-ju.net.
[67] Egyptian Penal Code 1937.
[68] Added to the Egyptian Penal Code by Law No. 117 of 1946.
[69] جلسة 12 من فبراير سنة 1987، (38) الطعن رقم 5903 لسنة 56 القضائية
[February 12, 1987, (38) appeal no. 5903/56] *Mohamoon*, online: www.mohamoon-ju.net.
[70] *Ibid.*

The use of terror as an aggravating circumstance allowed the punishment to be increased from five years' imprisonment to hard labor.[71] Despite the political nature of communist activities, Egyptian authorities treated communists neither as political criminals nor as ordinary criminals. They received harsher punishments, and were not granted pardon. For instance, in the aftermath of the Egyptian Revolution of 1952 that abolished the monarchy, political prisoners were released. However, communists were not included because communism was a "social crime."[72] This makes communists fit best in the category of "enemies" rather than criminals.

The monarchy and its supporter the British had common interests in suppressing the emerging labor class that threatened the imperial order. However, when the carried out against communism. This observation requires a deeper look. Unlike the monarchy, President Nasser was a socialist who supported the working class and the peasants. He succeeded in introducing socialist principles into the constitution, not only of Egypt, but also of many other Arab states. This can be noticed in Article 98*bis*(a) of the Penal Code, which was added in 1956.[73] This article provides protection to socialist principles by condemning "acting against the fundamental principles underpinning the socialist system of the country."[74] The vague wording reflects the same mindset characteristic of the monarchy, except that it protects "socialist principles" instead of capitalism.

A judiciary decision issued during Nasser's era confirms the same exaggerating tendencies of the monarchy against communism. The Court of Cassation states that the threat of communism is derived from

> [its] principles that [. . .] absolutely are not consistent with the fundamental social system settled in Egypt that is based on respecting faith, family, and freedom of interaction [. . . The organization's] goals cannot be obtained [. . .] in any country without the use of force and violence.[75]

This decision creates a subjective modality that allows communists to be accused of being violent even when violence is not used. It exceeds the colonial rationale, which allowed political and exceptional regulations to be applied during periods of martial law, by normalizing vagueness within the criminal law.

With the gradual fading of the threat of communism, the Egyptian Court shifted its view by rejecting the accusation of suspects for mere membership in a communist movement. In 1986, the court issued a remarkable precedent stating that

---

[71] Article 98(a) of Egyptian Penal Code of 1937.
[72] Tareq Y. Ismael, *The Communist Movement in Egypt, 1920–1988* (New York: Syracuse University Press, 1990) at 73.
[73] Law No. 68 of 1956.
[74] Article 98*bis*(a) of the Egyptian Penal Code.
[75] جلسة 28 من مايو سنة 1956, (217) القضية رقم 470 سنة 26 قضائية, أحكام النقض.
    [May 28, 1956 (217) case no. 470/26, appealing decisions] *Mohamoon*, online: www.mohamoon-ju.net.

The defendants' announcing in itself that they are Marxists does not support the [Prosecution's] argument that their principle is the use of force and violence to achieve their goals; but [being Marxist] only refers to their political and economic views"[76]

In practice, this precedent was far from perfect. The court then charged the defendants with sedition. It states that:

The defendants held many of the prints that include [anti-regime] ideas in a large amount, which conclusively indicates that [the defendants] had prepared them for distribution. [...] The Court investigated the content of these prints and concluded that they aim to change the basic principles of the Constitution [...] so that a social class dominates over others, or [they aim] to change the fundamental social and economic system of the State.[77]

The verdict shows that the crime of sedition can be used flexibly against opponents. This flexibility is derived from colonial exceptional and military principles such as "minimum use of force" that do not precisely identify the boundary of applying such principles. The court's broad interpretation of these vague crimes normalizes the exception at a judicial level, which closes the door to unfairly convicted people to challenge the system. Such practices belong to "enemy criminal law"[78] that treats convicted people as second-class citizens who enjoy no basic rights.

Another important point is regarding evidence in criminal trials. The court shows its acceptance of intelligence testimony without requiring examining the testimony of the source, or, as the witness is referred to in this case, the "guide":

It is clear from reviewing the witness [the guide] testimony regarding the truth of the defendant, [the guide] ended up being confident that the defendant has undertaken criminal activities and that his frequent visits to other homes listed in the search warrant [... are] criminal communications inciting opposition protests.[79]

The use of intelligence in the war on communism has its origins in colonial practice. The experience shows that British intelligence was established in Egypt to

---

[76] February 12, 1987 (38) appeal no. 5903/56.

[77] *Ibid.*

[78] Enemy criminal law or *Feindstrafrecht* is a concept promoted by the German scholar Günther Jakobs, which classifies wrongdoers into two categories: criminals and enemies. Accordingly, anti-terrorism laws do not deal with criminals (citizens), but rather with enemies. Enemies lose their citizenship rights because they do not respect their duties. The enemy in this concept includes individuals who belong to groups that represent extreme threat, or, more precisely, those who are viewed as a source of extreme danger. Carlos Gómez-Jara Díez, "Enemy Combatants versus Enemy Criminal Law: An Introduction to the European Debate Regarding Enemy Criminal Law and Its Relevance to the Anglo-American Discussion on the Legal Status of Unlawful Enemy Combatants" (2008) 11:4 *New Criminal Law Review: International and Interdisciplinary Journal* 529 at 530–62.

[79] March 11, 1952 (208) case no. 419/21, appealing decisions.

track the communist movement. In 1921, the British appointed Major G. W. Courtney as head of the Secret Intelligence Service in Cairo, primarily to monitor communist movements.[80] After independence, Egypt followed in the footsteps of the British by relying heavily on secret intelligence to identify communist members even before they had committed any harmful offense. In this regard, court verdicts show that the evidence presented by the secret intelligence service was accepted without cross-examination, and the identity of the witnesses was surrounded with confidentiality that even the judge could not breach. For example, the following judgment states that:

> The political intelligence men (el qalam esiyasi) were monitoring the accused who frequently visited houses in different neighborhoods aiming to transfer the instructions to the leaders of the communist movement and its members. The monitoring continued [...] in order to identify the main center of the organization and to figure out the members of the communist cell[.][81]

The verdict shows that conviction was based on identity rather than criminal conduct, and that mere previous accusation could be used against anti-government opponents. It states:

> [The accused] intended to contact Mustafa Abbas Fahmi who was known for his communist activities, and who was previously accused in case no. 478 Military High Court in 1949, and was acquitted.[82]

Unfair accusations could result from such assumptions, especially with the knowledge that during the war on communism, the Egyptian government offered a financial reward to anyone who revealed information about communist activities.[83]

Furthermore, the Egyptian Court states in another verdict that "it does not affect the procedure if the identity of the source remains unknown."[84] The use of undisclosed witnesses affects the fairness of the trial and breaches the principle of equality of arms, in which each party has access to the evidence against him. As we will see later, this fundamental principle is violated by law in the current Egyptian and Tunisian anti-terrorism laws.

The communist wave in Egypt gradually dissolved with the diminishing of the global influence of communism. Later, the growing power and influence of Islamic extremists led to a shift in national and international efforts in the war on terror. Legislation and judicial practice directed against communism show some of the same tendencies of current anti-terrorism legislation.

[80] Keith Jeffery, MI6: The History of the Secret Intelligence Service 1909–1949 (New York: Penguin Press, 2010) at 206–7.
[81] March 11, 1952 (208) case no. 419/21, appealing decisions, 591.
[82] Ibid.
[83] جلسة 3 فبراير سنة 1959, (30) الطعن رقم 1013 لسنة 28 القضائية, أحكام النقض
[February 3, 1959 (30) appeal no. 1013/28] Mohamoon, online: www.mohamoon-ju.net.
[84] Ibid.

THE EGYPTIAN ANTI-TERRORISM APPROACH IN A NEO-COLONIAL ERA: THE PEAK OF AUTHORITARIANISM

Terrorism as a distinctive crime was only added to the Egyptian Penal Code in 1992, a few years before the adoption of the Arab Convention. This amendment to the Penal Code did not make a significant difference to the course of justice or the internal security for two reasons. First, the Penal Code already had many broad articles that could be applied flexibly against suspects. Second, the endless state of emergency allowed "terrorists" to be referred to special and military courts.[85] The already existing exceptional laws and measures related to national security paved the way for more draconian anti-terrorism laws. This section examines the overall policy of counter-terrorism by focusing on the constitutional amendments that affirmed exceptionalism and centralization.

In 2005, the Egyptian authorities announced their intention to establish a new anti-terrorism law.[86] The law purported to implement by the post-9/11 Western anti-terrorism laws[87] and to replace the state of emergency.[88] It is not clear whether the Egyptian intention is to follow the model set by the United Kingdom and other democracies, which adopt broad definitions that seem to continually serve their political interests rather than crime control and security, or whether the intention is to include human rights safeguards, however minimal.

The anti-terrorism experience of several Arab states, such as Egypt, Syria, Jordan and Bahrain, shows that states of emergency have been enforced under the pretext of combating terrorism. During such periods, most of the constitution's norms were suspended and a set of national security measures were enforced, including the establishment of military courts. These forms, which are supposed to be exceptional, became endless in some countries, including Egypt. A tactic that Arab executives take is to put pressure on the parliament to pass a broad anti-terrorism bill in return for abolition of, for instance, the state of emergency. In 1991, this tactic was used in Jordan, in which in order to cancel most provisions of martial law,[89] which had been imposed multiple times since 1957 and continuously enacted from 1970 to 1991, the parliament had to pass an amendment to the law on the State Security Court to ensure the court's jurisdiction over national security cases.[90] The alleged reason for

---

[85] Ahmed Mahmoud, "Egypt's Long History of Military Trials" (September 25, 2011) *Al-Ahram Online*, online: english.ahram.org.eg.

[86] Welchman, "Rocks, Hard Places and Human Rights," at 636.

[87] Roach, *The 9/11 Effect*, at 87.

[88] Nathan J. Brown, Michele Dunne & Amr Hamzawy, "Egypt's Controversial Constitutional Amendments" (March 23, 2007) *Carnegie Endowment for International Peace*, at 2.

[89] "Jordan Cancels Most Martial Law Rules" (July 8, 1991) *New York Times*, online: www.nytimes.com.

[90] Tujan Faisel, "qanoon mukafahat elrhab fi alordon: lawb da'e" ["Counter-terrorism Law in Jordan: Lost Game"] *Aljazeera Net*, online: www.aljazeera.net/opinions/pages/cdff9c16-becc-4611-8092-e6611e67736c.

keeping this special court was to avoid a legislation vacuum. This approach affirms a duality in crime control: terrorism is countered through the exception, whether through the state of emergency or by law, while all other crimes are dealt with under the umbrella of the penal code and criminal law principles. The use of special courts in Egypt was advanced by Mubarak's Presidential Decree No. 375 of 1992, which granted the president the authority to transfer terrorist cases to military courts.[91]

In 2013, Egypt's intention to enact a new anti-terrorism law that would replace the state of emergency was taken seriously after a series of terrorist attacks claimed to be carried out by the Brotherhood in the aftermath of the withdrawal of President Morsi and the army's takeover. The Brotherhood was immediately accused of these attacks before any investigation was started. Such accusations are built on a previous political and social judgment that the Brotherhood is a violent organization that aims to destroy public and social order.

At the constitutional level, in 2007 an article regarding the state's role in countering terrorism was introduced to the 1923 constitution. It excludes counter-terrorism laws and measures from ordinary criminal procedures and constitutional guarantees regarding arrest, preventive detention, search, and monitoring. It also grants the president the right to refer terrorist cases to any judiciary body, including military courts.[92] Article 179 states that:

> The State shall seek to safeguard public security and discipline to counter dangers of terror. The law shall, under the supervision of the judiciary, regulate special provisions related to evidence and investigation procedures stipulated in paragraph 1 of Article 41 and 44, and paragraph 2 of Article 45 shall in no way preclude such counter-terror action.
>
> The President may refer any terror crime to any judicial body stipulated in the Constitution or in law.[93]

The essence of this constitutional amendment is similar to the regulations of the endless state of emergency that was enacted over the last decades, and which allowed suspension of constitutional rights and activation of special and military courts.[94] According to the UN Special Rapporteur on Counter-terrorism and Human Rights, Martin Scheinin, "article 179 of the Constitution carries features of a permanent state of emergency, although under a new name."[95] Article 179

---

[91] Michael Farhang, "Recent Development: Terrorism and Military Trials in Egypt: Presidential Decree No. 375 and the Consequences for Judicial Authority" (1994) 35:225 *Harvard International Law Journal* 225 at 232.

[92] Article 179 of the 2007 amendment to the 1923 Egyptian Constitution.

[93] Translation quoted from United Nations Office on Drugs and Crime website, online: www .unodc.org/tldb/pdf/Egypt_const_1971.pdf.

[94] Welchman, "Rocks, Hard Places and Human Rights," at 636; Brown, Dunne & Hamzawy, "Egypt's Controversial Constitutional Amendments," at 2.

[95] UN Human Rights Office of the High Commissioner, Report of the Special Rapporteur on the promotion and protection of human rights and fundamental freedoms while countering terrorism, Martin Scheinin. Mission to Egypt (October 14, 2009).

demonstrates exceptionalism and dualism in dealing with domestic peacetime situations – terrorists are second-class citizens treated outside the umbrella of ordinary law.

The Egyptian Revolution of 2011 resulted in the overthrow of the 1923 constitution. The hope was to adopt a new constitution that did not use the war on terror as a pretext to enact a state of emergency and suspend rights and liberties. In an attempt to meet that hope, on March 30, 2011 the Supreme Council of the Armed Forces of Egypt adopted a Constitutional Declaration, which restricts the authority's ability to enact a state of emergency. It requires the approval of the majority of parliament members, limits the period of state of emergency to three months, and allows an extension once after the approval of two-thirds of the parliament members. These requirements were included in the Constitution of 2012[96] and the current Constitution of 2014.[97]

Adopting a new constitution after the "Arab Spring" suggests that the old constitutions no longer reflect the political and socioeconomic desires of the current generation of Egyptians. Nonetheless, the issue is not with the constitutions or their aims as a whole, but in the clauses their authors include that allow them to back out of their promised obligations. For instance, Article 237 of the Constitution of 2014 brought back the substance of Article 179, which was introduced to the constitution in 2007. The new article obliges the state to counter terrorism by stipulating that:

> The state commits to fighting all types and forms of terrorism and tracking its sources of funding within a specific time frame in light of the threat it represents to the nation and citizens, with guarantees for public rights and freedoms. The law organizes the provisions and procedures of fighting terrorism, and fair compensation for the damages resulting from it and because of it.[98]

The above article is the latest constitutional foundation that allows the state to justify its war on terror. It should be noted that this article follows the international obligations set by UN Security Council Resolution 1373 (2001). However, problems remain in the broad definition and the draconian measures that Egypt continues to adopt in the name of protecting society from terrorism.

More constitutional reforms were made in 2014 to suppress Islamists. Article 74 states that "no political parties may be formed on the basis of religion [...] or on a sectarian basis[.]"[99] This restriction on associations has raised many questions, especially because several Islamic political parties exist in Egypt, such as al-Wasat

---

[96] Article 148 of the Egyptian Constitution of 2012.
[97] Article 154 of the Egyptian Constitution of 2014.
[98] Article 237 of the Egyptian Constitution of 2014. Translation quoted in *International IDEA*, online: constituteproject.org.
[99] Article 74 of the 2014 Egyptian Constitution. This article was first included in the Egyptian constitution during Mubarak's rule in 2007.

and al-Nour. One Egyptian professor of constitutional law argues that this article will not affect the existence of parties since none of the existing parties includes religious clauses in their platforms.[100] However, there is a concern that this article will be interpreted differently based on the authority's view.

Following the removal of President Morsi in July 2013, the Egyptian authorities released a draft of a new anti-terrorism law. Unsurprisingly, the draft law included broad definitions and subjective regulations that could violate basic rights and freedoms. Despite the concerns that this draft has created, President el-Sisi ignored most of the criticism and issued Anti-Terrorism Law No. 94 of 2015.[101]

EVALUATING THE EGYPTIAN ANTI-TERRORISM LEGISLATION

Although Egypt adopted the new Anti-Terrorism Law No. 94 in 2015, this law did not include a statement on abolishing the previous laws. This may create a contradiction between the pieces of legislation. Since the previous anti-terrorism regulations adopted in 1992 are still active, I use a chronological order in examining these laws. This section starts by examining Law No. 97 of 1992, which was added to the Penal Code of 1937, followed by Law No. 8 of 2015 Regarding Regulating Terrorist Entities and Terrorists, and finally the most recent legislation, Anti-terrorism Law No. 94 of 2015. Additional focus is given to the latter law, which discusses the definition of terrorism, speech related to terrorism, terrorism financing, and procedural regulations.

Law No. 97 of 1992 (Penal Code)

Egypt considers itself one of "the first states to deal with the phenomenon of terrorism and its causes[.]"[102] In 1992, Egypt decided to criminalize terrorism within its Penal Code by adopting Law No. 97 of 1992.[103] According to the Parliamentary Report on the Penal Code, there was no necessity to adopt a separate law since "the Penal Code is the overall law of criminalizing and sentencing in Egypt, as well as incorporating the general rules that apply to all crimes."[104] Despite this claim, practice suggests that terrorist cases were excluded from the umbrella of criminal law and procedures. This legislation introduced a definition of terrorism, and

---

[100] "Ghmood hawla maser alhzab esiyasiya fi M'ser" ["*Vagueness around the Destiny of Islamic Parties in Egypt after the Constitutional Ban*"] (December 1, 2013) *Al Arabiya*, online: www .alarabiya.net.
[101] Egyptian Anti-Terrorism Law No. 94 of 2015. *Official Gazette*, 33*bis*, August 15, 2015.
[102] Egypt's CTC Report 2001.
[103] Law No. 97 of 1992. This legislation added new articles to the Penal Code and amended other laws including the Code of Criminal Procedures, the Law Regarding State Security Courts, the Law Regarding the Confidentiality of Bank Accounts, and the Law Regarding Weapons and Explosives.
[104] Preamble to *ibid.*

toughened punishments for terrorist acts, for which the death penalty is set for several acts that do not necessarily cause death.[105] Terrorism is defined in Article 86 as follows:

> [A]ny use of force or violence or threat or intimidation resorted to by the perpetrator in implementation of an individual or collective criminal undertaking aimed at disturbing public order or jeopardizing the safety and security of society, which is of such nature as to harm persons or sow fear among them or imperil their lives, liberty or security; or of such a nature as to damage the environment, or to damage, occupy or take over communications, transport, property, buildings or public or private realty; or to prevent or impede the exercise of their functions by public authorities or places of worship or institutions of learning; or to thwart the application of the Constitution or the laws or regulations.[106]

This definition is based on three elements. The first is the means, which include the use of force, violence, threat, or terror, none of which is clearly defined. The second is the objective, which relies on the individual or collective criminal project. The third is the result, which is disturbing public order, terrifying society, or any of the outcomes referred to by the unclear phrases used. The law lacks a clear and objective determination of the meaning of its terms and clauses, which makes the intent of the legislature and the utility of the law unclear.

Egypt has long borrowed clauses from other, particularly French, legislation. The question is whether Egypt borrowed the above definition of terrorism or its elements, and if so from where? Considering the timing, which is long after the end of colonialism and well before 9/11, it is challenging to find a conclusive answer to this question, especially since no Arab writer has addressed it. However, a general observation is that Egypt continues to counter terrorism with the same centralizing approach that it borrowed from France. A heavy reliance on centralizing powers in counter-terrorism is noticeable in the current French experience of counter-terrorism.

France has progressively adopted several anti-terrorism laws, including Act No. 86–1020 of September 9, 1986 on action against terrorism, amended in 2012, which outlines the judicial authorities and procedures for dealing with terrorism crimes. France also adopted several amendments in the aftermath of 9/11.[107] Yet the definition of terrorism is regulated within the Penal Code, having been added to the Penal Code in 1996 and 1998.[108] This means that the French definition cannot be the source of the 1992 Egyptian definition. According to Article 421–1 of the French

---

[105] Article 86*bis*(c), *ibid.*
[106] Article 86, *ibid.* Translation quoted in Welchman, "Rocks, Hard Places and Human Rights," at 634.
[107] French Act No. 2001–1062 of November 15, 2001 on Everyday Security; Act No. 2003–239 of March 18, 2003 on Internal Security; Act No. 2004–204 of March 9, 2004 Bringing Justice into Line with New Patterns of Crime.
[108] Act No. 96–647 of July 22, 1996; Act No. 98–348 of May 11, 1998. See [French] Criminal Codes, *Legislationline*, online: www.legislationline.org/documents/section/criminal-codes/country/30.

Penal Code, offenses constitute acts of terrorism when "committed intentionally in connection with an individual or collective undertaking the purpose of which is seriously to disturb public order through intimidation or terror."[109] Acts considered to be terrorism include, among other acts, attacks on life and the physical integrity of persons, unlawful detention, hijacking of planes, theft, extortion, destruction, defacement and damage, computer offenses, transport of weapons, and money-laundering offenses. The French definition is less complex than the Egyptian, but it can be equally flexible.

Earlier French penal statutes include several phrases that allow a flexible interpretation and application of its regulations. For instance, the French Penal Code of 1810 uses the phrase "disturbances of public order" (*des Troubles apportés à l'ordre public*).[110] The same phrase is used in the French Law Regarding the State of Siege of 1849 (mentioned in Chapter 1). It should be noted that these codes were not directly transplanted into Egypt, but had a great influence over European and non-European territories, including the Ottoman Empire and Egypt. The current French definition of terrorism includes this clause by criminalizing the aim "to seriously disturb public order through intimidation or terror."[111] The vague concept of "disturbing public order" can be found repeatedly in the Egyptian and most Arab penal and penal-related statutes.[112]

Another concept that is used in the Egyptian definition of terrorism is "thwart[ing] the application of the Constitution." This concept can be traced back to the French 1810 Penal Code, which had a section titled "Crimes and Delicts against the Constitutions of the Empire" (*Crimes et délits contre les constitutions de l'Empire*). This Napoleonic concept criminalized, for example, conspiracies. It condemned individuals and public officers "concerted against the execution of the laws, or against the orders of the government."[113]

This short review of the Napoleonic and current French statutes does not directly answer the above question regarding the source of the Egyptian definition of terrorism, but it shows some similarities between the French and Egyptian punitive models. Similarly to France, the 1992 Egyptian anti-terrorism law was regulated by the Penal Code, and it remained that way until 2015. Also similarly to France, Egypt created a special judicial system and minimal procedures to deal with terrorist cases. While France abandoned some of the Napoleonic concepts, Egypt still clings to that

---

[109] Article 421–1 of the French Penal Code of Act No. 96–647 of July 22, 1996.
[110] Section III of the French Penal Code of 1810. English translation quoted in *The Napoleon Series*, online: www.napoleon-series.org/research/government/france/penalcode/c_penalcode .html.
[111] Article 421–22 of Act No. 1996–647 of July 22, 1996, Article 2 Official Journal July 23, 1996; Act No. 2004–204 of March 9, 2004, Article 8 Official Journal March 10, 2004.
[112] For instance, Article 21 (3) of the Kuwaiti Law No. 3 of 2006 regarding the Press and Publications; Article 1 of the Bahraini Law No. 58 of 2006 regarding Protecting Society from Terrorist Acts.
[113] Articles 123 and 124 of the French Penal Code of 1810.

imperial approach to crime control. On the other hand, the post-9/11 wave of legal modifications has been applied in both countries, especially regulating terrorism financing (this aspect of counter-terrorism financing is discussed below in the section on Anti-Terrorism Law No. 94 of 2015). Nonetheless, Egypt exceeded all national anti-terrorism laws by adopting an extremely broad definition and draconian measures.

Egyptian Law No. 97 of 1992 lists a set of ordinary crimes that can be treated harshly if terror was used as one of their means. These include establishing illegal organizations, membership in these organizations, and promoting and inciting terrorism. Article 86*bis* states that:

Shall be punished by imprisonment whoever establishes, founds, organizes or directs, in violation of the law, an association or body or organization or group or gang, the purpose of which is to call by any means for thwarting the provisions of the Constitution or the laws or preventing one of the government institutions or public authorities from exercising its functions, or attacking the personal freedom of the citizen or other public rights and freedoms guaranteed by the Constitution and the law, or harming national unity or social peace.

Shall be punished by hard labor whoever, with the knowledge of the purpose for which it calls, holds any kind of leadership within it, or supplies it with material or financial provisions.

Shall be punished by prison for a period not exceeding five years whosoever joins one of the associations, bodies, organizations, groups or gangs, with his knowledge of its purpose [...]

[... and] whoever promotes by saying, writing, or any other means for the purposes mentioned in the first paragraph [...] or holds publications or recordings promoting what has been stated, if it was prepared for distribution.[114]

This article condemns mere membership in illegal associations, even if violence has not been used.[115] Many individuals were detained and faced trials for belonging to NGOs that were not accurately registered to work in Egypt,[116] a pretext that Egypt used to weaken human rights groups. This article imposes high restrictions on the freedom of expression by criminalizing all forms of expression that "promote" almost anything the state conceives as illegal. This has led to the arrests and prosecutions of not only Islamic extremist members, but also journalists, demonstrators, and academics for their peaceful expression of their views.[117]

The danger of Law No. 97 of 1992 is increased by the tough penalties set by Article 86*bis*(a), which imposes life imprisonment or death if any of these illegal

---

[114] Article 86*bis* of Law No. 97 of 1992.
[115] Welchman, "Rocks, Hard Places and Human Rights," at 635.
[116] "Egypt: High Price of Dissent: Journalists, Protesters, Academics Charged over Speech Offenses" (February 19, 2014) *Human Rights Watch*, online: www.pri.org/stories/2013-01-25/egyptian-lawyer-trial-working-illegal-organization.
[117] *Ibid.*

associations adopts terrorism as a means to achieve its goals.[118] Hundreds of individuals were referred to military courts, accused of establishing and belonging to an illegal organization that used terrorism to achieve its objectives.[119] With this broad definition of terrorism, accusations can be easily fabricated against political opponents who do not necessarily carry out any violent acts.[120]

As well as the broad definition of terrorism and the harsh treatment of illegal associations that use terrorism as a means to their ends, Law No. 97 of 1992 treats other ordinary crimes as terrorism if committed for a "terrorist objective." For instance, Article 160[121] condemns disturbing religious celebrations or damaging buildings dedicated to religious practices or any religious symbols. Such acts are considered misdemeanors,[122] whereas if the same acts are committed for a terrorist objective they are considered felonies.[123] The same principle is applied in Articles 216–219, which consider making or using fraudulent traveling tickets or false names in renting hotel rooms as misdemeanors, but consider the same acts as felonies if used for a terrorist objective.[124] For some scholars, this terrorist objective is what makes terrorism a distinctive crime compared with ordinary ones,[125] yet there is a problem, particularly in Egyptian law, in the lack of a clear definition of the criminal term "terrorism" and other related terms like "terrorist objective."

Law No. 8 of 2015 Regarding Regulating Terrorist Entities and Terrorists

In December 2013, a terrorist attack was carried out against Dakahlia Governorate's Directorate of Security, northeast of Cairo. This attack resulted in the killing of 16 people and injuring of about 150 persons. The Council of Ministers responded by listing the Muslim Brotherhood, who did not claim responsibility for the attack but were assumed to be responsible, as a terrorist entity. A debate followed about the legal status of this listing. No explanation was provided by the Council of Ministers, and the debate was ended two years later when President el-Sisi issued

[118] Article 86*bis*(a) of Egyptian Law No. 97 of 1992.
[119] "Egypt: 7,400 Civilians Tried in Military Courts" (April 13, 2016) *Human Rights Watch*, online: https://www.hrw.org/news/2016/04/13/egypt-7400-civilians-tried-military-courts; "Trials of Civilians in Military Courts Violate International Law Executions Continue, No Appeal of Death Sentences to Higher Court" (July 3, 1993) *Human Rights Watch*, online: www.hrw.org/report/1993/07/02/egypt-trials-civilians-military-courts-violate-international-law/executions.
[120] Welchman, "Rocks, Hard Places and Human Rights," at 635.
[121] Egyptian Penal Code as amended by Law No. 97 of 1992.
[122] The punishment shall be a fine, imprisonment for no more than three years, or both. Article 160 of the Penal Code.
[123] The punishment shall be imprisonment for no more than five years. *ibid.*
[124] Penal Code as amended by Law No. 97 of 1992.
[125] Ben Saul, *Defining Terrorism in International Law* (New York: Oxford University Press, 2008), at 60–1.

Law No. 8 of 2015 Regarding Regulating Terrorist Entities and Terrorists (Terrorist Entities Law).[126]

This law establishes two terms: "terrorist entities" and "terrorist." The term "terrorist entities" is defined as:

> Any association, organization, group, gang, cell, or other entity whatever its legal or actual status, that practices or aims to call for by any means inside or outside the country to harm people, sow fear among them, or imperil their lives, liberty or security; or of such a nature as to damage the environment, natural resources, antiquities, financial resources, institutions, public or private property, or occupy or seize them, or prevent or obstruct public authorities or judicial bodies, governmental interests, local units, places of worship, hospitals or institutions of learning, or diplomatic and consular missions in Egypt from the exercise of all or some of their activities, or resist [them], or disrupt public or private transportation, or prevent, endanger or interrupt its movement; *or if it aims to disturb public order, endanger society's safety, interests, or security; or thwart the application of the Constitution or the laws*, or prevent any of the state's institutions or any of the public authorities from practicing their duties; or violate citizens' personal freedoms, or the other freedoms and rights granted by the constitution or by law; or harm national unity, social peace, or national security.[127] [emphasis added]

The term "terrorist" is defined as:

> Each natural person who commits, attempts to commit, incites, threatens, or plans inside [Egypt] or abroad a terrorist crime by any means even individually, or contributes to a joint criminal enterprise, or takes command, leadership, management, creation or establishment, or becomes a member of any of the terrorist entities stipulated in Article 1 of this law, or funds or participates in its acts with knowledge of [its purposes].[128]

Both definitions implicitly define terrorist crimes. They contain ambiguous terms that may be interpreted subjectively, such as "public order," "harm national unity," and "endanger the society's safety." These terms represent a repeated theme in the Egyptian national security laws. The Terrorist Entities Law is similar to Anti-Terrorism Law No. 97 of 1992, which both treat as terrorist acts harming people, damaging the environment or natural resources, public and private property, places of worship, and disturbing public order. In addition, both criminalize mere membership in a terrorist organization. This suggests that authoritarianism in Egypt, whether under Mubarak or el-Sisi, bore the same features of exceptionalism, centralization, and dualism.

The Terrorist Entities Law creates an arbitrary system of listing that does not belong to criminal law. Under this law, there are two ways to list terrorists and

[126] *Official Gazette* 7/58, no. 7bis, February 17, 2015.
[127] Article 1 of the 2015 Terrorist Entities Law.
[128] *Ibid.*

terrorist entities: The first is by a final court decision in a criminal case, which is the regular road of prosecution and sentencing. The second is by specified criminal courts within the Cairo Appeal Court. This can be done based on the Public Prosecution's request together with the investigation records and other supporting documents.[129] In both cases, the role of the court is not clear. Is it only judicial, or is it political? The constitution does not give an answer in this respect, but the practices of the Supreme Constitutional Court of Egypt have shown a tendency to issue decisions of a political nature, such as dissolving the parliament. Yet can a criminal court issue a political decision? Article 186 of the Constitution of 2014 states that "Judges are independent and immune to dismissal, and are subject to no other authority but the law."[130] This article creates by law a conditioned independence for the judiciary, and it empties the role of the constitution and the role of judges from any constitutionalist values.[131] As long as the law is politicized, the role of judges will automatically be politicized.

Experience has shown constant politicized decisions by the judiciary, whether during the monarchy or the republic. The Court of Cassation has played a politicized role in dealing with communists, as was shown earlier when discussing the emergence of the term "terror" during the war on communism. Such decisions were made based on an assumption that communism as derived from the Soviet Union uses force. Thus, Egyptian judges did not make an effort to look objectively at whether or not force or violence were actually used in each case. The same tendency has been evident in actions carried out against the Muslim Brotherhood. For instance, in 2014 a decision made by a criminal court sentenced 683 members of the Muslim Brotherhood to death.[132] Despite the fact that this mass death-sentence verdict was appealed, it sent a politically charged message by frightening ordinary people away from engaging with the Brotherhood or any act that could disturb "public order."

There are serious consequences of being listed as a terrorist or terrorist entity. These include: a ban on the entity, its practices and meetings; prohibition of financing the entity or raising its money; freezing funds; travel bans; passport seizure; and loss of reputation.[133] Moreover, until a final judicial decision is made, suspected entities remain on the list for three years, renewable for another term.[134] This law contradicts the presumption of innocence and creates terrorists well before a criminal trial. The law also allows the Public Prosecutor to rely on secret evidence,

[129] Article 3 of the 2015 Terrorist Entities Law.
[130] Egyptian Constitution of 2014.
[131] Brown, *Constitutions in a Nonconstitutional World*, at 89.
[132] Mai El-Sadany, "The Politicization of Egypt's Judiciary Amidst the 'War on Terror'" (April 29, 2014) *Tahrir Institute for Middle East Policy*, online: timep.org/commentary/politicization-egypts-judiciary-amidst-war-terror/.
[133] Article 7 of the 2015 Terrorist Entities Law.
[134] Article 4, *ibid.*

which is problematic. These measures transfer this law to a realm of exceptionalism normalized by unfair law.

This law raises concerns about basic rights and freedoms, including freedom of assembly and freedom of movement, especially with the broad authorities granted to the Public Prosecutor, which weaken the effectiveness of the judiciary. It seems that the Public Prosecutor is being included within the executive – a step toward expanding centralization. Following the overthrow of President Morsi, Public Prosecutor Hisham Barakat enabled the detention of thousands of Islamists and sent thousands of others for trial.[135] His approach of collective accusation and pretrial detention created concerns and discontent about the overlapping roles of the Public Prosecutor, which seemed to shift from bringing justice to satisfying those in power. On June 29, 2015, Barakat was assassinated in a car bombing.[136] This incident has sped up the adoption of a new anti-terrorism law.

Anti-Terrorism Law No. 94 of 2015

Following the assassination of Public Prosecutor Barakat, President el-Sisi announced at the funeral that "The arm of justice is chained by the law. We're not going to wait for this. We're going to amend the law to allow us to implement justice as soon as possible."[137] In the absence of a sitting parliament, President el-Sisi issued Anti-Terrorism Law No. 94 of 2015 – a solidification of the continuous centralization of powers. This law defines terrorism even more broadly than before,[138] creates a judiciary system that provides quick rather than just decisions,[139] grants the Public Prosecution vast authorities,[140] and allows the president to take all necessary measures whenever needed[141] – a confirmation of exceptionalism and even militarism. The following sections examine the overbroad definition of "terrorism" in this law as well as the problematic aspects of criminalizing speech related to terrorism and terrorism financing. The law also imposes special procedural regulations that challenge due process.

The Definition of "Terrorism"

Article 1 starts by defining a list of terms including "terrorist entity," "terrorist," and "terrorist crime," all of which are defined broadly and vaguely. Unlike in the Terrorist Entities Law, in the 2015 Anti-Terrorism Law the legislature attempted to

---

[135] "Egypt Prosecutor Hisham Barakat Killed in Cairo Attack" (June 29, 2015) *BBC*, online: www .bbc.com.
[136] *Ibid.*
[137] "Egyptian President 'to Change Law to Allow Faster Executions'" (June 30, 2015) *The Guardian*, online: www.theguardian.com.
[138] Articles 1, 2, 3 of Egyptian Anti-Terrorism Law No. 94 of 2015.
[139] Article 50, *ibid.*
[140] Articles 43, 46, 48, 49, 51, *ibid.*
[141] Article 53, *ibid.*

distinguish between "terrorist acts," "terrorist crimes," and "terrorist entities" by creating a definition for each instead of defining them all under one label. However, the attempt is limited to using separate titles with the same broad, vague terminology. The definition of "terrorist entity" refers to:

> [E]ach group, association, institution, organization, or gang composed of at least three persons, or any other entity proved to be [a terrorist group] regardless of its legal or factual status, whether inside or outside the country, and regardless of its nationality or the nationality of its members, [if it] aims to commit one or more terrorist crimes, or if [it takes] terrorism as a means to achieve or implement its criminal objectives.[142]

The 2015 Anti-Terrorism Law borrowed the definition of "terrorist entities" stipulated in the Terrorist Entities Law, but added a minimum number of members of "at least three persons."[143] It then added the phrase "regardless of its legal or factual status, whether inside or outside the country[.]" This attempt to broaden Egyptian jurisdiction could overlap with the legal and judicial practices in other jurisdictions, as will be explained later.

The Law then defines a "terrorist" as:

> [E]ach person who commits, attempts to commit, incites, threatens, or plans inside [Egypt] or abroad a terrorist crime by any means even individually, or contributes to a joint criminal enterprise, or takes command, leadership, management, creation or establishment, or becomes a member of any of the terrorist entities stipulated in Article 1 of the presidential decree of Law No. 8 of 2015 Regarding Regulating Terrorist Entities and Terrorists, or funds or participates in its acts with knowledge of [its purposes].[144]

According to the above definitions, a "terrorist group" and a "terrorist" are those who commit terrorist acts, as defined in Article 1(3) and Article 2, *or* those who the authority decides are terrorists based on the Terrorist Entities Law. This second clause is another flexible statement that adds ambiguity to the notion of terrorism and violates the principles and role of the criminal law. It should be noted that the definitions and regulations in this law do not replace the ones in the Terrorist Entities Law or those in Law No. 97 of 1992. This could create an overlap between the three laws. However, the primary issue remains the continuous adoption of broad definitions, vague terms, and arbitrary regulations.

Article 1 of the 2015 Anti-Terrorism Law of 2015 defines "terrorist act" as:

> [A]ny use of force, violence, or threat inside [Egypt] or abroad aiming to disrupt public order or endanger the safety, interests, security of the society; harm people,

---

[142] Article 1(1), *ibid.*
[143] *Ibid.*
[144] Article 1(2), *ibid.*

or horrify them, or risk their lives, liberties, public or private rights, their safety, or the other freedoms and rights granted by the constitution or by law; harm national unity, social peace, or national security; damage the environment, natural resources, antiquities, financial resources, institutions, public or private property, or occupy or seize them, or prevent or obstruct public authorities or judicial bodies, governmental interests, local units, places of worship, hospitals or institutions of learning, or diplomatic and consular missions in Egypt from the exercise of all or some of their activities, or resist [them], or thwart the application of the Constitution or the laws or regulations.

As well as all conduct committed with the intention of achieving one of the objectives shown in the first paragraph of this article, [including] preparing or incitement, if it caused damage to communication, information systems, financial or banking systems, national economy, energy storage, or security storage of goods, food and water, or their safety, or [against] medical services during disasters and crisis.[145]

This definition, while broader than the one created by Law No. 97 of 1992, shares some of its features. Neither requires any specific motive (e.g., religious, political, or ideological). Both require the use of "violence" or "threat," yet without providing a clear understanding of these terms. The definition in the 2015 Anti-Terrorism Law is exceedingly repetitious, and the two definitions also share this feature. They include the terms "violence," "damage," "harm," and "destroy," which sound similar but still do not have a clear meaning at a legal level. The two Egyptian definitions also include clauses like "disturb public order" or "thwart the application of the Constitution," which only add more ambiguity to the definition. Such clauses provide extra protection to tyrannical regimes. In fact, they can transfer the legitimacy of any unsuccessful revolution into acts of terrorism.

The 2015 definition provides protection to hospitals and other local services as well as diplomatic and consular missions in Egypt. However, it is not clear what kind of acts committed against or by these bodies form crimes of terrorism. For instance, if hospital employees carry out a strike related to their work, and the authorities view the strike as obstructing the "exercise of all or some of their activities" as the above article states, would this strike be considered terrorism? The wording of the article does not suggest any use of force. Thus, it implicitly allows the inclusion of strikes by labor unions and students that take place across governmental institutions and embassies, since such strikes could prevent these institutions from exercising "all or some of their activities," or even harm "communication" or "national unity," or may be considered as "occupying public or private property." The broad wording of the article allows the authority to treat peaceful political and civil activities as terrorism.

---

[145] Article 1, *ibid.*

The above definition explicitly includes acts committed or planned inside or outside Egypt. This is similar to Article 86*bis*(c) of the 1992 Egyptian anti-terrorism regulations, which states:

> Shall be punished with permanent hard labor, whoever seeks with a foreign country or an association, corporation, organization, group, or gang whose headquarters are abroad, or with any of those who work for the interest of any of them, or spies with them, or carries out a terrorist act in Egypt, or against its properties, its institutions, employees, diplomatic representatives, or its citizens in the course of their duties, or while they are abroad, or who joins in committing any of the foregoing.[146]

While criminalizing multi-national or cross-boundary terrorism seems to be a step toward globalization, it may cause difficulties regarding sovereignty and jurisdiction. With the absence of a unified international definition of "terrorism," and with the overbroad Egyptian definition, identifying the terrorist can be arbitrary. The lines between a political criminal, a peaceful protester, and a terrorist within the Egyptian anti-terrorism law are blurred. Besides, Egypt's poor human rights record and its constant use of torture[147] represent a concern regarding extradition.

Articles 1–4 of the Egyptian Penal Code specify its regional jurisdiction, which covers, besides crimes committed in Egypt, those that are committed abroad but harm the national security of Egypt. The 2015 Anti-Terrorism Law, however, expands Egyptian jurisdiction in a way that could interfere with other jurisdictions and violate the principle of sovereignty. For example, the new law gives Egypt the authority to prosecute those who commit crimes that cause "damage to any international or regional organization."[148] The article is not clear about the purpose of broadening its jurisdiction over crimes committed against organizations with which Egypt may or may not have any relationship. The law also does not require that the criminal holds Egyptian citizenship. This does not serve crime control as much as creating unreasonable interference with other jurisdictions.

Speech Related to Terrorism

Egypt has long restricted the freedom of expression through criminalizing sedition and other ill-defined activities. However, the global tendency toward criminalizing speech linked to terrorism was taken into account in the 2015 Egyptian anti-terrorism law. The law criminalizes incitement in three articles, all of which use vague language.

---

[146] Article 86*bis*(c) of the 1992 amendment added to the Egyptian Penal Code.
[147] "Egypt: Hundreds Disappeared and Tortured Amid Wave of Brutal Repression" (July 13, 2016) *Amnesty International*, online: www.amnesty.org/en/latest/news/2016/07/egypt-hundreds-disappeared-and-tortured-amid-wave-of-brutal-repression/.
[148] Article 4(b) of the 2015 Anti-Terrorism Law.

Incitement is first mentioned as part of the definition of "terrorist acts" provided in Article 1 (addressed above). This article condemns inciting any of the listed terrorist acts, from damaging property to disturbing public order. With the overbroad wording of this definition, any speech that criticizes the government, corruption, or socioeconomic issues including poor living conditions can be misinterpreted as inciting to harm national unity, social peace, or public order.

The application of this article is flexible and depends on the identity of the accused. For instance, in a TV interview in January 2016, Egyptian Justice Minister Ahmed al-Zind encouraged killing all members of the Muslim Brotherhood, stating that for each member of the Egyptian security forces who died during counter-terrorism campaigns, "I swear by God almighty that, personally, the fire in my heart will not be extinguished unless for each one there's at least 10,000 [of the Muslim Brotherhood killed]."[149] Al-Zind continued, "I'm saying the Brotherhood and who-ever aids them and whoever loves them and whoever pleases them and whoever takes bribes from them and whoever lives off their ill-gotten funds from Turkey and Qatar and Iran [should be killed]."[150] Human Rights Watch conceived these statements as hate speech.[151] Despite this explicit aggressive language against the Brotherhood and their sympathizers, the Egyptian authorities did not condemn al-Zind for incitement or hate speech. This selectivity in applying the law creates a sharp line between elite criminals, who can act and express their immoderate opinions freely, and "enemies," who have not necessarily engaged in any criminal activity yet are condemned as terrorists because of their identity.

Article 6 is the next to condemn incitement. It attempts to define incitement as terrorism by stating that,

> shall be punished for inciting a terrorist crime with the same punishment for the full crime, whether the incitement is directed toward a particular person or group, or whether it is general, made in public or in private, and whatever the means used, even if no effects have resulted from this incitement.[152]

The roots of this restriction can be found in Article 88 of the 1883 Penal Code, which was modeled on the French Press Law of 1881 (both addressed in Chapter 2). This attempt to define incitement fails to provide a clear meaning for its framework. By condemning speech expressed in private, it risks basic human rights and encour-ages false accusations. By punishing incitement as a full crime, it advances an anti-insurgency orientation that focuses on ideas rather than on harmful acts.

---

[149] "Egypt: Condemn Justice Minister's Hate Speech: Suggested Mass Killing of Brotherhood Supporters" (February 8, 2016) *Human Rights Watch*, online: www.hrw.org/news/2016/02/08/egypt-condemn-justice-ministers-hate-speech.

[150] *Ibid.*

[151] *Ibid.*

[152] Article 6 of Egyptian Anti-Terrorism Law of 2015.

The third article that regulates incitement is Article 18. This article treats attempting to overthrow the regime as terrorism and punishes such attempts with life imprisonment or hard labor. The article defines these acts as terrorism by stating that, "Whoever tried through force, violence, threat, intimidation, or any other methods of terrorist acts to overthrow the government, change the state constitution, the Republican system, or the form of government" shall be punished with life imprisonment for no less than ten years.[153] The origin of this article goes back to the Penal Code of 1904, which criminalizes "dissemination of revolutionary ideas"[154] and "advocating changing the basic social system through force or terror."[155] Similar wording is also found in Article 98(b) added to the Penal Code in 1946, which at that time was applied against communists.[156] Both of these articles are drawn from Section IV of the French Penal Code of 1810 on "Resistance, Disobedience, and other Defaults, in regard to the Public Authority" (discussed earlier in this chapter under the crimes of rebellion and sabotage). Restrictions on speech have a colonial origin, which has strongly reemerged in the neo-colonial global war on terror.

The definition of "incitement" in Article 18 of the Egyptian 2015 anti-terrorism law does not clarify the limits of its meaning. It seems to target all acts including mere criticism by academics and journalists, or any form of political pressure used by activists to modify the constitution. Such practices are legal and protected in democracies. Treating these practices as wrongdoing, and worse as terrorism, is another way of utilizing law as a suppressive tool. Post-9/11, there is a global tendency to narrow freedom of expression, but Egypt has gone far beyond any Western clampdown on freedom of expression.

Another restriction on speech and expression is listed in Article 35, which targets journalists and media. It condemns "publishing, forecasting, displaying, or promoting false news or information about terrorist acts that are committed in Egypt, or about the countering measures in opposition to the official statements issued by the Ministry of Defense."[157] The origin of this text goes back to Article 102*bis* added to the Penal Code in 1957, which is found in DORA (1914), both of which condemn spreading false reports or news (discussed at the beginning of this chapter under the crime of sedition). Article 35 of the 2015 Egyptian anti-terrorism law enacts a high penalty of a fine of between 200,000 and 500,000 Egyptian pounds ($25,550–$64,000), as well as depriving the involved journalist or the institution from practicing for a year. This article empties journalism of its monitoring role by effectively making the abusive authoritarian regime immune to accountability.

[153] Article 18, *ibid.*
[154] Article 151(2) of Law No. 37 of 1923 on Adding Provisions to the Penal Code No. 3 of 1904.
[155] Article 151(3), *ibid.*
[156] A detailed evaluation of Article 98(b) is provided in the section regarding the emergence of the term "terror" during the war on communism.
[157] Article 35 of Egyptian Anti-Terrorism Law of 2015.

Restrictions on the use of the internet are among the latest of the counter-terrorism tactics. Article 29 criminalizes use of the internet that aims to "promot[e] ideas or beliefs that call to commit terrorist acts" or "mislead security authorities" or "influence the course of justice."[158]

The internet has made communications easier among terrorists worldwide. A report by the United Nations Office on Drugs and Crime shows that the internet is a useful place for secret intelligence services to gather information about terrorists by monitoring online discussions and websites, which helps prevent terrorist acts.[159] However, monitoring already published information in websites is one thing, whereas monitoring unpublished forms of communication, including in emails and chat rooms, is a violation of the right to privacy and to confidential communication. The global restrictions on speech, especially those imposed by UN Security Council Resolution 1624 (2005), encourage authoritarian regimes to become more oppressive and arbitrary, which in turn affects international peace and security.

Terrorism Financing

Since 9/11, the theme of terrorism financing has become an essential part of the global war on terror. The international obligations listed in UN Security Council Resolution 1373 (2001) are clear in calling upon states to criminalize terrorism financing. Egypt has adopted several legal modifications to meet the requirements of Resolution 1373, and more importantly the FATF's standards (discussed in Chapter 2).

Egypt was ahead of this international obligation. It had already criminalized terrorism financing in Law No. 97 of 1992. Article 86*bis* condemns "whoever, with the knowledge of the purpose for which [the terrorist group] calls, holds any kind of leadership within it, or supplies it with material or financial provisions."[160] Despite this text, the 2015 Anti-Terrorism Law dedicated two articles to this theme. Article 3 of the 2015 Anti-Terrorism Law defines "terrorism financing" as:

> Collecting, receiving, holding, supplying, transferring, or providing funds, weapons, ammunition, explosives, missions,[161] machines, data, information, materials, or other things directly or indirectly, and by any means including digital and electronic forms, with the intention to use all or some of it to commit any terrorist crime, or knowing that it will be used for this purpose, or to provide a safe haven to terrorists or to financers of terrorists in any of the ways mentioned above.

Unlike Article 86*bis* of Law No. 97 of 1992, this article does not require knowledge of the terrorist purpose of the group or its actions. This puts anyone who

---

[158] Article 29, *ibid.*
[159] United Nations Office on Drugs and Crime, "The Use of the Internet for Terrorist Purposes."
[160] Article 86*bis* of Law No. 97 of 1992.
[161] The article uses the word مهمات, which means "missions." Even though it is not clear what the meaning or purpose of this word is in this article, I translate it as it is.

associates with or helps terrorist groups at risk under this article. For instance, if a technician fixes the laptops of terrorists, even if he does not know about their criminal activities, he is, according to this article, a "terrorist financer." The 2015 Anti-Terrorism Law establishes tough punishments for terrorism financing. Article 13 states:

> Shall be punished with life imprisonment whoever commits a crime of terrorism financing if the funding was to a terrorist, and shall the death penalty be applied if the funding was to a terrorist group or terrorist act.
>
> And in the cases when the crime [of financing] is committed by a terrorist group, shall those responsible for the actual management of this group be punished with the motioned sentences in the previous paragraph as long as the crime was committed for the benefit of the group.
>
> And shall the terrorist group be punished with a fine not less than one hundred thousand and not more than three million pounds, and [shall the group] be jointly responsible for the payment of any financial penalties or compensation.

The severity of the punishment is an aspect inherited from exceptionalism and militarism, which prioritize discipline over justice. Egyptian national security and anti-terrorism laws have long included tough punishments, which have not resulted in reducing crimes or terrorist cells. This tough approach is also seen in the special procedural regulations that treat terrorist suspects as enemies rather than criminals.

Procedural Regulations

The 2015 anti-terrorism law is designed in a way that violates the procedural guarantees of the accused in the stages of arrest and investigation. It broadens the authorities of investigators, extends the period of remand, deprives detainees of their right to contact a lawyer, and allows monitoring of the homes, phone calls, and letters of any suspected person. Article 50 allocates specific criminal courts to deal with terrorist lawsuits. These courts are required to ensure expeditious trials.[162] This requirement can explain the state's substitution of special courts for ordinary courts. By transferring many of the judges' authorities to the Public Prosecutor, this anti-terrorism law has designed the role of the judiciary in a way that suits the interests of the executive.

All articles in this law that regulate investigation use the phrase "the Public Prosecution" followed directly by "or the competent investigation authority[.]"[163] The law does not clarify the meaning of this latter authority. The wording implicitly allows the establishment of a special investigation body for terrorist cases, or even their referral to military courts. Interpreting this measure required looking at the draft law.[164] The intention was to establish a special investigation body for terrorist

---

[162] Article 50 of Egyptian Anti-Terrorism Law of 2015.
[163] Articles 40, 43, 46, and 49, *ibid.*
[164] www.legal-agenda.com/article.php?id=581.

cases. Removing the explicit wording that was suggested in the draft law from this current law may have been done in order to eliminate objections to this plan. Only time will show the real utility of this vague phrase.

The law in Article 40 allows the arrest of any person and their retention whenever "a danger of terrorism emerges" or "for the necessity to counter this danger" if collecting evidence or searching for the criminals require it.[165] The wording of the article includes anyone, even non-suspects. The detention is allowed for up to 24 hours, but the Public Prosecution may extend this period for up to seven days. By not requiring serious suspicion in order to arrest, the law legalizes arbitrary arrests and detention and violates due process.

The Egyptian Criminal Procedures Law No. 50 of 1951 provides several guaranties for those under preventive custody. The person must be notified of the accusation and the reason for the detention, and must be allowed to contact a lawyer.[166] While these guarantees are included in Article 41 of Egyptian Anti-Terrorism Law of 2015, they are followed by the phrase "without violating the benefit of investigation."[167] This vague phrase allows, by law, the most fundamental procedural guarantees to be disregarded.

The law in Article 46 grants the Public Prosecution or the competent investigation authority the power to issue permits regarding monitoring and recording calls, videotaping private places, and monitoring emails. Such monitoring can be put in place for 30 days, and can be extended for longer periods. On the other hand, Article 57 of the Constitution of 2014 requires a justified court order in order to permit such monitoring. The anti-terrorism law thus violates the constitution and basic human rights under the pretext of counter-terrorism. Such practices are a reflection of exceptionalism that may be justified during wartime but not in civil peacetime life.

Article 8 excludes those who work on enforcing this law from any criminal accountability "if they use force during their duty or to protect themselves from an imminent danger that is about to harm lives or property, as long as the use of this right is essential and sufficient to counter the risk."[168] The root of such immunities may be found in British martial law, which provided immunity to military members and protected their actions from legal accountability. Article 8 is not clear about the meaning of "danger" and endangering "lives or properties." It overprotects the authority and its persons, which results in creating two opposing groups without necessarily any actual opposition. Anyone who does not support the regime and its practices is a potential target, whereas those in power and their supporters are protected. The situation becomes more problematic with Egypt's security forces,

---

[165] Article 40 of Egyptian Anti-Terrorism Law of 2015.
[166] Articles 40, 41, 124, and 139 of Egyptian Criminal Procedures Law No. 50 of 1951.
[167] Article 40 of Egyptian Anti-Terrorism Law of 2015.
[168] Article 8, *ibid.*

which are known for their unjustified use of coercion,[169] and this article implicitly encourages more use of force against the "enemy," whether armed terrorists or peaceful opponents.

Egyptian counter-terrorism law and policy elevate the protection of the government over all other values. They intentionally turn a blind eye to the fact that there are tyrannical and corrupt governments that could be faced with anti-government revolutionary groups. While the acts of these groups are considered by part of the society as morally right, they will always be considered by corrupt governments as legally wrong.[170] This policy serves the Egyptian authoritarian government that maintains its power through superseding its political opponents by treating them as terrorists. The convicting of terrorist crimes has serious consequences from travel bans to freezing funds at both national and global levels. Such measures would discourage many people from engaging in sociopolitical discourses to avoid being a potential suspect of "terrorism." Egypt's authoritarianism is also supported by the West, which indirectly supports Egypt in its war on terror against the common enemy.

Other Authoritarian Laws and Measures

Egypt continues to issue and prepare suppressive laws that indirectly combat terrorism-related crimes but directly violate human rights. One of the most controversial laws is the infamous Law for Regulating the Work of Associations and Other Institutions Working in the Field of Civil Work (NGOs Law),[171] issued in March 2017. Another law is related to cyber crime, which at the time of writing is still a draft law.

The NGOs Law grants the government vast powers to monitor and restrict the work of NGOs. This Law establishes a National Commission for the Regulation of Foreign Non-Governmental Organizations. The commission includes representatives of several authorities, including the Ministry of Foreign Affairs, the Ministry of Defense, the Ministry of Interior, the General Intelligence Service, the Central Bank, and the Money Laundering Unit. This combination places charity and civil society work side by side with transnational crimes by criminal organizations. The law places great attention on the establishment of NGOs and their funding. Articles 70 and 71 grant the commission the authority to decide on all matters relating to the establishment, renewal, and operation of foreign NGOs in Egypt.[172] Funding for

---

[169] "Egypt: State-Sanctioned Pattern of Excessive Use of Force by Security Forces" (October 14, 2013) *Amnesty International,* online: https://www.amnesty.org/en/latest/news/2013/10/egypt-state-sanctioned-pattern-excessive-use-force-security-forces/.
[170] See C. A. J. Coady, "Terrorism and Innocence" (2004) 8:1 *The Journal of Ethics* at 40.
[171] Law for Regulating the Work of Associations and Other Institutions Working in the Field of Civil Work (NGOs Law), March 24, 2017, *Official Gazette* 2 (f).
[172] Article 70, *ibid.*

Egyptian or foreign NGOs or funding by these NGOs cannot be done without the commission's permission.[173] NGOs cannot hire, permanently or temporally, foreign employees or experts without the commission's permission.[174] These restrictions treat "foreigners" as aliens that should not be trusted. Through such a policy of suspicion, the Egyptian authorities bring back the spirit of emergency periods, including wars, which allows people and entities to be placed into black-and-white categories of citizens and aliens, friends and enemies. In its endless official or nominal state of emergency, Egypt allows laws to be issued that belong to the exception, prioritizing the security of the state over the liberty of people and civil society.

Among the security-related restrictions is the prohibition of NGOs from conducting acts that "harm national security, public order, public morality, or public health[.]"[175] The wording of this prohibition can be found in the 1966 International Covenant on Civil and Political Rights (ICCPR). Article 19 of the ICCPR states that "Everyone shall have the right to freedom of expression[,]" but the exercise of this right can be restricted "by law and as necessary" "[f]or the protection of national security or of public order (*ordre public*), or of public health or morals."[176] This article includes vague words, which reflects a weakness of the ICCPR. However, these clauses were clarified in 1985 by the United Nations' Economic and Social Council in the Siracusa Principles on the Limitation and Derogation Provisions in the International Covenant on Civil and Political Rights (Siracusa Principles). According to the Siracusa Principles, the phrase "public order" as used in the ICCPR is defined as "the sum of rules which ensure the functioning of society or the set of fundamental principles on which society is founded. Respect for human rights is part of public order (*ordre public*)."[177]

The above principle categorizes human rights as part of public order. However, authoritarian regimes could argue that the right to life allows the restricting of freedom of expression. The Siracusa Principles provided additional explanation to minimize the misuse of such clauses by stating that "National security cannot be used as a pretext for imposing vague or arbitrary limitations and may only be invoked when there exists adequate safeguards and effective remedies against abuse."[178] Another principle states that all limitation clauses "shall not be interpreted so as to jeopardize the essence of the right concerned."[179] Thus, these principles aim to balance security and rights.

---

[173] Articles 70 and 71 (A) and (B), *ibid.*
[174] Article 66, *ibid.*
[175] Articles 13 and 62, *ibid.*
[176] Article 19 of the ICCPR.
[177] Principle 22 of the United Nations' Economic and Social Council in the Siracusa Principles on the Limitation and Derogation Provisions in the International Covenant on Civil and Political Rights (Siracusa Principles).
[178] Principle 31, *ibid.*
[179] Principle 1(A.2), *ibid.*

In the Arab world, practice shows a one-sided understanding and application of restriction clauses. Arab governments have been abusing the vague clauses of "national security" and "public order" in justifying censorship and restricting freedom of expression and association. For instance, in 2011 a Lebanese human rights activist who documented torture by security forces was referred to a military investigative judge for having "published information harmful to the reputation of the Lebanese Military."[180] Many cases in Egypt show that civilians are frequently tried before military courts for criticizing the government, as such criticism is seen as a threat to "national security."[181] In Egypt, "national security" has a narrow meaning, which focuses on the security of the political regime and those in power, neglecting the human rights of individuals and groups. These practices are a misuse of the universal standards of restriction clauses on freedoms. In this respect, Rashid Al-Anezi argues that states may restrict freedom of expression and association in some occasions, such as dismissing an actual protest that provoke racial or ethnic hatred. However, permanent restriction on rights and freedoms in the name of countering terrorism lack legitimacy.[182] Expanding the limits and understanding of the above restriction clauses allows for replacing legal principles with the rule of exceptionalism.

In another article of the NGOs Law, NGOs are prohibited from conducting activities "that may result in violation of national unity, national security, public order or public morals"[183] or "opinion polls, publishing them or making their results available, or conducting field research or presenting their results before they are submitted to the Commission to ensure their integrity and impartiality."[184] Such restrictions empty the role of NGOs of its essence and importance, which should be a useful tool in researching and evaluating governmental policies and human rights abuses. For instance, Egyptian authorities may easily suppress reports by NGOs and even consider their field studies as a threat to public order.

The law also prohibits NGOs from "Advocating for the support or financing of violence or terrorist organizations."[185] With the overbroad definition of terrorism

---

[180] "Lebanon: Cease Harassment of Human Rights Activist for Documenting Torture" (August 4, 2011) *Amnesty International*, online: www.amnesty.org/en/press-releases/2011/08/lebanon-cease-harassment-human-rights-activist-documenting-torture-2011-08/; "Egypt Steps Up Vicious Onslaught against NGOs with Arrest of Minority Defender" (May 19, 2016) *Amnesty International*, online: www.amnesty.org/en/press-releases/2016/05/egypt-steps-up-vicious-onslaught-against-ngos-with-arrest-of-minority-rights-defender/.

[181] "Egypt: Hisham Genina's Sentence a Serious Setback for Freedom of Expression under al-Sisi" (April 24, 2018) *Amnesty International*, online: www.amnesty.org/en/latest/news/2018/04/egypt-hisham-geninas-sentence-a-serious-setback-for-freedom-of-expression-under-al-isi/.

[182] Rashid Al-Anezi, "Human Rights in the Light of International Opportunism: A Study of the Impact of the War on Terrorism on Human Rights" (2010) 24:41 *UAE University Journal of Sharia and Law* 101 at 146.

[183] Article 14(B) of the NGOs Law.

[184] Article 14(G), *ibid.*

[185] Article 14(I), *ibid.*

provided in the Anti-Terrorism Law discussed earlier in this chapter, the crime of supporting or financing terrorist organizations is not clear. In 2011, a case regarding an Egyptian NGO that received over $1.5 million from external donors was looked at by Cairo Criminal Court. The court ordered the cash and properties of activists involved in the case to be seized. The activists were also banned from traveling until 2012, when seventeen foreign people related to the case, including seven Americans, were allowed to leave Egypt. In 2013, the court ordered the closure of five NGOs that worked on defending human rights and that received funding for this task. Trials in absentia also resulted in foreigners involved in the case being charged with impressment.[186] Despite its harsh judgment, in 2016 the court ordered the case to be opened again, allegedly after receiving further information about NGOs, including those related to the Brotherhood, receiving foreign funds. Orders of travel bans have been issued against a large number of people, not all of whom were directly involved in this case.[187] In addition, the investigation authority issued an order prohibiting publishing about this case in any manner,[188] adding more ambiguity regarding its procedures and the final fate of the suspects.

The practice in Egypt suggests that, well before adopting the Law for Regulating the Work of Associations and Other Institutions Working in the Field of Civil Work of 2017, Egyptian authorities were targeting NGOs. This law further tightened freedom of association by strictly monitoring NGOs' work. The law also imposes harsh penalties of up to five years' imprisonment and up to one million Egyptian pounds in fines (about $56,700). In addition, if NGOs function in Egypt without registration, their members shall be punished with the above penalties,[189] even if the NGOs' activities are lawful. Such restrictions and penalties suggest an official policy of authoritarian intimidation toward civil society in Egypt.

Another recent authoritarian tendency in Egyptian lawmaking is the preparation of a cyber crime draft law. Many countries have adopted laws in this regard, especially with the increased abuse of the internet by hackers and scam businesses. However, my concern is the potential use of the cyber crime law to narrow the space for freedom of expression under the pretext of countering terrorism or national security.

---

[186] "The Egyptian Organization for Human Rights (EOHR) Calls for Closing the File on the Case of NGOs' Foreign Funding" (August 16, 2016) *Egyptian Organization for Human Rights,* online: http://en.eohr.org/2016/08/16/the-egyptian-organization-for-human-rights-eohr-calls-for-closing-the-file-on-the-case-of-ngos-foreign-funding/.
[187] "Qadiyat atamweel al ajnabi: Tawasou al man'a min as afar" "[Foreign Funding Case: Expansion of Travel Ban]" (November 26, 2016) *The New Arab [news],* online: www.alaraby.co.uk/politics/2016/11/25.
[188] "Al qadiya '173 tamweel ajnabi' qissat ehkaam al hissar ala al monathamat al ahliya" "[Case '173 Foreign Funding' a Story of Tightening the Siege on NGOs]" (March 23, 2016) *Masrawy [news],* online: www.masrawy.com/News/News_Reports/details/2016/3/23/774212.
[189] Article 87(D) of NGOs Law.

The draft law does not include the crime of terrorism, but refers to all crimes listed in the Penal Code, which includes terrorism crimes and inciting of terrorism. The draft law prohibits establishing websites that are used in inciting any crime stipulated in the Penal Code.[190] And if any of these crimes have the aim of "disturbing public order or endangering the safety and security of the nation [...] or harming national unity[,]" the punishment shall be life imprisonment or imprisonment of a minimum of three years and maximum of fifteen years.[191] Without a precise meaning for "disturbing public order," the draft law represents a threat to any opinions posted online that oppose the authorities, especially by journalists and users of social media.

CONCLUSION: COLONIAL HERITAGE AND NEO-COLONIAL APPROVAL OF AUTHORITARIANISM

Egyptian counter-terrorism policy is rooted in colonialism, informal imperialism, and indigenous authoritarianism. The colonial influence is seen in the British state of emergency and the use of special courts that were transplanted into postcolonial Egypt. In post-independence Egypt, exceptionalism and the interference of the military or the militarized security forces in everyday civil life has become the norm. Such normalization of the exception serves the authoritarian ambition of the Egyptian government.

The influence of informal imperialism is seen in the Egyptian Penal Code, which is built on the French model. France did not place direct pressure on Egypt to incorporate aspects of France's laws into its anti-terror legislation. According to Nathan Brown, Egypt found the French system attractive because of its feature of centralization, which serves the ruling class and the elite.[192] In addition to centralization, the French law codified the crimes of rebellion and sabotage. Criminalizing these acts gave the Egyptian government legal protection, especially after its tough experience with the 'Urabi revolt that was only ended with the British occupation of Egypt. Sedition is another crime that the Egyptian Penal Code of 1883 borrowed from the French Press Law. This was the beginning of speech restrictions in Egypt.

Egypt first adopted the term "terror" in Article 98(a) of the 1937 Penal Code. In this article, "terror" was considered an aggravating circumstance rather than a crime by itself. Egyptian ordinary courts used this and other vague articles against communists, who were assumed to use force and terror. Such an assumption belongs to the approaches of exceptionalism and militarism, which aim to preempt crimes through identifying the enemy before a crime or a threat of a crime occur.

[190] Article 14 of the cyber crimes draft law.
[191] Article 22, *ibid.*
[192] Brown, "Retrospective: Law and Imperialism," at 116.

Egyptian laws were extremely broad well before 9/11 because of colonial influence, but they have become even broader under the neo-colonial influence that continues the indirect Western support and encouragement of authoritarianism. Roger Owen has examined inter-state relations, making the important point that in the Arab world the boundary between domestic politics and foreign relations is far more porous than in most other regions. This can be seen in the American role in shaping counter-terrorism policy in the region post-9/11.[193] Thus, external political pressure plays a role in reshaping the policy of the war on terror. For example, the American approval of arbitrary Middle Eastern counter-terrorism policy began well before 9/11. Roach shows the connection between Egypt and the United States in their use of extraordinary rendition, when the American authorities transferred terrorist suspects into Egyptian custody.[194] Egypt is infamous for its willingness to use torture and other extra-legal measures, and the cooperation between the West and Egypt in extraordinary renditions therefore suggests Western approval of Egyptian authoritarianism.

The 2015 Egyptian anti-terrorism law is similar to post-9/11 Western laws in one respect: proposing a broad definition of terrorism. Other than that, it excessively disregards human rights and criminal law principles and safeguards. In the face of rising violence and terrorist attacks, this approach advances the authoritarian regime by centralizing powers in the president or other bodies, away from the ordinary course of governing. Egypt criminalizes incitement of terrorism and financing terrorism in its 1992 anti-terrorism law. However, it emphasizes these two themes in its 2015 anti-terrorism law, which reflects compliance with the post-9/11 global regulations. While satisfying the neo-colonial powers, represented by the UN Security Council and FATF, Egypt's new anti-terrorism measures allow it to enhance the centralization and exceptionalism of its authoritarian powers.

[193] Owen, *State, Power and Politics*, at 219–24.
[194] Roach, *The 9/11 Effect*, at 80–1.

6

The Colonial and Neo-Colonial Experience in Tunisia

The Republic of Tunisia is a small state that is bordered by Algeria to the west, Libya to the southeast, and the Mediterranean Sea to the north and east. Although it is located in North Africa and Arabic-speaking Sunni Muslims represent 98 percent of the population, at a social and cultural level Tunisia reflects Europe's strong influence.[1] Its location on the Mediterranean coast has linked it culturally and economically to France, Italy, and Spain.[2]

Before the establishment of the republic, Tunisia was an extension of the Ottoman Empire known as the province of Tunis (1574–1705). It was ruled by monarchs, known as beys, from 1631 to 1956. Like Egypt and the Ottoman Empire during that time, Tunisia, under the rule of Ahmad I ibn Mustafa, sought modernizing reforms in state institutions and the economy.[3] This chapter is concerned with modern Tunisia. It examines chronologically four main periods: informal imperialism (1850–70s), which represents European political and economic control; colonialism under the French protectorate of Tunisia and its legacies of centralization and exceptionalism (1881–1956); postcolonialism and the falling back into authoritarianism (1950s–present); and, finally, neo-colonialism and the economic dependence on and political submission to the West (1990s–present).

INFORMAL IMPERIALISM: POLITICAL AND ECONOMIC CONTROL (1850S–1870S)

During the 1850s, European countries considered Tunisia a place for agricultural and other investments, and established railways, ports, and lending companies

---

[1] Christopher Alexander, *Tunisia: Stability and Reform in the Modern Maghreb* (Milton Park, UK: Routledge, 2010) at 1.
[2] *Ibid.*
[3] Julia A. Clancy-Smith, *Rebel and Saint: Muslim Notables, Populist Protest, Colonial Encounters (Algeria and Tunisia, 1800–1904)* (Berkeley, CA: University of California Press, 1997) at 157.

there.[4] Through informal imperialism, Britain and France placed pressure on the bey to issue the Fundamental Pact ('Ahd al-Amān) in 1857.[5] This document served foreigners by granting them the right to conduct business activities and own property in the country.[6]

The Fundamental Pact paved the way for the adoption of the Tunisian Constitution of 1861 – a more sophisticated legal framework for governing, rights and duties. This document is considered the first constitution in the Arab world.[7] Even though it centralized authority in the bey and his ministers,[8] it made the bey accountable to a Grand Council if he violated the law.[9] Another aspect of the constitution is that, unlike the Fundamental Pact, which stated in its introduction the validity of Islamic Sharia, the constitution did not mention Islam. Instead, it emphasized the equality between citizens and foreign subjects of all religions before the law.[10] It also stated foreigners' rights to own land and practice business activities.[11]

Nathan Brown argues that the timing of adopting the constitution and its content suggest that it was designed to serve two categories: foreign subjects and the political elite.[12] Foreign subjects enjoyed unconditional rights, and the political elite enjoyed centralized administration. Leon Carl Brown argues that the constitution was a sham step that aimed "more to curry favor and suppress criticism from abroad than to regularize the actual balance of political forces within Tunisia."[13] The constitution was permanently suspended by a beylical order in 1864 as a response to a revolution known as the Ali Ben Ghdahem Revolt.[14]

European control was more evident in Tunisia's economic life. Britain, France, and Italy invested their financial surplus by offering loans to the bey. The lending agreements included unfavorable rates and terms, displaying unequal positions of

---

4   Aḥmad Maḥmūd Khalīl, *Jarā'im amn al-dawlah al-'Ulyā b mu'allaqan 'alayhā bi-aḥkām Mahkamat al-Naqḍal-Miṣrīyah [National Security Crimes Commentated with Judgments of the Court of Cassation]* (al-Azārīṭah, al-Iskandarīyah: al-Maktab al-Jāmi ī al-Ḥadīth, 2009) at 43–5.

5   Brown, *Constitutions in a Nonconstitutional World*, at 16.

6   Articles 9 and 10 of the Tunisian 1857 Fundamental Act ('Ahd al-Amān), December 10, 1857. See "'Ahd al-Amān Text," *Higher Committee for Human Rights and Fundamental Freedoms in Tunisia*, online: www.droitsdelhomme.org.tn/?page_id=105.

7   Brown, *Constitutions in a Nonconstitutional World*, at 16.

8   Articles 12, 13, 16, 18 of the 1861 Tunisian Constitution, April 26, 1861. See "Dustor (qanon adawla aTunisia)" ["Constitution of Tunisia"], *Higher Committee for Human Rights and Fundamental Freedoms in Tunisia*, online: www.droitsdelhomme.org.tn/?page_id=106.

9   Article 11, *ibid.*

10 Articles 86–90, *ibid.*

11 Articles 98, 112, 113, *ibid.*

12 Brown, *Constitutions in a Nonconstitutional World*, at 18.

13 Quoted in *ibid.*

14 Ali Muhafitha, "Reform and Modernization in Nineteenth Century Tunisia" (August 16, 2009) *Addustor Newspaper*, online: www.addustour.com.

power.[15] As a result, in 1869 Tunisia declared bankruptcy.[16] This led to the establishment of a European commission (Commission Financière Internationale) in 1871, formed by France, Britain, and Italy, to supervise Tunisia's budget and protect European investors.[17] According to Leon Carl Brown, European powers were aware of Tunisia's increasing debt but paid no attention to it until Tunisia reached a complete deficiency and the need to protect European stakes became a necessity.[18] Brown suggests that European financial control in both Egypt and Tunisia "was the last stage before outright western control."[19] The European powers ignored the debt until they needed to protect their interests, which justified taking direct control. This suggests that a pattern of informal imperialism placed Arab countries in a subordinate position. This pattern of imperial control starts with economic and political control, then military control.

The economic crisis weakened the Tunisian government and made Tunisia more vulnerable to external threat. France, Italy, and the Ottoman Empire all had ambitions to control Tunisia. In 1881, France presented itself to the bey as a protector ally, and an era of direct French control lasted until 1956.

THE FRENCH PROTECTORATE OF TUNISIA (1881–1956)

On April 24, 1881, the French sent 35,000 of its troops from Algeria to Tunisia, and invaded several Tunisian cities with limited resistance.[20] The representative of the French Republic, General Bréart, reached the Tunisian Bardo Palace on May 12, 1881, promising to restore Tunisia's economic stability.[21] Thereafter, the bey signed the Treaty of Bardo, granting the French the right to supervise Tunisia's financial, foreign, and military matters.[22]

The French, at least at the beginning, ruled Tunisia based on a system of sharing powers with the bey. The bey was granted his authority and, as a result, Tunisia remained an absolute and centralized monarchy.[23] For instance, the bey had unlimited right – without an authorizing legal text – to punish those he

---

[15] 'Alī al-Maḥjūbī, *ʿĀlam al-ʿArabī al-ḥadīth wa-al-muʿāṣir: takhalluf fa-istiʿmār fa-muqāwamah* [*Modern and Contemporary Arab World: Backwardness, Colonialism, Resistance*] (Beirut: al-Intishār al-ʿArabī, 2009) at 43–5.

[16] Lisa Anderson, *The State and Social Transformation in Tunisia and Libya, 1830–1980* (Princeton, NJ: Princeton University Press, 1986) at 70.

[17] Leon Carl Brown, *International Politics and the Middle East: Old Rules, Dangerous Game* (London: I. B. Tauris, 1984) at 75.

[18] *Ibid.*

[19] *Ibid.*

[20] 'Alī al-Maḥjūbī, *Modern and Contemporary Arab World*, at 118–19.

[21] Charles William Olson, *Decolonization in French Politics (1950–1956): Indo-China, Tunisia, Morocco* (Ann Arbor, MI: University Microfilms, 1966) at 111.

[22] *Ibid.*

[23] Arfawi, *The Judiciary and Politics in Tunisia during French Colonialism*, at 73.

considered rebels against his authority.[24] According to one Tunisian scholar, because there were no constitutional regulations, the bey had absolute legislative and administrative power.[25]

Despite the autocratic position that the bey enjoyed, the French gradually expanded their powers. In 1883, the bey signed the French-proposed Convention of La Marsa, which officially established a French protectorate over Tunisia.[26] The convention granted the French Resident General additional financial and political control.[27] According to Lars Rudebeck, the French Resident General ruled Tunisia "through the bey if he cooperated and without him if he occasionally tried to oppose his will to that of the French government."[28] The bey's government was required to put into action French recommendations regarding administrative, judicial, and financial reforms.[29] These conditions undermined local authority without destroying it, and centralized powers on the French.

France ruled the three Maghreb countries, Algeria, Morocco, and Tunisia, but each of these colonies presented a unique case. For instance, Algeria was administered as an integral part of France, whereas the rest of the Maghreb was never considered part of France. This difference arose from the various French political interests and economic ambitions in each country, which led to the use of different policies in each case. Algeria differed from the others insofar as, unlike in the other Maghreb countries, there was a deep-rooted enmity between the Kingdom of France and the government of Algeria.[30] The timing of the invasion of Algeria was essentially related to domestic issues in France. The invasion was a tactic that the French King Charles X used to turn the attention of his people to this external victory.[31] By considering Algeria as part of France, the French used a destructive policy that included disposing of thousands of Algerians and completely replacing the local social and political structure with a French model. This also resulted in the specific form of resistance that arose in Algeria. Algerian nationalists faced the French as guerrilla fighters,[32] and the French systematically responded with coercive counter-insurgency policy and measures.[33]

The long period of French colonization of Algeria led to a nationalist struggle and a revolutionary war, in which both sides used every kind of violence. France

---

[24] *Ibid.*
[25] *Ibid*, at 72–3.
[26] Olson, *Decolonization in French Politics*, at 111.
[27] Alexander, *Tunisia*, at 20.
[28] Quoted in *ibid*.
[29] *Ibid.*
[30] For more, see Jamil M. Abun-Nasr, A History of the Maghrib in the Islamic Period (Cambridge: Cambridge University Press, 1987) at 250.
[31] *Ibid.*
[32] Alexander, *Tunisia*, at 19, 34.
[33] French, *The British Way in Counter-Insurgency*, at 163, 173.

developed counter-insurgency as a military–political doctrine. By looking at Algeria, we learn that the French doctrine in Algeria was extended to Tunisia, yet to a lesser extent. The French in Tunisia were aware that relying solely on a military doctrine might be counterproductive. Therefore, in order to prevent Tunisia from splitting into an Islamic country – as was the case in Algeria – a tolerant policy was required regarding social and cultural matters such as education. The tolerant French policy, however, was only considered in the first few years in Tunisia. With the emergence of opposition, a more coercive policy was adopted. Post-independence, Tunisia mimicked the latter French approach by adopting tough national security and anti-terror laws to prevent Tunisians from becoming radical Islamists and to counter all forms of political opposition.

Counter-insurgency was used in Tunisia, but it involved the use of military courts more than direct military campaigns. Many exceptional measures were taken to suppress nationalists, regardless whether they were considered insurgents or political criminals. Exceptionalism included declaring a state of siege, establishing military committees and military courts, imposing executive and military censorship, and applying French rather than Tunisian laws.

This section examines the exceptional and militarized measures adopted during colonialism. The themes examined are censorship, state of siege, and military courts. France has long used press legislation and measures to preempt crimes. This tendency is seen in the French Press Law of 1881 and the exceptional measures adopted in the protectorate of Tunisia. The other theme is the state of exception, which includes the state of siege as well as military courts.

The French Legacy of Censorship

The French colonial government used censorship in suppressing free speech that could threaten national security and order. In this section, I address censorship as an exceptional measure, on the basis of the source that regulated it, which was the executive or the military, and the suppressive nature of the speech and press regulations. According to Tunisian scholar Khamis Arfawi, French colonialism used censorship in Tunisia to monitor journalism, books, cinema, theater, and radio. Censorship focused particularly on expression that addressed or criticized the political system.[34] Arfawi indicates that censorship in Tunisia was an exceptional system largely regulated by executive and military orders during the state of siege and the two World Wars.[35]

---

[34] Khamis Arfawi, "aSahafa wa raqaba fi Tunis 1938–1953" ["Journalism and Censorship in Tunisia: 1938–1953"] (September 25, 2016) *Alawan*, online: www.alawan.org/content/الصحافة-والرقابة-في-تونس-1938-1953.
[35] *Ibid.*

With a growing number of French and Tunisian newspapers, the French adopted an order on October 14, 1884 referring to the French Press Law of 1881 as the pertinent law. This law prohibits incitement, through speech or written words,[36] of hatred or violence,[37] and defamation of the president,[38] the army, or court.[39] The decree of October 14, 1884 created two additional crimes: criticizing the bey or his family, and criticizing France.[40]

The French Press Law and the 1884 order were not sufficient to suppress nationalists and communists. Consequently, more regulations were adopted. In 1911, Tunisians carried out violent protests against the French in an event known as the Jellaz Conflict, which led the French to declare a state of siege.[41] During the state of siege, Arabic newspapers were banned.[42] This ban continued during World War I.[43] The French added additional exceptional precautionary measures by adopting the order of August 29, 1939 regarding publications and the order of September 1, 1939 regarding the state of siege.[44] Accordingly, the military authority could ban newspapers that they considered able to provoke disorder. In addition, no newspaper, whether Tunisian or foreign, could be published without a license. In Algeria, the French established a central agency to monitor news, and branches of this agency were established in Tunisia in 1943.[45] Axis forces dominated parts of Tunisia from November 1942 until May 1943. Once they were expelled, a decree was adopted on August 19, 1944 transferring censorship authorities during wartime to the French Resident General. According to this decree, the French Resident General had the authority to ban all news and publications that could endanger the security of the army or the safety of civilians.[46]

According to Arfawi, the rationale for censorship in Tunisia was divided into two parts. The first regards national security during wartime. This led to regulations that prohibit disclosure of military, diplomatic, or economic information. This sort of censorship prohibits criticism of the state's institutions, or comments that could affect the morale of army and civilians. Any criticism of other French colonies, including Syria, Lebanon, and Indochina, was referred to the French Resident General. In addition, it was prohibited to publish news that showed reprehensible

---

[36] Article 23 of the 1881 French Press Law.
[37] Article 24, *ibid.*
[38] Article 31, *ibid.*
[39] Article 30, *ibid.*
[40] Arfawi, *The Judiciary and Politics in Tunisia during French Colonialism*, at 47.
[41] Aljelani ben Haj & Muhamad alMarzuqi, *Ma'rakat alzalaj [Jellaz War]* (Tunis: Asharika atunisia letawzie) at 38.
[42] *Ibid.*
[43] Arfawi, "Journalism and Censorship in Tunisia."
[44] *Ibid*, at 53.
[45] *Ibid*, at 720.
[46] *Ibid.*

acts by the French army. Censorship regarding national security also included prohibiting the publicization of ideological beliefs.[47]

The second rationale for censorship was protecting the colonial regime. Arfawi argues that protecting colonialism required isolating Tunisians from revolutionary events in the Arab world. Accordingly, criticism of the French Resident General, the bey, or the security services was prohibited. News regarding public strikes and social struggle were referred to the French Resident General to take appropriate action.[48] Other restrictions included a prohibition of the use of the term "constitution," which could remind people of the banned Constitutional Liberal Party.[49]

When whole or parts of newspaper columns were deleted by the French authority, the papers filled the blank areas with the words like "censored."[50] Arfawi observes that the French censorship policy produced counterproductive results. In his view, while censorship forced newspapers to delete some parts and leave them blank, which made them unattractive and difficult to read, it led people to find other means of expression. These included secret leaflets and underground newspapers, such as the communist newspaper *Altaleea*.[51]

The use of censorship shows that this measure was an exceptional politicized tool centralized in the military or the French Resident General and used for social and mind control. This measure might have been necessary during wartime, but the experience in protectorate Tunisia suggests that its use exceeded this necessity. This contention is supported by that fact that even though World War II ended in 1945, censorship continued under the regulations of state of siege until 1955.[52]

The French Legacy of State of Siege and Military Courts

The French declared a state of siege in Tunisia in two cases of internal disorder in 1911 and 1938, and during the two World Wars.[53] Before that, transferring authority to the army was done without the declaration of state of siege by beylical decree. For example, the Bey of Tunisia issued a decree on June 10, 1882 authorizing French military commanders to use deterrent powers against whoever showed dissent or disobeyed military orders. The above beylical order of 1882 also enabled the establishment of military councils. These councils were the first French judicial system in Tunisia. The councils had the power to try Tunisians for attacks against French residents and against the French army.[54]

[47] *Ibid.*
[48] *Ibid.*
[49] *Ibid.*
[50] These included *"censuré," "X lignes censures,"* and *"Un article censure."* See *ibid.*
[51] *Ibid.*
[52] Arfawi, *The Judiciary and Politics in Tunisia during French Colonialism*, at 103.
[53] *Ibid*, at 101, 103.
[54] *Ibid*, at 100.

In France and colonized Tunisia, both military courts and ordinary courts were active in viewing sensitive cases. For instance, in its homeland France adopted the Law of March 9, 1928 replacing the war councils established during World War I with military tribunals.[55] These military tribunals became responsible for specific crimes committed during peacetime, including rebellion.[56] Other crimes remained within the jurisdiction of ordinary courts.[57] The jurisdiction of these military tribunals was expanded by a decree of July 29, 1939 to include crimes that affect the external security of the state, such as treason and other vague crimes such as "enterprise of demoralization."[58] The French Law of March 9, 1928 was applied in Tunisia, replacing the earlier military councils with military courts.[59]

During the state of siege in Tunisia,[60] the jurisdiction of military courts included crimes against the state or against the authorities, and crimes against public peace and security.[61] Among these crimes were sabotage and insurgency. For instance, on May 31, 1953, 15 Tunisians were accused of bombing a hospital (sabotage), and attempting to kill solders and the Tunisian Minister of Commerce, Ben Raice. Accordingly, the military court sentenced one person to the death penalty, two to hard labor for life, and the rest to two to 20 years of imprisonment.[62] Another case involved a group of nationalists who were accused of being "rebels" or "insurgents." During a search in May 1953, security forces found weapons and a printing machine with the signature of the "resistance committee." The investigation showed that the group was divided into two parts, one responsible for assassination and sabotage, and the other for making weapons and hiding rebels. Accordingly, they were accused of several bombings that were committed during February and March 1952. On November 3, 1953, the suspects were referred to a military court. The suspects claimed their confessions had been induced through coercion. Despite that, the military court sentenced one person to death, another to hard labor for life, eight to 20 years of imprisonment, and 11 others to hard labor for one to five years.[63] Another group of nationalists were accused of engaging in acts of sabotage between 1952 and 1953. These acts included damaging buildings, phone lines, power stations, and streetcars. They were also accused of acts of insurgency against French army and security forces. On January 14, 1954, a military court sentenced two to

---

[55] Yves Beigbeder, *Judging War Crimes and Torture: French Justice and International Criminal Tribunals and Commissions (1940–2005)* (Leiden: Martinus Nijhoff, 2006) at 12.
[56] *Ibid.*
[57] *Ibid.*
[58] *Ibid.*
[59] Arfawi, *The Judiciary and Politics in Tunisia during French Colonialism*, at 102.
[60] State of siege in Tunisia was issued by beylical decrees based on the French Resident General's orders. See Jacob Abadi, *Tunisia since the Arab Conquest: The Saga of a Westernized Muslim State* (Cornwall: Apollo Books, 2012) at 379.
[61] Arfawi, *The Judiciary and Politics in Tunisia during French Colonialism*, at 101.
[62] *Ibid,* at 394.
[63] *Ibid,* at 396.

death, another two to death in absentia, six others to hard labor for life, and two to hard labor for 20 years. Many Tunisian nationalists and political activists were labeled as "rebels" without a trial, and thus were exiled based on an administrative decision by the French Resident General.[64]

It should be noted that crimes of sabotage and insurgency were not necessarily defined by law. This is because the state of siege suspended ordinary laws and instead applied the French laws and other decrees adopted in Tunisia by the French army and the French Resident General.[65] The related articles of the French law are addressed in Chapter 7. Nonetheless, a general observation is that the French Penal Code of 1810, which is also referred to as the Napoleonic Code, had a revolutionary and vengeful nature that primarily served the empire.

In addition, in its homeland France adopted the Law of August 14, 1941, which established special courts that combined civil and military judges to try communists.[66] In Tunisia, a decree adopted on September 29, 1941 established special courts to try communists.[67] According to Arfawi, these special courts in Tunisia were formed by military officers and had special procedures that allowed suspects caught *in flagrante* to be tried directly without prior interrogation. In other cases, the investigation took no longer than eight days, and judgments were final.[68] Despite the fact that the communist movement in Tunisia was small in size and with limited influence, measures that were taken in France were implanted in Tunisia without consideration of actual necessity. This direct involvement of French laws in Tunisia is not seen in the case of colonized Egypt. The British in Egypt had exceptional powers, but they did not apply or implant their legal and judicial system.

POSTCOLONIALISM: THE CENTRALIZATION OF A "WESTERNIZED" AUTHORITARIAN REGIME (1950S–PRESENT)

French intervention in local affairs provoked the rage of Tunisians. Nationalists, under the leadership of Habib Bourguiba, did not seek negotiations with the French protectorate for redistribution of power, but pursued complete independence. Even though Bourguiba was arrested several times and was exiled more than once, his strategy suggested adopting an approach of gradual transition that ensured not only peaceful independence, but also a strong long-term relationship with France.[69]

Tunisia achieved independence in 1956, and Bourguiba came to power as a nationalist hero. Bourguiba sought a secular state that could bring Tunisia to the

[64] *Ibid*, at 398.
[65] *Ibid*, at 103.
[66] Sarah Fishman, *The Battle for Children: World War II, Youth Crime, and Juvenile Justice in Twentieth-Century France* (Cambridge, MA: Harvard University Press, 2002) at 105.
[67] Arfawi, *The Judiciary and Politics in Tunisia during French Colonialism*, at 103.
[68] *Ibid*.
[69] Alexander, *Tunisia*, at 31.

level of development of European countries. At the legal level, Bourguiba introduced the most liberal family and personal status law in North Africa. But at the
political level, he modernized the state selectively. Bourguiba turned Tunisia into a
single-party authoritarian regime. At a cultural level, he worked on weakening
Islamic traditions and developed a "secular national identity."[70] This included
closing the historical Islamic school Zitouna University.[71] Jennifer Noyon describes
modernization in Tunisia as a self-styled secularism: a rejection of higher laws,
with a continuous old-style Eastern mentality in treating people as subjects rather
than citizens.[72]

The lower classes continued to live according to their traditional Arab-Islamic
culture. Yet they felt marginalized. This led to a deepening of the social and cultural
gap between the Westernized classes and the traditional Arab-Islamic class, as
also happened in post-independence Algeria.[73] Rashid al-Ghannouchi, who is an
Islamic thinker and the co-founder of the En-Nahda Movement, describes this gap:

> The attack against religious institutions was one of the first decisions after independ-
> ence. My generation felt thus that it had been made extraneous, subjected to a very
> strong alienation, the victims of a kind of banishment[.]
>
> At independence, those who attended institutions dependent on Zitouna were
> about 25[,000] to 27,000. Those who were studying at secondary schools, created
> under the French occupation, were less than 4,500 to 5,000. So it was the majority
> which felt that it had been marginalized by the minority [. . .;] it was an effective
> minority because it could understand the West, and understand foreigners and
> communicate with the new international order.[74]

It should be noted that Tunisian Islamic movements are different than any other
Islamic movement in the Arab world. Unlike the Egyptian Muslim Brotherhood
and Algerian Islamic Salvation Front, Tunisian Islamists are moderate, with a liberal
approach to Islamic politics.[75] This moderate approach, however, did not save
Tunisian Islamists from the government's suppressive policy against Islamic movements and their potential influence. This included denying legal recognition to
their political parties, waves of arrests, and sentences of up to 11 years for no clear
wrongdoing.[76]

---

[70] Jennifer Noyon & Royal Institute of International Affairs, *Islam, Politics and Pluralism: Theory
     and Practice in Turkey, Jordan, Tunisia and Algeria* (London: Royal Institute of International
     Affairs, Middle East Programme, 2003) at 96.
[71] *Ibid* at 97.
[72] *Ibid* at 96.
[73] *Ibid*.
[74] Quoted in François Burgat & William Dowell, *The Islamic Movement in North Africa* (Austin,
     TX: Center for Middle Eastern Studies, University of Texas at Austin, 1993) at 54–5.
[75] Noyon & RIIA, *Islam, Politics and Pluralism* at 100.
[76] *Ibid*, 102.

The unrest between Bourguiba and the Islamists paved the way for the overthrow of Bourguiba, whose health was declining. In 1987, Prime Minister Zine El Abidine Ben Ali seized the presidency in a bloodless coup. The early stages of Ben Ali's rule witnessed some reforms, including abolishing the infamous state security court, and a new code regarding associations was adopted that allowed legal opposition parties. However, the substance of these reforms was bound by Article 7 of the constitution, which allowed citizens' rights to be limited for the sake of "public order, national defense, the development of the economy and social progress."[77]

At the beginning of his presidency Ben Ali showed tolerance toward Islamists, which led to reopening Zitouna University, releasing thousands of political prisoners, and promising a pluralist political environment capable of embracing both secular and religious thought.[78] Despite this political openness, Ben Ali was not expecting a serious challenge to his power. Once En-Nahda showed strong representation in the election of July 1989, it once again lost its legal recognition as a legitimate political party, and no party that mixed religion with politics was allowed.[79] From 1989 to 1992, violence was carried out by Islamists, which led to widespread arrests and repression. Charges included membership in an illegal organization and holding unauthorized meetings.[80]

This anti-Islamist campaign was later escalated by linking En-Nahda to terrorism. In this respect, Noyon observes that

> By carefully emphasizing the alleged terrorist character of En-Nahda, the regime was able to undermine the movement's legitimacy in the eyes of the people and to jail and repress its members. As "terrorists," they could be viewed as less than human or as carriers of a "disease," as the regime has since termed Islamism."[81]

Tunisia thus fell into authoritarianism. Bourguiba and Ben Ali had made Tunisia a *de facto* one-party state, discarding the values of republican life and democratic practices.

Although some claim that, politically, Tunisia has been relatively stable,[82] the 2010 uprising brought to the surface the consequences of the failure of the post-colonial authoritarian regime. From 2010 until the time of writing this book, the political life of Tunisia has been difficult to predict. People in Tunisia, Egypt, and elsewhere have staged massive populist revolutions, protesting for greater individual rights in the hope that the latter would additionally give rise to greater benefits for the population as a whole. Arab peoples have always remonstrated with social and

---

[77] Article 7 of the Tunisian Constitution of 1959.
[78] Kenneth Perkins, *A History of Modern Tunisia* (New York: Cambridge University Press, 2014) at 189.
[79] Noyon & RIIA, *Islam, Politics and Pluralism*, at 102–3.
[80] *Ibid*, at 106.
[81] *Ibid*, at 110.
[82] See Alexander, *Tunisia*, at 1–3.

political suppression; however, during the Arab Spring, protesters expressed their will by sacrificing their lives, in light of the high stakes – to live free or die with dignity. By the year 2010, Tunisia was suffering government corruption, high rates of unemployment, food inflation, and poor living conditions.[83] This economic decline provoked the whole population, including the Westernized elite, to oppose Ben Ali's reckless policy.

The starting point was in Tunisia when a street-cart vendor, Mohamed Bouazizi, immolated himself in protest against his continuous mistreatment by the police, who forcibly took his cart on December 17, 2010. The event led to a series of protests over unemployment and political restrictions, which led to what is known as the Jasmine Revolution. The protests continued despite the aggressiveness of the police in their use of live ammunition against mostly peaceful demonstrators.[84] The biggest achievement of this revolution was forcing Ben Ali to give up his presidency on January 14, 2011.

During Ben Ali's 23-year rule, Tunisia was turned into a police state in which thousands of political opponents had been jailed. Ben Ali sought to secure himself with a long-lasting authoritarian presidency, which required a suppressive policy against opposing political parties, particularly the Islamist party En-Nahda. The global wave of efforts to counter Islamist terrorism made any legal or extra-legal anti-terrorism efforts in Tunisia more acceptable.

NEO-COLONIALISM: ECONOMIC DEPENDENCE AND POLITICAL
SUBMISSION (1990S–PRESENT)

France has long feared the wave of violence related to the Algerian civil war that started in 1991. Algeria suffered bloody massacres undertaken by the Algerian Islamic Salvation Front and other Islamic groups and gangs. As an extension of this struggle, Algerian Islamist groups carried out terrorist attacks in France in 1995.[85] This regional threat required more efforts by the Tunisian government to secure itself and to satisfy France. In the 1990s, France and Europe supported Ben Ali's government by financial aid.[86] Aside from the strong relationships between France and Tunisia, Tunisia represents an important tourist spot for Europeans. This has required a strict national security policy that ensures the safety of tourists.

Tunisia continues to receive financial aid from France and the European Union. In January 2016, France promised to provide Tunisia with one billion euros over the

---

[83] Ibid.
[84] "World Report 2012: Tunisia, Events of 2011" Human Rights Watch, online: www
      .hrw.org/world-report-2012/world-report-2012-tunisia.
[85] Pia Christina Wood, "French Foreign Policy and Tunisia: Do Human Rights Matter?" (2002)
      9:2 Middle East Policy Council, online: www.mepc.org/journal/middle-east-policy-archives/
      french-foreign-policy-and-tunisia-do-human-rights-matter?print.
[86] Ibid.

next five years to support its economy. Yet some of the French financial aid has been directed to bankroll special military forces and cooperation between the two countries to counter terrorism.[87]

Another source of financial aid is the United States. Between 2012 and 2015, the United States loaned Tunisia one billion dollars and promised another $500 million. Tunisia was described by American officials as a "great model"[88] in a part of the world where democracy seems impossible. In July 2015, the United States designated Tunisia a major non-NATO ally, a status that could bring military cooperation.[89]

The lack of democracy in the Arab world is partially a result of the Western interest in maintaining the status quo. The constant Western financial and military support for Tunisia also represents approval of its suppressive policies. Such a Western–Tunisian relationship is thus transactional: Tunisia receives support as long as it complies with the neo-colonial requirements of counter-terrorism. Tunisia's submission to the West also leads it to drift into an overreactive approach in dealing with terrorist crimes, especially those aimed at Westerners.

CONCLUSION: DIRECT FRENCH TRANSPLANTING OF LAWS AND MEASURES

Unlike the British in Egypt, the French were directly involved in transplanting their laws into the Tunisian legal system. This had a major impact on postcolonial Tunisian ordinary laws and exceptional measures. During British colonialism Egypt had a parliament – regardless of how active it was – and a constitution, both of which empowered Egyptians to willingly adopt a system based on a French model to counter the British imperial order. Tunisia, on the other hand, had no parliament and no constitution, factors that allowed the French to easily control the autocratic ruler and his centralized powers. In addition, the French revolutionary way of ruling, derived from the French Revolution, requires changing the system of government in their colonies in accordance with their mindset. This is a differentiating feature between French and British colonialism of the late nineteenth and twentieth centuries. The British often supervised and advised, an implicit method of control, whereas the French did not hesitate in depriving the local authority of its powers. The direct involvement of the French in Tunisia normalized the colonial policy in this region. Thereafter, after colonialism, Tunisia continued to use exceptional measures even during peacetime.

---

[87] "Tunisia: 20 mil Euro in Aid from France against Terrorism" (October 6, 2015) *ANSAmed*, online: www.ansamed.info/ansamed/en/news/nations/tunisia/2015/10/06/tunisia-20-mil-euro-in-aid-from-france-against-terrorism_c6d04f24-ee1e-488a-adea-d1831bac8536.html.

[88] Julie Hirschfeld Davis, "John Kerry Says U.S. Will Give Tunisia More Financial Aid" (November 13, 2015) *New York Times*, online: www.nytimes.com.

[89] *Ibid.*

In addition, the Napoleonic Penal Code that was transplanted into Tunisia was known for its severity. Above all other interests, it aimed to protect the French Empire and the emperor himself. In this respect, Gerhard O. W. Mueller and Jean F. Moreau observe that

> The severity of the Penal Code of 1810 was remarkable [. . .] We are no longer facing a Code of Revolution or even of the "Consulate," but, in fact, a Code of the Empire, enacted at the apogee of Napoleon's reign [. . .;] this code was marked by some authoritarian ideas, and the felonies and misdemeanors against the state as such were repressed with harshness.[90]

The harsh nature of this law has been extended to the current Tunisian laws.

[90] *The French Penal Code*, translated by Gerhard O. W. Mueller & Jean F. Moreau (South Hackensack, NJ: F. B. Rothman, 1960) at 9.

7

Counter-Terrorism in Tunisia

Tunisia has had a less dramatic history than Egypt. Communism was less influential and Islamic movements are generally moderate in Tunisia. Despite this relative stability, Tunisia had strict national security and counter-terrorism laws and measures well before 9/11. This chapter starts by examining the early Tunisian national security laws. Tunisia has fewer national security laws and concerns than Egypt, but a stronger colonial heritage. French colonialism had direct influence over Tunisia, which was practiced through transplanting and applying French laws in protectorate Tunisia. After independence, with French approval, Tunisia selected the most arbitrary aspects of the French system and combined them with local regulations that served the indigenous authoritarian ambition.[1]

This chapter will first look at the relevant laws and measures introduced under colonialism. It examines the Penal Code of 1913, particularly the crimes of plotting and inciting, sabotage and rebellion or insurgency, which are specified in the Penal Code. The Tunisian Penal Code, which is still active, was framed by a French–Tunisian committee – a factor that affected the signification of the articles. The chapter then examines exceptionalism and militarism in Tunisia. Postcolonial Tunisia did not use the state of emergency extensively as Egypt did, but relied on military courts in trying civilians in national security cases. However, with the outbreak of the Revolution of 2011, a state of emergency was imposed from 2011 to 2014, and later from November 2015 till the date of writing this book, to deal with internal disorder and terrorist attacks.[2] During the state of emergency, military courts were established to try those involved in terrorism. These measures find their

---

[1] Arfawi, *The Judiciary and Politics in Tunisia during French Colonialism*, at 28.
[2] "Tunisia's Moncef Marzouki Lifts State of Emergency" (March 6, 2014) *BBC*, online: www .bbc.com; "Tunisia's President Extends Nationwide State of Emergency" (July 19, 2016) *Press TV*, online: www.presstv.com/Detail/2016/07/19/475982/Tunisia-Essebsi-Habib-Essid-Daesh-Libya-Algeria.

roots in the French colonial experience in Tunisia, which tried "subversions" before military courts.

The chapter then examines the Tunisian approach to counter-terrorism in the neo-colonial era, which is influenced by the global post-9/11 efforts to counter terrorism. Tunisia is the first Arab country that responded to Resolution 1373 (2001) by adopting a new anti-terrorism law. Nonetheless, Islamic terrorism was not an issue in Tunisia until recently. The fact that Tunisia is a neighbor of the strict Islamic Algeria, as well as the disordered Libya, makes Tunisia vulnerable to terrorist attacks and influx of arms. The regional instability and the Revolution of 2011 also shaped the more recent Tunisian legal attempts to counter terrorism. Right after the 2011 revolution, groups like Al-Qaeda in the Islamic Maghreb (AQIM) and Ansar al-Shari'a in Tunisia (AAS-T) took advantage of Tunisia's instability by establishing training camps in the country's suburbia.[3] They have been disturbing the peace and security of the post-revolutionary state and later the elected government through bombings and assassinations that target the army and the police, political figures, embassies, and civilians.[4] Tunisia responded to these threats by adopting draconian counter-terrorism law and measures.

The chapter examines the 2015 anti-terrorism law, with a focus on the definition of terrorism and crimes related to terrorism. It evaluates the broad definitions and harsh penalties and their usefulness in counter-terrorism. It also evaluates the special procedural regulations that could undermine the outcome of a fair trial. The chapter then examines other authoritarian laws and measures related to national security. These include Decree No. 115 of 2011 Concerning Freedom of the Press, Printing and Publishing (Press Law), and a cyber crime draft law. The focus of both is on censorship combined with the use of exceptional measures.

LAWS AND MEASURES REGARDING NATIONAL SECURITY: THE INFLUENCE OF COLONIALISM

French colonial expansion produced contradictory results that exist until this day. While France developed an advanced legal system, it established or allowed the establishment of oppressive laws in its colonies. For example, a new Tunisian Penal Code was adopted in 1913. This law reflects the overall principles of French law, but with some Tunisian features that are derived from both Islamic law and the earlier beys' arbitrary system. For instance, unlike the French Penal Code of 1810, which treats crimes of bodily harm against heads of state and their families as public order crimes, the Tunisian Penal Code of 1913 considers such crimes as crimes against the

[3] Oussama Romdhani, "Terror and Politics in Tunisia" *World Affairs Journal*, online: www.worldaffairsjournal.org/article/terror-and-politics-tunisia.
[4] "Country Reports on Terrorism 2013: Tunisia" *Embassy of the United States in Tunisia*, online: tunisia.usembassy.gov/country-reports-on-terrorism-2013-tunisia.html.

state, similar to the Islamic crime of *baghi*, which is basically carrying out assaults and violating imams. The next section addresses this double standard through examining the Tunisian Penal Code.

The Penal Code

Tunisia first adopted its modern Penal Code, which is still active, in 1913.[5] After independence the law was amended several times.[6] These amendments were made, as the code's preamble states, "to support the foundations of the Republican system and to respect all elements of national sovereignty and the establishment of the state of law and institutions and human rights[.]" This was in order to "refine the terminology and the form and to clear them of extraneous phrases associated with political and administrative systems no longer in line with independent Tunisia."[7] Despite this statement, the French influence can still be seen in the current law in the crimes of plotting and incitement, sabotage and rebellion/insurgency.

Plotting and Incitement

The crime of "plotting" is one of the oldest crimes in Tunisia, which provides special protection to the ruler and the royal family as part of the state. This approach vanished with the fading of imperialism and the emergence of democracy. However, Tunisia, as well as the rest of the Arab world, still clings to the earlier system of imperial protection for heads of state. The Tunisian Penal Code of 1913 defines the crime of plotting as an act that "occurs once there is an agreement, decision, or intention [to carry out] the action between two persons or more."[8] This text, which is still active, is derived from Articles 88 and 89 of the 1810 French Penal Code:

> 88. Such an attempt [*attentat*] exists, whenever any act is committed or commenced, in order to execute of those crimes, though they have not been actually effected.[9]
>
> 89. Such a plot [*complot*] exists, whenever the purpose of acting is concerted and resolved upon, between two or more conspirators, though there may not have been an attempt.[10]

In a subsequent article, the Tunisian Penal Code combines the crimes of plotting and incitement. Article 70 states that

---

[5] Tunisian Penal Code of 1913 (October 1, 1913) *Official Gazette* 79.
[6] Tunisian Penal Code amended in 1956, 1964, 1966, 1989, 1999, 2003, and 2005.
[7] Preamble of the Penal Code as amended by Law 46 of 2005.
[8] Article 69 of the Tunisian Penal Code.
[9] Article 88 of the French Penal Code of 1810.
[10] Article 89, *ibid.*

Expressing an opinion [proposing][11] to form a plot in order to commit any attacks [against the internal security of the State] as stated in Articles 63, 64 and 72 of this Code, shall be punished with ten years in exile and two years imprisonment[.][12]

This article shows the early speech restrictions in Tunisia. This article refers to three other articles that specify the values that are to be protected from plotting. Articles 63 and 64 consider assaults against the president a crime against the state,[13] whereas Article 72 considers "changing the form of the state, encouraging people to attack each another with weapons, or provoking disorder, murder and pillage."[14] The basis for these crimes is Article 87 of the 1810 French Penal Code, which criminalizes plotting "against the person of the emperor" or "to destroy or change the government."[15] It should be noted that when the Third French Republic was established, crimes against the life or safety of the president became ordinary crimes. Nevertheless, Tunisia did not adopt this amendment, reflecting a combination of the colonial heritage and a local authoritarian ambition.

Another article from the French Penal Code of 1810 that could be a basis for the Tunisian crime of plotting is Article 202, which condemns "any direct incitement to disobedience of the laws, or any other acts of the public authority, or if it tends to stir up or arm a part of the citizens against the others[.]"[16] This is an early speech regulation that goes back to the Napoleonic era. The wording of this article suggests a preemptive approach to countering potential rebellions. During colonialism, this approach provided protection to the Tunisian government and to the existence of the French in Tunisia.

The French not only transplanted their tough laws into Tunisia, but also created new, more arbitrary regulations that applied in colonies but not in France. For example, Tunisia adopted its Penal Code in 1913 under the supervision of the French colonists.[17] This law created the crimes of "Hatred or contempt of the President, the government, or the international administration[,]"[18] "Provoking people's anger in a way that confuses public security[,]"[19] and "Incit[ing] people to non-compliance with the country's laws[,]"[20] all punished with five years' imprisonment and a fine. This article was abolished in 1956; however, its essence still exists in other arbitrary articles within the Penal Code and other national security laws, as examined throughout this chapter.

---

[11] The text in the Tunisian Code, written in French, focuses on the actor, "l'auteur de la proposition," whereas the Arabic text focuses on the opinion. Both texts, however, are vague.
[12] Article 70 of the Tunisian Penal Code of 1913.
[13] Articles 63 and 64, *ibid.*
[14] Article 72, *ibid.*
[15] The full article is mentioned in Chapter 3 of this book.
[16] Article 202 of the French Penal Code of 1810.
[17] Arfawi, *The Judiciary and Politics in Tunisia during French Colonialism*, at 40.
[18] Article 81 of the Tunisian Penal Code of 1913, quoted in *ibid*, at 42.
[19] *Ibid.*
[20] *Ibid.*

Both the French and Tunisian legislatures seem to take the crime of inciting very seriously, even though they do not clarify its meaning. It is not clear whether illegal speech is limited to serious plans or includes sarcastic comments and jokes, or whether it depends on whether the other person accepts the proposal or rejects it. In fact, the wording of the mentioned articles suggests that committing a crime based on incitement is not required. Thus peaceful activities like criticizing the government can be arbitrarily condemned under the crime of "incitement."

Sabotage and Rebellion/Insurgency

Sabotage has no uncontroversial meaning, but it consists of attacks and damages of property primarily for political advantage. The Tunisian Penal Code describes this crime as, for example, "burning" or "destroying" state property, "attacking" private property," or "as, for example, 'burning,' 'destroying,' or 'attacking' property." This section also considers the crime of insurgency, which the Penal Code defines as disobeying orders, or attacking or threatening to attack law enforcement officers. This crime requires an interaction between "insurgents" and officers. Attacks on public property and attacks on public authority are listed in the Tunisian Penal Code under "attacks on public order."[21] As mentioned earlier, "Disturbances of Public Order"[22] is a notion established in the Napoleonic Penal Code of 1810. This suggests that Tunisia borrowed this notion – willingly or under French pressure – from the French model and implanted it into its own Penal Code.

The penalties associated with some cases of sabotage are severe: the Tunisian Penal Code considers destroying public property as sabotage that requires the death penalty. Article 76 states: "Shall be punished with death whoever burns or destroys by using explosive materials buildings or military ammunition stores or other state property."[23] The root of the crime of sabotage is Article 95 of the French Penal Code (addressed in Chapter 5), which condemns setting fires and the use of explosions to destroy public property. The wording for the Tunisian crime of sabotage is simpler than in Egyptian and French law; however, it is equally broad and flexible. This flexibility reflects a colonial rationale that desires the ability to interpret and apply the law selectively against opponents.

Another article addresses sabotage against private property. It states: "if an armed or non-armed group attacked the residence of a person or his work place [...] with the intention of assaulting, each [member of the group] shall be punished with three years imprisonment."[24] The Tunisian Penal Code considers attacks on private property as attacks on public order. This is not the case in the Napoleonic Code, which considers such attacks as crimes against individuals.[25] According to

---

[21] See Tunisian Penal Code of 1913, Book the Second, Chapter 2, Section 1 and 4.
[22] See French Penal Code of 1810, Book the Third, Title 1, Chapter 3, Section 3.
[23] Article 76 of the Tunisian Penal Code.
[24] Article 78, *ibid.*
[25] Article 436 of the French Penal Code of 1810.

Article 436 of the French Penal Code of 1810, "The threat of burning a habitation, or any other property, shall be punished with the penalty provided against the threat of assassination[.]"[26] The punishment ranges from the death penalty to no more than five years' imprisonment.[27] Another article about sabotage in the French Penal Code of 1810 states that:

> Whoever shall wilfully set fire to any buildings, ships, boats, warehouses, dock or timber yards; woods, undergrowth, or crops, either standing or cut down; and whether the wood be in heaps or cords, and the crops in heaps or stacks; or to combustible materials, so placed as to communicate the fire to such objects, or any of them; shall be punished with death.[28]

Even though sabotage in the above two cases is listed as a crime against individuals and not against the state, the punishment is severe in a way that makes the distinction between crimes against the state and crimes against individuals insignificant. Nonetheless, in some crimes against the state, the judge may apply other punitive measures, such as civic degradation and interdiction from some civil rights.[29] These measures are also found in the Tunisian Penal Code, and they are particularly applied in crimes against the state.[30] Analyzing the connection between the French and Tunisian penal codes indicates that Tunisian law selectively adopts harsh crimes from the French model and regards them as crimes against state security, a tendency that suggests an authoritarian ambition justified under the pretext of Westernization of law. Sabotage is the basis for other acts that are penalized, such as subversion, coup, and terrorism.

Rebellion is another crime against public order in Tunisian Penal Code. The Tunisian use of the word *'esyan*[31] can also be translated as "insurgency," but this book prefers the term "rebellion" in accordance with the French translation of the Tunisian law, which uses *rébellion*. This crime is regulated in nine articles of the Tunisian Penal Code,[32] giving it exaggerated emphasis. Unlike the Egyptian crime of rebellion, which focuses on the overthrow of the regime, the Tunisian law understands rebellion as the use of violence against public authority or security forces during their application of law and regulations. A rebel is defined in Article 116 as "whoever attacks with violence or threatens to do so an employee during his duty or person who is legally invoked to help the employee [. . .] or whoever attacks with violence or threatens to do so an employee to force him to do or not do something that is part of his job[.]"[33] Another article states: "whoever took part in an

---

[26] Article 436, *ibid.*
[27] Article 436 refers to the punishments imposed in Articles 305, 306, and 307. *Ibid.*
[28] Article 434, *ibid.*
[29] Articles 8 and 9 of the French Penal Code of 1810.
[30] *See* Articles 5, 70, and 141 of the Tunisian Penal Code.
[31] عصيان.
[32] Articles 116–24 of the Tunisian Penal Code.
[33] Article 116, *ibid.*

insurgency, with or without the use of weapons, assaulted a public employee during his duty, they shall be punished for their participation[.]"[34] The law also criminalizes inciting insurgency by condemning "whoever called for it in public places or public meetings or in advertisements or publications[,]" even if acts of insurgency did not occur.[35]

These articles have their origin in the Napoleonic model. The French Penal Code of 1810 in Article 209 considers "Every attack or resistance, by force or violence, against ministerial officers" as rebellion "according to the circumstances."[36] Articles 210–221 show that rebellion can be committed individually or by a group of people, armed or unarmed. In addition, inciting a rebellion is considered a full crime of rebellion.[37] The broadness and vagueness of this definition of rebellion is one of the noticeable features of the "flexibility" of the French Penal Code in regard to crimes against the state. This feature is also clear in the Tunisian Penal Code, which combines the inherited colonial rationale with local authoritarian ambition.

State of Emergency and Military Courts

The history of postcolonial Tunisia shows no use of state of siege. However, the French enacted the state of siege in Tunisia for sixteen years (1938–54).[38] The state of siege allowed the suspension of Tunisian laws and the application of French law and military courts. The long period of state of siege left a strong colonial heritage regarding exceptionalism and militarism in Tunisia.

In the postcolonial era, Tunisia replaced the state of siege with the state of emergency. The state of emergency is regulated by Presidential Decree of January 26, 1978. Emergency cases include imminent danger that threatens public order or disasters.[39] The president can declare a state of emergency in all or part of the state for a maximum period of 30 days, which may be extended by another decree. The state of emergency grants the authority to arrest and detain suspects, ban meetings, impose curfews, search places, and censor without prior permission from the judiciary.[40]

A state of emergency was declared five times between 1957 and 1984.[41] Both internal and external security threats were behind these declarations of the state of emergency. For instance, a state of emergency was declared three times from 1957 following

---

[34] Article 119, *ibid.*
[35] Article 212, *ibid.*
[36] Article 209 of the French Penal Code of 1810.
[37] Article 217, *ibid.*
[38] Arfawi, *The Judiciary and Politics in Tunisia during French Colonialism*, at 103.
[39] Article 1 of Tunisian Presidential Decree of January 26, 1978.
[40] Article 4, *ibid.*
[41] These were Law No. 29 of 1957 issued on September 9, 1957 declaring a state of emergency in five Tunisian governorates; Law No. 57 of 1958 issued on May 12, 1958 extending the previous state of emergency; Law No. 59 of 1958 issued on May 25, 1958 declaring a state of emergency

French threats and attacks by the French air force against Tunisia.[42] Threats to internal security were represented by general strikes.[43] In all of these cases, the state of emergency was declared for a limited time and was ended after the end of the emergency. Therefore, no observations regarding the misuse of state of emergency can be made in these cases. A second phase of the use of state of emergency started as a response to the uprising of 2011. At this time, the state of emergency was enforced for more than three continuous years, and declared occasionally in later years. As a result of the constant use of state of emergency, civilians were referred to military courts. However, despite this recent use of state of emergency, Tunisia relied on military courts well before 2011. This section examines the early use of military courts chronologically followed by the more recent use of state of emergency and its consequences.

Military courts are regulated by the Penal and Procedures Military Code No. 92 of 1957, adopted one year after independence. In 1979, Tunisia amended this law by expanding the military court's jurisdiction to include crimes of rebellion committed during peacetime. The jurisdiction of this court is derived from the colonial experience in following the French model, in which military courts targeted crimes against the state, particularly rebellion. Article 123 of the Tunisian Penal and Procedures Military Code states that:

> Shall be punished with the death penalty, any Tunisian who is enrolled in favor of a state that is at war with Tunisia, or joins rebels.
>
> And every Tunisian who puts himself during peacetime under the dominance of a foreign army or terrorist organization operating abroad, shall be punished with ten years of hard labor and banned from exercising civic rights and confiscation of all or part of his property [...].
>
> And shall be punished with the same penalty whoever incites to commit these crimes.[44]

This article represents the first codification of a crime of terrorism in Tunisia. It condemns mere membership in a "terrorist organization." The timing of adopting the above article requires a deeper look. An important event in the year of 1979 is the Iranian Islamic Revolution. Jacob Abadi argues that this revolution affected Tunisian Islamists in a way that concerned Bourguiba's regime.[45] Accordingly, Islamic movements were suspended and not allowed to form political parties.[46] The rise of Islamic movements represented a threat to Bourguiba's regime and France, and it

---

in all Tunisia; Order No. 49 of 1978 issued on January 26, 1978; Order No. 1 of 1984 issued on January 3, 1984 declaring a state of emergency in all Tunisia.

[42] Martin S. Alexander & J. F. V. Keiger, *France and the Algerian War, 1954–1962: Strategy, Operations and Diplomacy* (New York: Routledge, 2013) at xiii.

[43] Abadi, *Tunisia since the Arab Conquest*, at 495.

[44] Article 123 as amended by Decree-Law of Penal and Procedures Military Code No. 12 of 1979, issued on October 10, 1979.

[45] Abadi, *Tunisia since the Arab Conquest*, at 496.

[46] *Ibid*, at 498–9, 509.

was considered justified to reactivate colonial methods of social control within the Tunisian Penal and Procedures Military Code. The direct application of military courts in accordance with the above article of the Penal and Procedures Military Code has not been documented, probably because of the confidential and exceptional nature of such courts. However, Human Rights Watch observes that, since the mid-1990s, under the above article the authorities have accused hundreds of civilian Tunisians who live abroad and have come back home of "serving terrorist organizations operating abroad."[47] According to Human Rights Watch, most were sentenced to not less than eight years' imprisonment, even though the court, in most of the cases, did not accuse them of committing any violent acts.[48]

In 2011, Ben Ali's regime was overthrown, and a state of emergency was declared that lasted from January 15, 2011 until March 6, 2014. In 2015 and 2016, a number of terrorist attacks were committed, leading the state to declare the state of emergency again. During these periods of state of emergency, several exceptional measures were taken, including speech restrictions and trying civilians by military courts.[49] Journalists criticizing state policy through writing or even caricature were accused of crimes against "public order."[50] Comments by civilians on social media were also considered crimes against the state.[51] Civilians were constantly referred to military courts for their speech crimes. This approach has its roots in colonial practice, as we showed in Chapter 6. The problem with this approach is that it does not aim to deter crimes as much as to impose control and discipline.

In 2015, Tunisia issued a new anti-terrorism law that defines terrorism over-broadly. The Tunisian authority has been misusing this law by accusing hundreds of Tunisians of terrorism for their political opinions and without committing or planning to commit any violent action.[52] The following section examines the recent Tunisian anti-terrorism law and policy in more detail.

THE TUNISIAN ANTI-TERROR APPROACH IN A NEO-COLONIAL ERA: THE PEAK OF AUTHORITARIANISM

Although the recent increase of terrorist violence in Tunisia is related to post-revolution instability, Tunisia's counter-terrorism measures have a long history.

---

[47] *Human Rights Watch World Report, 2003* (New York: Human Rights Watch, 2003) at 489–90.
[48] *Ibid*, at 489.
[49] "Tunisia: Events of 2015" *Human Rights Watch*, online: www.hrw.org/world-report/2016/coun try-chapters/tunisia.
[50] "Tunisia: Severe Restrictions on Liberty and Movement Latest Symptoms of Repressive Emergency Law" (March 17, 2016) *Amnesty International*, online: www.amnesty.org/en/press-releases/2016/03/tunisia-severe-restrictions-on-liberty-and-movement-latest-symptoms-of-repres sive-emergency-law/.
[51] *Ibid*.
[52] *Ibid*.

During the reign of President Bourguiba, Islamist identity was fought against as part of ensuring a secular state. President Ben Ali also applied the same rationale. And since the "global war on terror" was primarily directed against Islamic groups, Ben Ali found it a useful tool against Tunisian Islamists in general who represented a considerable competitor in the parliamentary and presidential elections. As in Egypt, Ben Ali's tactics included banning religious parties from standing for election and jailing Islamic and other political opponents.

Ben Ali used the constitution as a tool to express his politicized desire to protect his position. For instance, with the increasing power of Islamists, a constitutional reform was adopted in 1997 that prohibited establishing political parties on the basis of religion.[53] This restriction no longer exists in the 2014 Tunisian constitution.

In the aftermath of 9/11, Tunisia responded to Security Council Resolution 1373 by adopting the 2003 Law in Support of International Efforts to Fight Terrorism and the Repression of Money Laundering. This law was established regardless of the fact that in Tunisia from 1991 until 2005 only one terrorist attack was carried out. That was on Djerba Island in April 2002, and targeted the Ghriba synagogue, resulting in the deaths of around 19 people, including tourists and citizens.[54] Other incidents were announced by the Tunisian government in December 2006 and January 2007, in which security forces engaged in clashes with armed militants.[55] However, since the revolution of 2011, terrorist attacks have become uncountable.

In the aftermath of the 2011 uprising in Tunisia, there were calls to amend the 2003 anti-terrorism law.[56] As a response, in May 2013, Minister of Human Rights and Transitional Justice Samir Dilou announced that a draft law was being prepared. Chakib Darwish, a spokesperson for the Ministry, promised that the draft law would contain "a precise and clear definition of terrorist crime, unlike the old law, where the definition of the crime of terrorism was loose and open to many interpretations [.]"[57] Also, there was a promise that the new law would respect human rights.[58]

In March 2015, as response to terrorist attacks, Tunisia imposed arbitrary travel restrictions primarily on males under 35 years old. To ensure that the intended trip was not intended for jihad, the restrictions require written authorization from the traveler's parents. These restrictions are based neither on law nor an order from a

---

[53] The fifth paragraph of Article 8 of the Tunisian Constitution. Added by Constitutional Law No. 65 of 1997, October 27, 1997.

[54] "Al-Qaeda Claims Tunisia Attack" (June 23, 2002) *BBC*, online: news.bbc.co..

[55] William Mark Habeeb, *The Middle East in Turmoil: Conflict, Revolution, and Change* (Santa Barbara, CA: ABC-CLIO, 2012) at 158.

[56] "Tunisia: Amend Counterterrorism Law, Reforms Necessary to Protect Fundamental Rights" (May 29, 2013) *Human Rights Watch*, online: www.hrw.org/news/2013/05/29/tunisia-amend-counterterrorism-law.

[57] "Tunisia Gearing Up to Implement New Anti-Terrorism Bill" (January 6, 2014) *AFK Insider*, online: afkinsider.com/36751/tunisia-anti-terrorism-bill/#sthash.L1QhxLbl.dpuf.

[58] *Ibid.*

court.[59] These restrictions violate constitutional and international human rights, but the war on terror seems to justify all means in Tunisia.

Such restrictions, however, rely on implicit support in Security Council Resolution 2178, which encourages states to impose restrictions on traveling. The neo-colonial powers, represented by the permanent members of the Security Council, are directing not only the war on terror, but also the course of democracy worldwide, and particularly in Third World countries. The rationale of the Tunisian anti-terrorism measures suggests selectivity: while influenced by the imperfect obligations of Security Council resolutions, it also embodies a colonial logic, all of which serves authoritarian ambition rather than human security.

In August 2015, Tunisia adopted a new anti-terrorism law, which reflects the same combination of colonial legacy and neo-colonial policy. The new law so far has not deterred the frequent terrorist crimes carried out throughout 2016, 2017, and 2018. In addition, it did not provide human rights guarantees as promised. This retreat in criminal justice is examined in the following section.

EVALUATING THE TUNISIAN ANTI-TERRORISM LEGISLATION

Even though Tunisia had no history of jihadism, the secular governments of Bourguiba and Ben Ali adopted tough national security laws that particularly suppressed Islamists. During Ben Ali's presidency, two legal steps to counter terrorism were taken: adopting a definition of terrorism in 1993 within the Penal Code and adopting a separate anti-terrorism law in 2003. After the overthrow of Ben Ali's regime in 2011, the new government sought a new anti-terrorism law to counter the unprecedented wave of terrorism in Tunisia. A new law was adopted in 2015. This section is divided into two parts: anti-terrorism laws prior to 2015, and the anti-terrorism law of 2015.

Counter-Terrorism Prior to 2015

Tunisia first added a definition of "terrorism" to the Penal Code in 1993. Accordingly, terrorist acts included "all actions relating to individual or collective initiatives, aiming at undermining individuals or properties, through intimidation or terror" and "acts of incitement to hatred or to religious or other fanaticism, regardless of the means used."[60] This article does not clarify the meaning of "terror." In addition, by condemning inciting hatred, this definition of terrorist acts overlaps with hate crime. The focus on incitement of terror or hatred suggests that Tunisia

---

[59] "Tunisia: Arbitrary Travel Restrictions: Apparent Effort to Prevent Recruiting by Extremists" (July 10, 2015) *Human Rights Watch*, online: www.hrw.org/news/2015/07/10/tunisia-arbitrary-travel-restrictions.

[60] Article 52*bis*, amended by Law 93–112 of November 22, 1993, and abolished in 2003.

was ahead of the international regulations in targeting speech associated with terrorism. It should be noted that the criminalization of inciting hatred is drawn from the French Press Law, which condemns inciting hatred or violence based on religious or other grounds.[61]

In 2002, Tunisia had its first significant terrorist act on Djerba Island (mentioned above). This resulted in Tunisia rushing into responding to UN Security Council Resolution 1373 (2001) by adopting a separate anti-terrorism law in 2003. This made Tunisia the first Arab country to respond to the above resolution. In December 2003, Tunisia passed the Law Concerning Support for International Efforts to Combat Terrorism and Prevent Money-Laundering.[62] Article 4 defines terrorism as:

> Shall be categorized as terrorist, every offense, regardless of its motives, related to an individual or collective undertaking liable to intimidate a person or group of persons or spread alarm among the population with the intention of influencing the policy of the state and prompting it to do or abstain from doing any action, disturbing public order or international peace and security, causing harm to persons or property, damaging the headquarters of diplomatic and consular missions and international organizations, inflicting serious harm on the environment so as to endanger the life or health of inhabitants, or damaging vital resources, the infrastructure, transport, communications, information system or public amenities.[63]

This broad definition is similar to the Egyptian definition in including vague terms such as "disturbing public order" and "causing harm to persons or property." It includes the crime of sabotage by condemning causing damage to properties, as well as rebellion/insurgency by condemning forcing authorities to act or prevent them from acting in a certain way. It also criminalizes mere membership without requiring specific acts of violence to be committed.

Despite the fact that no major terrorist attacks were carried out in Tunisia for several years, a report by Human Rights Watch shows that under Ben Ali's regime, over 3,000 people were prosecuted under this law.[64] This huge number of prosecutions in a relatively safe country suggests that anti-terrorism law serves the authoritarian government rather than the safety of the nation.

In 2015, Tunisia adopted a new anti-terrorism law. The 2015 anti-terrorism law abolished the earlier law of 2003. Therefore, we will limit the discussion of the 2003 law to the above paragraphs and will address the 2015 law in detail in the following section.

---

[61] Article 24 of the French Press Law of 1881.
[62] Tunisian Act No. 75 of 2003 (December 10, 2003).
[63] Translation quoted in Welshman, "Rocks, Hard Places and Human Rights," at 648.
[64] "Tunisia: Amend Counterterrorism Law, Reforms Necessary to Protect Fundamental Rights" (May 29, 2013) at 830.

Law No. 26 of 2015 Regarding Anti-Terrorism and Money-Laundering

After a series of terrorist attacks in 2015, on August 7 of that year Tunisia adopted a new anti-terrorism law. This law defines "terrorism" and "terrorist offenses" over-broadly. It focuses on terrorism financing and speech crimes in a way that combines post-9/11 neo-colonial logic and authoritarian ambition. It also creates special procedural regulations similar to the exceptional regulations inherited from coloni-alism. This section discusses these themes consecutively, starting with the definition of terrorism, followed by speech related to terrorism, terrorism financing, and finally the procedural regulations.

The Definition of "Terrorism"

The anti-terrorism law of 2015 is similar to the previous law of 2003 in adopting broad definitions and vague terms. Terrorism is defined in Article 13 as:

> [Acts] deliberately implemented by any means an individual or collective project to commit any act listed in articles 14 to 36 aiming by its nature or context to spread terror among the population or to unduly compel a State or an international organization to do what it is not obliged to do or refrain from doing what it is obliged to do.

The Tunisian definition, unlike the Egyptian, requires spreading fear or terror as an essential element of terrorism. Spreading fear is a controversial element. Some consider it, from a linguistic point of view, as part of the term "terrorism" that reflects the feeling of terror,[65] while others reject adding this element to terrorist offenses and suggest confining the definition to attacking civilians.[66] Even if the effect of an explosion is limited to one place, its psychological and social effects (fear) are globally generated among people. What makes the element of fear controversial as part of a definition of terrorism is that the feeling of terror or fear is a psychological element that cannot be confined to terrorist crimes. School shootings, among other crimes, accidents, and tragedies, also terrify the whole society. The role of the media should also be considered in focusing on tragedies and in anticipating investigations by using big labels like "terrorists" and "enemies." This not only provokes people's emotions, but also manipulates them to believe whatever is being transplanted into their minds without being able to engage in a social dialogue. This is particularly true considering the fact that civil society organizations often either get into trouble or are seen as troublemakers. This irrational social chain of actions (e.g., violence) and immediate reactions (e.g., media judgments) maximizes the spread of fear.

---

[65] Saul, *Defining Terrorism in International Law*, at 62.
[66] Coady, "Defining Terrorism," at 39.

"Terrorism offenses" are listed in Article 14 of the 2015 Law as:

1- Killing a person;
2- Injuring, assaulting, or other forms of violence contemplated by Articles 218 and 319 of the Penal Code;
3- Causing other forms of injury, assault or violence;
4- Damaging the buildings of diplomatic or consular missions, or international organizations;
5- Causing harm to food security and to the environment in a way that unbalances ecosystems or natural resources or puts the life or health of its inhabitants in danger;
6- Intentionally opening flood discharge from dams or pouring chemicals or biological materials into those dams or into water facilities to cause harm to inhabitants;
7- Causing harm to public or private property, vital resources or infrastructure or means of transport or communication means or computer systems or public services[.]

This broad definition does not require the use of violence and does not elucidate the level of damage that is considered terrorism. Damaging property, which is a form of the crime of sabotage, is becoming a common clause in many Arab definitions of terrorism. The origin of these crimes is the Napoleonic Penal Code of 1810, which treats most of the crimes of "destruction, spoil, and damage" under the title of crimes against individuals.[67] As we mentioned earlier, the Tunisian legislature has long treated these crimes as crimes against the state and public order.

Another article of the 2015 anti-terrorism law suggests that the definition of terrorism is not limited to violent crimes like murder and sabotage, but also includes membership in terrorist entities and receiving "training" domestically or abroad for the purpose of committing terrorist crimes. Article 32 states that:

> Shall be considered a perpetrator of a terrorist crime and shall be punished with imprisonment of six years up to twelve years and a fine of twenty thousand up to fifty thousand dinar, whomever intentionally joined [...] inside or outside the Republic, a terrorist organization or agreement associated with terrorist crimes, or received training [...] with the intention to commit any of the crimes listed in this law.[68]

The article condemns mere membership in a terrorist organization without requiring committing violent acts. It is also not clear what kind of training is prohibited. This article leaves the door open for political interpretation of who is a terrorist or belongs to a "terrorist organization" or is involved in a terrorist agreement.

---

[67] Articles 434–42 of the French Penal Code of 1810.
[68] Article 32 of the 2015 Tunisian Anti-Terrorism Law.

Speech Related to Terrorism

As part of the definition of "terrorist offenses," Article 14 of the 2015 law condemns "*Takfir* or advocating for [excommunication], or incitement of or calling for hatred or loathing among races, religions and faiths."[69] The meanings of the terms "*takfir*" and "incitement" both leave the door open for broad and arbitrary interpretations. Even though the criminalization of incitement seems to follow the post-9/11 regulations, its origin goes back to colonialism, as mentioned earlier in our discussion of the definition of terrorism that was added in 1993 to the Tunisian Penal Code.[70]

The origin of criminalizing *takfir* is most likely Sharia law, which condemns excommunication among Muslims. Nevertheless, religious-based speech restrictions are found in the Napoleonic Penal Code. For instance, Article 201 of this code states,

> Ministers of religion, who shall pronounce, in the exercise of their ministry, and in a public assembly, any discourse, containing any criticism upon, or censure of, government, or of any law, imperial decree, or other act of the public authority, shall be punished with an imprisonment of from three months to two years.

Article 202 of the Napoleonic Penal Code follows, stating that:

> If the discourse contains any direct incitement to disobedience of the laws, or any other acts of the public authority, or if it tends to stir up or arm a part of the citizens against the others; the minister of religion who shall have pronounced it, shall be punished with an imprisonment of from two to five years, if the provocation has not been followed by any effect; and with banishment, if it has caused any disobedience, other than such as shall have ended in sedition or revolt.

The tension between the state and religion has a long history, which goes beyond the scope of this book. However, long-term solutions require more than legal restrictions. The criminal law should not be the only tool for promoting security. Sociopolitical solutions must be provided to deal with hate speech and incitement, which can be symptoms of an imbalanced social system.

Another article of this law that criminalizes incitement states that "It is considered a terrorist crime and shall be punished with half the original penalties, whoever incites by any means to commit [terrorist crimes.]"[71] This article does not require that the terrorist act is committed, but "the possibility of committing it"[72] is considered a sufficient basis for condemnation. According to a paper by the International Court of Justice (ICJ), this article fails to explain the boundaries of

---

[69] Paragraph 8 of Article 14, *ibid.*
[70] Article 52*bis* of the Tunisian Penal Code.
[71] Article 5 of the 2015 Tunisian Anti-Terrorism Law.
[72] *Ibid.*

incitement and its subjective intent.[73] Applying this article becomes more problematic when looking at the broad definition of terrorism in this law, which has the capacity to include any violent and non-violent acts.

Article 31 of the 2015 anti-terrorism law criminalizes speech that apologizes for terrorism. According to this article, speech is considered a terrorist act when a person "inside or outside the Republic, by any means, praises and glorifies, in a public, clear and manifest manner, a terrorist offense or its perpetrator or an organization or a conspiracy related to terrorist offenses or its members or its activities."[74] This article is drafted overbroadly in a way that reflects the spirit of the French Press Law of 1881 and censorship during colonialism (discussed earlier in this chapter).

Contrary to the above approach, the UN Special Rapporteurs on Counter-terrorism and on Freedom of Expression suggest that because of the consequences of the criminalization of these offenses, criminalizing "glorification" offenses should be avoided. Such offenses "must be proscribed by law in precise language, including by avoiding reference to vague terms such as 'glorifying' or 'promoting' terrorism[.]"[75]

Terrorism Financing

The 2015 anti-terrorism law combines counter-terrorism and anti-money laundering. In this respect, it follows the previous law of 2003. The 2003 law took that form partially to satisfy the Financial Action Task Force's requirements. In other words, it was a formality rather than an effective act of crime control. The new law also emphasizes financing regulations, but combining terrorism financing and money laundering in one law and sometimes within the same articles has caused an overlap between the two.

In 2003, Tunisia reported its financing regulations to the Counter-Terrorism Committee. According to the Tunisian report, the 2003 anti-terrorism law allows freezing of funds "even if no suspicious or unusual operation or transaction is reported, if authorized by the president of the Tunis Court of First Instance on the basis of a request from the Attorney-General to the Tunis Court of Appeal."[76] This regulation is transferred to the 2015 anti-terrorism law.[77] Freezing funds without an actual crime having been committed or planned is an arbitrary measure that

---

[73] International Commission of Jurists, Position Paper: "Tunisia's Law on Counter-Terrorism in Light of International Law and Standards" (August 6, 2015) *International Commission of Jurists*, online: icj.wpengine.netdna-cdn.com/wp-content/uploads/2015/08/Tunisia-CT-position-paper-Advocacy-PP-2015-ENG-REV.pdf. at 6.

[74] Article 31 of the Tunisian Anti-Terrorism Law of 2015.

[75] Special Rapporteur on the Promotion and Protection of Human Rights and Fundamental Freedoms while Countering Terrorism, para 31.

[76] "Note verbale dated 15 September 2003 from the Permanent Mission of Tunisia to the United Nations addressed to the Chairman of the Security Council Committee established pursuant to Resolution 1373 (2001) concerning counter-terrorism" (October 27, 2003) S/2003/1038 [Tunisia's Report to the CTC, 2003]. In this report, Tunisia refers to the regulations of Article 94 of the 2003 Tunisian anti-terrorism law.

[77] Article 133 of Tunisian Anti-Terrorism Law of 2015.

belongs to the logic of enemy criminal law. The CTC showed no criticism of such measures. This passive attitude is an implicit neo-colonial license to continue using unfair measures without fear of being criticized.

The law prohibits funding terrorist entities or terrorist activities.[78] It also prohibits accepting funds from unknown sources or from entities involved in terrorism.[79] While these regulations are reasonable, without a clear definition of terrorism any opposition group can be listed as a potential terrorist entity. In 2013, Tunisia declared the radical Ansar al-Sharia a terrorist group.[80] The news spread about this decision, but without clarifying the actual body or person who made this decision.

The 2015 anti-terrorism law established an executive body that has the authority to freeze funds, without a clear reference to procedures for listing and de-listing. This body is called the National Commission to Combat Terrorism, which includes representatives of the Prime Minister, Ministry of Justice, Ministry of Interior Affairs, Ministry of Foreign Affairs, and many others. This commission has many nominal tasks, such as "preparing a national study on identifying the phenomena of terrorism and terrorism financing" and "cooperating with international organizations and civil society" to counter terrorism.[81] However, the importance of this commission, as mentioned earlier, is in its authority to freeze the funds of suspected terrorists and terrorist entities.[82] According to Article 103 of the Tunisian Anti-Terrorism Law of 2015, "The National Commission to Combat Terrorism shall within its framework to fulfill Tunisia's international obligations decide to freeze the funds of persons or organizations that appear to it or to the specialized international bodies to be in association with terrorist offenses."[83] The article does not show the basis for and evidence relied upon in the commission's decisions.

Centralizing powers within the executive is a theme inherited from French colonialism and combined with authoritarian ambition. Since 9/11, centralization is being reimposed in Tunisia by supra-national practices required by the UN Security Council and its right to list and de-list. Such a system undermines the role of ordinary judicial review.

Procedural Regulations

The 2015 anti-terrorism law establishes within the ordinary Tunisian judicial system a specialized court for terrorist cases.[84] This court can be seen as an extension of the colonial legacy, which dealt with crimes against the state within an exceptional

---

[78] Article 98, *ibid.*
[79] Article 99, *ibid.*
[80] "Tunisia Declares Ansar al-Sharia a Terrorist Group" (August 27, 2013) *BBC*, online: www .bbc.com.
[81] Article 68 of the Tunisian Anti-Terrorism Law of 2015.
[82] Article 103, *ibid.*
[83] Article 103, *ibid.*
[84] Article 40, *ibid.*

framework. The court established by this law also has an exceptional nature regarding due process, extradition, and its exclusion of security forces members from criminal accountability, as will be explained in this section.

According to Article 40, a Counter-Terrorism Judicial Pole is established in the Court of Appeal in Tunis. Until September 2017, the court has eight judges, a small number that has affected the speed of trials.[85] In February 2017, the UN Special Rapporteur on the promotion and protection of human rights and fundamental freedoms while countering terrorism, Ben Emmerson, raised concerns after visiting Tunisia. He was informed that more than 1,500 individuals had been investigated and prosecuted of terrorist crimes. Less than 10 percent of those had been charged, whereas the rest remained in detention.[86] The Special Rapporteur points out the consequences of long detention, which would particularly affect "those charged with terrorism because they are less likely to be granted provisional release, because their cases sometimes take years to come to trial and because they receive the longest sentences."[87] Among the Special Rapporteur's concerns are the conditions of the Mornaguia Prison, which "is approximately 150 % over capacity[.]"[88] Such practices reflect a dangerous decline of Tunisian criminal justice system, with little or no improvement of security relating to counter-terrorism.

So far, the court has issued several tough verdicts, including the death penalty.[89] It is worrisome to see that the death penalty is still applied in a country that has, overall, a moderate policy and has been taking some serious steps toward democracy. Although Tunisia largely follows the French legal system, and although France abolished the death penalty in 1981, Tunisia still clings to the Napoleonic model and its vengeful nature.

Another point concerns the court's jurisdiction over terrorist cases. The court's jurisdiction covers crimes committed inside or outside Tunisia. According to Article 83,

> The court of first instance of Tunis, through the judges appointed to the Judicial Pole of Counter-terrorism, is competent to examine terrorist crimes stipulated in this law and related offenses committed outside the national territory in the following cases:
> – If they are committed by a Tunisian citizen,
> – If they are committed against Tunisian persons or interests,

---

[85] "19 qadiyan fi qutbay al eqtisad wa wl erhab" "[19 Judges in the Poles of Economy and Terrorism]" (September 9, 2017) *Tunisie Telegraph*, online: tunisie-telegraph.com, www .ohchr.org/EN/NewsEvents/Pages/DisplayNews.aspx?NewsID=21156&LangID=E.

[86] UN Human Rights Office of the High Commission, Special Rapporteur on the Promotion and Protection of Human Rights and Fundamental Freedoms while Countering Terrorism Concludes Visit to Tunisia (February 3, 2017).

[87] *Ibid.*

[88] *Ibid.*

[89] "Mahkama Tunisia tusder ahkam bil e'dam dud annassir irhabia" ["Tunisian Court Sent Terrorist Members to Death"] (March 3, 2016) *ASharaq Al-Awsat*, online: http://aawsat.com/ home/article.

– If they are committed against foreign persons or interests, by a foreigner or a stateless person whose habitual residence is Tunisia, or by a foreigner or stateless person on the national territory, and the relevant foreign authorities have not requested his extradition before a final judgment is rendered against him by the competent Tunisian courts.

The same tendency is found in the Egyptian Anti-Terrorism Law (examined in Chapter 5). The problem of including crimes committed outside Tunisia under Tunisian jurisdiction arises in particular in relation to the group of crimes of speech related to terrorism. Opponents who freely and legally express their political opinion outside Tunisia might still be found guilty under Tunisia's Anti-Terrorism Law.

The Tunisian Anti-Terrorism Law explicitly states that "'Terrorist crimes are in no way considered political offenses,'"[90] and "'Terrorist financing crimes are in no way considered as fiscal offenses[.]'"[91] Therefore, extradition for terrorist crimes is mandatory.[92] However, the Law does not include safeguards relating to extradition, especially regarding prisoners of conscience who might face harsh penalties according to the Tunisian Anti-Terrorism Law. The Special Rapporteur raised concerns about allegations of the Tunisian authority's use of torture or other forms of ill-treatment against terrorist suspects.[93] Nonetheless, Article 88 of the Anti-Terrorism Law states that Tunisia shall not grant extradition to another country "if there are substantial grounds for believing that the person subject to the extradition request would be at risk of being subjected to torture or the request for extradition intended to track or punish a person for his race, color, origin, religion, sex, nationality or political opinions."[94]

This article suggests that Tunisia is able or willing to protect terrorist suspects from other jurisdictions if there might be a risk of torture or discrimination based on political opinion. However, the law does not provide such safeguards inside Tunisia, suggesting a disparity between Tunisia's internal lack of human rights and its external ambition for political control.

In Article 39 the Anti-Terrorism Law allows judicial police officers to keep suspects in custody for five days. Article 41 allows the Public Prosecutor to extend the detention for a maximum of 15 days.[95] These periods of detention may be renewed twice. On the other hand, the Tunisian Criminal Procedure Code as amended in 2016 limits the period of custody to a maximum of 48 hours based on permission from the Public Prosecutor, which may be renewed once.[96] Despite the

---

[90] Article 87 of the Tunisian Anti-Terrorism Law of 2015.
[91] *Ibid.*
[92] *Ibid.*
[93] *Ibid.*
[94] Article 88, *ibid.*
[95] Article 41, *ibid.*
[96] Article 13*bis* of the Tunisian Criminal Procedure Code as amended in 2016 (Law No. 5 of 2016).

guarantees of the Criminal Procedure Code, the latest amendment of this code in 2016 created an exception for terrorist cases. Article 57 of the Criminal Procedure Code states that "for the needs of investigating terrorist cases, the investigative judge may not allow the lawyer to visit the suspect, attend the hearing, or view the documents for a maximum period of 48 hours, unless the Public Prosecutor has previously taken a decision on this ban."[97] This duality in applying the law, in which suspects of ordinary crimes are granted procedural rights whereas suspects of terrorism are treated as enemies, belongs to the colonial strategy of exceptionalism that was justified during wartime or state of siege. As we showed earlier in this chapter when discussing the state of exception, French colonialism suspended law and applied a set of exceptional orders that ensured the suppression of opponents.[98]

Another article shields members of security forces from criminal accountability when using force while performing their duty in countering terrorism. This is similar to the Egyptian anti-terrorism law of 2015 that we discussed in Chapter 5. The Tunisian law was issued nine days before the Egyptian law, which suggests there was no direct influence between the two. Article 72 of the Tunisian Anti-Terrorism Law of 2015 stipulates that:

> In addition to self-defense cases, internal security forces, military personnel and assistance officers are not criminally liable when they use force or give orders to use force if that was necessary to perform tasks within the limits of the law, or internal regulations and instructions given on a legal basis in the framework of fighting terrorist crimes provided by this law.[99]

The article does not impose any explicit restrictions or any specific requirements regarding proportionality.[100] By placing the authority of its security forces above other values, this article reflects the spirit of colonialism and authoritarianism in countering rebellion and insurgency. The above article leaves the door open for the use of coercion and shoot-to-kill tactics – a possibility that is not far from the actual Tunisian experience.

Other Authoritarian Laws and Measures

After the "Arab Spring," Tunisia adopted new legal and political reforms aiming to respect civil liberties and rights. This was part of the revolutionary reaction to the suppressive era of Ben Ali. During that era, the Tunisian press was one of the most monitored in the Arab world. The media was subject to strict censorship that did not

---

[97] Article 57, *ibid.*
[98] Arfawi, *The Judiciary and Politics in Tunisia during French Colonialism*, at 103–5.
[99] Translation quoted in International Commission of Jurists, Position Paper: "Tunisia's Law on Counter-Terrorism in Light of International Law and Standards," at 845.
[100] *Ibid.*

tolerate criticism. After the revolution, the need to break these old chains required the regulation of the press.

On November 2, 2011, Tunisia adopted Decree No. 115 of 2011 Concerning Freedom of the Press, Printing and Publishing (Press Law). The Law aimed to regulate the profession of journalism and respect journalists' rights. Article 1 states that:

> The right to freedom of expression is guaranteed and exercised in accordance with the provisions of the International Covenant on Civil and Political Rights and other relevant international treaties ratified by the Republic of Tunisia, and the provisions of this decree.
>
> The right to freedom of expression includes the free circulation, dissemination and reception of news, opinions and ideas of any kind.
>
> Restrictions on freedom of expression can be done only by legislative provision and provided that:
>
> – The purpose of which is to achieve a legitimate interest in respect for the rights and dignity of others, the maintenance of public order or the protection of national defense and security.
>
> – And to be necessary and proportionate in accordance with regulations of a democratic society without jeopardizing the essence of the right to freedom of expression and information.

This article acknowledges freedom of expression yet within legal limitations, which include maintaining "public order" and the "protection of national defense and security." These restrictions could be proportionate and useful if they are limited to cases like disclosing military secrets, but the practice in Tunisia shows flexibility in interpreting these restriction clauses. For instance, a journalist who quoted information from the *Washington Post* about the establishment of an American military base in Tunisia was accused of harming national defense.[101]

The problem in Tunisia is not limited to the vague wording of restriction clauses such as the one above, but is reflected in the justice system as a whole. In Tunisia, practice shows that journalists are not charged in accordance with the Press Law, which includes penalties of a maximum of three years' imprisonment, but with the Penal Code, Anti-Terrorism Law, and – worst of all – the Code of Military Justice. These laws include the death penalty for "harming national defense."[102] The practice of trying civilians before military courts has been particularly justified since 2015 with the declaration of the state of emergency. Tunisia's systematic use of military and exceptional measures combined with draconian laws does not foster hope for a democratic society.

---

[101] "Tunisia: Journalists Before Military Tribunal: Prosecuted for Criticizing the Army" (November 30, 2016) *Human Rights Watch*, online: www.hrw.org/news/2016/11/30/tunisia-journalists-military-tribunal.
[102] *Ibid.*

Tunisia intends to issue a cyber crime draft law, but no draft law has yet been realized. Despite that, social media has become a monitored "trap" for potential terrorists, as a Tunisian journalist describes it.[103] From 2011 to 2016, Tunisian authorities announced the arrest of a total of 62 persons for terrorist activities on social media.[104] One of these announcements states:

> The Ministry of Interior has managed to arrest 8 individuals that are inciting the following activities: carrying out terrorist attacks targeting touristic areas, the assassination of security and political figures, and supporting a terrorist organization via social media on the internet. In collaboration with the public prosecutor, the investigation continues.[105]

Such arrests bring us back to the core issue of the lack of a clear definition of terrorism. As long as "terrorism" is widely defined, the actual danger of terrorism-related crimes carried out on social media is questionable. Without the first being clearly defined, glorifying extremism or peaceful opposition can be considered as terrorism crime.

CONCLUSION: COLONIAL HERITAGE AND NEO-COLONIAL APPROVAL OF AUTHORITARIANISM

Well before 9/11 and the Tunisian Revolution of 2011, Tunisia had tough national security laws and policies. The French colonial legacy played a significant role in this regard. The direct implanting of tough colonial laws and exceptional measures created a *de facto* state of subordination in which Tunisia is unable or unwilling to detach from its colonial heritage. Unlike colonized Egypt, which had an independent parliament and an active constitution, at least partially implemented, colonized Tunisia had neither. This paved the way for more centralization for both the bey and the colonial power. While the bey continued to enjoy absolute authority, whether actual or nominal, the French Resident General and the French army enjoyed superior centralization. After colonialism, the Tunisian regime reimposed the system of centralization, ensuring the president absolute powers similar to those of the bey, and exceptional powers similar to those of the French Resident General and the French army. This duality is a common outcome in postcolonial political life.[106]

While colonialism established the legal foundation of national security laws and measures, postcolonial Tunisia used these measures to protect the authoritarian

[103] Muhamad Muamri, "Facebook 'mesyaday el erhabiyeen' fi Tunis" "[Facebook is a 'Trap for Terrorists' in Tunisia"] (December 4, 2017) *The New Arab [news]*, online: www.alaraby.co.uk/medianews.
[104] Eva Gaperin, "The Crime of Speech: How Arab Governments Use the Law to Silence Expression Online" (September 9, 2016) *Electronic Frontier Foundation*, online: www.eff.org/wp/crime-speech-how-arab-governments-use-law-silence-expression-online#ct_law.
[105] Quoted in *ibid.*
[106] Owen, *State, Power and Politics*, at 10–12.

regime and to satisfy France. Differentiating Tunisia from Algeria, which long contained militant Islamist groups, was a French priority. Therefore, Tunisian Islamists were targeted regardless of their moderate approach. Exceptionalism continued through the use of military courts during peacetime and for domestic crimes. France turned a blind eye to Tunisia's weak human rights record and violations against Islamists. This can be taken as an implicit indication of Western approval of Tunisia's authoritarianism.

Since 9/11, Tunisia has responded to neo-colonial pressure by adopting a counter-terrorism financing framework based on UN Security Council resolutions and FATF regulations. This neo-colonial pressure aims to stop domestic terrorism in Tunisia, in part to protect European tourists, and in part to cooperate in the fight against ISIS. The neo-colonial agenda of counter-terrorism requires imposing exceptionalism, which repeals elements of democracy – the promised outcome of the so-called Arab Spring. This agenda serves the entrenched authoritarian ambition of the Tunisian government.

Conclusions

This book has argued that anti-terrorism legislation and policy in Egypt and Tunisia criminalize many lawful acts and include exceptional measures that primarily support the authoritarian governments. Anti-terrorism and national security laws allow targeting of opponents and unjustifiably undermine freedoms in the name of national security. This book argues that this situation has been shaped by the colonial past of Egypt and Tunisia along with continuing neo-colonial influence and the indigenous authoritarian ambition of its rulers. The book has traced the emergence in colonial times of four aspects of control (economic expansion, centralization, militarism, and exceptionalism), which continue to operate in Egyptian and Tunisian anti-terror legislation and policy today. They continue to be encouraged through neo-colonialism, as Western powers emphasize global counter-terrorism. Western powers also help support authoritarian governments, which have eagerly adopted these measures. Anti-terrorism legislation includes broad definitions that can be applied selectively to whomever the state chooses. This is a result of the lack of a definition of terrorism at the international level.

This conclusion begins by showing the problems arising from the lack of a comprehensive definition of terrorism at the international level. It then moves to examining the problems with anti-terrorism legislation in Egypt, Tunisia, and worldwide, focusing on the broad definitions of terrorism and the overly broad categories of crimes related to terrorism. Crimes related to terrorism, which include terrorism financing, speech related to terrorism, and membership in a terrorist organization, are themes of the current global war on terror.

The second section of the conclusion traces the roots of these measures in colonial counter-insurgency, neo-colonial influence, and postcolonial authoritarian ambition. I argue that these influences have resulted in disproportionate responses. This disproportionateness is addressed in terms of three concepts: colonial implanting and imperial migration of law, neo-colonial migration of law, and postcolonial authoritarian migration of law. I argue that such migration, while it aims to unify contemporary anti-terrorism laws and efforts, may be an additional challenge in enhancing national and international security.

The third section investigates the underlying reasons for current anti-terrorism rationales, found in colonialism, neo-colonialism, and authoritarianism. The book argues that the exceptional nature of the colonial states produced exceptional measures, which became acceptable in the postcolonial world. In addition, the exceptional war on terror has allowed a return to the colonial rationale by neo-colonial powers. I suggest that the current approaches – while differing in degree – share an authoritarian ambition. States worldwide have become more obsessed with identifying terrorists than identifying wrongdoings. This has justified adopting flexible laws and measures that allow the capture of suspects rather than wrongdoers.

The fourth section examines the tendency of states to adopt "flexible" anti-terrorism laws that allow a "catch-all" logic. The aim of this logic is to create a threat-free environment through suppressing not only crimes, but also threats of crimes well before they emerge or are even planned. The task of the criminal law is changed from crime control into threat control, which is often difficult to predict. And in order to create a society free from threat, a disciplined approach is needed to make sure that nothing challenges the status quo. I argue that too much flexibility undermines the role of the criminal justice system as a whole.

As a result of these features of the colonial and neo-colonial rationale, the modern Arab world is faced with multiple restrictions of freedoms and political activities through unnecessary laws that allow the authority to selectively arrest and charge its enemies in the name of national security. Restricting and prohibiting various nonviolent activities in the form of political and economic pressure, such as strikes and protests, have become tools to suppress certain groups. Countering terrorism and maintaining a climate of order have allowed the return of the colonial rule of the exception.

PROBLEMS WITH NATIONAL AND GLOBAL ANTI-TERRORISM LEGISLATION

National and global anti-terrorism laws have been criminalizing a wide range of acts related to terrorism without clearly defining terrorism. Such breadth and lack of precision have led to ambiguity in the boundaries of terrorist acts. Many supposedly lawful acts can be selectively condemned as terrorist-related crimes, which belongs to a preemptive approach. What I mean by a preemptive approach in counter-terrorism is the willingness to regulate speech and associations well before any act of terrorism has emerged or even been planned. I therefore distinguish between preventive measures within the criminal law that aim to protect the public from actual harm, and other preemptive measures that suppress speech and association in the name of counter-terrorism. Such unclear crimes may only reflect the overbroad definitions that make the indictment process arbitrary.

The Definition of "Terrorism"

The main problem with national and international anti-terrorism legislation is the lack of a clear objective definition of terrorism. Most, if not all, national laws are broad and vague. Determining what terrorism is remains the crucial underpinning of any successful discussion of counter-terrorism, and of the future success of counter-terrorist measures. A number of problems arise from building counter-terrorism measures on the foundation of a vague definition of terrorism.

This problem is becoming more complex because of the post-9/11 global demands imposed by the UN Security Council and FATF. These neo-colonial powers have been encouraging states to adopt anti-terrorism laws, yet without insisting on the importance of defining terrorism. This global neglect of the importance of the definition has allowed states to adopt broad definitions of terrorism that do not serve the common goal of national and international security.

Defining the crime of terrorism is important because it sends a clear message to society about what is legally wrongful. By outlawing particular acts and determining their illegal elements, criminal law sends a clear message to society to avoid these specific wrongdoings. Fair warning is essential in a criminal legal system so that the audience is able to understand the message behind the criminalization of such acts and recognize its elements clearly.[1] From this perspective, precise labeling is vital: a wrongdoer should be convicted for the specific act committed, so that justice is not only being done but also seen by the public as being done.[2] This process would ensure that the values protected by criminalizing terrorism were clear to all members of society, so individuals could unambiguously recognize what type of wrongdoing was to be avoided.

Current national definitions are not only broad and vague; they also vary from one jurisdiction to another. Efforts to define terrorism within the UN General Assembly took decades without reaching an international agreement. UN Security Council Resolution 1373 (2001), adopted in the aftermath of 9/11, called on states to condemn terrorism and terrorism financing, but without providing a definition of terrorism. Some Western and Commonwealth countries, including Australia, Canada, and South Africa, rushed into adopting the British model. Other countries that already had broad criminal laws, like Egypt and Arab states in general, only rushed into adopting counter-terrorism financing laws. This has resulted in the adoption of broad national definitions of terrorism, which lack precision and objectivity.

The complexities involved in defining terrorism have caused scholars to question the possibility of defining these activities objectively. In fact, achieving a united definition of terrorism might be impossible. When criticizing national and global

---

[1] Andrew Simester & Andreas Von Hirsch, *Crimes, Harms, and Wrongs: On the Principles of Criminalisation* (Oxford: Hart, 2011) at 198–9.
[2] *Ibid*, at 202.

counter-terrorism frameworks, the aim is not to let criminals go free; they must be brought to justice. However, a first step in this regard must be to identify crimes and their elements in order to correctly charge wrongdoers in accordance with their actual wrongdoing. A murderer and a protester should not be equally labeled "terrorists." International guidance on defining terrorism is essential in encouraging states to define this notion within a framework that ensures respect for human rights and minimum guarantees according to the principles of criminal law.

This attempt requires the depoliticization of the definition of terrorism. An observation regarding current definitions of terrorism is that they have been designed to target those who are against the ruling authority, wrongdoers and peaceful opponents alike. This can be found, for example, in Article 29 of the Egyptian Anti-Terrorism Law of 2015, which criminalizes use of the internet that "incite[s] thoughts or ideas that call to commit terrorist acts" or "to mislead security forces" or "to affect the course of justice."[3] This article includes vague concepts, which allows the authority to condemn anyone who uses their freedom of expression in a way that does not resonate with the state's view.

The application of a broad definition of terrorism in national laws allows groups to be targeted on the basis of their identities and their political or religious activities rather than on wrongdoing and criminal conduct. For instance, the experience in Egypt and Tunisia shows that the government captured and detained Islamists based on their association, regardless of whether or not they had committed terrorist acts. For example, Egypt has long targeted those who associate with the Muslim Brotherhood, whether or not they are involved in criminal activities. This suggests that people are often biased against minorities or those who do not conform to mainstream social or political ideology. This political bias has made the overbroad politicized definition of terrorism acceptable since it is directed against "them," not "us." The "other," who shares the same human nature and values as "us," but differs in his or her political beliefs, is the suspected terrorist. Being charged with a crime of terrorism has dangerous consequences, which include travel bans and freezing of funds, and these risks mean it is important to have a precise definition that distinguishes between an ordinary criminal and a terrorist. The line between lawful and wrongful acts is blurred in current definitions of terrorism, and this requires a reevaluation of the current national definitions of terrorism.

Terrorism-Related Crimes

A lack of a clear definition of "terrorism" has led to broadening the scope of terrorism-related crimes. This can be found in prohibiting speech inciting terrorism, financing terrorism, and membership in a terrorist organization. These acts, while

---

[3] Article 29 of the Egyptian Anti-Terrorism Law of 2015.

they threaten the state's power, do not directly or necessarily cause harm. The rationale behind treating them as terrorism is that this is argued to preempt terrorism in its violent forms before they occur.[4] The concept of preemption suggests that the legislature's strategy is to target potential threats in their peaceful forms. Therefore, "potential" wrongdoers, rather than wrongdoers, become the targets of anti-terrorism law. The preemptive approach is problematic because it is threat-based rather than crime-based,[5] which therefore risks the course of justice. I discuss these issues in the next subsections.

Membership in Terrorist Organizations

Membership in terrorist groups is one activity that has been criminalized globally. This is a complex problem because even if the group in question is involved in terrorist activities, members may not be aware of this. For instance, Maher Arar, a Syrian-born Canadian citizen, is an example of the subjectivity of the term "terrorism." Canadian officials had information about Arar because of his associations with targeted groups. As a result, he was apprehended by American officials and deported to Syria, where he was tortured and detained for almost a year. The collected information was not based on his actions or intentions, but rather on his association with others who were the targets of a national security investigation.[6] Listing decisions at the national and international levels are highly politicized, risking wrongfully listing political opponents or other innocent people.

The UN Security Council and some countries, including the United States, have blacklisted many organizations, some of which run schools and hospitals. Criminalizing mere membership allows states to consider doctors, teachers, and others providing social services in charities as terrorists. Condemning mere membership in these organizations is likely to be misapplied, especially considering the biased standards for the definition of terrorism and the standards for blacklisting.

The criminalization of mere membership in terrorist groups can be linked to the colonial experience of targeting individuals based on their associations. Associations that have been criminalized in the past include those that are either ideological, such as communism in colonized Greece and Iraq, or religious, such as Catholicism in Northern Ireland. Colonial methods of control included legal reforms, such as the Restoration of Order in Ireland Act of 1920 that targeted Irish rebels. Another example would be the establishment of special courts to try communists in France and colonized Tunisia in 1941.

---

4   Hocking, *Beyond Terrorism*, at 25–6; McCulloch & Pickering, "Counter-Terrorism," at 17.
5   McCulloch & Pickering, *ibid.*
6   See Canada, Commission of Inquiry into the Actions of Canadian Officials in Relation to Maher Arar, *Report of the Events Relating to Maher Arar: Analysis and Recommendations* (Ottawa: Public Works and Government Services Canada, 2006).

Speech Related to Terrorism

Terrorism crimes include speech that encourages, glorifies or apologizes for terrorism. These crimes are not clear and could interfere with lawful disagreement or with racial or religious hate speech.[7] I am limiting my argument to speech crimes as such and not when associated with violent attacks. Still, extreme or false speech could harm people's dignity and provokes hatred among society. The problem, however, is in states misusing speech crimes in selectively targeting opponents or even minorities for matters of political opinion. States worldwide have adopted legal restrictions on the freedom of expression for purposes related to "public order" and "national security." For practical reasons, it is unwise to ask for all restrictions to be abolished; however, such limitations must be taken within a precise and narrow sense. Limitation clauses should be interpreted in favor of the right concerned and without jeopardizing its essence.[8] The essence of freedom of expression is violated when states subjectively suppress political opposition.

The Arab world and the West are similar in their use of speech regulation as a form of counter-terrorism. The difference between the two is in degree: the Arab world uses excessive censorship and provides limited criminal procedural safeguards. In many Arab states, demands for political and socioeconomic reforms are considered terrorism-related acts. With the "Arab Spring" and the following unrest, terms like "terrorists," "opponents," and "revolutionaries" complicate further the broad and nebulous understanding of what legally comprises "terrorism." The use of restriction clauses in Egyptian and Tunisian laws has shown that opposition political opinions have become narrowed in a way that deprives freedom of expression of its essence. It is impossible for university students, journalists, and NGO members to express their political views without the risk of being arrested or even accused of ambiguous acts like glorifying or inciting terrorism.

The tendency in the West is also toward selectively tightening freedom of expression. The aim of criminalizing glorifying and incitement of terrorism is supposedly to combat jihadist attacks, but anti-terrorism laws cover speeches and expressions more broadly than this aim.[9] In 2017, Germany adopted a new law on online hate speech, which requires online platforms to remove "illegal content" – a broad clause that could selectively target particular groups.[10] Another action to restrict freedom of expression has been taken by the British and French governments; together they have been developing a plan to identify and remove online

---

[7] Sara Savage and Jose Liht, "Radical Religious Speech: The Ingredients of a Binary World View" in Ivan Hare & James Weinstein, eds, *Extreme Speech and Democracy* (New York: Oxford University Press, 2009) at 125–7; Al-Anezi, "Human Rights in the Light of International Opportunism," at 145–7.
[8] Principles 2 and 3 of Siracusa Principles.
[9] Sarah Sorial, "Can Saying Something Make It So? The Nature of Seditious Harm" (2010) 29:3 *Law and Philosophy* 273 at 273.
[10] Netzwerkdurchsetzungsgesetz (NetzDG) law, adopted in June 2017 and coming into force in January 2018.

material that they view as "terrorist, radical, or hateful."[11] Such attempts, while undermining freedom of expression, also send a wrong message to the rest of the world of current Western and supposedly democratic approaches to handle speech crimes.

Terrorism Financing

Post-9/11, UN Security Council Resolution 1373 (2001) and the FATF placed great international attention on counter-terrorism financing. The aim of preventing financing terrorist groups and freezing their funds is to weaken terrorists' ability to conduct their criminal plans. However, terrorist acts, on many occasions, do not require large funds. Handguns, blades, and homemade bombings are all inexpensive. Unlike tax evasion, which is purely financial, and money laundering, which is combined with other costly underlying crimes, terrorism can survive with or without funding. For instance, the 9/11 Commission report shows that Al-Qaeda's primary source of funds was donations.[12]

Nonetheless, not all terrorist crimes are inexpensive. For instance, ISIS needs large assets to continue funding its military operations, as well as providing its men with heavy arms and motors. Since 2015, ISIS has been using hundreds of Toyota pickup trucks and SUVs in Iraq.[13] American and Iraqi officials have been questioning how ISIS obtained all these vehicles. Although Toyota defended its position, stating that it does not sell its cars for the use of terrorist activities, it stated that it cannot "control indirect or illegal channels [... or vehicles being] re-sold by independent third parties."[14] The lack of control over such deals makes counter-terrorism financing more challenging.

Despite the difficulty of monitoring terrorist financing, countries worldwide have responded to UN Security Council Resolution 1373 by adopting new anti-terrorism financing regulations. Resolution 1373 required states to update the CTC with their counter-terrorism financing laws and measures. This suggests that, regardless of the efficiency of terrorism financing laws, the obligation listed in Security Council Resolution 1373 must be adhered to, and states must adopt new laws to satisfy the neo-colonial powers that dominate the Security Council. The obligations of

---

Philip Oltermann, "Tough New German Law Puts Tech Firms and Free Speech in Spotlight" (January 5, 2018) *The Guardian*, online: www.theguardian.com/world/2018/jan/05/tough-new-german-law-puts-tech-firms-and-free-speech-in-spotlight.

[11] "Germany: Flawed Social Media Law: NetzDG Is Wrong Response to Online Abuse" (February 14, 2018) *Human Rights Watch*, online: www.hrw.org/news/2018/02/14/germany-flawed-social-media-law.

[12] The 9/11 Commission Report, at 172.

[13] "Officials: How Did ISIS Get So Many Toyotas?" (October 6, 2015) *ABC News*, online: https://www.youtube.com/watch?v=sq_iP5lQsAU.

[14] "Why does Isis Have so Many Toyota Trucks?" (October 7, 2015) *Independent*, online: www.independent.co.uk/news/world/middle-east/why-does-isis-have-so-many-toyota-trucks-a6684336.html.

Resolution 1373 allow the controlling of terrorist groups more than terrorist activities, and this in turn accords with a counter-insurgency approach, which attempts to control through politics.

This book has argued that the collective adoption of laws regarding anti-terrorism financing was more than mere adherence to UN Security Council Resolution 1373. The adoption of counter-terrorism financing regulations was a fear-based action taken by states to satisfy the FATF and avoid being placed on its blacklist. Blacklisting became a neo-colonial method of control and maintaining unequal positions of power.

The fact that listing and de-listing of "terrorists" are politicized decisions made by executive-like bodies, not the court, makes the blacklisting mechanism injudicious. This is a one-sided mechanism that lacks transparency, adding an authoritarian nature to its decisions. The fact that it provides no due process protections and no right to appeal increases the chance of wrongful freezing of funds of innocent people.

WHERE DO THESE PROBLEMATIC ASPECTS OF ANTI-TERRORISM LAW COME FROM?

States have long been countering and defining terrorism in accordance with their experiences or by borrowing elements of the definition from other countries and complying with global obligations. This section addresses the findings about the origins of legislation and exceptional powers used in the war on terror in Egypt and Tunisia.

Colonial Implanting and Informal Imperialism Migration of Law

British and French powers implanted many of their laws and measures into their colonies, including Egypt and Tunisia. Such legacies include martial law or state of siege, state of emergency, and special courts. Imperial migration refers to European influence during the nineteenth and early twentieth centuries, which spread into countries that were not colonies. This applies particularly in Egypt, which willingly borrowed the French legal system while it was under British colonialism.

Arab states, whether willingly under external compulsion, built their criminal laws based on the French model, and often express pride in having adopted this model. These states adopted the French system as the embodiment of liberty and modernity. However, the French model has developed over the decades, while these states still cling to the Napoleonic model. The reputation of the French Penal Code of 1810 differs from that of the French Civil Code of 1804. The latter is often appreciated for its fairness, whereas the former is noted to be outdated.[15] Part of this

---

[15] See Mueller & Moreau's argument in their translation of *The French Penal Code*, at 9.

reputation is derived from the Penal Code's severity. For instance, the early version of the Napoleonic Penal Code treated any attack against the person of the emperor as high treason.[16] Yet in 1853 the French code abolished this article, and no special protection is provided to the person of the emperor or the president. On the other hand, the Egyptian and Tunisian penal codes are still based on the early version of the Napoleonic Penal Code, and both provide special protection to the president and his family. Arab penal codes are similar to and sometimes worse than the Napoleonic model. They reflect the severity of that model by using harsh punishments and creating second-class citizens by depriving them of their civil rights.

Informal Imperialism Migration and Colonial Implanting of Law in Egypt

Egyptian national security laws and measures are shaped by French imperial influence and British colonial heritage. As mentioned earlier, Egypt willingly borrowed legal reforms from the French laws. The book treats this migration of law as a form of informal empire. In Egypt, the informal imperial heritage regarding the definition of terrorism is indirect yet strong. Egypt first defined "terrorism" in 1993; it did not borrow the definition from any other jurisdiction. However, it borrowed some of its elements from French law. This can be found in its inclusion of vague concepts that are derived from the Napoleonic Penal Code of 1810, such as "disturbances of public order" and "thwart the application of the Constitution." In addition, the crime of "incitement" as regulated in the French Press Law of 1881 is also seen in the Egyptian definition of terrorism. Other acts, including damaging property (sabotage) and rebellion – all broadly and vaguely defined – are derived from the French Penal Code of 1810 and also form part of the Egyptian definition of terrorism.

These acts were earlier included in the first Egyptian Penal Code of 1883. Egypt prepared the draft of this law based on the Napoleonic model while it was independent, and issued it while under British colonialism. Egypt, although under colonial pressure, had a constitution and a parliament, which partially empowered Egypt against the British authority. The Egyptian Penal Code was not a colonial product; rather, it represents the Egyptian will as influenced by French imperialism in the late nineteenth century. Most of the articles in the Egyptian Penal Code of 1883 still exist in the current Penal Code of 1937 and its amendments. The Egyptian Penal Code of 1883 is therefore the direct bedrock for the later definitions of terrorism in Egypt.

British colonial influence in Egypt, while limited, has been significant in shaping current anti-terrorism law policy. This influence can be found in the British transplanting of exceptionalism into the Egyptian system. The British not only declared martial law in Egypt several times, but also insisted on regulating martial law within the Egyptian Constitution of 1923.[17] Martial law allowed the rule of the

---

[16] Article 86 of the French Penal Code of 1810.
[17] Brown, *The Rule of Law in the Arab World*, at 111; Reza, "Endless Emergency," at 535–7.

military with limited or no accountability for military actions. According to Reza, the Egyptian ruling class and the elite found martial law a useful tool that protected its position.[18] This suggests a combination of colonial legacy and local authoritarian ambition. Martial law, however, was seen as an extreme system. Therefore, the British invented the state of emergency. According to David French, "The British threw a veneer of legality over their operations by avoiding imposing martial law and instead employing emergency powers regulations to create a legal framework within which their security forces operated."[19]

Another form of exceptionalism during colonialism was the use of military and special courts. The British established several special courts, including the special court to try 'Urabi in 1882, the special courts to try offenses against the British army during the period of colonialism, and the martial law courts established during World War I.[20] During colonialism the British imposed their special tribunals whenever they felt discomfort about national courts.[21] The impact of such a dual legal system was to create a notion of "us" versus "them," "good citizens" versus "evil enemies."

In the postcolonial era, Egypt limited its use of martial law,[22] but replaced it with extensive use of state of emergency. Egypt continuously declared a state of emergency from 1967 to 2012, with an 18-month break in 1980 and 1981.[23] After the assassination of Sadat in 1981, President Mubarak deployed the state of emergency in the name of national security and counter-terrorism. State of emergency allowed the use of many emergency powers, including searches and arrests without warrant, detention without trial, and the use of special courts.

During both ordinary times and emergencies, Egypt has relied heavily on military and special courts. Right after the overthrow of the Egyptian monarchy, the newborn government, run by the Free Officers, established several special courts, including the Court of Treason set up in 1952 and the special Court against Egyptian Communists in 1953. These courts had broad procedural guidance, were run by political and military figures without legal backgrounds, and had a broad politicized mandate.[24] The justification for these courts was to secure the new government. However, the same tendency continued in the 1990s in the name of counter-terrorism. In 1992, Mubarak issued a presidential decree that allowed him to

---

[18] Reza, *ibid*, at 535.
[19] French, *The British Way in Counter-Insurgency*, at 75.
[20] Brown, "Retrospective: Law and Imperialism," at 121.
[21] Cromer, *Flawed Diplomacy*, at 32–3.
[22] Martial law was declared three times: from 1952 to 1956 as a response to clashes with British troops at the Suez Canal; in 1956 due to the Suez War; and in 1958 to secure what was then the United Arab Republic – the union between Egypt and Syria. See Reza, "Endless Emergency," at 536.
[23] Reza, *ibid*, at 537.
[24] Brown, *The Rule of Law in the Arab World*, at 72.

transfer terrorist cases to military courts.[25] This duality, which existed under colonialism, was transferred to postcolonial authoritarian Arab regimes. The experience of Egypt shows that many judicial bodies were established to deal with the same wrongdoings but under different labels. This practice enabled the authoritarian regime to categorize their enemies as second-class citizens and deprive them of some civil rights, including the rights to establish political parties and run for parliament.

Colonial Implanting of Law in Tunisia

In the case of Tunisia, colonialism has had a direct yet limited role in shaping the definition of terrorism. The French colonial influence on the definition of terrorism can be found in the Tunisian legislation in the use of vague concepts derived from the 1810 French Penal Code, such as "disturbing public order" and "thwart the application of the Constitution." However, unlike Egypt, which willingly adopted the French model, Tunisia had limited choice in this respect. The French colonials were directly involved in lawmaking in Tunisia. For instance, a French–Tunisian committee drafted the Tunisian Penal Code of 1913 based on the Napoleonic model. Tunisia's Penal Code has been amended several times, but the basic provisions remain the same. This law includes the crimes of plotting, incitement, sabotage, and rebellion (or insurgency), all of which include vague terminology and broad definitions. The specification of these crimes in the 1913 Penal Code is the direct foundation of Tunisia's current definition of terrorism adopted in 2015.

Prior to colonialism, Tunisia was ruled by an autocratic bey, who suspended the Tunisian Constitution of 1861 and centralized powers within his authority. This autocratic system allowed the French to easily control the country by controlling the will of one man. The French experience in Tunisia shows that the bey had nominal authority, signing decrees as designed by the French army or the French Resident General. For example, in 1882, the bey issued a decree granting the French army suppressive powers against those who disobeyed military orders.[26] This was the beginning of military involvement in civil life in Tunisia.

The state of siege was a militarized way of ruling that provided the French army and the Resident General exceptional powers. The French imposed the state of siege in Tunisia for over sixteen years.[27] During a state of siege, French laws as issued and applied in France replaced Tunisian laws. These included replacing the Tunisian Penal Code with the French Penal Code from 1938 to 1954. In addition, military courts were established to try civilians for crimes against the state. Among these crimes was the crime of rebellion. According to the French Penal Code of

---

[25] Egyptian Presidential Decree No. 375; see Farhang, "Recent Development," at 226.
[26] Arfawi, *The Judiciary and Politics in Tunisia during French Colonialism*, at 100.
[27] *Ibid*, at 103.

1810, "Every attack or resistance, by force or violence, against ministerial officers" can count as rebellion "according to the circumstances."[28] Chapter 7 of this book showed that cases held by the military courts often condemned nationalists for rebellion and acts of sabotage, which included acts of damaging public property. The authority interpreted acts of rebellion and sabotage as "insurgency," justifying the use of military action.

Another form of direct French colonial involvement in the legal and political life of Tunisia was the application of strict censorship. During the state of siege, the French colonials applied the French Press Law of 1881 in Tunisia rather than allowing Tunisia to adopt its own legislation. This law condemns inciting hatred or violence against religions, the president, the army, or the courts.[29] The French Press Law of 1881 is still active in France, suggesting that incitement is a crime that has consistently been taken seriously by the French. This legacy is seen in post-colonial Tunisia, which continues to criminalize incitement within its Penal Code as a crime against the state or a crime against public order.[30]

Postcolonial Tunisia continued to adopt the colonial forms of exceptionalism. Tunisia replaced the use of state of siege with state of emergency, which was used five times between September 1957 and 1984 for specific cases and for limited periods and areas. Although Tunisia limited its use of state of emergency, it relied more extensively on military courts. Military courts were established one year after independence by the Penal and Procedures Military Code No. 92 of 1957. In 1979, the jurisdiction of these courts was expanded to include crimes of rebellion committed during peacetime, and membership in a "terrorist organization operating abroad."[31]

This book has argued that by referring "rebels" and "terrorists" to military courts, Tunisia embodies the colonial legacy of counter-insurgency in a contemporary counter-terrorism framework. The direct involvement of the French colonials in Tunisia, creating and implementing legislation, specifically the long period of state of siege and the application of military courts, undermined Tunisia's long-term ability to establish ordinary regulations and a jurisprudence that reflects its civil identity. Ben Ali, relying on this colonial heritage, turned Tunisia into a police state by supervising civilian activities, especially those by journalists and Islamists. This policy imposed strict censorship that allowed the government to monitor the internet and mosques.[32] Tunisians who published columns on French websites

---

[28] Article 209 of the French Penal Code of 1810.
[29] Articles 23, 24, 30, and 31 of the French Press Law of 1881.
[30] Articles 70 and 81 of the Tunisian Penal Code of 1913.
[31] Article 123 as amended by Tunisian Decree-Law of the Penal and Procedures Military Code No. 12 of 1979. Issued on October 10, 1979.
[32] "The Development of Tunisian Terrorism" (October 11, 2015), *Rawabet Center for Research and Strategic Studies*, online: rawabetcenter.com/archives/13067.

criticizing Ben Ali's policies were charged with crimes against the state.[33] While censorship has its roots in colonialism, the postcolonial use of this tool reflects an authoritarian ambition that serves those in power, as discussed below.

In 1993, Tunisia established a definition of "terrorism" within its Penal Code. This definition condemns "all actions relating to individual or collective initiative, aiming at undermining individuals or properties, through intimidation or terror" and "acts of incitement to hatred or to religious or other fanaticism, regardless of the means used."[34] As mentioned earlier, the criminalization of inciting hatred is drawn from the French Press Law of 1881. The continuous reliance on French regulations, particularly those established during colonialism, weakens contemporary criminal justice systems.

Neo-Colonial Migration of Law

The United Kingdom is one of the most influential powers in counter-terrorism. This derives from its long colonial history of countering insurgency and all other violent and nonviolent forms of resistance. Its experience in Northern Ireland, India, and many other colonies allowed it to develop a sophisticated counter-terrorism model. In the aftermath of 9/11, the British Terrorism Act of 2000 had a global influence over many common law countries and former British colonies.[35] Roach observes that the migration of the British definition of terrorism to other Western countries and former British colonies was "a voluntary process."[36] In a neo-colonial era, the United Kingdom does not force states to adopt its model. Does this willingness suggest that states prefer to follow what is familiar rather than to create new models? This point requires further investigation. The United Kingdom built a model for counter-terrorism based on its own experience of counter-insurgency, which may not be appropriate to other countries. This means a collection of several laws, rather than a united counter-terrorism law, could be more useful and effective. However, each crime should be clearly and precisely defined in any anti-terrorism law. Terrorism includes multi-national and cross-boundary acts, and this requires states to cooperate rather than to mimic other states' tendencies in adopting broad definitions and tough measures.

Post-9/11, however, states have become more tightly bound by global obligations. UN Security Council Resolution 1624 (2005), adopted in the aftermath of the 2005 London bombing, emphasizes speech related to terrorism. The resolution

---

[33] "Reporters without Borders in Tunisia: A New Freedom That Needs Protecting" (February 10, 2011 updated in January 20, 2016) *Reporters without Borders*, online: rsf.org/en/news/reporters-without-borders-tunisia-new-freedom-needs-protecting.
[34] Article 52*bis*, amended by Law 93–112 of November 22, 1993, and abolished in 2003.
[35] Countries that rushed into adopting the British model include Australia, Canada, and South Africa.
[36] Roach, "Comparative Counter-Terrorism Law Comes of Age," at 18.

condemns "the incitement of terrorist acts and *repudiat*[*es*] attempts at the justification or glorification (*apologie*) of terrorist acts that may incite further terrorist acts."[37] The colonial experience showed a tendency to target speech that could threaten the imperial position. This was applied by the British in Northern Ireland[38] and in India,[39] where incitement to hatred, whether against the government or against other races or religions, was considered a hate crime. Another example is drawn from the French experience in Tunisia, which showed a strict censorship policy that granted the French colonial elite the power to monitor newspapers before they were published and to delete parts of or whole columns. The reemergence of speech restrictions in the name of counter-terrorism and with the approval of the Security Council does not change the suppressive nature of these restrictions. Furthermore, history shows limited effectiveness if not a counterproductive impact of speech regulations.

UN Security Council Resolution 1373 (2001) calls upon states to prevent the financing of terrorism[40] and to freeze the funds of terrorists.[41] Monitoring financing has its colonial roots, yet to a lesser extent than speech crimes. A colonial example of counter-terrorism financing can be seen in the British experience in Northern Ireland. The British enforced the Prevention of Terrorism (Temporary Provisions) Act (PTA) issued in 1974 and renewed until 1989. This Act criminalizes receiving or giving funds "in connection with, acts of terrorism."[42] The global impact of Security Council Resolution 1373 raises the question of the proportionality and efficiency of colonial practices in our current era. If this Security Council resolution and other related resolutions are rooted in colonial practice, then they reflect an antiquated way of crime control, which does not serve the evolution of law and humanity.

The problem with the approach of imitating other countries' legislation instead of developing one's own approach based on the specific situation in each country is not limited to the issue of neo-colonial influence in domestic affairs and encouraging of puppet governments. It also, crucially, disregards the unique geopolitical features of each regime, each of which may call for a very different set of rules. An effective, informed global counter-terrorism effort can only be structured around a comprehensive geographical and political analysis. A reactive or transplanted approach to counter-terrorism cannot expect to meet success in every state. The resolutions adopted by the UN Security Council, however, suggest that the accepted approach to supposed global security is largely restricted to Western security, with little attention paid to the unique needs and demands of other regions.

[37] UN Security Council Resolution 1624 (2005), para 1.
[38] Prevention of Incitement to Hatred Act 1970 (Northern Ireland).
[39] Section 295A, added to the Indian Penal Code in 1927.
[40] UN Security Council Resolution 1373 (2001), para 1(a).
[41] *Ibid*, para 1(c).
[42] Part III, "Financial Inimical Assistance for Terrorism," Prevention of Terrorism (Temporary Provisions) Act (PTA) issued in 1974.

The neo-colonial influence practiced by Western powers through the UN Security Council and the FATF have shaped current anti-terrorism approaches worldwide. The following sections discuss this influence in the case studies of Egypt and Tunisia.

Neo-Colonial Migration of Law in Egypt

Post-9/11, neo-colonialism spread its influence over the Egyptian anti-terrorism framework. Neo-colonial powers, working primarily through the UN Security Council and FATF, have imposed global anti-terrorism obligations, including counter-terrorism financing, condemning speech that encourages or apologizes for terrorism, travel restrictions, and blacklisting. Even though Egypt had tough anti-terrorism laws well before 9/11, it complied with the Security Council and FATF obligations regarding terrorism financing. In 2001, Egypt was listed by FATF as a non-cooperative country.[43] As a result, it adopted an Anti-Money Laundering Law in 2002,[44] and was de-listed in 2004.[45] However, the usefulness of counter-terrorism financing, especially in Egypt, is questionable. For example, a report by the FATF shows that in Egypt, most financial operations are done in cash, and only 20 percent are done within the official banking system.[46] This indicates that this globally applicable measure is not appropriate in Egypt.

Egypt has adhered to other Security Council obligations, but did not make further changes to legislation immediately after 9/11. This is because Egypt already had broad anti-terrorism laws. However, in 2015 Egypt adopted two laws regarding anti-terrorism. The first is the Terrorist Entities Law,[47] which creates an executive mechanism to blacklist terrorists and terrorist entities. Blacklisting – whether by states or by the Security Council – allows the freezing of funds and imposition of travel bans without providing a fair judicial review mechanism. The second, a new Anti-Terrorism Law,[48] includes an overbroad definition of terrorism with an emphasis on inciting terrorism.[49] While drafting this law, Egypt claimed that it aimed to meet Western and post-9/11 standards. However, it went beyond such standards by adopting a draconian law that includes broad articles and harsh penalties, including the death penalty. This suggests that Egypt is making use of the obligations imposed by the neo-colonial powers to enhance its authoritarian ambition. The converging of neo-colonial and indigenous authoritarian interests is a

---

[43] Financial Action Task Force, "Review to Identify Non-Cooperative Countries or Territories: Increasing the Worldwide Effectiveness of Anti-Money Laundering Measures, " June 22, 2001.
[44] Egyptian Law No. 80 of 2002 on Anti-Money Laundering.
[45] Egypt's Report to the CTC, 2005.
[46] Mutual Evaluation Report: "Anti-Money Laundering and Combating the Financing of Terrorism, Egypt," at 18.
[47] Egyptian Law Regarding Regulating Terrorist Entities and Terrorists of 2015.
[48] Egyptian Anti-Terrorism Law of 2015.
[49] Articles 1, 6, and 18, *ibid.*

common feature in many anti-terror measures in Egypt and elsewhere, discussed in more detail below.

Neo-Colonial Migration of Law in Tunisia

Post-9/11, Tunisia responded to Security Council Resolution 1373 by adopting its 2003 Law in Support of International Efforts to Fight Terrorism and the Repression of Money Laundering. The law defines "terrorism" broadly by including acts that "disturb public order." This phrasing is derived from the Napoleonic Penal Code. The law also emphasizes incitement of terrorism, mere membership in a terrorist organization, and terrorism financing. The former two activities were criminalized in Tunisia well before 9/11, whereas the latter was adopted post-9/11. Counter-terrorism financing can thus be seen as a reflection of both colonial and neo-colonial influence.

Prior to the "Arab Spring," Tunisia had no history of extremism or jihadism. However, in the aftermath of the Tunisian uprising of 2011, it became a vulnerable target for ISIS, who accessed Tunisia through its neighbors, Libya and Algeria. As a response, Tunisia declared a state of emergency from 2011 to 2014, and declared it occasionally in 2015 and 2016. During a state of emergency, crimes against the state are referred to military courts, now in the name of counter-terrorism.

In 2015, Tunisia adopted a new law regarding anti-terrorism and money laundering. Similarly to the 2003 Anti-Terrorism Law, the new law defines terrorism broadly. A few new regulations were added to this law, including further emphasis on incitement. For instance, Article 14 condemns *"Takfir* [calling for excommunication], or incitement of or calling for hatred or loathing among races, religions and faiths."[50] This is a reflection of the French colonial legacy as well as the post-9/11 neo-colonial emphasis on incitement. Another addition to the Tunisian 2015 anti-terrorism law is the establishment of an executive commission, the National Commission to Combat Terrorism, which is authorized to blacklist terrorist entities and freeze their funds. This is an instance of direct neo-colonial influence derived from the UN Security Council and FATF's obligations.

Neo-colonialism imposes global obligations regarding the definition of terrorism and terrorism-related crimes, which places pressure on Tunisia to take action against foreign terrorist fighters and terrorism aimed at Western tourists. Tunisia's anti-terrorism framework combines a colonial legacy with neo-colonial regulations and an internal authoritarian ambition, in which Tunisia selectively borrows anti-terrorism regulations from the French system and the post-9/11 regulations imposed by the UN Security Council. This selectivity empowers the authoritarian system under the cloak of international legality and anti-terrorism necessity. The next section will look more closely at the influence of authoritarian ambition on current anti-terror legislation in Egypt and Tunisia.

---

[50] Paragraph 8 of Article 14, *ibid.*

Postcolonial Authoritarian Development of Law

In addition to the impact of colonial and neo-colonial powers on counter-terrorism, the authoritarian ambitions and desire to consolidate powers of rulers in Arab countries influences their adoption of oppressive measures and their tendency to centralize powers. The authoritarian ambition allows the government to use methods of social and political control, which includes relying on censorship, diminishing political pluralism, and the use of intelligence and suppressive laws.

The experience of the Arab world shows that authoritarian laws and measures are adopted in two ways: borrowing measures from other countries and combining them with other locally created practices. Arab states have borrowed from France the Napoleonic model of criminal law and the French pattern of centralization. For instance, in both Egypt and Tunisia, the president holds the position of the Supreme Commander of the Armed Forces[51] and is the head of the National Security Council[52] and of the National Defense Council.[53]

Militarizing national security policies is another aspect of Arab authoritarian ambition. This can be seen in the overlap between the civil state and the police–military state. Owen shows that, just as the colonial power used the military to secure its occupation and its political control, modern Arab states widely depend on the police and the military to secure the political regime.[54] The priority of the security and stability of the colonial state created a culture of ruling and resisting by force. This culture was carried into the postcolonial Arab world. After colonialism, Egypt and Tunisia established larger police forces that primarily protect the government rather than the society.

As for the locally created measures, they include above all the broad definitions of terrorism. By including vague terms and broad definitions, current anti-terrorism law is easily manipulated to punish those who challenge state power. Egypt and Tunisia adopt definitions of terrorism that allow suppressing political activities by civil society organizations and journalists. Both Egypt and Tunisia continue using military and special courts in trying civilians in the name of counter-terrorism.

Regionally, Egypt plays an influential role regarding security legislation. Many Arab states have willingly adopted the Egyptian definition of terrorism, or at least the main elements of this definition. Egypt's leadership regarding counter-terrorism goes back to its influence on Arab states in signing the 1998 Arab Convention on the Suppression of Terrorism. This means that Egypt and the Arab world were ahead of the West in their legal efforts to counter terrorism.

---

[51] Article 152 of the 2014 Egyptian Constitution; Article 77 of the 2014 Tunisian Constitution.
[52] Article 205 of the 2014 Egyptian Constitution; Article 77 of the 2014 Tunisian Constitution.
[53] Article 203 of the 2014 Egyptian Constitution.
[54] Owen supports his argument by showing the budget indicated for security compared to education and other substantial sectors. Owen, *State, Power and Politics*, at 10–12.

There are historical reasons for this influence of Egypt. While Egypt did not colonize the rest of the Arab world, it has long been ahead of other Arab countries at the legal and political levels. It was among the first to adopt the French model in its challenge against British colonialism. Nathan Brown argues that in the last quarter of the nineteenth century, Egypt realized that in order to counter colonialism peacefully, a strong state had to be built that derived its power from its legal order and organized institutions. Brown describes this period as the emergence of liberal legality, in which the unlimited authority of the Egyptian ruler was restricted or at least regulated.[55]

Many Arab countries imitated the Egyptian model in order to be considered "modern," and thus be able to develop diplomatic and economic relations with the West. This, however, is a general observation that has its exceptions. For instance, Lebanon and the Maghreb countries have long borrowed their laws directly from France. Iraq was also ahead of other Arab states in developing its own legal and political systems based on Western models.

My analysis of postcolonial Egypt shows that when leaders came to power, the Egyptian approach of liberal legality that had developed during colonialism became a lost glory. The new government selectively chose centralization and harsh Napoleonic punitive measures, combined these with the British colonial legacy of exceptional powers, and formed a highly authoritarian system. Nationalists, communists, and Islamists felt betrayed, and thus opposed the government in many ways. Whether violent or nonviolent groups, they were and still are equally suppressed by the government in order to maintain the postcolonial authoritarian system. Counterterrorism laws and measures have been useful tools to the Egyptian authoritarian government. The event of 9/11 added an additional justification for the coercive Egyptian laws. This tendency also extends to other Arab countries, including Jordan, Bahrain, and Qatar, which defined "terrorism" in their anti-terrorism laws in accordance with the Egyptian definition of terrorism, specifically by borrowing vague concepts, including "disturbing public order" and "threatening national unity."[56]

Post-9/11, Arab states came under neo-colonial pressure to adopt further counterterrorism measures, especially regarding terrorism financing. Egypt already had a tough counter-terrorism model within its Penal Code, and in 2015 developed this model in a way that exceeded post-9/11 global regulations. Nevertheless, Western powers have not criticized the Egyptian Anti-Terrorism Law of 2015, which could be an indication of approval. With this implicit approval of Egypt's draconian laws, Arab states found it safe to adopt the Egyptian model rather than developing their own.

The authoritarian ambition survives through maintaining a circle of order and uncertainty about the nation's security. Authoritarian leaders attempt to convince

---

[55] Brown, *The Rule of Law in the Arab World*, at 8.
[56] Roach, "Comparative Counter-Terrorism Law Comes of Age," at 35–7.

their nations that exceptional measures, such as the use of secret intelligence and arbitrary arrests, are the normal way to establish security in the face of unpredictable national threats like terrorism. The political uncertainty fuels a cycle of coercion that, in places like Egypt, has become inescapable. Authoritarian leaders can thus justify the "normalized" exceptional practices as the ideal way to deal with threats like terrorism.

UNDERLYING REASONS FOR CURRENT ANTI-TERRORISM RATIONALES

This book has argued that counter-terrorism laws and measures in Egypt and Tunisia are influenced by colonial and neo-colonial practices. These practices, while they serve the global war on terror, also serve Arab authoritarian regimes. This combination of political interests has resulted in a utilitarian approach to crime control that strengthens neo-colonial powers and authoritarian regimes in the name of counter-terrorism. In order to understand reasons behind embracing current anti-terror legislation as they reflect particular rationales, this section separates these chains of political interests into three: the colonial rationale, neo-colonialism, and authoritarianism and the authoritarian ambition.

On the Colonial Rationale

I asked in the introduction of this book whether Arab and Western states' rationale in counter-terrorism represents an aspect of the modern state or a return to colonial state strategies and conceptions. In order to answer this question, one should be clear whether the colonial state was an exceptional form of government, or a normal – yet having its own unique characteristics – form of government that developed into a modern state.[57] Scholars who glorify the imperial "civilizing mission" consider colonialism a normal form of government that transformed backward nations into modern countries.[58] Others argue that the colonial state is exceptional, thus not a form of the modern state, because of the special framework applied in the colonies that was based on policies of segregation and suppression.[59] I have argued that the colonial state is an exceptional form of government because it was not an organic system. It did not evolve gradually inside the colonized country, but was an unwelcome sudden event or series of events imposed by an external power. Even when "protection" agreements were signed between a powerful empire

---

[57] Partha Chatterjee, *The Nation and Its Fragments* (Princeton, NJ: Princeton University Press, 1993) at 14.

[58] Peter Fitzpatrick, "Custom as Imperialism" in J. M. Abun-Nasr & U. Spellenbert, eds, *Law and Identity in Africa* (Hamburg: Helmut Buske, 1990) at 15; Philip Darby, *The Three Faces of Imperialism* (New Haven, CT: Yale University Press) at 31.

[59] Chatterjee, *The Nation and Its Fragments*, at 19.

and a weaker state, such agreements represented unequal positions of power. In the case of Egypt and Tunisia, the colonial powers were not invited; they occupied these countries then offered their protection. Compliance in these cases does not represent the free will of the country and its people.

These events brought about sudden changes at the political and legal levels, yet with limited preparation for constitutionalism.[60] And when the people of a particular nation valued constitutionalism, it was undermined by a system of elitism that served the local elite and the colonial power. Constitutionalism was also undermined through the use of exceptional powers. Even in cases where colonialism lasted for decades or even over a century (for instance, the French remained in Algeria for 132 years and the British in India for 89 years), exceptionalism and militarism were at the heart of colonial practice. Ruling through the exception is an oppressive process that resulted in oppressive postcolonial actions. The same culture of control has continued since the demise of colonialism but in a different form, just as the tree looks different from the seed.

Apart from problems with the colonial rationale in counter-terrorism described throughout this book, there is this issue of inappropriateness of the colonial heritage. Measures that developed during the periods of colonialism should be part of the past. Colonialism can be understood as a historical series of events, from which we can draw lessons. The problem is in clinging to the colonial rationale without realizing its exceptional nature. A conscious choice to detach from the colonial heritage requires an open mind that dares to challenge inherited understandings.

On the Neo-Colonial Rationale

Exceptionalism and militarism are not exclusive to the colonial experience. Britain and France applied exceptional measures in their mainland. V. G. Kiernan argues that measures that were carried out in colonies reflect practices carried out in Europe. He refers to the competitive attitude between the British and French empires, which enlarged their military to be the most dominant regionally and globally.[61] This preparedness allowed the British and French empires to face external and internal unrest firmly. The two World Wars and the emergence of fascism, communism, and anarchism in Europe required or justified exceptional and military measures.

In the aftermath of World War II, Western Europe, while backing away from militarism, clung to restricting speech and other rights of expression and association. Roach argues that the European approach is based on a militant democracy that is intolerant with those considered enemies of the democratic life.[62] This is reminiscent of Frank Kitson, the British counter-insurgency thinker, who believed

---

[60] Brown, *Constitutions in a Nonconstitutional World*, at 12, 19–20.
[61] See Brown, "Retrospective: Law and Imperialism," at 31–2.
[62] Roach, *The 9/11 Effect*, at 57.

that insurgency starts with nonviolent acts, including strikes and all forms of disturbance, which he thought should be suppressed in order to ensure a threat-free environment.[63]

The Western approach found its way to global domination through neo-colonialism. Both colonialism and imperialism affected the neo-colonial distribution of power. Practices justified during imperialism in mainland Britain and France reemerged in the neo-colonial era. For instance, at a supra-national level, European militant democracy explains the focus of the Security Council –and the European Union – on the theme of speech related to terrorism.

The anti-terrorism laws of both Egypt and Tunisia are hardly questioned by the neo-colonial powers, above all permanent members of the UN Security Council. One reason for this may be that current anti-terrorism laws serve Arab states and neo-colonial powers in suppressing the common enemy – increasingly ISIS, which has had significant success in recruiting, particularly in Tunisia. This would explain the implicit neo-colonial approval of Arab anti-terrorism policy. Responses including blacklisting serve the neo-colonial powers by monitoring their enemy, and Arab governments by suppressing opponents. In effect, global counter-terrorism responses are informed by a neo-colonial rationale, which implicitly allows – by not question-ing – Arab authoritarian regimes and their continuous clinging to a repressive way of ruling that stands in the way of developing authentic Arab democracies.

On Authoritarianism and Authoritarian Ambition

To secure their newly independent states, Arab rulers transferred the former colon-ized regimes into authoritarian governments. The duality in the modern Arab legal systems, which adopted a European legal model but with a colonial model in regard to national security, could be a consequence of an ambivalent colonial policy: Preparing states for independence and at the same time protecting imperial interests in the colonies led to policies as paradoxical as these two goals.

Authoritarianism is the postcolonial Arab way of ruling. It reflects the precolonial patriarchal autocratic practices, which emphasized the obligation of obedience to the ruler. Whether titled king, bey, or sultan, those who ruled the Arab world before colonialism were mostly autocrats. Even when they adopted the Islamic principle of *shura*, or consultation, decisionmaking remained largely within the authority of one person. This was clear in precolonial Tunisia, as shown in Chapter 7.

On the other hand, authoritarianism, compared to autocracy, is a functional system capable of dealing with the complexity of the postcolonial modern state. Postcolonial Arab countries have political institutions, justice systems, and capitalist markets. One person (the ruler) cannot control and regulate all of these modern institutions. Arab states found their salvation in French centralization, which at

---

[63] Kitson, *Low Intensity Operations*, at 3.

some level maintains the essence of autocracy. By adopting the colonial rationale of centralizing power in the executive and the use of the military in counter-terrorism, the Arab world in fact serves the Western-capitalist ideology. Authoritarian regimes are more interested in securing their positions than in any ideological goals. Through continuously obeying the Western agenda of the war on terror, both Western governments and authoritarian regimes are maximizing their interests. I have argued that this utilitarian approach will not work in the long run, as it threatens the essence of human security. The "Arab Spring," which overthrew two authoritarian presidents, is a recent example of this short-term regime stability.

While authoritarianism is a form of political government, this book has suggested that authoritarian ambition can be an underlying reason behind states' obsession with control. Restrictions on speech and association, travel bans, and monitoring of financial transactions, are all forms of authoritarian ambition that contradict liberal legality and democratic values. For instance, one of the problems of listing terrorists and terrorist entities is the mechanism of blacklisting. At the national level, decisions on blacklisting and freezing funds are left to the executive, and at a supra-national level, the UN Security Council has absolute authority in this regard. Centralizing power is a form of a collective authoritarian ambition. One could argue that practicality requires the use of this kind of mechanism. However, I have argued that practicality is overshadowing the legal principles that aim to protect rather than undermine human values.

Similar erosions of rights and freedoms in the name of anti-terrorism are occurring within legal systems in both Western democracies and authoritarian regimes like those in the Arab world. Post-9/11, we are witnessing a convergence between the ruling strategies of authoritarian and democratic governments.[64] This convergence is seen in the preventive measures taken and control orders given with regard to counter-terrorism. In the last century, preventive detentions without charge or trial have not typically been common in Western democracies as they have been in authoritarian regimes. However, post-9/11 these practices are seen to be justified in both types of system. For example, former Egyptian president Hosni Mubarak has claimed that the shifts in American counter-terrorism policy post-9/11 prove that Egypt was "right from the beginning in using all means, including military tribunals, to combat terrorism."[65] Anti-terrorism laws as used under Mubarak's regime threaten the development of the criminal legal system and the development of society as a whole. The adoption of such measures in the West raises the concern of both undermining Western legal systems and societies and legitimizing further oppression in the Arab world.

[64] Tom Ginsburg & Tamir Moustafa, *Rule by Law: The Politics of Courts in Authoritarian Regimes* (Cambridge: Cambridge University Press, 2008) at 3.
[65] Roach, *The 9/11 Effect*, at 80.

THREAT-FREE ENVIRONMENT AND THE "FLEXIBILITY" OF ANTI-TERRORISM LAW

This book has suggested that authoritarian ambition is not limited to authoritarian regimes, but also can emerge in democracies. This can be found in the excessive need to identify terrorists, as can be seen in the use of blacklisting by states and the UN Security Council. Other examples include laws prohibiting speech inciting terrorism and membership in a terrorist organization, which allow the authorities to intervene with the aim of preventing terrorism well before a crime occurs. The events of September 11 demonstrated that the war on terror is a war against two enemies, both of which continue to be vaguely defined: terrorists and fear. In the context of the war on terror, fear is commonly interpreted as collective feelings of outrage and insecurity. Within the language of law and politics, these feelings are translated into the terms "security gap" or "lack of security." Both legal and extra-legal measures continue to be taken to overcome this gap. The results have been of limited effectiveness: it remains impossible to absolutely ensure security. This has led officials to demand tougher and, crucially, more flexible anti-terrorism laws and measures. For instance, in the aftermath of the November 2015 Paris attacks, President Hollande asked for more flexible anti-terrorism and emergency laws.[66] Similar measures in the recent past have resulted in a temporary sense of security; however, these measures are not reliably effective in eliminating crimes.

While criminal law must remain capable of adaptation as circumstances and situations change, the driving of states toward increased "flexibility" can undermine efforts to run a state according to the rule of law. In other words, an excess of adaptation – an excess of flexibility – risks undermining the rule of law. The content and form of criminal law has never been fixed or static, nor is this thought to be desirable. The role of criminal law is not tethered solely to political purposes; it remains essential to shaping public policy and maintaining the conventions that are associated with a safe society. But the further the criminal law strays from its conventional core, as flexible measures are adopted by judicial and legislative bodies – which has increasingly happened in the area of counter-terrorism – the greater the strain becomes on the rule of law. The supposed benefits of these flexible laws in countering terrorism are unproven, and the fracturing of the foundational rule of the law in these states could have negative long-term consequences.

The aim of the current approach to crime control in Arab states such as Egypt and Tunisia, as well as elsewhere, as it relates to terrorism is not only to eliminate the fear of deadly acts of violence, but seemingly to allay feelings of insecurity. This latter goal is what redirects the stream of counter-terrorism by targeting the fear of potential threats and of acts that have not yet been committed; this is all-important

---

[66] Henry Samuel, "France Wants to Change Constitution to Extend Powers in State of Emergency" (December 3, 2015), *The Telegraph*, online: www.telegraph.co.uk.

among decisionmakers. This has led to counter-terrorism measures around the world becoming increasingly flexible and exceeding traditional legal boundaries. At the legislative level, repressive laws are justified to maintain a climate of order free from threats.

This book has offered a theoretical framework for understanding national and international counter-terrorism frameworks. Challenges regarding countering terrorism within a legal rather than a politicized framework require further efforts at all levels. While I invite politicians and lawmakers to reevaluate national and global anti-terrorism regulations, I also invite individuals and civil society organizations to understand that there is nothing worse than fearing fear itself. I leave space for the reader to apply the suggested theoretical framework in accordance with their receptivity and with the unique geopolitics of their countries.

Egyptian Anti-Terrorism Law No. 94 of 2015

ANTI-TERRORISM LAW

Section 1 *Substantive Provisions*

Chapter 1 General Provisions

ARTICLE 1 In the application of the provisions of this Law, the following expressions and words shall bear the meaning indicated next to them:

1- **Terrorist entity:** Each group, association, institution, organization, or gang composed of at least three persons, or any other entity proved to be [a terrorist group] regardless of its legal or factual status, whether inside or outside the country, and regardless of its nationality or the nationality of its members, [if it] aims to commit one or more terrorist crimes, or if [it takes] terrorism as a means to achieve or implement its criminal objectives.

2- **Terrorist:** Each person who commits, attempts to commit, incites, threatens, or plans inside [Egypt] or abroad a terrorist crime by any means even individually, or contributes to a joint criminal enterprise, or takes command, leadership, management, creation or establishment, or becomes a member of any of the terrorist entities stipulated in Article 1 of the presidential decree of Law no. 8 of 2015 Regarding Regulating Terrorist Entities and Terrorists, or funds or participates in its acts with knowledge of [its purposes].

3- **Terrorist act:** Any use of force, violence, or threat inside [Egypt] or abroad aiming to disrupt public order or endanger the safety, interests, security of the society; harm people, or horrify them, or risk their lives, liberties, public or private rights, their safety, or the other freedoms and rights granted by the constitution or by law; harm national unity, social peace, or national security; damage the environment, natural resources, antiquities, financial resources, institutions, public or private property, or occupy or seize them, or prevent or obstruct public authorities or judicial bodies, governmental interests, local units, places of worship, hospitals or institutions of learning, or diplomatic and consular missions in Egypt from the exercise of all or some of their activities, or resist [them], or thwart the application of the Constitution or the laws or regulations.

As well as all conduct committed with the intention of achieving one of the objectives shown in the first paragraph of this article, [including] preparing or incitement, if it caused damage to communication, information systems, financial or banking systems, national economy, energy storage, or security storage of goods, food and water, or their safety, or medical services during disasters and crisis.

ARTICLE 2 A terrorist act shall refer to any use of force, violence, threat, or intimidation domestically or abroad for the purpose of disturbing public order, or endangering the safety, interests, or security of the community; harming individuals and terrorizing them; jeopardizing their lives, freedoms, public or private rights, or security, or other freedoms and rights guaranteed by the Constitution and the law; harming national unity, social peace, or national security or damaging the environment, natural resources, antiquities, money, buildings, or public or private properties or occupying or seizing them; preventing or impeding public authorities, agencies or judicial bodies, government offices or local units, houses of worship, hospitals, institutions, institutes, diplomatic and consular missions, or regional and international organizations and bodies in Egypt from carrying out their work or exercising all or some of their activities, or resisting them or disabling the enforcement of any of the provisions of the Constitution, laws, or regulations.

A terrorist act shall likewise refer to any conduct committed with the intent to achieve, prepare, or instigate one of the purposes set out in the first paragraph of this article, if it aims to harm communications, information, financial or banking systems, national economy, energy reserves, security reserves of goods, food and water, or their safety, or medical services in disasters and crises.

ARTICLE 3 Funding terrorism shall refer to collecting, receiving, holding, supplying, transferring, or providing funds, weapons, ammunition, explosives, equipment, machines, data, information, materials, or other things directly or indirectly, and by any means including digital and electronic forms, with the intention to use all or some of it to commit any terrorist crime, or knowing that it will be used for this purpose, or to provide a safe haven to terrorists or to financers of terrorists in any of the methods mentioned above.

ARTICLE 4 Without prejudice to the provisions of Articles (1), (2), (3), and (4) of the Penal Code, the provisions of this Law shall apply to any perpetrator of a terrorist crime outside Egypt in the following cases:

1. If the crime is committed aboard a means of transportation by air, land, sea, or river, registered in Egypt or carrying the flag thereof.
2. If such a crime is committed or aims to:
   (A) Harm any of the citizens or residents of Egypt, its security, any of its interests or properties domestically or abroad, the headquarters and offices of its diplomatic or consular missions, its institutions, or the branches of its institutions abroad.
   (B) Harm any international or regional organizations or bodies.
   (C) Push the state or any of its authorities or its institutions to carry out an act or abstain therefrom.
3. If the victim is an Egyptian abroad.
4. If the perpetrator is a foreigner or stateless person present in Egypt.

ARTICLE 5 An attempt to commit a terrorist crime shall be punished by the same penalty prescribed for the completed offense.

ARTICLE 6 Shall be punished for inciting a terrorist crime with the same punishment for the full crime, whether the incitement is directed towards a particular person or group, or whether it is general, made in public or in private, and whatever the means used, even if no effects have resulted from this incitement.

ARTICLE 7 Any person who facilitates for a terrorist or terrorist group, by any direct or indirect means, the perpetration or preparation of any terrorist crime or knowingly provides housing, shelter, a place to hide or to use for meetings, or other facilities for the perpetrator shall be punished as an accomplice.

ARTICLE 8 Enforcers of the provisions of this Law shall not be held criminally accountable if they use force during their duty or to protect themselves from an imminent danger that is about to harm lives or property, as long as the use of this right is essential and sufficient to counter the risk.

[...]

Chapter 2 Offenses and Penalties

ARTICLE 12 Whoever establishes, founds, organizes, or manages a terrorist group or assumes command or leadership thereof shall be punished by the death sentence or life imprisonment.

Whoever joins or participates in any manner in a terrorist group, while being aware of its purposes shall be punished by imprisonment with hard labor. The penalty shall be imprisonment for no less than ten years if the offender received military, security, or technology training by the terrorist group to achieve its objectives or if the perpetrator is a member of the armed forces or the police.

Whoever coerces or obliges a person to join a terrorist group or prevents his separation therefrom shall be punished by life imprisonment.

The penalty shall be the death sentence if the coercion, obligation, or prevention results in this person's death.

ARTICLE 13 Shall be punished with life imprisonment whoever commits a crime of terrorism financing if the funding was to a terrorist, and shall the death penalty be applied if the funding was for a terrorist group or terrorist act.

And in the cases when the crime [of financing] is committed by a terrorist group, shall those responsible for the actual management of this group be punished by the penalty prescribed in the preceding paragraph of this Article provided that the crime is committed on behalf of the group or to its advantage.

And shall the terrorist group be punished with a fine not less than one hundred thousand and not more than three million pounds, and [shall the group] be jointly responsible for the payment of any financial penalties or compensation.

ARTICLE 14 Whoever seeks to communicate or communicates with a foreign country or any association, body, organization, group, gang, or other entities based inside or outside Egypt or with someone who works for the benefit of such foreign state or any of the parties cited with the aim of committing or preparing for a terrorist crime inside Egypt or against any of its citizens, interests, or properties, the headquarters and offices of diplomatic or consular missions, its institutions, the branches of its institutions abroad, or against any of the employees in any of the above bodies or persons enjoying international protection shall be punished by life imprisonment.

The penalty shall be the death sentence if the terrorist crime subject of the communication or espionage attempt is carried out or attempted.

ARTICLE 15 Whoever, in any manner, directly or indirectly, and with the intent to commit a terrorist crime domestically or abroad, prepares or trains people to manufacture or use conventional or unconventional weapons, wired, wireless, or electronic means of communication, or any other technical means or teaches them martial arts, combat, technology, skills, tricks or other methods in whatever form to be used to commit a terrorist crime or instigates to any of the above shall be punished by life imprisonment or imprisonment with hard labor for no less than ten years.

Whoever receives the training or education provided for in the preceding paragraph of this Article or is present in such locations in order to prepare or commit one of the offenses referred to in the first paragraph of this Article shall be punished by imprisonment for no less than seven years.

ARTICLE 16 Whoever captures, attacks, enters by force or violence, threatens, or intimidates presidential headquarters, parliamentary headquarters, the Cabinet, ministries, governorates, the armed forces, courts, prosecution offices, security directorates, police stations, prisons, security or regulatory bodies or agencies, archaeological sites, public facilities, places of worship or education, hospitals, or any public buildings or facilities, with intent to commit a terrorist crime, shall be punished by life imprisonment or imprisonment for no less than ten years.

The provisions of the first paragraph of this Article shall apply to whoever places devices or materials in any of the above-mentioned headquarters with the intent to damage or destroy them or any of the people present in or who frequent them, or whoever threatens to commit any of these acts.

The penalty shall be life imprisonment if the act was carried out using a weapon or by more than one person or if the perpetrator destroys or damages the headquarters or resists by force public authorities while performing their duty to guard the headquarters or recapture it. If the perpetration of any of the previous acts results in the death of a person, the penalty shall be the death sentence.

ARTICLE 17 Whoever enters by force or resistance the headquarters of a diplomatic or consular mission, an international or regional body or organization, or the official offices or private residences of their members in Egypt or abroad for the purpose of committing a terrorist crime shall be punished by life imprisonment or imprisonment with hard labor for no less than ten years.

Whoever resorts to the use of force to attack or simply threatens to attack any of the headquarters set forth in the first paragraph of this Article or means of transport of a person under international protection shall be punished by the same penalty if such an attack jeopardizes the latter's security or freedom.

The penalty shall be life imprisonment if the act was carried out with the use of weapons by one or more individual. If the act results in the death of a person, the penalty shall be the death sentence.

ARTICLE 18 Whoever tried through force, violence, threat, intimidation, or any other methods of terrorist acts to overthrow the government, change the state constitution, the Republican system, or the form of government shall be punished by life imprisonment or imprisonment with hard labor for no less than ten years.
[. . .]

ARTICLE 21 Any Egyptians who, without written permission from the relevant authority, cooperate with or enlist in the armed forces of a foreign state or any militant groups, associations, bodies, or organizations based outside Egypt, and use terrorism, military training, military arts, combat methods, tricks or skills as means to achieve their objectives in the perpetration or preparation of terrorist crimes shall be punished by imprisonment for no less than ten years, even if the actions of these entities do not target Egypt.

If the offender receives any kind of training or education referred to in the preceding paragraph of this Article, the penalty shall be life imprisonment.

Whoever facilitates others to cooperate, join, or transit outside Egypt in order to join the armed forces of a foreign state or any armed groups, associations, bodies, or organizations shall be punished by the same penalty set forth in the first paragraph of this Article.

ARTICLE 22 Whoever arrests, abducts, detains, imprisons, or limits the freedom of a person in any manner shall be punished by imprisonment for no less than ten years if the purpose is to force a State body or authority to take or refrain from an action or to obtain an advantage or benefit of any kind.

The penalty shall be life imprisonment if the offender commits any of the acts set forth in Article (2) of this Law or if he makes false impersonations, unduly wears an official uniform or bears a card or insignia distinctive of a profession or function, conducts a job in accordance with the requirements of these professions, presents false documents, claiming they are issued by a State authority, if the act results in an injury, or if the offender resists public authorities during the performance of their function while releasing the victim.

The penalty shall be the death sentence if the act results in the death of a person.

ARTICLE 23 Without prejudice to any other aggravated penalty, whoever makes, designs, acquires, achieves, provides, offers, or facilitates the obtainment of a conventional weapon to be used or prepared for use in the perpetration of a terrorist crime shall be punished by aggravated imprisonment for no less than ten years.

The penalty shall be life imprisonment if the weapon subject of the crime is unconventional.

The penalty shall be the death sentence if the use of the conventional or unconventional weapon or the mentioned material results in the death of a person.

ARTICLE 24 Whoever captures by force, violence, threat, or intimidation any means of air, land, sea, or river transport or fixed platforms installed permanently on the bottom of the sea for the purpose of discovering or exploiting resources or for any other economic purposes in order to achieve a terrorist purpose shall be punished by aggravated imprisonment for no less than seven years.

The penalty shall be life imprisonment if the means of transport or the fixed platform is for the armed forces or the police, if the perpetrator commits an act of violence against a person present in any of such installations, or if he destroys or causes damage to the means of transport or fixed platform in a manner that results in a permanent or temporary disruption.

The penalty shall be the same provided for in the second paragraph of this article for whoever places on the means of transport or fixed platform devices or materials that destroy or harm lives or property or whoever destroys or vandalizes transportation installations and facilities or resists by force or violence the public authorities during the performance of their duty to restore the means or the fixed platform or prevents such authorities from carrying out their duties.

The penalty shall be the death sentence if the act results in the death of a person.

ARTICLE 25 Whoever intentionally damages, ruins, destroys, disrupts, cuts, or breaks a network, tower, or power line, oil or natural gas pipe, or the buildings or installations necessary for any of such buildings or whoever seizes by force any of these facilities shall be punished by imprisonment with hard labor for no less than seven years.

If the perpetrator uses force or violence to commit any of the acts described in the first paragraph of this Article or deliberately prevents specialists from repairing any of the above, or if the crime results in interruption of the supply of electricity, petroleum products, or natural gas, even if temporarily, the penalty shall be life imprisonment.

If the perpetration of the crimes referred to in the two preceding paragraphs of this Article results in the death of a person, the penalty shall be the death sentence.

In all cases, the court shall order the confiscation of the machinery and tools used in the crime and the restoration of the situation to the state prior to the crime at the expense of the convicted person who will be ordered to pay the value of the damage.

[. . .]

ARTICLE 27 Without prejudice to any other aggravated penalty provided for in this Law or any other law, whoever attacks the people in charge of the application or enforcement of the provisions of this Law or resists them by force, violence, or threat of use of force during or due to the application or enforcement of the provisions of this Law, shall be punished by imprisonment with hard labor for no less than seven years.

The penalty shall be life imprisonment if the assault or resistance results in a permanent disability that is impossible to treat or if the offender bears a weapon, kidnaps or detains any of those in charge of the application or enforcement of the provisions of this law.

If the act results in the death of a person, the penalty shall be the death sentence.

The provisions of this Article shall apply if the victim is a spouse of someone in charge of the application or enforcement of the provisions of this law or one of his predecessors or descendants.

ARTICLE 28 Whoever promotes or prepares to promote, directly or indirectly, the perpetration of any terrorist crime, whether verbally, in writing, or by any other means, shall be punished by imprisonment for no less than five years.

Indirect promotion shall include the promotion of ideas and beliefs inciting the use of violence by any of the means set forth in the preceding paragraph of this Article.

The penalty shall be imprisonment for no less than seven years if the promotion occurs inside houses of worship, among members of the armed or police forces, or in locations belonging to such forces.

Whoever possesses or acquires any public means of printing or recording used or intended for use, even if temporarily, for the purpose of printing, recording, or broadcasting the aforementioned shall be punishable by the same penalty set forth in the first paragraph of this Article.

ARTICLE 29 Whoever establishes or uses a communications site, website, or other media for the purpose of promoting ideas or beliefs that call to commit terrorist acts or broadcasts material intended to mislead security authorities, influence the course of justice in any terrorist crime, exchange messages and issue assignments among terrorist groups or their members, or exchange information relating to the actions or movement of terrorists or terrorist groups domestically and abroad shall be punished by imprisonment with hard labor for no less than five years.

Whoever unduly or illegally accesses websites affiliated with any government agency in order to obtain, access, change, erase, destroy, or falsify the data or information contained therein in order to commit an offense referred to in the first paragraph of this Article or prepare it shall be punishable by imprisonment with hard labor for no less than ten years.

ARTICLE 30 Whoever participates in a criminal conspiracy for the purpose of committing a terrorist crime shall be punished by life imprisonment or imprisonment with hard labor for no less than seven years.

The penalty shall be life imprisonment if the perpetrator is one of the instigators of this conspiracy or is an accomplice in its administration.

[. . .]

ARTICLE 33 Whoever is aware of the perpetration or preparation of a terrorist crime or has information or data related to one of the perpetrators and was able to report the same to the relevant authorities but failed to do so shall be punished by imprisonment for no less than three months and a fine of no less than 100,000 Egyptian pounds and no more than 300,000 Egyptian pounds or either of the two penalties.

The provision of the preceding paragraph of this Article shall not apply to the husband, wife, predecessors, or descendants of the offender.

ARTICLE 34 Whoever prepares to commit a terrorist crime shall be punished by imprisonment for no less than one year, even if his work does not exceed the preparation stage.

ARTICLE 35 Whoever intentionally, by any means, publishes, forecasts, displays, or promotes false news or information about terrorist acts that are committed in Egypt, or about the countering measures in opposition to the official statements issued by the Ministry of Defense shall be punishable by a fine of no less than 200,000 Egyptian pounds and no more than 500,000 Egyptian pounds, without prejudice to the disciplinary penalties prescribed.

In cases where the crime is committed through a juridical person, the person in charge of the actual management of such juridical person shall be punished by the same penalty set forth in the first paragraph of this Article, provided that the crime is committed on his own account or for his own benefit. The juridical person shall be jointly liable for the fines and compensation sentenced.

In all cases, the court shall prohibit the convicted party from practicing the profession for a period not exceeding one year if the crime is a breach of the ethics of the profession.

[...]

ARTICLE 37 In relation to any terrorist crime, and in addition to imposing the prescribed penalty, the court may impose one or more of the following measures:

1) Deportation of foreigners.
2) Prohibition of residence in a particular place or specific area.
3) Obligation to reside in a particular place.
4) Prohibition from approaching or frequenting certain places or areas.
5) Obligation to be in certain places at certain times.
6) Prohibition of work in certain places or in specific activities.
7) Prohibition of the use of certain means of communication or prevention of their acquisition or possession.
8) Obligation to participate in rehabilitation sessions.

With the exception of the first measure, the duration of measures may not exceed five years.

Whoever violates the above measure taken against him shall be punished by imprisonment for no less than six months.

In all cases, conviction of a terrorist crime shall result in the loss of good reputation and behavior that is a condition for assuming public office or running for representative councils.

ARTICLE 38 Offenders who inform the relevant authorities before pursuing the execution of the crime shall be exempted from the penalties of the crimes referred to in this Law. The court may exempt from punishment if the reporting occurs after the execution of the crime and before the start of investigations, if the perpetrator enables the authorities to arrest other perpetrators of the crime or perpetrators of another crime of a similar type and danger.

[…]

Section 2 *Procedural Provisions*

Article 40
In the case that a danger of terrorism emerges that needs to be confronted, law enforcement officers shall have the right to collect information on such danger, search for the perpetrators, and keep them in custody for a period not exceeding 24 hours.

Law enforcement officers shall prepare reports on the procedures and the detainee(s) shall be referred along with the report to the public prosecutor or the competent investigation authority, according to the case.

For the same necessity set forth in the first paragraph of this Article and before the expiration of the period specified, the Public Prosecution or the competent investigation authority may order the extension of custody once for a period not exceeding seven days. The order shall be issued with the causes by at least an Attorney General or the equivalent.

The custody period shall be calculated as part of the precautionary detention, and the accused shall be kept in a legally-designated area.

The provisions of the first paragraph of Article (44) of this Law shall apply to grievances against continuation of custody.

[…]

Article 43
During the investigation of a terrorist offense, and in addition to the legally-prescribed competencies thereof, the Public Prosecutor or the competent investigation authority, according to the case, shall have the jurisdiction of investigation judges and the Court of Appealed Misdemeanors convened in consultation chambers, according to the same jurisdiction, restrictions, and periods provided for in Article (143) of the Criminal Procedure Code.

[…]

Article 46
The Public Prosecutor or the competent investigation authority in a terrorist crime, according to the case, may authorize a reasoned warrant for a period not exceeding thirty days to monitor and record the conversations and messages received on wired, wireless, and other means of modern telecommunications, record and film what is

happening and being written in private premises or across communication and information networks or websites, and seize ordinary or electronic correspondence, letters, publications, parcels, and cables of all kinds.

The warrant referred to in the first paragraph of this Article may be renewed for one or more similar periods.

[...]

Article 48

The Public Prosecutor, the commissioned attorney generals, or the competent investigation authority, according to the case, may order the access or acquisition of any data or information related to accounts, deposits, safes, or transactions related thereto if it is necessary to uncover the truth as part of evidence-gathering or investigation of the role of the accused in the crime or his participation in any terrorist crime proven to have occurred regarding which there exists sufficient evidence.

Article 49

With regards to the crimes set forth in Articles (12), (15), (19), and (22) of this Law, the Public Prosecutor or the competent investigation authority, according to the case, shall issue an interim order to close headquarters, premises, housing, and residencies, provided a decision is issued by at least a chief prosecutor.

Luggage and furniture seized shall be considered items seized administratively as soon as they are seized until a final decision is issued in the case. After an inventory is prepared and they are recorded in a report, they shall be handed over to the guard assigned to guard the seals placed on the closed headquarters, premises, housing, and residencies. In the event that there were no seizures, he shall be assigned to guard the seals in the same manner. The issuance of a verdict of acquittal shall result in the abolition of the closure order.

The Public Prosecutor or the competent investigation authority shall stop the sites provided for in the first paragraph of Article (29) of this Law, block them, or block their content to prevent any aspect of use set forth in this Article. It shall also retain the devices and equipment used in the crime.

Article 50

One or more circuit of the criminal courts, each headed by a judge of at least the grade of Chief Judge of a Court of Appeals, shall be dedicated to hear terrorist crime felonies and crimes associated with such crimes.

Circuits of the First Instance Courts, presided over by a judge of at least the grade of Chief Judge, shall be dedicated to hear terrorist crime misdemeanors and crimes associated with such misdemeanors.

Circuits of the First Instance courts, presided over by a judge of at least the grade of Chief Judge and with the membership of two judges, one of whom is at least at the grade of Chief Judge, shall be dedicated to hear the appeals of the judgments issued for such crimes.

Cases referred to in this Article shall be decided promptly and in accordance with the procedures set forth in this Law and the Code of Criminal Procedure.

Article 51

The public prosecution or the competent investigation authority, according to the case, or the court that is hearing any terrorist crime or to which such a crime was referred, shall rule on the crimes associated therewith.

Article 52

Criminal cases for terrorist crimes shall not expire and the sentence imposed shall not lapse with the passage of time.

Article 53

In the event of danger of terrorist crimes or consequent environmental disasters, the President of the Republic may issue a decree to take appropriate measures to maintain security and public order, including the evacuation or isolation of some areas or imposition of a curfew, provided the decree identifies the region it applies to for a period not exceeding six months.

This decree shall be presented to the House of Representatives within the next seven days to decide on it. If the House of Representatives is not in ordinary session, it shall be called to convene immediately. If the House of Representatives is not yet formed, the approval of the Cabinet shall be taken and the decree presented to the new House of Representatives at its first meeting. The decree shall be approved by a majority of the members of the House of Representatives. If the decree is not presented within the aforementioned time limit or it is presented and not approved, it shall be considered as null and void unless the House of Representatives sees otherwise.

The President may extend the duration of the measure referred to in the first paragraph of this Article, upon the approval of a majority of the members of the House of Representatives.

In urgent cases, the measures referred to in this Article shall be taken under verbal orders, provided they are supported in writing within eight days.

Tunisian Law No. 26 of 2015 regarding Anti-terrorism and Money-laundering[1]

ARTICLE 1

This law aims to confront and prevent terrorism and money laundering, and to support the international efforts in this field in accordance with international standards and within the framework of international, regional and bilateral agreements ratified by the Republic of Tunisia.

ARTICLE 2

The public authorities implementing this law shall respect the constitutional guarantees, international and regional treaties, and the bilateral treaties ratified by the Republic of Tunisia in the field of human rights, refugee protection and international humanitarian law.

ARTICLE 3

The following terms shall mean:

- [Conspiracy] agreement: Any conspiracy for any period regardless of the number of its members, with the intention of committing one of the offenses provided in this law, without the need for a structural organization or a specific and formal distribution of roles between them, or the continuation of their membership.
- Organization: A group with an organizational structure of three or more people formed for any period and that works in a joint manner, with the

---

[1] *Official Gazette* no. 63, August 7, 2015.

intention of committing one of the offenses provided in this law, inside or outside the national territory.
– [. . .]

[. . .]

CHAPTER 1 ON COUNTERING AND SUPPRESSING TERRORISM

Section 1 *General Provisions*

Article 5
Shall be considered perpetrators of terrorist crimes as stipulated in this law and shall be punished by half the penalties whoever incites by any means to commit [a terrorist act] when such [incitement] by its nature or its context creates a danger of the possibility of committing it.

And if the punishment is the death sentence or life imprisonment, they shall be replaced by imprisonment for twenty years.

And shall be considered perpetrators of terrorist crimes and shall be punished by half the penalties whomever intends to commit such acts, if accompanied by any preparatory work to commit it.

Article 6
Administrative monitoring shall be imposed over perpetrators of terrorist crimes as stipulated in this law, which shall not be less than three years and not more than ten years, unless the court decides to reduce it.

This shall not preclude the imposition of any or all of the collateral consequences of criminal conviction prescribed by law.

[. . .]

Article 8
Shall be exempted from being punished those who belong to a terrorist organization or a [conspiracy] agreement or who has an individual project aiming to commit a terrorist act as stipulated in this law or crimes related to it by providing the relevant authority with guidance or information that enables discovering and preventing the crime.

The court is obliged to impose administrative monitoring over this person or to prevent him from staying in certain places for a period of not less than two years and not more than five years, unless the court decides to reduce it.

Article 9
Shall be punished by half the penalties those who belong to a terrorist organization or a [conspiracy] agreement or who has an individual project aiming to commit a

terrorist act as stipulated in this law or crimes related to it, if they provide the relevant authority with guidance or information in connection with the initial investigation, investigation or trial that enables putting an end to terrorist crimes or crimes related to them, or prevents killing a human, or leads to discovering all or some of the [terrorist] members or to arrest them.

And the punishment shall be twenty years imprisonment if the punishment prescribed for the offense is the death sentence or life imprisonment.

[...]

Section 2 *Terrorist Crimes and their Punishments*

[...]

Article 13
Shall be considered a perpetrator of a terrorist crime whomever deliberately implemented by any means an individual or collective project to commit any act listed in articles 14 to 36 aiming by its nature or context to spread terror among the population or to unduly compel a State or an international organization to do what it is not obliged to do or refrain from doing what it is obliged to do.

Article 14
Shall be considered a perpetrator of a terrorist crime whomever commits any of these acts:

1- Killing a person;
2- Injuring, assaulting, or other forms of violence contemplated by Articles 218 and 319 of the Penal Code;
3- Causing other forms of injury, assault or violence;
4- Damaging the buildings of diplomatic or consular missions, or international organizations;
5- Causing harm to food security and to the environment in a way that unbalances ecosystems or natural resources or puts the life or health of its inhabitants in danger;
6- Intentionally opening flood discharge from dams or pouring chemicals or biological materials into those dams or into water facilities to cause harm to inhabitants;
7- Causing harm to public or private property, vital resources or infrastructure or means of transport or means of communication or computer systems or public services.
8- *Takfir* or advocating for [excommunication], or incitement of or calling for hatred or loathing among races, religions and faiths.

Shall be punished by the death sentence and a fine of two hundred thousand dinar whomever commits the crime stipulated in the first paragraph or if the act stipulated in the other paragraphs leads to causing death to a person.

And shall be punished by life imprisonment and a fine of one hundred and fifty thousand dinar whomever commits the act listed in the third paragraph or if the acts listed in the fourth, fifth, sixth, seventh, and eightieth paragraphs cause severe physical damage.

And shall be punished by imprisonment for twenty years and a fine of 100,000 dinars if the acts listed in the fourth, fifth, sixth, seventh and eighth paragraphs cause physical damage of the type prescribed in the second paragraph.

And shall be punished by imprisonment for ten to twenty tears and a fine of 50,000 to 100,000 dinar whomever commits any of the acts listed in the fourth, fifth, sixth and seventh paragraphs.

And shall be punished by imprisonment for a year to five years and a fine of 5,000 to 10,000 dinar whomever commits any of the acts listed in the second and eighth paragraphs.

[...]

Article 31
Shall be considered a perpetrator of a terrorist crime, and shall be punished by imprisonment of one to five years or a fine of five to ten thousand dinars, whomever inside or outside the Republic deliberately and openly by any means expresses praise or glorification of a terrorist offense or

its perpetrators or an organization or a [conspiracy] agreement connected to terrorist offenses, its members, activities, opinions or ideas associated with such terrorist offenses.

Article 32
Shall be considered a perpetrator of a terrorist crime, and shall be punished by imprisonment of six years up to twelve years and a fine of twenty thousand up to fifty thousand dinar, whomever intentionally joined, at any address inside or outside the Republic, a terrorist organization or [conspiracy] agreement associated with terrorist crimes, or received training, at any address, with the intention to commit any of the crimes stipulated in this law.

And the punishment shall be imprisonment for ten to twenty years and a fine of one thousand to one hundred thousand dinars for the establishers of such organizations.

Article 33
Shall be considered a perpetrator of a terrorist crime, and shall be punished by imprisonment of six to twelve years and a fine of 20,000 to 50,000, whomever intentionally commits any of the following acts:

1- Using the land of the Republic or the land of a foreign country to recruit or train a person or a group with the intention to commit one of the crimes stipulated in this law, inside or outside the Republic.
2- Using the land of the Republic to commit one of the crimes stipulated in this law against another country or its citizens or doing preparatory work.
3- Traveling outside the Republic with the intention to commit any of the terrorist crimes stipulated in this law, or to incite them, or to receive or provide training to commit such acts.
4- Entering the land of the Republic or passing through it with the aim of traveling outside it to commit one of the terrorist crimes stipulated in this law, or to receive or provide training to commit such acts.

[…]

Article 36

Shall be considered a perpetrator of a terrorist crime, and shall be punished by imprisonment of six to twelve years and a fine of 50,000 to 100,000 dinars, whomever intentionally by any means directly or indirectly commits any of the following acts:

1- Donating, collecting, providing or offering funds with the knowledge that the objective is to finance persons, organizations or activities that are related to terrorist crimes stipulated in this law, regardless of the legitimacy or illegitimacy of the source of such funds.
2- Donating, collecting, providing or offering funds with the knowledge that the objective is to finance the traveling of persons outside the land of the Republic with the aim to join a terrorist organization or [conspiracy] agreement, or to commit any terrorist crimes, or aiming to receive or offer training to commit [such crimes].
3- Concealing or facilitating the concealment of the real source of movable [funds] or immovable property, income or profit that belong to natural persons or juridical persons whatever its form, or accept deposit under a fictitious name, or incorporate it with the knowledge that it is intended to finance persons or organizations or activities related to terrorist crimes, regardless of the legitimacy or illegitimacy of the source of such funds.

The amount of the fine may be increased to five times the value of the money subject to the offenses set forth in this article.

Article 37

Shall be considered a perpetrator of a terrorist crime, and shall be punished by imprisonment for one to five years and a fine of 5,000 to 10,000 dinars, whomever refrains, even if he is subject to professional secrecy, from immediately notifying the relevant authorities about the acts and information he has obtained, or of instructions regarding the committing or potential committing of any of the terrorist crimes stipulated in this law.

Shall be excluded from the provisions of the above paragraph parents, children and partners.

And shall be excluded lawyers and doctors regarding such secrets if they know them in the course of their duties.

And shall be excluded journalists in accordance with the provisions of Decree No. 115 of 2011 of November 2, 2011 relating to the Freedom of Press, Printing and publishing.

These exceptions do not include the information that could by notifying the authority prevent the commission of terrorist crimes in the future.

No criminal charges can be taken against whomever with good faith notified the authorities.

[. . .]

Section 3 *Judicial Police Officers*

[. . .]

Article 39
Judicial police officers are obliged to notify, without delay, the Prosecutor to whom they belong about the terrorist offenses which they have been dealing with. And they cannot keep the suspect in [custody] for more than five days.

They must also inform the authorities concerned without delay if the defendant is a member of the armed forces, internal security forces or customs officers.

Prosecutors in the courts of first instance are obliged to forward, immediately, the above-mentioned cases to the General Prosecutor of the Tunisian court of first instance to decide the [following step].

Section 4 *On the Counter-terrorism Judicial Pole*

Article 40
Shall a Counter-terrorism Judicial Pole be established in the Court of Appeal in Tunis to hear cases of the terrorist crimes stipulated in this law.

The Counter-terrorism Judicial Pole consists of representatives of the public prosecution, investigating magistrates, judges of the prosecution services, and judges in the felony and the misdemeanor courts of first instance and appeal, and they shall be chosen based on their composition and experience in cases related to terrorist crimes.

Subsection 1 On the Public Prosecution

ARTICLE 41 The public prosecutor at the Republic Court of First Instance has sole jurisdiction to initiate and prosecute terrorist crimes stipulated in this law and crimes related to them.

He is assisted by at least second-tier substitutes, who have been appointed to the Counter-terrorism Judicial Pole.

The public prosecutors of the Republic's other courts of first instance are authorized to carry out urgent preliminary investigations to ascertain the offense, gather the evidence and investigate the perpetrators. They shall receive voluntary denunciations, complaints, reports and statements relating thereto, interrogate the accused summarily upon his appearance, and decide to place him at the disposal of the public prosecutor at the court of first instance in Tunisia with the reports, the written minutes and the [other] reserved objects [that help the investigation in] revealing the truth.

The public prosecutor at Tunisia's Court of First Instance has sole jurisdiction to extend the duration of the custody twice for the same period provided by article 39 of this law, by a written order which includes the legal grounds and facts that justify it.

The Public Prosecutor at the Republic's Court of First Instance must immediately notify the General Prosecutor at the Court of Appeal in Tunis of all terrorist offenses that have been detected and immediately ask the related investigating judge to proceed with the [provided] information.

[...]

ARTICLE 46 In exceptional cases that require the protection of the witness, or at the request of the witness, or if the testimony presented is not the only or most important evidence to prove the indictment, the investigating judge may decide not to confront the witness with the suspect or with another witness.

ARTICLE 47 If the witness has failed to meet the requirements of the testimony, the investigating judge shall issue an independent report to the General Prosecutor to consider referring the witness to the competent court in accordance with direct referral procedures and without investigating.

ARTICLE 48 Shall be punished by imprisonment for three to six months and a fine of one hundred to two thousand dinars the witness who lacks the requirements of testimony in any of the terrorist crimes.

[...]

Section 5 *Special Investigation Techniques*

Subsection 1 – Interception of Communications

ARTICLE 54 In cases where the necessity of the inquiry so requires, the public prosecutor or the investigating judge may resort to the interception of the communications of the suspect, by a written and reasoned decision.

Interception of communications includes data streams, eavesdropping, or access to the content of communications, reproduction or recording with the help of appropriate technical means and by using, when necessary, the Telecommunications Technical Agency, the operators of public telecommunications networks, access networks, and telecommunications service providers, each depending on the type of service provided.

A Data stream is data that can identify the type of service, the source of the communication, its destination, and the transmission network, the time, date, volume, and duration of the communication.

The decision of the General Prosecutor or the investigating judge shall include all the elements that allow the identification of the communications subject to the interception request, as well as the acts that justify it and its duration.

The duration of the interception cannot exceed four months from the date of the decision. It can be renewed once for the same duration by reasoned decision.

The authority responsible for the implementation of the interception is obliged to inform the public prosecutor or the investigating judge, depending on the case, by any written means about the arrangements made to accomplish the mission and the actual date of the interception operation.

The decision stipulated in this article may be withdrawn at any time.

[. . .]

Subsection 3 – Audiovisual Monitoring

[. . .]

ARTICLE 63 When the necessities of the investigation so require, the General Prosecutor or the investigating judge may, according to the case, by a written and reasoned order authorize the officers of the judicial police responsible for ascertaining the offenses stipulated in this Law to place a technical device in the personal belongings of the suspect, in private or public places, premises or vehicles in order to capture, prove, transfer and record discreetly their words and photos and locate them.

The decision of the General Prosecutor or investigating judge shall include, depending on the case, the authorization to access private places, premises, or vehicles, even outside the hours provided by the Criminal Procedure Code and without the knowledge or without the consent of the owner or any person entitled to the place or vehicle.

The decision shall include all the elements that identify the personal belongings, private or public places, premises, or vehicles concerned for audiovisual monitoring and the acts that justify it and its duration.

The duration of the audiovisual monitoring cannot exceed two months from the date of the decision, and it can be renewed once for the same duration by reasoned decision.

The decision stipulated in this article may be withdrawn at any time.
[…]

Section 6 *National Commission to Combat Terrorism*

Article 66
A Commission called the "National Commission to Combat Terrorism" shall be established by the Prime Minister, and shall acts as its permanent secretariat.

Article 67
The National Commission to Combat Terrorism shall consist of:

- Representative of the Prime Minister as President, one full-time member,
- Representative of the Ministry of Justice as Vice-President, one full-time member,
- Representative of the Ministry of Justice on the General Administration of Prisons and Reform, one member,
- Representatives of the Ministry of the Interior Affairs, two members,
- Representative of the Ministry of Defense, one member,
- Representative of the Ministry of Foreign Affairs, one member,
- Representative of the minister responsible for human rights, one member,
- Representative of the Ministry of Financing, one member,
- Representative of the Ministry of Youth and Sports, one member,
- Representative of the Ministry of Agriculture on Forest Management, one member,
- Representative of the Ministry of Women, Family and Childhood, one member,
- Representative of the Ministry of Religious Affairs, one member,
- Representative of the Ministry of Culture, one member,
- Representative of the Ministry of Education on Program Management, one member,
- First investigative judge specializing in terrorism cases, one member,
- Expert from the Intelligence, Security and Defense Agency, one member,

– Expert from the Technical Communications Agency, one member,

– Expert from the Tunisian Financial Analysis Commission, one member,

The members of the National Commission to Combat Terrorism shall be appointed by a government order, [and they shall be chosen in accordance with] a proposal by the relevant ministries and bodies for a period of six years, with the renewal of one-third of the members of the Commission every two years.

The President of the Commission may invite any person of competence and experience or representative of civil society to attend the meetings of the Commission and to consult his views on the raised issues.

The expenses of the Commission shall be part of the Prime Minister's budget.

The Commission shall be organized and operated by a governmental order.

Article 68

The National Commission to Combat Terrorism shall, in particular, undertake the following tasks:

– Follow-up and evaluation of the implementation of the decisions of the competent international bodies related to counter-terrorism in the context of the fulfillment of Tunisia's international commitments,

– Proposing the necessary measures to be taken about organizations or persons connected with the terrorist crimes stipulated in this law in light of the information collected and case law in the reports directed to the President of the Republic and the President of the People's Assembly and the Prime Minister and the administrative authorities concerned,

– Give an opinion on the draft legal texts relating to counter-terrorism,

– Prepare a national study to identify the phenomenon of terrorism and its financing and the criminal phenomena associated with it to determine their characteristics and causes, assess their risks and propose ways to combat them. The study shall identify the national priorities in addressing this phenomenon,

– Issue guidelines to prevent and combat terrorism and to support the international effort to combat all its manifestations,

– Assist in the development of programs and policies aimed at preventing terrorism and proposing mechanisms to implement them,

– Coordinate and follow-up with national efforts in the application of procedures for the protection of persons concerned with the application of this law as well as measures to help the victims,

– Facilitate communication between the different ministries and coordinate their efforts,

– Cooperate with and assist international organizations and civil society in combating terrorism,

– Collect data, information and statistics related to combating terrorism to create a database to exploit them in accomplishing the tasks assigned to them. The concerned parties are committed to empowering the Commission with the data and statistics mentioned for the completion of its work,
– Spread social awareness about the dangers of terrorism through awareness campaigns, cultural and educational programs, holding conferences and symposia, issuing pamphlets and guides,
– Organize training courses and supervize programs to develop expertise at the internal and external levels,
– Contribute to the revitalization of research and studies to update the legislation areas related to terrorism to achieve the implementation of state programs in addressing this phenomenon.
[…]

Section 7 *Protection Mechanisms*

Article 71
Necessary measures shall be taken for the protection of persons who preview and repress terrorist crimes as stipulated in this law, including judges, judicial police officers, military officers, assistance officers and agents of public authority.

Protective measures shall also be applicable to court officers, undercover agents, informants, victims, witnesses and any other person who in any way have a duty to notify the relevant authorities of the offense.

Such measures shall be extended, where appropriate, to the family members of the persons referred to in the above paragraphs and to all those who are to be targeted among their relatives.

Article 72
In addition to self-defense cases, internal security forces, military personnel and assistance officers are not criminally liable when they use force or give orders to use force if that was necessary to perform tasks within the limits of the law, or internal regulations and instructions given on a legal basis in the framework of fighting terrorist crimes provided by this law.
[…]

Section 9 *On Terrorist Crimes Committed Outside the National Territory*

Article 83
The court of first instance of Tunis, through the judges appointed to the Judicial Pole of Counter-terrorism, is competent to examine terrorist crimes stipulated

in this law and related offenses committed outside the national territory in the following cases:

- If they are committed by a Tunisian citizen,
- If they are committed against Tunisian persons or interests,
- If they are committed against foreign persons or interests, by a foreigner or a stateless person whose habitual residence is Tunisia, or by a foreigner or stateless person on national territory, and the relevant foreign authorities have not requested his extradition before a final judgment is rendered against him by the competent Tunisian courts.

[...]

Article 86
Public prosecution may not be instituted against the perpetrators of terrorist crimes stipulated in this law and related offenses if proven that a judiciary abroad has issued a final decision, in the case that a sentence is imposed, the entire sentence has been served, or the sentence is prescribed or is covered by amnesty.

Section 10 *Extradition*

[...]

Article 87
Terrorist crimes are in no way considered political offenses that makes extradition not obligatory.

Terrorist financing crimes are in no way considered as fiscal offenses that make extradition not obligatory.

Article 88
Terrorist crimes stipulated in the law shall be extraditable in accordance with the provisions of the Criminal Procedure Code, if committed outside the territory of the Republic against a foreigner or against foreign interests by a foreigner or stateless person who is in Tunisian territory.

Extradition shall be granted only in the event that the Tunisian authorities receive a legal request from a competent state in accordance with its domestic law.

And extradition shall not be granted if there are substantial grounds for believing that the person subject to the extradition request would be at risk of being subjected to torture or the request for extradition intends to track or punish a person for his race, color, origin, religion, sex, nationality or political opinions.

Article 89
If it is decided not to extradite a person to be prosecuted abroad for a crime stipulated in this law, the case shall be brought up and heard before the Tunisian Court of First Instance.

Section 11 *Expiration Periods of Public Prosecution and Penalties*

Article 90
The public prosecution for the terrorist crimes stipulated in this law shall be dropped after twenty years for a felony and after ten years for a misdemeanor.

Article 91
Sentences for terrorist crimes are expired for felonies after thirty years. Nevertheless, it is not permissible for the convicted person to reside in the area of the state where the crime was committed without a license from the competent administrative authority, otherwise penalties shall be applied for violating the residence ban.
Sentences for misdemeanor are expired after ten years.
[...]

CHAPTER 3 JOINT PROVISIONS BETWEEN COUNTER-TERRORISM FINANCING AND MONEY-LAUNDERING

Section 1 *On Preventing Illegal Financial Routes*

Article 98
Shall be prohibited all forms of support and financing to persons, organizations or activities related to the terrorist crimes stipulated in this law and other illegal activities, whether done directly or indirectly, through natural or legal persons, regardless of the form or objective, and even if gaining profit is not among their goals.

Article 99
Legal persons must adopt the following prudent conduct requirements:

- Refrain from receiving any donations or grants whose origin is unknown or from illegal acts that the law describes as a crime or from natural or legal persons or organizations or bodies involved, inside or outside the territory of the Republic, in activities related to terrorist offenses,
- Refrain from accepting any contributions beyond the legally prescribed ceiling,

– Refrain from accepting any donations or other financial assistance, whatever their amount, except in the exceptions prescribed by special legal provision,
– Refrain from accepting any money derived from abroad, except through an acceptable broker based in Tunisia, and that the current law does not prevent such transfer,
– Refrain from accepting any amounts in cash equal to or exceeding the equivalent of five thousand dinars, even if this is done under multiple payments if suspected to be related to each other.

[...]

Article 103
The National Commission to Combat Terrorism shall, within the framework of the fulfillment of Tunisia's international obligations and based on [the National Commission to Combat Terrorism] or the competent international bodies' findings, decide to freeze the assets of persons or organizations linked to terrorist crimes.

The procedures for implementing the decisions of the competent international bodies shall be regulated by a government order.

Those responsible for implementing the freezing decision must take the necessary measures immediately after its publication in the Official Gazette of the Republic of Tunisia and inform the National Commission to Combat Terrorism of the initiating and freezing measures that have been taken and all useful information to implement its decision.

No allegation for damages or criminal liability may be accepted against any natural or legal person for having performed, in good faith, the duties incumbent on him, in execution of the decision of the freezing.

Article 104
The person concerned by the freezing order or his representative may request the National Counter-Terrorism Commission to order the use of part of the funds frozen to cover the expenses necessary for the payment of foodstuffs, rents or repayment of mortgages, drugs and medical care, taxes, insurance premiums and utility or service fees, or fees to be paid for reasonable professional services, and payments regarding legal services or expenses related to the normal keeping and management of the frozen funds.

The National Commission to Combat Terrorism may authorize the use of part of the funds frozen to cover these basic expenses.

If the freezing is based on a decision of the competent international bodies, they shall be notified about this authorization by diplomatic means, and the [international bodies] may object within two days from the date of the notification, [and the objection] shall then suspend the decision.

Article 105

A person who is included in the freezing decision or his representative may request the National Commission to Combat Terrorism to authorize the lifting of the freezing of his assets if the measure is proved to be wrong.

The Commission shall respond to this request in no later than 10 days from the date of its submission. In case of refusal, the decision may be appealed to the Administrative Court.

If the freezing is based on a decision of the competent international bodies, the National Commission to Combat Terrorism shall not take the decision to lift the freeze unless the competent international body is informed and agreed.

Select Bibliography

LEGISLATION

International Conventions, Declarations, & Resolutions

Declaration on the Granting of Independence to Colonial Countries and Peoples Adopted and Proclaimed by United Nations General Assembly Resolution 1514 (XV) of December 14, 1960.

"Charter of the United Nations" (October 24, 1945) 1 UNTS XVI.

International Convention on Suppression of Terrorism Financing, United Nations in Resolution 54/109 of December 9, 1999.

International Law Commission, "Draft Code of Offences against the Peace and Security of Mankind" (Part I), in ILC 6th Session Report (June 3–July 28, 1954), UN Doc A/2693, as requested by UNGA res 177(II) (1947).

UN General Assembly Resolution 3034 (XXVII) adopted in 18 December 1972 Measures to prevent international terrorism which endangers or takes innocent human lives or jeopardizes fundamental freedoms, and study of the underlying causes of those forms of terrorism and acts of violence which lie in misery, frustration, grievance and despair and which cause some people to sacrifice human lives, including their own, in an attempt to effect radical changes.

UN Security Council, Security Council Resolution 1267, 1999 SC Res. 1267, UN SCOR, S/RES/1267.

UN Security Council, Security Council Resolution 1373, 2001 SC Res. 1373, UN SCOR, S/RES/1373 [Resolution 1373].

UN Security Council, Security Council Resolution 1566, 2004 SC Res. 1566, UN SCOR, S/RES/1566 [Resolution 1566].

UN Security Council Resolution 2178, 2014 SC Res. 2178, UN SCOR, S/RES/2178.

UN Security Council, Security Council Resolution 2253, 2015 SC Res. 2253, UN SCOR, S/RES/2253.

Regional Conventions

Arab Convention for the Suppression of Terrorism, adopted by the Council of Arab Ministers of the Interior and the Council of Arab Ministers of Justice, Cairo, April 1998 [Arab Convention].

Council of Europe Convention on the Prevention of Terrorism (CECPT), No. 196, May 16, 2005.

National Legislation

Egypt

Constitution of 1882.

Constitution of 1923.

Constitution of 2012.

Constitution of 2014.

Penal Code of 1883.

Penal Code of 1904.

Law No. 37 of 1923 on Adding Provisions to the Penal Code No. 3 of 1904.

Penal Code of 1937.

Law No. 117 of 1946 amending the Penal Code of 1937.

Law No. 79 of 1992 amending the Penal Code of 1937 (crimes of terrorism).

Law No. 15 of 1923 on the System of Martial Law.

Law No. 37 of 1923 on Adding Provisions to the Penal Code No. 3 of 1904.

Criminal Procedures Law No. 50 of 1951.

Law No. 112 of 1957 of amending the Penal Code of 1937.

Law No. 80 of 2002 on Anti-Money Laundering.

Law No. 8 of 2015 Regarding Regulating Terrorist Entities and Terrorists (Terrorist Entities Law).

Anti-terrorism Law No. 94 of 2015.

Presidential Decree No. 375 of 1992 regarding transferring terrorist cases to military courts.

France

Constitution of 1958

Penal Code of 1810.

Press Law 1881.

Law Regarding the State of Siege of 1849.

Law Regarding State of Siege of 1878.

Law No. 55–385 of 1955 regarding the State of Emergency.

Penal Code of Act No. 96–647 of July 22, 1996.

Penal Code of Act No. 98–348 of May 11, 1998.
Act No. 2001–1062 of November 15, 2001 on Everyday Security.
Act No. 2003–239 of March 18, 2003 on Internal Security.
Act No. 2004–204 of March 9, 2004 Bringing Justice into Line with New Patterns of Crime.

Tunisia
Fundamental Act ('Ahd al-Amān) 1857.
Constitution of 1861.
Constitution of 1959.
Constitution of 2014.
Constitutional Law No. 65 of 1997.
Penal Code of 1913.
Law No. 29 of 1957 issued on September 9, 1957 declaring a state of emergency.
Law No. 57 of 1958 issued on May 12, 1958 extending the state of emergency.
Law No. 59 of 1958 issued on May 25, 1958 declaring a state of emergency in all Tunisia.
Decree-Law of the Penal and Procedures Military Code No. 12 of 1979.
Act No. 75 of 2003 concerning Support for International Efforts to Combat Terrorism and Prevent Money-Laundering.
Anti-Terrorism Law of 2015.
Law No. 5 of 2016 amending Criminal Procedure Code.
Presidential Decree of January 26, 1978 Declaring State of Emergency.
Order No. 49 of 1978 issued on January 26, 1978 Declaring State of Emergency.
Order No. 1 of 1984 issued on January 3, 1984 Declaring State of Emergency.

United Kingdom & Northern Ireland
Defence Regulation 18B, 1939.
Defence of the Realm Consolidation Act (DORA) 1914.
Prevention of Incitement to Hatred Act (Northern Ireland) 1970.
Northern Ireland (Emergency Provisions) Act 1973.
Civil Authorities (Special Powers) Act (Northern Ireland) 1922.
Terrorism Act 2006.

Other Countries
Bahraini Law No. 58 of 2006 regarding Protecting Society from Terrorist Acts.
Kuwaiti Law No. 106 of 2013 regarding Combating Money Laundering and Terrorism Financing.
Kuwaiti Press and Publication Law No. 3 of 2006.
Lebanese Penal Code No. 340 of 1943.

Lebanese Law No. 318 of 2001 on Combating Money Laundering.
Singapore Internal Security Act 18 of 1960 amended by Act 15 of 2010.
United Arab Emirates Law No. 1 of 2004 regarding Combating Terrorist
   Crimes.

Other Countries

State Security Case No. 237:33 (May 30, 2005), UAE University Press,
   Ministry of Justice, vol 61:27 (2005).

UN DOCUMENTS

"Letter dated 14 July 2006 from the Permanent Representative of France to
   the United Nations addressed to the Chairman of the Counter-Terrorism
   Committee" S/2006/547.
"Letter dated 19 May 2015 from the Chair of the Security Council Com-
   mittee pursuant to Resolutions 1267 (1999) and 1989 (2011) concerning
   Al-Qaida and associated individuals and entities addressed to the Presi-
   dent of the Security Council."
"Letter dated 2 September 2015 from the Chair of the Security Council
   Committee established pursuant to Resolution 1373 (2001) concerning
   counter-terrorism addressed to the President of the Security Council"
   S/2015/683.
UN Human Rights Office of the High Commission, Special Rapporteur on
   the Promotion and Protection of Human Rights and Fundamental Free-
   doms while Countering Terrorism, A/HRC/16/51 (December 22, 2010).
UN Human Rights Office of the High Commissioner, Report of the
   Special Rapporteur on the promotion and protection of human rights
   and fundamental freedoms while countering terrorism, Martin Scheinin.
   Mission to Egypt (October 14, 2009).
UN Human Rights Office of the High Commission, Special Rapporteur on
   the Promotion and Protection of Human Rights and Fundamental
   Freedoms while Countering Terrorism Concludes Visit to Tunisia (Feb-
   ruary 3, 2017).

GOVERNMENT DOCUMENTS AND REPORTS

Canada, Commission of Inquiry into the Actions of Canadian Officials in
   Relation to Maher Arar, *Report of the Events Relating to Maher Arar:*

Analysis and recommendations (Ottawa: Public Works and Government Services Canada, 2006).
"Country Reports on Terrorism 2013: Tunisia," Embassy of the United States in Tunisia, online: tunisia.usembassy.gov/country-reports-on-terror ism-2013-tunisia.html.
National Commission on Terrorist Attacks upon the United States (9–11 Commission) [The 9/11 Commission Report] (2004) online: National Commission on Terrorist Attacks Upon the United States www.9–11 commission.gov/report/.

COUNTRIES' REPORTS TO THE CTC

"Letter dated 20 December 2001 from the Permanent Representative of Egypt to the United Nations addressed to the Chairman of the Security Council Committee established pursuant to Resolution 1373 (2001) concerning counter-terrorism" S/2001/1237 [Egypt's Report to the CTC, 2001].
"Letter dated 13 December 2001 from the Permanent Representative of the Syrian Arab Republic to the Chairman of the Security Council Committee established pursuant to Resolution 1373 (2001) concerning counter-terrorism" (December 13, 2001), S/2001/1204 [Syria's Report to the CTC, 2001].
"Note verbale dated 30 August 2002 from the Permanent Mission of Tunisia to the United Nations addressed to the Chairman of the Security Council Committee established pursuant to Resolution 1373 (2001) concerning counter-terrorism," S/2002/1024 [Tunisia's Report to the CTC, 2002].
"Letter dated 20 January 2003 from the Permanent Representative of Egypt to the United Nations addressed to the Chairman of the Security Council Committee established pursuant to Resolution 1373 (2001) concerning counter-terrorism" S/2003/277 [Egypt's Report to the CTC, 2003].
"Note verbale dated 15 September 2003 from the Permanent Mission of Tunisia to the United Nations addressed to the Chairman of the Security Council Committee established pursuant to Resolution 1373 (2001) concerning counter-terrorism" (October 27, 2003) S/2003/1038 [Tunisia's Report to the CTC, 2003].
"Note verbale dated 29 April 2005 from the Permanent Mission of Egypt to the United Nations addressed to the Chairman of the Counter-Terrorism Committee," S/2005/288 [Egypt's Report to the CTC, 2005].

REPORTS BY INTERNATIONAL NON-GOVERNMENTAL &
INTER-GOVERNMENTAL ORGANIZATIONS

Amnesty International

"Egypt: Hundreds Disappeared and Tortured Amid Wave of Brutal Repression" (July 13, 2016) *Amnesty International*, online: www.amnesty.org/en/
latest/news/2016/07/egypt-hundreds-disappeared-and-tortured-amid-wave-
of-brutal-repression/.

"Egypt: Hisham Genina's Sentence a Serious Setback for Freedom of
Expression under al-Sisi" (April 24, 2018) *Amnesty International*, online:
www.amnesty.org/en/latest/news/2018/04/egypt-hisham-geninas-sentence-
a-serious-setback-for-freedom-of-expression-under-al-isi/.

"Egypt: State-Sanctioned Pattern of Excessive Use of Force by Security
Forces" (October 14, 2013) *Amnesty International*, online: www
.amnesty.org/en/latest/news/2013/10/egypt-state-sanctioned-pattern-exces
sive-use-force-security-forces/.

"Egypt Steps Up Vicious Onslaught against NGOs with Arrest of Minority
Defender" (May 19, 2016) *Amnesty International*, online: www.amnesty
.org/en/press-releases/2016/05/egypt-steps-up-vicious-onslaught-against-ngos-
with-arrest-of-minority-rights-defender.

"Egypt: Systematic Abuses in the Name of Security" (April 2007), *Amnesty
International*, online: amnesty.org/resources/Egypt/pdf/2007_04_
amnesty_international_egypt_report.pd.

*Upturned Lives: The Disproportionate Impact of France's State of
Emergency*, 2016.

"Lebanon: Cease Harassment of Human Rights Activist for Documenting
Torture" (August 4, 2011) *Amnesty International*, online: www.amnesty
.org/en/press-releases/2011/08/lebanon-cease-harassment-human-rights-
activist-documenting-torture-2011-08/.

"Sahrawi Activists on Trial for Visiting Refugee Camps" (October 13, 2010)
Amnesty International, online: www.amnesty.org.

"The Arab Convention for the Suppression of Terrorism: A Serious Threat
to Human Rights" (January 9, 2002) online: amnestyinternational.org.

"Tunisia: Severe Restrictions on Liberty and Movement Latest Symptoms
of Repressive Emergency Law" (March 17, 2016) *Amnesty International*,
online: www.amnesty.org/en/press-releases/2016/03/tunisia-severe-restric
tions-on-liberty-and-movement-latest-symptoms-of-repressive-emergency-
law/.

Tunisia: 'We Want an End to the Fear': Abuses under Tunisia's State of
Emergency" (February 13, 2017) *Amnesty International*, online: www
.amnesty.org/en/documents/mde30/4911/2017/en/.

"Tunisia: Open Letter Urges Government to End Impunity for Security Forces" (March 13, 2018) *Amnesty International*, online: www.amnesty .org/en/latest/news/2018/03/tunisia-open-letter-urges-government-to-end-impunity-for-security-forces/.

Human Rights Watch

"Egypt: Condemn Justice Minister's Hate Speech: Suggested Mass Killing of Brotherhood Supporters" (February 8, 2016) *Human Rights Watch*, online: www.hrw.org/news/2016/02/08/egypt-condemn-justice-ministers-hate-speech.
"Egypt: High Price of Dissent: Journalists, Protesters, Academics Charged over Speech Offenses" (February 19, 2014) *Human Rights Watch*, online: www.pri.org/stories/2013-01-25/egyptian-lawyer-trial-working-illegal-organization.
"Egypt: 7,400 Civilians Tried in Military Courts" (April 13, 2016) *Human Rights Watch*, online: www.hrw.org/news/2016/04/13/egypt-7400-civilians-tried-military-courts.
"Germany: Flawed Social Media Law: NetzDG Is Wrong Response to Online Abuse" (February 14, 2018) *Human Rights Watch*, online: www.hrw.org/news/2018/02/14/germany-flawed-social-media-law.
Human Rights Watch World Report, 2003 (New York: Human Rights Watch, 2003).
"Media Blocked, Threatened in Dispute with Qatar: Actions by Other Middle Eastern Countries a Blow to Free Speech" (June 14, 2017) *Human Rights Watch*, online: www.hrw.org/news/2017/06/14/media-blocked-threatened-dispute-qatar.
"Preempting Justice: Counterterrorism Laws and Procedures in France" (July 1, 2008) *Human Rights Watch*, online: www.hrw.org.
"Saudi Arabia: New Counterterrorism Law Enables Abuse: Criminalizes Criticisms of King and Crown Prince as Terrorism Offense" (November 23, 2017), *Human Rights Watch*, online: www.hrw.org/news/2017/11/23/saudi-arabia-new-counterterrorism-law-enables-abuse.
"Trials of Civilians in Military Courts Violate International Law Executions Continue, No Appeal of Death Sentences to Higher Court" (July 3, 1993) *Human Rights Watch*, online: www.hrw.org/report/1993/07/02/egypt-trials-civilians-military-courts-violate-international-law/executions.
"Tunisia: Amend Counterterrorism Law, Reforms Necessary to Protect Fundamental Rights" (May 29, 2013) *Human Rights Watch*, online: www.hrw.org/news/2013/05/29/tunisia-amend-counterterrorism-law.

"Tunisia: Arbitrary Travel Restrictions: Apparent Effort to Prevent Recruiting by Extremists" (July 10, 2015) *Human Rights Watch*, online: www
.hrw.org/news/2015/07/10/tunisia-arbitrary-travel-restrictions.
"Tunisia: Events of 2015" *Human Rights Watch*, online: https://www.hrw
.org/world-report/2016/country-chapters/tunisia.
Tunisia: Journalists before Military Tribunal: Prosecuted for Criticizing the
Army" (November 30, 2016) *Human Rights Watch* www.hrw.org/news/
2016/11/30/tunisia-journalists-military-tribunal.
"World Report 2012: Tunisia, Events of 2011" *Human Rights Watch*, online:
www.hrw.org/world-report-2012/world-report-2012-tunisia.
"Yemen: Events of 2017" *Human Rights Watch*, online: www.hrw.org/
world-report/2018/country-chapters/yemen.

FATF

Financial Action Task Force, "Review to Identify Non-Cooperative Coun-
tries or Territories: Increasing the Worldwide Effectiveness of Anti-
Money Laundering Measures," June 22, 2001.
"Financial Action Task Force on Money Laundering 2000–2001 Report
Released," PAC/COM/NEWS (2001)58 Paris, June 22, 2001.
"Mutual Evaluation Report: Anti-Money Laundering and Combating the
Financing of Terrorism, Egypt" (May 19, 2009) *MENAFATF*.
Special Recommendations on Terrorist Financing, FATF IX Special Rec-
ommendations, October 31, 2001.

Other Organizations

International Commission of Jurists, Position Paper: "Tunisia's Law on
Counter-Terrorism in Light of International Law and Standards" (August
6, 2015) *International Commission of Jurists*, online: icj.wpengine
.netdna-cdn.com/wp-content/uploads/2015/08/Tunisia-CT-position-
paper-Advocacy-PP-2015-ENG-REV.pdf.
"Reporters without Borders in Tunisia: A New Freedom That Needs
Protecting" (February 10, 2011, updated in January 20, 2016) *Reporters
Without Borders*, online: rsf.org/en/news/reporters-without-borders-
tunisia-new-freedom-needs-protecting.

BOOKS, BOOK CHAPTERS, AND JOURNAL ARTICLES

Abadi, Jacob, *Tunisia since the Arab Conquest: The Saga of a Westernized Muslim State*
(Cornwall: Apollo Books, 2012).
Abū al-Rūs, Aḥmad, *al-Irhāb wa-al-taṭarruf wa-al-ʿunf fī al-duwal al-ʿArabīyah [Terrorism and
Extremism in Arab States]* (Alexandria: al-Maktab al-Jāmiʿī al-Ḥadīth, 2001).

Abun-Nasr, Jamil, A History of the Maghrib in the Islamic Period (Cambridge: Cambridge University Press, 1987).

Agamben, Giorgio, State of Exception (Chicago: University of Chicago Press, 2005).

Al-Anezi, Rashid, "Human Rights in the Light of International Opportunism: A Study of the Impact of the War on Terrorism on Human Rights" (2010) 24:41 UAE Univ J Sharia and Law, pp. 101–84.

Alexander, Christopher, Tunisia: Stability and Reform in the Modern Maghreb (Milton Park, UK: Routledge, 2010).

Alexander, Martin S. & Keiger, J. F. V., France and the Algerian War, 1954–1962: Strategy, Operations and Diplomacy (New York: Routledge, 2013).

Al-kitab al-dahabi li-lmahakim al-ahliyya [The Gold Book of the National Courts], vol 2 (Cairo: Al-matba'a al-amiriyya bi-bulaq, 1937).

Al-Maḥjūbī, 'Alī, ʿĀlam al-ʿArabī al-ḥadīth wa-al-muʿāṣir: takhalluf fa-isti'mār fa-muqāwamah [Modern and Contemporary Arab World: Backwardness, Colonialism, Resistance] (Beirut: al-Intishār al-'Arabī, 2009).

Al-Mūsawī, Sālim Rawḍān al-Mūsawī, Fi 'l al-irhāb wa-al-jarīmah al-irhābīyah: dirāsah muqāranah mu ʿazzazah bi-taṭbīqāt qaḍā'īyah [Terrorism and Terrorist Crime: Comparative Study Supported by Judiciary Decisions] (Beirut: Manshūrāt al-Ḥalabī al-Ḥuqūqīyah, 2010).

Alnasseri, Sabah, "Understanding Iraq" in Panitch, Leo & Leys, Colin, eds, Global Flashpoints: Reactions to Imperialism and Neoliberalism (Wiltshire: Merlin Press, 2007).

Andaya, Barbara Watson, A History of Malaysia (Honolulu: University of Hawai'i Press, 2001).

Anderson, Lisa, The State and Social Transformation in Tunisia and Libya, 1830–1980 (Princeton, NJ: Princeton University Press, 1986).

Andrés-Sáenz-De-Santa-María, Paz, "Collective International Measures to Counter International Terrorism" in Fernández-Sánchez, Pablo Antonio, ed, International Legal Dimension of Terrorism (Leiden: Martinus Nijhoff, 2009).

Arfawi, Khamis, Al-Qaḍā' wa-al-siyāsah fī Tūnis zaman al-isti'mār al-Faransī, 1881–1956 [The Judiciary and Politics in Tunisia during French Colonialism: 1881–1956] (Ṣafāqis: Ṣāmid lil-Nashr wa-al-Tawzī', 2005).

"aSahafa wa raqaba fi Tunis 1938–1953" ["Journalism and Censorship in Tunisia: 1938–1953"] (September 25, 2016) Alawan, online: www.alawan.org/content/ الصحافة-و-الرقابة-في-تونس-1938-1953.

ARifa'ee, Abdu-rahman, Tareakh alharaka alqawmiya wa tatawur nitham alhukom [History of Nationalist Movement and the Development of the Ruling System] (Cairo: Matabie' alhaya' almasriya alama' lilkitab, 2000).

Aydin, Cemil, The Idea of the Muslim World: A Global Intellectual History (Cambridge, MA: Harvard University Press, 2017).

Badawi, Jamal, Muhamad Ali wa awladah [Muhamad Ali and His Sons] (Cairo: Matabie' alhaya' almasriya alama' lilkitab, 1999).

Barak-Erez, Daphne & Scharia, David, "Freedom of Speech, Support for Terrorism, and the Challenge of Global Constitutional Law" (2011) 2 Harvard Nat Sec J, pp. 1–32.

Baring, Evelyn, The Government of Subject Races (Cambridge: Cambridge University Press, 2011 [1913]).

Barton, A. Gregory, Informal Empire and the Rise of One World Culture (London: Palgrave Macmillan, 2014).

Beckert, Sven, Empire of Cotton: A Global History (New York: Vintage Books, 2014).

Beigbeder, Yves, Judging War Crimes and Torture: French Justice and International Criminal Tribunals and Commissions (1940–2005) (Leiden: Martinus Nijhoff, 2006).

Beinin, Joel & Lockman, Zachary, *Workers on the Nile: Nationalism, Communism, Islam, and the Egyptian Working Class, 1882–1954* (Cairo: American University in Cairo Press, 1998).

Ben Haj, Aljelani & alMarzuqi, Muhamad, *Ma'rakat alzalaj [Jellaz War]* (Tunis: Asharika atunisia letawzie).

Birkhimer, William E., *Military Government and Martial Law* (Kansas City, MO: F Hudson, 1914).

Brown, Leon Carl, *International Politics and the Middle East: Old Rules, Dangerous Game* (London: I. B. Tauris, 1984).

Brown, Nathan, "The Precarious Life and Slow Death of the Mixed Courts of Egypt" (1993) 25:1 *Intl J Middle East Stud*, pp. 33–52.

"Retrospective: Law and Imperialism: Egypt in Comparative Perspective" (1995) 29:1 *Law & Soc Rev*, pp. 03–126.

The Rule of Law in the Arab World (New York: Cambridge University Press, 1997).

Constitutions in a Nonconstitutional World: Arab Basic Laws and the Prospects for Accountable Government (New York: State University of New York Press, 2002).

Brown, Nathan, Dunne, Michele & Hamzawy, Amr, "Egypt's Controversial Constitutional Amendments" (March 23, 2007) *Carnegie Endowment for International Peace*.

Burgat, François & Dowell, William, *The Islamic Movement in North Africa* (Austin, TX: Center for Middle Eastern Studies, University of Texas at Austin, 1993).

Busky, Donald F., *Communism in History and Theory: Asia, Africa, and the Americas* (Westport, CT: Greenwood Publishing Group, 2002).

Chabal, Patrick, *Power in Africa: An Essay in Political Interpretation* (New York: Springer, 2016).

Chatterjee, Partha, *The Nation and Its Fragments* (Princeton, NJ: Princeton University Press, 1993).

Chen, Albert H. Y., "Emergency Powers: Constitutionalism and Legal Transplants: The East Asian Experience" in Ramraj, Victor V. & Thiruvengadam, Arun K., eds, *Emergency Powers in Asia* (Cambridge: Cambridge University Press, 2010).

Chilcote, Ronald H., "Globalization or Imperialism?" (2002) 29:6 *Latin Amer Persp*, pp. 80–4.

Chomsky, Noam & Vltchek, Andre, *On Western Terrorism: From Hiroshima to Drone Warfare* (Toronto: BTL, 2013).

Clancy-Smith, Julia A., *Rebel and Saint: Muslim Notables, Populist Protest, Colonial Encounters (Algeria and Tunisia, 1800–1904)* (Berkeley, CA: University of California Press, 1997).

Cleveland, William L. & Bunton, Martin P., *A History of the Modern Middle East* (Boulder, CO: Westview Press, 2013).

Coady, C. A. J., "Defining Terrorism" in Primoratz, Igor, ed, *Terrorism: The Philosophical Issues* (Basingstoke: Palgrave Macmillan, 2004).

Cole, Juan, *Colonialism and Revolution in the Middle East: Social and Cultural Origins of Egypt's 'Urabi Movement* (Princeton, NJ: Princeton University Press, 1993).

Napoleon's Egypt: Invading the Middle East (Basingstoke: Palgrave Macmillan, 2007).

Comras, Victor D., *Flawed Diplomacy: The United Nations and the War on Terrorism* (Dulles, VA: Potomac Books, 2010).

Cromer, Earl of, *Modern Egypt*, 2 vols (New York: The Macmillan Company, 1908).

Damais, Alien, "The Financial Action Task Force" in Muller, Wouter H., Kalin, Christian H. & Goldsworth, John G., eds, *Anti-Money Laundering: International Law and Practice* (London: John Wiley & Sons, 2007).

Darby, Philip, *The Three Faces of Imperialism* (New Haven, CT: Yale University Press).

Degefu, Gebre Tsadik, *The Nile: Historical, Legal and Developmental Perspectives* (Victoria, BC: Trafford, 2003).

Dyzenhaus, David, "The Puzzle of Martial Law" (2009) 59 *Univ Toronto Law J*, pp. 1–64.

Fadlallah, Mohammad Hussain, *Hiwarat filfikr wa esyasa wa elejtima* ' *[Dialogues in Thought, Politics and Sociology]* (Beirut: Dar al-Malak: 1997).

Farhang, Michael, "Recent Development: Terrorism and Military Trials in Egypt: Presidential Decree No. 375 and the Consequences for Judicial Authority" (1994) 35:225 *Harvard Intl Law J*, pp. 225–37.

Feldman, William, "Theories of Emergency Powers: A Comparative Analysis of American Martial Law and the French State of Siege" (2005) 38:3 *Cornell Int Law J*, pp. 1021–48.

Fishman, Sarah, *The Battle for Children: World War II, Youth Crime, and Juvenile Justice in Twentieth-Century France* (Cambridge, MA: Harvard University Press, 2002).

Fitzpatrick, Peter, "Custom as Imperialism" in Abun-Nasr, J. M. & Spellenbert, U., eds, *Law and Identity in Africa* (Hamburg: Helmut Buske, 1990).

Foucault, Michel, *Discipline and Punish: The Birth of the Prison* (New York: Pantheon Books, 1977).

French, David, *The British Way in Counter-Insurgency: 1945–1967* (Oxford: Oxford University Press, 2011).

French Penal Code, translated by Gerhard O.W. Mueller & Jean F. Moreau (South Hackensack, NJ: F. B. Rothman, 1960).

Friedrich, Carl J., *Constitutional Reason of State: The Survival of the Constitutional Order* (Providence, RI: Brown University Press, 1957).

Galula, David, *Counterinsurgency Warfare: Theory and Practice* (New York: Praeger, 1964).

Garland, David, *The Culture of Control* (New York: Oxford University Press, 2001).

Ghanoushi, Rashid, *al-Ḥurrīyāt al-'āmmah fī al-dawlah al-Islāmīyah [Public Liberties in the Islamic State]* (Beirut: Markaz Dirāsāt al-Waḥdah al-'Arabīyah, 1993).

Gilligan, George, "Multilateral Regulatory Initiatives – A Legitimation-based Approach" in O'Brien, Justin, ed, *Governing the Corporation: Regulation and Corporate Governance in an Age of Scandal and Global Markets* (Hoboken, NJ: John Wiley & Sons, 2005).

Ginsburg, Tom & Moustafa, Tamir, *Rule by Law: The Politics of Courts in Authoritarian Regimes* (Cambridge: Cambridge University Press, 2008).

Go, Julian, *Patterns of Empire: The British and American Empires, 1688 to the Present* (New York: Cambridge University Press, 2011).

Postcolonial Thought and Social Theory (New York: Oxford University Press, 2016).

Gómez-Jara Díez, Carlos, "Enemy Combatants Versus Enemy Criminal Law: An Introduction to the European Debate Regarding Enemy Criminal Law and Its Relevance to the Anglo-American Discussion on the Legal Status of Unlawful Enemy Combatants" (2008) 11:4 *New Crim Law Rev: An International and Interdisciplinary J*, pp. 529–62.

Griffin, Christopher, "French Military Interventions in Africa: Realism vs. Ideology in French Defense Policy and Grand Strategy" (2007) Paper prepared for the International Studies Association Annual Convention, 28 February–3 March 2007, *Chicago*.

Habeeb, William Mark, *The Middle East in Turmoil: Conflict, Revolution, and Change* (Santa Barbara, CA: ABC-CLIO, 2012)

Hajjar, Lisa and Niva, Steve, "(Re)Made in the USA: Middle East Studies in the Global Era" (1997) 205 *Middle East Report*, pp. 2–9.

Hardin, Russell, "Civil Liberties in the Era of Mass Terrorism" (2004) 8:1 *J of Ethics*, pp. 77–95.

Hegghammer, Thomas, "The Rise of Muslim Foreign Fighters: Islam and the Globalization of Jihad" (2010/11) 35:3 *Intl Sec*, pp. 53–94.

Hinsley, F. H. & Simkins, C. A. G., *British Intelligence in the Second World War: Volume 4. Security and Counter-Intelligence* (Cambridge: Cambridge University Press, 1990).

Hobson, J. A., *Imperialism: A Study* (New York: Gordon Press, 1975 [1902]).

Hocking, Jenny, "Orthodox Theories of 'Terrorism': The Power of Politicised Terminology" (1984) 19:2 *Austral J Pol Sci*, pp. 103–10.

Beyond Terrorism: The Development of the Australian Security State (St Leonards, NSW: Allen & Unwin, 1993).

Hoffman, Bruce, *Inside Terrorism* (New York: Columbia University Press, 2006).

Hussain, Nasser, *The Jurisprudence of Emergency: Colonialism and the Rule of Law* (Ann Arbor, MI: University of Michigan Press, 2003).

Ismael, Tareq Y., *The Communist Movement in Egypt, 1920–1988* (New York: Syracuse University Press, 1990).

James, Lawrence, *The Rise and Fall of the British Empire* (New York: Abacus, 1995).

Jeffery, Keith, *MI6: The History of the Secret Intelligence Service 1909–1949* (New York: Penguin Press, 2010).

Joffé, George, *Islamic Radicalisation in Europe and the Middle East: Researching the Case of Terrorism* (London: I. B. Tauris, 2013).

Kalhan, Anil, "Constitution and 'Extraconstitution': Colonial Emergency Regimes in Post-Colonial India and Pakistan" in Ramraj, Victor V. & Thiruvengadam, Arun K., eds, *Emergency Powers in Asia* (Cambridge: Cambridge University Press, 2010).

Kelly, George A., *Struggles in the State: Sources and Patterns of World Revolution* (New York: Wiley, 1970).

Kelly, Joseph B. & Pelletierm, George AJr, "Theories of Emergency Government" (1966) 11 *South Dakota Law Rev*, pp. 42–54.

Kenney, Jeffery T., *Muslim Rebels: Kharijites and the Politics of Extremism in Egypt* (Oxford: Oxford University Press, 2006).

Kepel, Gilles, *Muslim Extremism in Egypt* (Berkeley, CA: University of California Press, 1986).

Jihad: The Trail of Political Islam, trans Anthony F. Roberts (London: I. B. Tauris, 2006).

Khalil, Aḥmad Maḥmud, *Jarā'im amn al-dawlah al-'Ulyā: [b mu'allaqan 'alayhā bi-aḥkām Maḥkamat al-Naqḍal-Miṣrīyah. [High State Security Crimes with Judgments of the Court of Cassation]* (al-Azārīṭah, al-Iskandarīyah: al-Maktab al-Jāmi'ī al-Ḥadīth, 2009).

Kiernan, V. G., *The Lords of Human Kind: European Attitudes towards the Outside World in the Imperial Age* (Harmondsworth, UK: Penguin Books, 1972).

"Tennyson, King Arthur, and Imperialism" in Harvey, J. Kaye, ed, *Poets, Politics, and the People* (London: Verso, 1989).

Imperialism and Its Contradictions (New York: Routledge, 1995).

Kitson, Frank, *Low Intensity Operations* (London: Faber and Faber, 1971).

Kramer, Hilde Haaland & Yetiv, Steve A., "The UN Security Council's Response to Terrorism: Before and After September 11, 2001" (2007) 122:3 *Pol Sci Q*, pp. 409–32.

Laqueur, Walter, *The New Terrorism* (New York: Oxford University Press, 1999).

Lévy, René, "Pardons and Amnesties as Policy Instruments in Contemporary France" (2007) 36:1 *Crime and Justice*, pp. 551–90.

Lippman, Thomas W., *Egypt after Nasser: Sadat, Peace and the Mirage of Prosperity* (New York: Paragon House, 1989).

Loewenstein, Karl, *Political Power and the Governmental Process* (Chicago: University of Chicago Press, 1957).

Loughlin, Martin, *Sword and Scales: An Examination of the Relationship between Law and Politics* (Oxford: Hart, 2000).

Lyngaas, Sean, "Ahmad Urabi: Delegate of the People's Social Mobilization in Egypt on the Eve of Colonial Rule" (Spring 2011) *The Fletcher School Online Journal for Issues Related to Southwest Asia and Islamic Civilization*, online: fletcher.tufts.edu/Al-Nakhlah.

Mahfouz, Naguib, *Palace Walk* (New York: Anchor Books, 1991).

Malashenko, Alexey, "Russia and the Arab Spring" (October 2013) *Carnegie Moscow Center*.

Mann, Michael, *The Sources of Social Power, Volume 3: Global Empire and Revolution, 1890–1945* (New York: Cambridge University Press, 2012).

Martínez, Luis Miguel Hinojosa, "The Legislative Role of the Security Council in Its Fight against Terrorism: Legal, Political and Practical Limits" (2008) 57:2 *Int & Comp Law Q*, pp. 333–59.

McCulloch, Jude & Pickering, Sharon, "Suppressing the Financing of Terrorism: Proliferating State Crime, Eroding Censure and Extending Neo-colonialism" (2005) 45:4 *British J Crim*, pp. 470–86.

"Pre-Crime and Counter-Terrorism: Imagining Future Crime in the 'War on Terror'" (2009) 49:5 *British J Crim*, pp. 628–45.

"Counter-Terrorism: The Law and Policing of Pre-emption" in Lynch, Andrew, McGarrity, Nicola & Williams, George, eds, *Counter-Terrorism and Beyond: The Culture of Law and Justice after 9/11* (New York: Routledge, 2010).

McGregor, Andrew, *A Military History of Modern Egypt: From the Ottoman Conquest to the Ramadan War* (Westport, CT: Praeger Security International, 2006).

Menon, Rajan, *The Conceit of Humanitarian Intervention* (New York: Oxford University Press, 2016).

Mitchell, Richard P., *The Society of the Muslim Brothers* (London: Oxford University Press, 1969).

Moore, Clement Henry, "Authoritarian Politics in Unincorporated Society: The Case of Nasser's Egypt" (1974) 6:2 *Comp Pol*, pp. 193–218.

Murray, Mark J., "Extraordinary Rendition and U.S. Counterterrorism Policy" (2011) 4:3 *J Strat Sec*, pp. 15–28.

Nardo, Don, *The European Colonization of Africa* (Greensboro, NC: Morgan Reynolds Pub., 2010).

Neely, Mark E., "In the Highest Degree Odious: Detention without Trial in Wartime Britain by A. W. Brian Simpson" (Spring 1995) 13:1 *Law and Hist Rev*, pp. 177–78.

Neocleous, Mark, "From Martial Law to the War on Terror" (2007) 10:4 *New Crim Law Rev*, pp. 489–513.

Nicholls, David, *Napoleon: A Biographical Companion* (Santa Barbara, CA: ABC-CLIO, 1999).

Njoh, Ambe, "Colonial Philosophies, Urban Space, and Racial Segregation in British and French Colonial Africa" (2008) 38:4 *J Black Stud*, pp. 579–99.

Nolan, Victoria, *Military Leadership and Counterinsurgency: The British Army and Small War Strategy since World War II* (London: I. B. Tauris, 2012).

Nordbruch, Götz, *Nazism in Syria and Lebanon: The Ambivalence of the German Option, 1933–45* (London: Routledge, 2009).

Noyon, Jennifer & Royal Institute of International Affairs, *Islam, Politics and Pluralism: Theory and Practice in Turkey, Jordan, Tunisia and Algeria* (London: Royal Institute of International Affairs, Middle East Programme, 2003).

Nutting, Anthony, *Nasser* (New York: E. P. Dutton, 1972).

Oehmichen, Anna, *Terrorism and Anti-terrorism Legislation: The Terrorised Legislator? A Comparison of Counter-terrorism Legislation and Its Implications on Human Rights in the Legal Systems of the United Kingdom, Spain, Germany, and France* (Antwerp: Intersentia, 2009).

Olson, Charles William, *Decolonization in French Politics (1950–1956): Indo-China, Tunisia, Morocco* (Ann Arbor, MI: University Microfilms, 1966).

Owen, Roger, *State, Power and Politics in the Making of the Modern Middle East* (London: Routledge, 2004).

Palan, Ronen, Murphy, Richard & Chavagneux, Christian, *Tax Havens: How Globalization Really Works* (New York: Cornell University Press, 2013).

Parkman, Tim, *Mastering Anti-Money Laundering and Counter-Terrorist Financing* (Harlow: Pearson, 2012).

Perkins, Kenneth, *A History of Modern Tunisia* (New York: Cambridge University Press, 2014).

Post, Robert, "Hate Speech and Democracy" in Hare, Ivan & Weinstein, James, eds, *Extreme Speech and Democracy* (New York: Oxford University Press, 2009).

The Quarterly Review 75 (London: John Murray, Albemarle Street, 1845).

Qutab, Said, *Fi Zilal Al-Qur'an [In the Shade of the Qur'an]* (Beirut: Al Shurooq: 2003).

Radin, Max, "Martial Law and the State of Siege" (1942) 30:6 *Cal Law Rev*, pp. 634–47.

Rajah, Jothie, *Authoritarian Rule of Law: Legislation, Discourse and Legitimacy in Singapore* (New York: Cambridge University Press, 2012).

Ramraj, Victor V., Hor, Michael & Roach, Kent, eds, *Global Anti-Terrorism Law and Policy* (New York: Cambridge University Press, 2012).

Rejwan, Nissim, *Arabs Face the Modern World: Religious, Cultural, and Political Responses to the West* (Gainesville, FL: University Press of Florida, 1998).

Reza, Sadiq, "Endless Emergency: The Case of Egypt" (2007) 10:4 *New Crim Law Rev*, pp. 532–53.

Roach, Kent, *September 11: Consequences for Canada* (Montreal: McGill-Queen's University Press: 2003).

"Defining Terrorism: The Need for a Restrained Definition" in Forcese, Craig & Violette, Nicole La, eds, *The Human Rights of Anti-Terrorism* (Toronto: Irwin Law, 2008).

The 9/11 Effect: Comparative Counter-Terrorism (New York: Cambridge University Press, 2011).

"The Criminal Law and Terrorism" in Ramraj, Victor, Hor, Michael & Roach, Kent, eds, *Global Anti-Terrorism Law and Policy* (New York: Cambridge University Press, 2012).

"Comparative Counter-Terrorism Law Comes of Age," in Roach, Kent, ed, *Comparative Counter-Terrorism Law* (New York: Cambridge University Press, 2015).

Rodinson, Maxime, *Marxism and the Muslim World* (London: Zed Press, 1979).

Rosand, Eric, "The UN Security Council's Counter-Terrorism Efforts" in Lee, Roy, ed, *Swords into Plowshares: Building Peace through the United Nations* (Leiden: Martinus Nijhoff, 2006).

Rossiter, Clinton, *Constitutional Dictatorship: Crisis Government in the Modern Democracies* (New York: Harcourt Brace & World, 1963).

Rutledge, Ian, *Enemy on the Euphrates: The Battle of Iraq and The Great Arab Revolt 1914–1921* (London: Saqi, 2015).

Said, Edward W., *Culture and Imperialism* (New York: Knopf, 1993).

Orientalism, 1st Vintage Books edn (New York: Vintage Books, 1979).

Samy, Mahmoud, "The League of Arab States" in Nesi, Giuseppe, ed, *International Cooperation in Counter-Terrorism* (Aldershot: Ashgate, 2006).

Saul, Ben, *Defining Terrorism in International Law* (New York: Oxford University Press, 2008).

Schmitt, Carl, *Dictatorship* (Cambridge: Polity Press, 2014).

Political Theology: Four Chapters on the Concept of Sovereignty (Chicago: University of Chicago Press, 2005 [1922]).

Sharmen, J. C., "The Agency of the Peripheral Actors: Small State Tax Havens and International Regimes as Weapons of the Weak" in Hobson, John M. & Seabrooke, Leonard, eds, *Everyday Politics of the World Economy* (Cambridge: Cambridge University Press, 2007).

Shohat, Ella, "Notes on the 'Post-Colonial'" (1992) 31/32 *Third World and Post-Colonial Issues*, pp. 99–113.

Simester, Andrew & Hirsch, Andreas Von, *Crimes, Harms, and Wrongs: On the Principles of Criminalisation* (Oxford: Hart, 2011).

Simpson, A. W. Brian, "Round up the Usual Suspects: The Legacy of British Colonialism and the European Convention on Human Rights" (1953) 41:4 *Loyola Law Rev*, pp. 629–712. "Detention without Trial in the Second World War: Comparing the British and American Experiences" (1988) 16:2 *Florida State Univ Law Rev*, pp. 225–68. *In the Highest Degree Odious: Detention without Trial in Wartime Britain* (Oxford: Clarendon Press, 1992).

Smithers, William W., "The Code Napoléon" (1901) 49:3 *Amer Law Reg*, pp. 127–47.

Sorial, Sarah, "Can Saying Something Make It So? The Nature of Seditious Harm" (2010) 29:3 *Law and Philosophy*, pp. 273–305.

Steil, Benn & Litan, Robert E., *Financial Statecraft: The Role of Financial Markets in American Foreign Policy* (New Haven, CT: Yale University Press, 2008).

Stern, Jessica & Berger, J. M., *ISIS: The State of Terror* (New York: Ecco Press, 2015).

Strathern, Paul, *Napoleon in Egypt* (New York: Bantam Books Trade Paperbacks, 2009).

Ṣubḥī, Aḥmad M. & Wālī, Zāmiliā, *Judhūr al-irhāb fī al-'aqīdah al-Wahhābīyah [The Roots of Terrorism in Wahhabism]* (Beirut: Dār al-Mīzān, 2008).

Tal, Nichman, *Radical Islam in Egypt and Jordan* (Brighton: Sussex Academic Press/Jaffee Center for Strategic Studies, 2005).

Talmon, Stefan, "The Security Council as World Legislature" (2005) 99:1 *Amer J Int Law* pp. 175–93.

Talmon, Stefan & Krisch, Nico, "The Rise and Fall of Collective Security: Terrorism, US Hegemony, and the Plight of the Security Council," in Walter, Christian et al, eds, *Terrorism as a Challenge for National and International Law: Security versus Liberty?* (Berlin: Springer Science & Business Media, 2004).

Tan, Kevin, *Marshall of Singapore: A Biography* (Pasir Panjang: Institute of Southeast Asian Studies, 2008). "From Myanmar to Manila" in Ramraj, Victor V. & Thiruvengadam, Arun K., eds, *Emergency Powers in Asia: Exploring the Limits of Legality* (New York: Cambridge University Press, 2010).

Thompson, Elizabeth F., *Justice Interrupted: The Struggle for Constitutional Government in the Middle East* (Cambridge, MA: Harvard University Press, 2013).

Thompson, Robert, *Defeating Communist Insurgency: Experiences from Malaya and Vietnam* (New York: F. A. Praeger, 1966).

Tollefson, Harold, *Policing Islam: The British Occupation of Egypt and the Anglo-Egyptian Struggle over Control of the Police, 1882–1914* (London: Greenwood Publishing Group, 1999).

Townsend, Mary Evelyn, *European Colonial Expansion since 1871* (Chicago: J. B. Lippincott, 1941).

Urābī, Aḥmad, *Mudhakkirāt al-Za'īm Aḥmad 'Urābī: kashf al-sitār 'an sirr al-asrār fī al-naḍah al-Miṣrīyah, al-Mashhūrah bi-al-Thawrah al-'Urābīyah, fī 'āmay 1298 wa-1299 al-hijrīyatayn, wa-fī 1881 wa-1882 al-mīlādīyatayn [Ahmad Urabi's Memoir]* (Cairo: Dār al-Hilāl, 1989).

Weiss, Michael & Hassan, Hassan, *Isis: Inside the Army of Terror* (New York: Regan Arts, 2015).

Welchman, Lynn, "Rocks, Hard Places and Human Rights: Anti-Terrorism Law and Policy in Arab States" in Ramraj, Victor, Hor, Michael & Roach, Kent, eds, *Global Anti-Terrorism Law and Policy* (New York: Cambridge University Press, 2012).

Wheeler, Charles B., "The Code Napoleon and Its Framers" (1924) 10:3 *Amer Bar Ass J*, pp. 202–06.

Wilkinson, Paul, *Terrorism versus Liberal Democracy* (London: Institute for the Study of Conflict, 1976).

Yates, Douglas Andrew, *The Rentier State in Africa: Oil Rent Dependency and Neocolonialism in the Republic of Gabon* (Trenton, NJ: Africa World Press, 1996).

Young, James T., "Administrative Centralization and Decentralization in England" (1897) 10 *Annals Amer Acad Pol and Soc Sci*, pp. 39–57.

Young, James T., "Administrative Centralization and Decentralization in France" (1898) 11 *Annals Amer Acad Pol and Soc Sci*, pp. 24–43.

Záhořík, Jan & Piknerová, Linda, eds, *Colonialism on the Margins of Africa* (London: Routledge, 2018).

Index